THE RISE AND DECLINE OF THE POST-COLD WAR INTERNATIONAL ORDER

The Rise and Decline of the Post-Cold War International Order

Edited by

HANNS W. MAULL

OXFORD
UNIVERSITY PRESS

OXFORD
UNIVERSITY PRESS

Great Clarendon Street, Oxford, OX2 6DP,
United Kingdom

Oxford University Press is a department of the University of Oxford.
It furthers the University's objective of excellence in research, scholarship,
and education by publishing worldwide. Oxford is a registered trade mark of
Oxford University Press in the UK and in certain other countries

First Edition published in 2018

Impression: 1

Published in the United States of America by Oxford University Press
198 Madison Avenue, New York, NY 10016, United States of America

British Library Cataloguing in Publication Data
Data available

Library of Congress Control Number: 2018939295

ISBN 978–0–19–882894–5

Printed and bound by
CPI Group (UK) Ltd, Croydon, CR0 4YY

Preface

The project behind this book started more than four years ago with an internal working group at the German Institute for International and Security Affairs (Stiftung Wissenschaft und Politik, SWP) in Berlin. In this group, we reviewed the literature on the evolution and the state of the international order, and in a series of discussions developed the basic ideas and the analytical concepts we intended to use in a systematic exploration of how the international order has evolved since 1990 and where it seems to be headed.

Generous financial support provided by the Fritz-Thyssen Foundation, and additional funding from the German Foreign Ministry (Auswärtiges Amt, AA) and the Friedrich Ebert Foundation (Friedrich-Ebert-Stiftung, FES) enabled us to organize an international conference in late 2014; the papers produced and discussed at that two-day meeting represent the basis of this book. In the process of preparing this volume, we unfortunately lost some of our original contributors, but we also were able to recruit some new ones and thus complete the substance of our exploration of international order largely as we had envisaged it originally. The internal working group of SWP continued after the conference to prepare this book, as well as a shorter study in German, which used the analytical framework presented in the Introduction in this volume and drew on its Conclusions, but broadened the perspective by the inclusion of several new case studies that dealt with what we call "functional partial orders" beyond the cases presented here.[1]

During the course of this project, I have benefitted greatly from, and have accumulated a great debt to, the many people who not only helped me enormously to bring this project to completion but also made the work on it an intellectual adventure and a personal pleasure. My gratitude goes to all those who contributed to make this volume possible—directly, by writing and repeatedly revising the individual chapters to this book and the German language report, and indirectly, by providing the critical financial and logistical support for this project, notably the Fritz-Thyssen Foundation, the German Foreign Ministry, the Friedrich Ebert Foundation and the leadership and staff of the German Institute for International and Security Affairs under its able director Volker Perthes. The task of an editor involves persistently getting on authors' nerves with suggestions, queries, and reminders about deadlines; all of you put up with this with good grace, remarkable patience,

[1] This study, entitled: "Auflösung oder Ablösung? Die internationale Ordnung im Umbruch," also edited by Hanns W. Maull, appeared in December 2017; it is available on the homepage of SWP at https://www.swp-berlin.org/fileadmin/contents/products/studien/2017S21_mul_hg.pdf.

and great effectiveness! Thank you, Chaesung Chun, Daniel Deudney, Myriam Dunn Cavelty, Joyeeta Gupta, Bernard Hoekman, Iris Hunger, Daniel Krahl, Charles E. Morrison, Marco Overhaus, Pang Zhongying, Volker Perthes, Wolfgang Richter, and William Walker.

Special thanks are due to Petra Rettig and her colleagues at the SWP conference unit for their, as always, immaculate organization of the international conference in late November and early December 2015, as well as to Denise Rüttinger and her colleague Heike Perscheid for their patient and efficient management of the project finances through the thickets of administrative and bureaucratic regulations and deadlines.

I would like to thank all those who provided invaluable intellectual and practical input to our project: the colleagues and friends of SWP who provided additional analyses to our project, notably Steffen Angenendt and Anne Koch, Marcel Dickow, Susanne Dröge, Oliver Meier, and Jonas Schneider, as well as Günther Maihold, Bettina Rudloff, Peter Rudolf, and Stefan Steinicke, and the other participants in our working group session for their prepared written and oral contributions and their many suggestions. My gratitude extends to all the other authors of conference papers and the commentators and chairs of the conference, notably Annegret Bendiek, Mustafa El-Labbad, Ilona Kickbusch, Ivan Krastev, Fyodor Lukyanov, Umma Salma Bava, and Volker Stanzel, as well as our rapporteurs Leonie Beining, Arno Bratz, Johannes Gabriel, and Stefan Steinicke. Special thanks are due to Muthiah Alagappa whose work inspired our project and whose contribution throughout the conference provided particularly valuable insights, and to Thomas Bagger, then head of the AA Planning Staff, now in the Federal President's Office, for his support for the whole project throughout and his keynote speech at the occasion of our welcoming dinner on November 29, 2015. At the German Foreign Office, I would also like to thank Patricia Flor for her encouragement and the opportunities to discuss with her and her colleagues. At the Friedrich Ebert Foundation, I would like to thank Christoph Karg, Katrien Klüver, Thomas Mättig, Christoph Pohlmann, and Jochen Steinhilber.

Volker Perthes, the director of SWP, and his colleagues Barbara Lippert and Günther Maihold have supported this ambitious endeavor throughout with advice, assistance, and contributions, and have made it possible for us at various important stages of the project to get help from young colleagues. I was very fortunate to find excellent supporters in Arno Bratz, Philipp Joseph Nock, and Corinna Weiler, who in many ways helped this project to move forward and this book to take shape. We were also fortunate to find such a friendly and efficient editorial team with Dominic Byatt, Sarah Parker, and Olivia Wells at Oxford University Press, and with Santhosh Palani of SPi Global and, particularly, freelance copy editors Brian North and Joanna North.

My own contributions to this book owe a great deal to the friends and colleagues who helped me in developing and polishing my thoughts. My heartfelt thanks go to Johannes Gabriel, Sebastian Harnisch, Charles Heck, Achim von Heynitz, Friedemann Müller, Desmond Ryan, William Wallace and Reinhard Wolf, as well as to the three anonymous reviewers of Oxford University Press. All of them have helped me enormously to sharpen my own views and to avoid errors of fact and judgment. If there is still much that could be improved it is certainly not their fault, but mine alone.

Hanns W. Maull

Contents

PART III. "ORDERING POWERS"

List of Figures

List of Tables

List of Abbreviations

ABM	Anti-Ballistic Missile (Treaty)
ACFE	Adaptation Agreement to the Conventional Armed Forces in Europe Treaty
AFT	Aid for trade
AIDS	Acquired Immune Deficiency Syndrome
AIIB	Asian Infrastructure Investment Bank
ALBA	Bolivarian Alliance for the Peoples of our America (in Spanish)
APEC	Asia Pacific Economic Cooperation
APTs	Advanced persistent threats
ASEAN	Association of Southeast Asian Nations
BASIC	Grouping formed by Brazil, South Africa, India, and China in the context of UNFCCC climate change policy negotiations
BIS	Bank for International Settlements
BRI	Belt and Road Initiative
BRICS	Acronym of Brazil, Russia, India, China, and South Africa
CACAM	rainforest coalition, Central Asia, Caucasus, and Moldova
CBDR	common but differentiated responsibilities (principle agreed in UNFCCC)
CCP	Chinese Communist Party
CDM	Clean Development Mechanism (of the Kyoto Protocol)
CFE	Treaty on Conventional Armed Forces in Europe
CICA	Conference on Interaction and Confidence-Building Measures in Asia
CMAs	Critical mass agreements
COP	Conference of the Parties (of the UN Framework Convention on Climate Change)
CORDS	Connecting Organizations for Regional Disease Surveillance
CSBMs	Confidence- and Security-Building Measures
CSCE	Conference for Security and Cooperation in Europe
CTBT	Comprehensive Nuclear Test-Ban Treaty
DDA	Doha Development Agenda
DPRK	Democratic People's Republic of Korea
EU	European Union
EUCOM	European Command
FAO	Food and Agriculture Organization

FDI	foreign direct investment
FMCT	Fissile Material Cut-off Treaty
FOCAC	Forum of China Africa Cooperation
FTA	Free Trade Agreement
G4	Group of Four (Brazil, India, Japan and Germany)
G7	Group of Seven (Canada, France, Germany, Italy, Japan, the United Kingdom, and the United States)
G8	Group of the seven largest advanced economies and Russia
G20	Group of Twenty
GATS	General Agreement on Trade in Services
GATT	General Agreement on Tariffs and Trade
GAVI	Global Alliance for Vaccines and Immunization
GCC	Gulf Cooperation Council, today usually known as Cooperation Council for the Arab States of the Gulf
GDP	Gross Domestic Product
GEIS	US Department of Defense Global Emerging Infections Surveillance and Response System
GHG	Greenhouse gases
GHSA	Global Health Security Agenda
GHSI	Global Health Security Initiative
GOARN	Global Outbreak Alert and Response Network (of the WHO)
IAEA	International Atomic Energy Agency
IFIs	international financial institutions
IHL	International Humanitarian Law
IHR	International Health Regulations
IISS	International Institute for Strategic Studies, London
IMF	International Monetary Fund
INDC	Intended Nationally Determined Commitments (contributions to international efforts to slow global warming)
IPCC	Intergovernmental Panel on Climate Change
IPHE	International Public Health Emergency
ISO	International Organization for Standardization
ITA	Information Technology Agreement
ITO	International Trade Organization
JCPOA	Joint Comprehensive Plan of Action, known commonly as Iran nuclear deal
KP	Kyoto Protocol
LDC	Least developed countries

LIO	Liberal international order
MCM	medical countermeasures
MDB	Multilateral development bank
MFN	Most favored nation
MSC	Munich Security Conference
MSF	Médecins Sans Frontières, Doctors Without Borders
NATO	North Atlantic Treaty Organization
NDB	New Development Bank (BRICS)
NGO	Non-governmental organization
NPT	(Nuclear) Non-Proliferation Treaty
NSA	National Security Agency
NSS	American National Security State
OBOR	One Belt One Road
OECD	Organization for Economic Co-operation and Development
OIE	World Organization for Animal Health, originally Office international des epizooties
OSCE	Organization for Security and Cooperation in Europe
PA	Paris Agreement
PAs	Partnership agreements
PESCO	Permanent Structured Cooperation
PHEIC	Public health emergency of international concern
PLO	Palestine Liberation Organization
PRC	People's Republic of China
PTAs	Preferential trade agreements
R&D	Research and development
RCEP	Regional Comprehensive Economic Partnership
SARS	Severe acute respiratory syndrome
SCO	Shanghai Cooperation Organization
SCS	South China Sea
SDG	Sustainable development goals
SDT	Special and differential treatment (principle in UNFCCC)
SICA	Central American Integration System
TFA	Trade Facilitation Agreement
TIO	*The* international order
TiSA	Trade in Services Agreement
TPP	Transpacific Partnership
TRIPS	Trade-Related Aspects of Intellectual Property Rights

UN	United Nations
UNCLOS	UN Convention on the Law of the Sea
UNFCCC	UN Framework Convention on Climate Change
UNMEER	UN Mission for Ebola Emergency Response
UNSC	United Nations Security Council
US	United States of America
WHA	World Health Assembly
WHO	World Health Organization
WMD	Weapons of mass destruction
WTO	World Trade Organization

List of Contributors

Chaesung Chun, Seoul National University

Daniel Deudney, Johns Hopkins University Baltimore

Myriam Dunn Cavelty, Center for Security Studies (CSS), ETH Zürich

Joyeeta Gupta, University of Amsterdam

Bernard Hoekman, European University Institute, Florence

Iris Hunger, Federal Information Centre for Biological Threats and Special Pathogens (IBBS), Robert Koch Institute Berlin

Daniel Krahl, Social Democratic Party (SPD) Berlin

Hanns W. Maull, German Institute for International and Security Affairs of the Foundation for Science and Policy (SWP), and Mercator Institute for China Studies (MERICS) Berlin

Charles E. Morrison, East-West Center, Hawaii

Marco Overhaus, German Institute for International and Security Affairs Berlin

Zhongying Pang, distinguished university Professor of Global Studies/International Relations, and Dean, The Marine Development Studies Institute, Ocean University of China in Qingdao, Beijing

Volker Perthes, German Institute for International and Security Affairs Berlin

Wolfgang Richter, German Institute for International and Security Affairs Berlin

William Walker, University of St. Andrews

Introduction

The International Order: A Framework for Analysis

Hanns W. Maull

The origins of the postwar liberal international order were hardly auspicious. In August 1941, its two architects, US President Franklin D. Roosevelt, and British Prime Minister Winston Churchill, sailed to a remote naval base off the coast of Newfoundland on two warships, the USS *Augusta* and HMS *Prince of Wales*. The meeting and its location were kept strictly secret. The United States had not formally entered the war against Germany yet, while Britain had just barely defeated the German Air Force in the Battle of Britain. In the Atlantic, the submarine war was raging. The German Wehrmacht had just begun its attack on the Soviet Union and was advancing rapidly. Against this backdrop, Roosevelt and Churchill finalized the "Joint Statement" which later became known as the Atlantic Charter. Published on August 14, 1941 simultaneously in Washington and London, the Charter became the blueprint for the liberal international order (LIO) that shaped much of world politics during the second half of the twentieth century and into the twenty-first.

A functioning international order is, to adapt a felicitous metaphor from Joseph S. Nye, Jr., like oxygen in the air: you do not take notice of it until it begins to disappear.[1] During the first half of the last century, two world wars, with about fifteen million and fifty million deaths respectively,[2] made clear the cost of a collapse of international order in terms of human suffering and material destruction. The search for a functioning international order that would be able to prevent major war therefore was taken up with increasing urgency during the late nineteenth and early twentieth centuries, from below,

[1] Joseph S. Nye, Jr., East Asia: The Case for Deep Engagement, *Foreign Affairs* 74:4 (July/August 1995), pp. 90–102 (90).

[2] Matthew White, Necrometrics, Part of the Historical Atlas of the Twentieth Century, available at http://necrometrics.com/20c5m.htm#Second [accessed January 15, 2017].

by civil society, but also by governments. Those efforts inter alia produced the League of Nations and the Briand–Kellogg Pact (officially the General Treaty for Renunciation of War as an Instrument of National Policy), but they were unable to prevent World War II. It was the course initiated with the Atlantic Charter by America and Britain that succeeded in establishing a viable international order that shaped world politics for the next seventy-five years.

The outlines of this international order took up elements of the Pax Britannica—the first liberal international order that Great Britain had orchestrated during the middle of the nineteenth century.[3] The basic orientations of this new LIO included the principles of free trade, individual rights, including property rights, rule of law, democracy, and justice; it was "orderly" in supplementing the anarchy of international politics with an expanding body of international law (with the Charter of the United Nations at its core) and with a plethora of global and regional institutions (again, with the United Nations family of institutions at the core, but also with vibrant regional institutions such as the European Community (EU), North Atlantic Treaty Organization (NATO), or Association of Southeast Asian Nations (ASEAN)). It also was sustainable, for two major reasons: the LIO rested on the considerable material power of the United States and its political will to use it in support of the LIO, and it enjoyed considerable legitimacy—that is, it was accepted and supported by other states.[4] In the aftermath of World War II, the LIO built on the Atlantic Charter was rather quickly supplanted by the Cold War that dominated world politics from 1947 onward and confined the LIO to the countries and regions outside the Communist bloc. When the Cold War ended in 1989/90, however, the LIO as it had developed as a partial order since 1947 now was the only game in town. It thus became *the* international order—we call it the LIO 2.0. This order ambitiously tried to include Russia and China within it.

Over the last decade, this international order has come under increasing stress,[5] and by the end of 2016, the LIO 2.0 arguably already had died quietly

[3] Ian Clark, *Hegemony in International Relations*, Oxford: Oxford University Press, 2011, ch. 5.

[4] See ibid. and David A. Lake, *Hierarchy in International Relations*, Ithaca, NY: Cornell University Press, 2011.

[5] On this topic, there has been an avalanche of publications in recent years: see, e.g., David Held and Charles Roger (eds.), *Global Governance at Risk*, Cambridge: Polity Press, 2013; Henry Kissinger, *World Order: Reflections on the Character of Nations and the Course of History*, New York: Penguin, 2014; Bruce Jones and Thomas Wright, *The State of the International Order*, Washington, DC: Brookings (Policy Paper 33), February 2014; Maximilian Terhalle, *The Transition of Global Order: Legitimacy and Contestation*, London: Palgrave Macmillan, 2015; Amitav Acharya (ed.), *Why Govern? Rethinking Demand and Progress in Global Governance*, Cambridge: Cambridge University Press, 2016; Robert Kagan, *The Twilight of the Liberal World Order*, Washington, DC: Brookings: January 24, 2017, available at https://www.brookings.edu/research/the-twilight-of-the-liberal-world-order/?utm_campaign=Brookings+Brief&utm_source=hs_email&utm_medium=email&utm_content=41517002 [accessed January 30, 2017]. The most recent important addition to this literature is Richard Haass, *A World in Disarray: American Foreign Policy and the Crisis of the Old Order, With a New Afterword*, New York: Penguin Press, 2018.

from exhaustion, making way for a new, as yet undefined and rather precarious transitional state of world order. This did not mean, of course, that nothing remained of the LIO 2.0. Most of its principles, rules, norms, and institutions continue to exist, but they have lost much of their effectiveness and legitimacy, and the political center of gravity in world politics no longer is to be found in the United Nations (UN) Security Council in New York (now again frequently blocked by vetoes threatened or even actually cast by one or two of the permanent members) or in Washington, DC, in the buildings of the US government. By 2016, the West had been severely weakened by internal upheavals and dislocation in the wake of the financial and economic crises of 2008–10. At the same time, it was also challenged increasingly from outside by the rising power China and by the frustrated old power Russia. The international order therefore has to be, and already is, renegotiated between the West, still led by the United States, and its challengers. The result will be a different international order.[6]

This transformation takes place at a time when a functioning universal international order is desperately needed to collectively manage the opportunities and risks of globalization and rapid technological change. World politics therefore faces a dilemma: while a more effective international order is urgently needed to deal with a range of pressing global issues, agreement on the basic principles, norms, and rules to guide such cooperation is becoming more difficult to establish as all concepts of international order, regardless of who promotes them, are contested as a result of power shifts and power diffusion.

Against this background, this volume aims to assess what has been happening with the international order over the last quarter of a century since the end of the Cold War. It will do so by looking into the developments in some of its major parts, and the role of two of its "ordering powers," the United States and China. Our assumption is that this focus on the components, rather than on the international order itself, allows a comparative evaluation and will provide fresh insights with respect to the following major questions:

(1) *What exactly happened in and with the LIO 2.0 since 1990?* This question is *descriptive*; it aims at a better understanding of events and changes affecting those components of international order.

(2) *What are major identifiable longer-term trends? Are we observing an overall transition from "more" to "less" international order? Which particular arrangements of order have proven most, and which least resilient?* The focus of this second question is the *evaluation* of international order.

[6] This is the central insight of Terhalle, *Transition of Global Order*.

(3) *What strategies and policies have the major ordering powers the United States and China pursued with regard to international order?* This question is centered on the key actors and their policies.

Those three questions are at the heart of the chapters that follow. The remainder of this introduction defines our key concepts, clarifies assumptions, and develops the analytical framework that will guide the following chapters and make their findings comparable. We begin with the term "the international order" itself.

1. "THE INTERNATIONAL ORDER": CONCEPTUAL CLARIFICATIONS AND NORMATIVE FOUNDATIONS

1.1. "The International Order" (TIO)

Is it at all meaningful to talk about "*the* international order"? Or is this but an abstraction, a figment of internationalist hopes that have never been able to triumph over the realities of world politics?[7] While "international order" has been an important topic for the discipline of international relations and has inspired a number of important scholarly efforts in the past,[8] in recent years, the term seems to have been superseded by the more fashionable concept of "global governance." It has made a strong comeback, however, since the financial crisis, not least in the universe of Western think tanks[9]—a symptom, perhaps, of the present crisis of the LIO 2.0.

We assume that the concept of *the* international order (TIO) is indeed meaningful. It describes more than the sum of all arrangements that together constitute the international order, but also its underlying logic, which gives the individual parts coherence and makes TIO more than just the sum of its parts. TIO consists of the structures, institutions, and arrangements in and through

[7] For an argument along those lines, see Richard Fontaine, Salvaging Global Order, *The National Interest*, March 10, 2015, available at http://nationalinterest.org/feature/salvaging-the-global-order-12390 [accessed July 22, 2016].

[8] Among the seminal works are Stanley Hoffmann (ed.), *Conditions of World Order*, Boston, MA: Houghton Mifflin, 1968; Hedley Bull, *The Anarchical Society*, London: Macmillan, 1977; Nicholas J. Rengger, *International Relations, Political Theory and the Problem of Order*, London: Routledge, 2000. The most recent systematic explorations are Andrew Hurrell, *On Global Order: Power, Values and the Constitution of International Society*, Oxford: Oxford University Press, 2007, and Terhalle, *Transition of Global Order*.

[9] Thus, the Brookings Institution has been running a Project on International Order and Strategy "...to understand the changing power dynamics in the international system and the implications for U.S. strategy and international cooperation" (see the website, available at https://www.brookings.edu/about-ios/ [accessed January 12, 2017]. The January/February 2017 issue of *Foreign Affairs* carried the title: Out of Order? The Future of the International System.

which world politics is or may be managed. "Global governance" describes something closely related, namely the politics and policies in the context of the international order (which could also be seen as the "world polity"), but it often simply takes TIO as a given, putting the emphasis on analysis of process. International order presupposes the existence of an international system, indeed an international society, in which "actors" (individuals and collectives, including nation-states) regularly interact with each other.

Following Stanley Hoffmann, we define *the* international order (TIO) as "... establishing the minimum conditions of coexistence" under which humankind would "... be able not merely to avoid destruction, but to live together relatively well in one planet."[10] Perhaps the most widely quoted definition of TIO is that of Hedley Bull, who describes it as "... a pattern of activity that sustains the elementary or primary goals of the society of states, or international society."[11] As Muthiah Alagappa has pointed out, this definition is somewhat tautological in that "international order" and "international society" are almost synonymous; he therefore proposes a slightly modified version of it, describing TIO as "... a formal or informal arrangement that sustains rule-governed interaction among sovereign states in their pursuit of individual and collective goals."[12] According to William Walker, however, both Bull's and Alagappa's definitions appear too static; they need to be broadened to encompass "... an order's creation, consolidation and decline."[13] We also integrate in our definition three other considerations that seem important to us: first, non-state actors have become relevant autonomous participants in world politics; second, TIO is a multi-layered phenomenon that is composed of regional and functional components; and third, TIO is a social construction that results from, and depends on, "... practices of shared meaning and collective intentionality."[14]

Thus, for the purposes of this volume we define TIO as follows:

> The international order is the sum of all formal or informal arrangements that sustain rule-governed interaction among sovereign states and non-state actors in their pursuit of individual and collective goals. The international order is a dynamic social construct that, like its components, is created through human interactions, changes over time, and is eventually transformed or dissolved.

[10] Hoffmann, *Conditions of World Order*, p. 2. The following definition draws on William Walker, *A Perpetual Menace: Nuclear Weapons and International Order*, London: Routledge, 2010, pp. 11–15.

[11] Bull, *Anarchical Society*, p. 8.

[12] Muthiah Alagappa, The Study of International Order: An Analytical Framework, in Alagappa (ed.), *Asian Security Order: Instrumental and Normative Features*, Stanford, CA: Stanford University Press, 2003, pp. 28–64 (39).

[13] Walker, *Perpetual Menace*, p. 14.

[14] Rengger, *International Relations*, p. 84, quoted in Walker, *Perpetual Menace*, p. 13.

What is to be ordered? International relations consist of the sum of human interactions across boundaries and the open spaces of the world; those interactions have been global in scope since at least the middle of the nineteenth century as a result of the two great revolutions of the eighteenth and nineteenth centuries: the French revolution and the industrial revolution.[15] The notion of a unitary international order finds its material base in an increasingly integrated global system of socio-economic, political, and cultural interactions. This system has been undergoing changes induced by the advances of science and technology commonly described as "modernization" or, today, "globalization."[16] It is characterized by three major trends that together may well make this an entirely new phase in the history of human civilization: the exponential growth of human economic activity's demand on global resources, including the environment, the rapid rise of interconnectivity across the globe, and the increasing homogenization of human culture.[17]

Politically, the LIO found expression in the Charter of the United Nations and the international institutions it has brought into life. The former may be seen as the constitution of the post-1945 international order, and defines its normative foundations; the UN family of institutions collectively serves as a rudimentary, incomplete world government. Both aim to establish and orchestrate "international ordering," but they lack the authority to do so. This order therefore has to rely largely on voluntary compliance and enforcement by the true arbiters of international order, the nation-states who are members of the UN and together form part of world society: the society of states. (The other part consists of the peoples and nations of the planet, of humankind.) Leadership is essential in this order to organize initiatives, bring together coalitions of countries willing and able to decide and implement them, and to assume the costs for public goods. The United States has played this role for the last twenty-five years. It could do so because it enjoyed authority—an authority that was based on its ability to get things done (i.e., its power) and the acceptance and support of others for its leading role.[18]

In sum, the notion of a unitary, integrated international order therefore seems meaningful for three reasons: it corresponds to the material reality of a globalized system of international relations; it manifests itself politically in a global power structure defined by cooperation and competition between major

[15] For a fascinatingly comprehensive treatment of this transformation, see Jürgen Osterhammel, *Die Verwandlung der Welt, Eine Geschichte des 19. Jahrhunderts*, Munich: C. H. Beck, 2009.

[16] David Held, Anthony McGrew, David Goldblatt, and Jonathan Perraton, *Global Transformations: Politics, Economics and Culture*, Stanford, CA: Stanford University Press, 1999.

[17] Ian Morris, *Why the West Rules—for Now: The Patterns of History, and What They Reveal About the Future*, New York: Farrar, Straus & Giroux, 2010, ch. 12 and *passim*; Thomas Homer-Dixon et al., Synchronous Failure: The Emerging Causal Architecture of Global Crisis, *Ecology and Society* 20:3 (2015): p. 6, available at http://dx.doi.org/10.5751/ES-07681-200306.

[18] Clark, *Hegemony*; Lake, *Hierarchy*.

states; and it finds normative, institutional, and political expression in the United Nations system.

Yet while the international order is unitary, it is certainly not undifferentiated, nor homogeneous. Our project distinguishes three different levels of international order: first, the global level of "international" order; second, regional or functional "partial orders"; and third, the political orders of individual states, which through their actions still play the most important (but no longer exclusive) role in shaping and implementing international order. International order thus consists of many different, partly overlapping regional and functional partial orders; these, in turn, rest on the national political order of nation-states. Together, these three levels form a continuum, a seamless web. Patterns of cooperation and competition between states are at the core of the politics of international order.

What happens within all those orders of different types and levels will sometimes reflect influences originating in other, adjacent or even completely separate orders. Those influences (we call them "interferences" to make clear that they may be unintended and even without specific actors) can contribute to order or its decay and dissolution (positive/negative interference).

The concept of "political order" (or simply: "order") is crucial for our analysis; it is also one of the oldest and most important terms in political science. From the very beginning of political thought, the concept had two different dimensions:

(a) Empirically, political order describes the sum of regulative features in a society (or any collective) that guide the way members of the collective interact with regard to its identity, its shared purposes, and desires (Who are we? How do we want to live? What are our collective aspirations?) across the four major issue areas of economics and welfare, security, culture, and institutional arrangements of political order. Those regulative features build on certain ideas, principles, and norms that serve to establish and justify specific arrangements of order and provide guidance on issues of collective identity and ambition. They may reflect a broad consensus among all members, or they may have been imposed by a few members of that society, or even from outside. Depending on how order is seen from within by its members or subjects, it may enjoy a high or low degree of acceptance or legitimacy. What principles and norms guide specific orders and what level of legitimacy they enjoy are key empirical issues in any analysis of political order. So are the exercise of power by individual actors and power relationships between them that shape the developments within any given order, but also the specifics of that order itself.

(b) What constitutes a good political order has long been a key question in political philosophy and political science. Beyond empirical assessments about the level of acceptance by the members of a political order and their satisfaction with existing arrangements, it is also possible, however, to compare the aspirations that political orders formulate with the realities of their policies, and from that comparison draw conclusions about their performance. More ambitious still are reflections on what would constitute an "ideal" order and how it could be brought about. All these are normative considerations that involve (inter-)subjective value judgments about what constitutes a "good" political order.

1.2. Partial Orders

Partial orders are our most important object of analysis in this volume. We decided to approach the study of international order by focusing on its regional and functional components and on two of its ordering powers, rather than on the international order itself to provide a different, "bottom-up" perspective on the LIO. In this approach, we look at what we call partial orders—a term chosen to make clear that we want to compare not only various functional orders (or international regimes) but also regional orders through the lens of a common framework of analysis that can also be used to study national orders and TIO.

Partial orders are regional and/or functional arrangements of cooperation and competition between states. Their existence reflects incentives for and constraints on nation-states, usually resulting from interdependence, that push them into cooperation (for example, to deal with collective action problems) or conflict, and/or the desire to realize shared aspirations. Partial orders can be competitive as well as cooperative: during the Cold War, for example, the international order as a whole, but also the regional orders, especially in East Asia and Europe, were shaped by the conflict between the two superpowers.

Functional partial orders, commonly called international regimes, are usually (though not necessarily always) cooperative. While *regional partial orders*, as mentioned, may be cooperative or even integrative, as in the case of the European Union (and the associated European states Norway, Iceland, Liechtenstein, and Switzerland), in this volume we focus on ambivalent, conflictual, or even antagonistic regional orders. As well as interdependence, transnational and international aspects of solidarity and shared identities across borders may also underpin such partial orders, as for example religious solidarity among Shi'ites or Sunnis (transnational solidarity) or pan-Arab solidarity (international solidarity) against Israel in the Middle East.

In any order, the behavior of actors displays certain patterns that make developments predictable, at least to some extent. Those patterns, in turn, reflect formal or informal principles, norms, and rules governing the order that are widely observed among its members. Those rules developed through, and are supported by, the exercise of power, persuasion, indoctrination, or mutual advantage.

Partial orders may contain sub-orders that can be analyzed in much the same way as partial orders themselves. Thus, the pan-European regional order has regional sub-orders (Western and Central Europe, with the EU and associated states; Eastern Europe, with the Eurasian Union), and the Nuclear Suppliers Club represents a functional sub-order to the nuclear order.

Partial orders exist in specific—and often specified—territorial and/or functional realms demarcated by boundaries. Boundaries may be precise or fuzzy boundary zones; they may change over time (e.g., enlargement of the European Union or the World Trade Organization (WTO); changing geographic definitions of what constitutes and who belongs to the Asia-Pacific region), overlap or intersect. Ultimately, boundaries are social constructions that are constitutive for partial orders; they reflect differences in the density of interactions within and across boundaries.

Principles, norms, rules, and organizations guide the behavior of actors within the respective partial order. They may be formal or informal. The Middle Eastern order, for example, or the pan-European security order before 1975 did not have any formal documents laying out comprehensively the rules for interaction, while the Helsinki document issued by the Conference for Security Cooperation in Europe (CSCE) in 1975 did spell out the principles, norms, and rules of interaction, albeit in a legally non-binding form. "Principles" are broad guidelines inspiring the norms and rules of behavior; in the context of the Cold War pan-European order, an important principle was recognition of the territorial status quo as "inviolable." "Norms" in that order stipulated the inadmissibility of the use of force or the protection of human rights. "Rules" concerned the way the order worked—for example, through regular review conferences of the member states, in which all countries had one vote with the same weight.

Full *compliance* with the principles, norms, and rules of orders will be exceptional. Non-compliance per se is not a sign that an order has broken down: only when non-compliance has no consequences and becomes widespread, and when those defying the principles, rules, and norms will not attempt to justify their behavior in terms relating to them, has it ceased to exist. The degree of compliance will vary, depending on the legitimacy and effectiveness of rule enforcement. The norms and rules may enjoy broad consensus or be contested within the order. Mechanisms for creating legitimacy and sanctions to enforce compliance may also differ widely.

1.3. Actors

Actors create, sustain, transform, or destroy order through their interactions. While we assume that states remain the most important actors in international order, we recognize the importance of non-state actors, including business and civil-society organizations but also terrorist groups and warlords, for the development of order in international relations. In our understanding, "actions" include words ("speech acts") as well as deeds ("behavior"). In the last analysis, all actors are individuals, but they may act not only on their own but also as representatives of collectives and assume roles in institutions. For our purposes, we will therefore consider states, international organizations, enterprises, and other non-state organizations as actors, and will include all actors with significant influence on the evolution of the respective order in our analysis, be they states, non-state actors, or individuals, and regardless of whether their influence on order is constructive or destructive.

One of the many challenges in upholding order in international relations is that there seems to be an important asymmetry between actions capable of sustaining and developing order and those that have the effect of weakening and undermining it. It thus may be easier to achieve a "significant" degree of influence over the trajectory of order for actors that strive to obstruct change or even to destroy existing orders. Nobody would pay much attention to North Korea if it were just one of the many member states of the Non-Proliferation Treaty (NPT) that observed the principles, norms, and rules of that partial order fully. By resigning from the NPT after having been caught developing nuclear weapons, and then bringing that program to fruition, North Korea became a very significant actor in that functional order, the non-proliferation regime. Similarly, some non-state actors like al-Qaida or ISIS have acquired significance for international order due to their carefully calculated use of excessive and gory violence.

1.4. Collective Sanctions

Compliance with the principles, norms, and rules of order usually is voluntary: actors have internalized them and tend to follow them as a matter of course. The need for enforcement is likely to be inversely related to the degree of legitimacy the order enjoys but even partial orders or regimes that are perceived as highly legitimate will probably need mechanisms of enforcement to be sustainable in the face of violation of key principles and norms. This can be done through the threat and use of force, through imposing costs, or through withholding benefits. The incentives and costs may be material (e.g., withdrawing financial transfers, imposing an oil export embargo) or immaterial (e.g., excluding a state from membership, boycotting Olympic Games, "naming and shaming").

Enforcing compliance depends on enforcers: there have to be states (or other actors) in the order that are willing and able to initiate and implement the required measures with sufficient determination and resources. Within states, the government usually has those resources; at the level of partial orders and the international order, however, this will usually require collective action, with all the well-known problems and political difficulties (such as free-riding) that implies.

1.5. Structural Characteristics

Any order will be defined by certain structural characteristics, such as the number of actors and the distribution of material and immaterial resources (equal/unequal) and of power (concentrated/diffuse) between them, the density of interactions and interdependence of formal institutions, and the distribution of status, rights, and responsibilities. Orders can be hierarchical (as state political orders usually are), amalgamated (as with the European Union), pluralistic, or antagonistic; in the latter case, the order will be built around enmity and the permissibility of the use of force. At the extreme, even war therefore can represent a form of political order. One of the most important structural aspects of partial orders is whether they function below or above the "threshold of violence," that is, whether compliance with or contestation within an order involves recourse to organized violence on a major scale.

1.6. Genesis and Evolution over Time

Muthiah Alagappa, who has provided much of the intellectual background for our approach in his seminal work on Asian security, distinguishes the following three "pathways" to create and uphold order, which are not necessarily mutually exclusive:[19]

(a) *Order through competition and power*: following the Realist tradition in international relations theories, arrangements of order will come about through the pathways domination and subjugation, hegemony, balance of power, and concert of powers;

(b) *Order through cooperation*: following the Liberal tradition in international relations theories, pathways to cooperation include collective security, international regimes, and deepening interdependence;

(c) *Order through transformation* relies on changes in the ideational or institutional context of interactions and in collective identities to produce new qualities of order along the pathways of nation-building, democratic peace, or international integration.

[19] Alagappa, The Study of International Order, pp. 53–64.

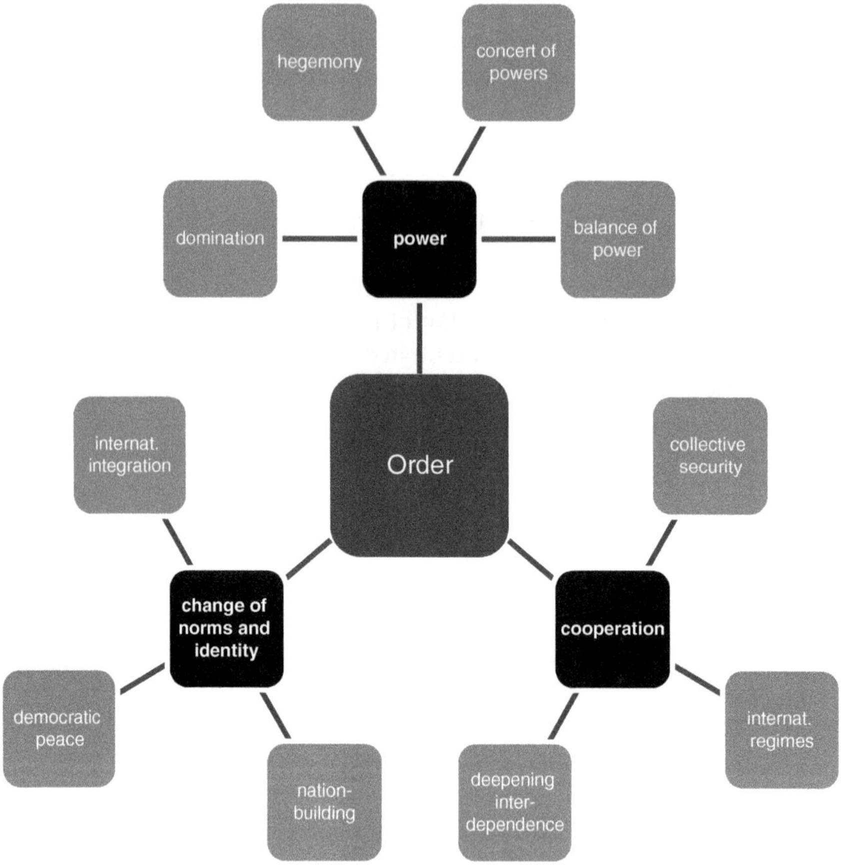

Figure 0.1 Arrangements of order and pathways to their development

Source: own design, based on Muthiah Alagappa, *Asian Security Order: Instrumental and Normative Features*, Stanford, CA: Stanford University Press, 2002

These "pathways to order" can be extended into "pathways within order" and "away from order" by recognizing that orders evolve over time: they may sustain themselves and grow stronger; weaken, decay, or collapse; or mutate into some other form of order through (a mixture of) power, cooperation, or transformation (Figure 0.1).

1.7. Interference between Orders

As we noted above, what happens in one partial order affects other partial orders. Interference between orders may be positive (i.e., mutually reinforcing) or negative (i.e., detrimental for one or all of the orders involved). It can be horizontal, that is, between orders of the same level, or vertical, across the divides between levels. Interference will be the result of interactions across boundaries separating orders; interaction between orders may take the forms of trade, travel, migration, or exchange of ideas. They may be mediated by power, through markets of all kinds, or by persuasion through indoctrination, socialization, or cultural adaptation. Interferences may be highly asymmetrical and unidirectional, or relatively balanced, that is, mutual. It may, but need not result from deliberate efforts by actors in other orders; interference may also reflect unintended side effects of actions and developments within one order on another.

Interference reflects high levels of connectivity across boundaries of states and partial orders, but also tells us something about the *resilience* and adaptability of orders. After all, the capacity to cope with external shocks, threats, or risks is a key function of any order; the phenomenon of interference thus suggests that the affected order has insufficient resilience to protect itself from the impact of interference. If that is the case, the order will have to rely on external resources. This presupposes that other orders will be capable of generating such resources and willing to make them available. If a particular order cannot cope adequately with challenges and is overwhelmed, this is likely to spill over into other orders in the form of unintended (and probably negative) interference.[20]

Figure 0.2 summarizes our framework for analysis.

1.8. Evaluating Orders

The simplest and most obvious way to evaluate the performance of orders is by comparing their declared or implicit objectives with their output and its impact on realizing those objectives, that is, their *effectiveness as well as their efficiency (inputs per unit of outputs) in achieving the results.* Since the attitudes of members towards an order will have significant influence on its effectiveness, a second path to evaluate orders is their *legitimacy*, as measured through

[20] The notion of exporting or importing the capacity to sustain political order is similar to the more familiar metaphor of an export/import of security. The following example may illustrate what the export of a capacity to create political order could mean. The international conference on Syria organized under the auspices of the United Nations and the activities of the UN Special Representative for Syria were efforts to recreate political order of the territory of the Syrian state, which had imploded in civil war. Those efforts relied on capacities to create order mobilized at the global level. In this case, the global level obviously was either unable or unwilling to make available resources sufficient to the task. Another aspect of interference in the case of Syria is the involvement of outside powers in the civil war in Syria, which in turn reflects characteristics of the regional order in the Middle East.

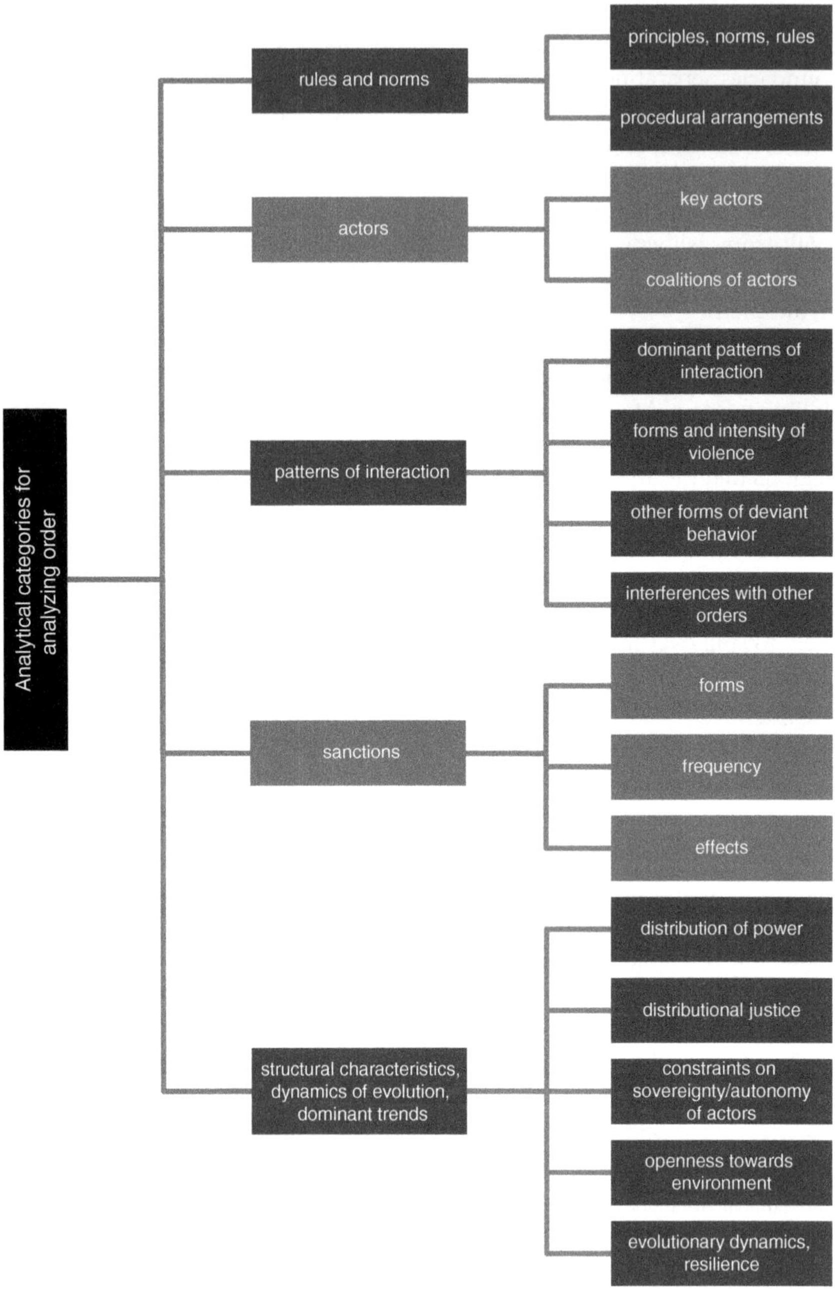

Figure 0.2 Analytical categories for analyzing order

Source: own design

the approval/disapproval and the overall level of support for that order. We are also, as mentioned, interested in the levels of violence. This mode of evaluation implies a shift away from the perceptions of those within the order towards those of outside observers. More generally, significant levels of effectiveness and legitimacy enable authoritative governance of political orders, a government (for nation-state orders), or some weak functional equivalent for partial orders and the international order as a whole. Again, Figure 0.2 summarizes our analysis framework.

2. NORMATIVE PREMISES

While we will empirically analyze the normative dimensions of any political order to find out the values at its base, we of course all also have our own ideas about how politics should be ordered. The editor and the authors of this volume will no doubt disagree about many details on this issue; however, we broadly share the body of principles and norms enshrined in the Charter of the United Nations, the constitution of the present international order that is recognized by all its member states—that is, the Liberal International Order 2.0 that emerged, largely as a result of American efforts, out of the debris of World War II and the implosion of the Cold War.[21] We assume that political order is sustainable when it is reasonably effective and enjoys legitimacy. It will then be able to rely on non-violent forms of conflict management and conflict resolution.

Somewhat paradoxically perhaps, in our view sustainable order will always contain significant elements and spheres of disorder, and should do so. Even in the most repressive and rigid order, actors will, through their interactions with others, not only affirm the principles, norms, rules, and regulations of any political order, but also reinterpret and subtly modify them, thus adapting them over time in line with changing circumstances and individual preferences. Moreover, some may simply disregard or even actively oppose specific aspects or the normative base of the order, probing the ability and will of those committed to its enforcement. The alternative for the regime then is to try to defeat or crush the opposition, or to respond by adapting the order to new circumstances and expectations. Better still are arrangements within the order that provide for adaptation by opening space for unexpected and unpredictable behavior and contestation—that is, for disorder.

[21] G. John Ikenberry, The Liberal International Order and its Discontents, *Millennium* 38:3 (2010), pp. 509–21; G. John Ikenberry, *Liberal Leviathan: The Origins, Crisis, and Transformation of the American World Order*, Princeton, NJ: Princeton University Press 2011.

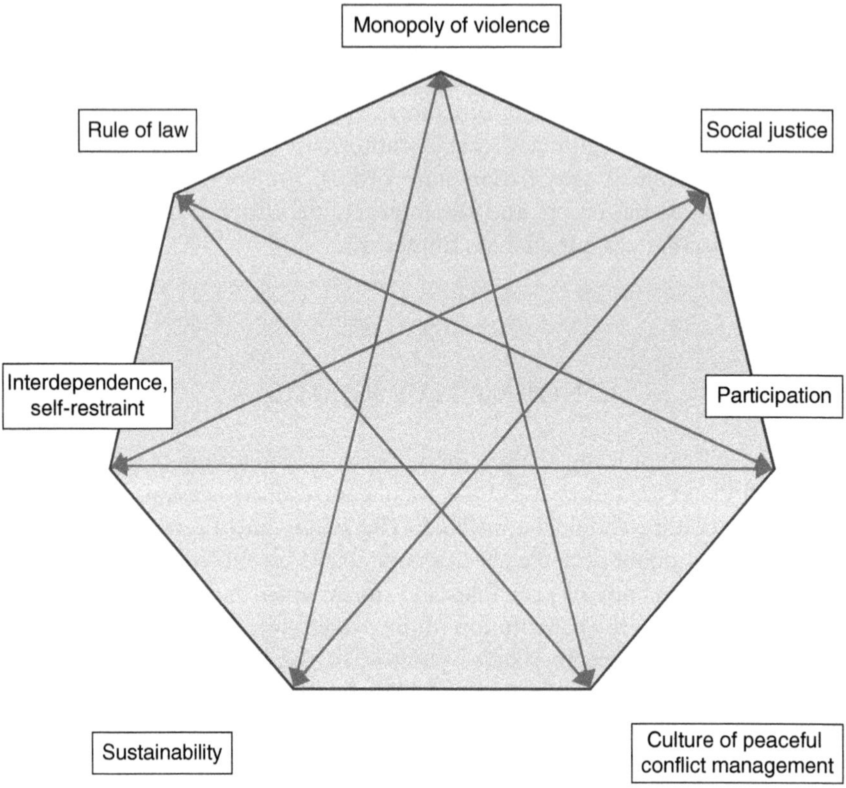

Figure 0.3 The civilizational heptagon
Source: own design, based on Dieter Senghaas, *Zum irdischen Frieden*, Frankfurt am Main: Suhrkamp, 2004

More specifically, we share the view that political order can and should move away from violent to "civilized" forms of conflict management. Following Norbert Elias' work on long-term change in European societies,[22] Dieter Senghaas has suggested the "civilizational hexagon" to capture the essence of such a transformation of political order, the six dimensions of which we have slightly modified by adding another seventh dimension: ecological sustainability (Figure 0.3).[23] Those seven dimensions of "civilized" political order are:

(1) an effective monopoly of the use of force,
(2) rule of law,
(3) interdependence and exercise of self-restraint on emotional impulses,

[22] Norbert Elias, *Über den Prozess der Zivilisation*, 2 vols., Frankfurt am Main: Suhrkamp, 1976.
[23] Dieter Senghaas, *Zum irdischen Frieden*, Frankfurt am Main: Suhrkamp, 2004, p. 39.

(4) a culture of peaceful conflict management,
(5) social fairness/justice,
(6) political participation,
(7) ecological sustainability.

As Figure 0.3 indicates, the seven dimensions of "civilized" or "civilizing" political order are interdependent and mutually supportive: advances in ensuring an effective monopoly of violence may go hand in hand with strengthening the rule of law, for example, and they will enable a collective to rely more effectively on division of labor, thus deepening interdependence.

The transformation of politics along the seven dimensions will usually not be linear and could take place in both directions, towards more or less civilized order. Breaks and setbacks are possible at any time; progress will always remain tenuous and reversible.

We consider an effectively functioning, legitimate, and sustainable "international order" as desirable and critically important as a prerequisite for shaping worldwide individual and collective behavior in ways that would allow mankind to cope with the huge risks and uncertainties, but also exploit the opportunities, of globalization. We doubt that this would be possible without significant political input, i.e., via spontaneous self-coordination through markets or civil society interaction. We are aware that a sustainable "international order" will be a very demanding political artifice, requiring comprehensive political input across the whole spectrum of politics, from within the nation-state to the United Nations. Moreover, the politics of international order do not comprise only states and international organizations, but also a whole range of non-state actors. Order develops, unfolds, transforms, and decays through the interaction of all those actors. The two most relevant aspects in the overall evolution of order are the distribution of power within the respective systems, and the legitimacy of the underlying principles of order.

"Order" may be created in very different ways. For our purposes, one very important dividing line separates peaceful from violent forms, in which actors who want to impose order resort to violence. We assume that sustainable forms of order rely on non-violent forms of conflict management and conflict resolution, such as negotiated compromises, the establishment of constitutional and legal norms, and institutionalized processes of conflict management.

We assume that changes in the international order reflect what is happening within its components, including the nation-state orders, as well as the positive and negative interferences between those components from national levels through regional and/or functional partial orders onto the global level of international order, and vice versa. We are interested in where the balance of influences on international order stands today and how they came about (empirical focus), but also how this order may be strengthened in the future (policy focus). The kind of sustainable international order that offers humankind the chance to cope with present uncertainties, risks, and opportunities will need to be legitimate, non-violent, effective, and adaptable.

3. THE PLAN FOR THIS BOOK

In the following chapters, we use the analytical framework developed above to look at a number of partial orders and two major ordering powers, the United States and China. In selecting our case studies, we focused on seven regional and functional partial orders that seemed to us particularly important for the overall evolution of international order. In one case, the East Asian order, we have two perspectives. As it turned out, one of our functional partial orders, the international climate change order, underwent what we consider a fundamental transformation into a different order, thus giving us a total of nine case studies.

We decided to ask for two different perspectives on each of the two major ordering powers, again with the aim to reflect, at least to some degree, different views about their respective roles. We also wanted to include different perspectives on some issues to recognize the fact that critical issues of international order today are deeply contested.

We also considered the question of which major powers to include. Apart from the United States and China, possible candidates included the European Union, India, and Russia. However, while the European Union may have the power potential to assume an important role as an ordering power, so far it fails the tests of coherence, consistency, and purpose: the EU has not yet displayed the political will to act as a major force in world politics.[24] This is confirmed by our analysis of partial orders, where the EU plays a significant role in only a single case—the world trade order. While it was able to exercise leadership in the first climate change order, it then lost this role to the USA and China in the Paris Agreement order; the US withdrawal announced by President Trump provides an opportunity for the EU to reclaim that position. Thus, the EU has a fighting chance to come back in the Paris Agreement climate change order and also in the cyberspace order due to US isolationism under the Trump administration—but only if it were able to overcome its

[24] Giles Merritt, *Slippery Slope: Europe's Troubled Future*, Oxford: Oxford University Press, 2016; John R. Gillingham, *The EU: An Obituary*, London and New York: Verso, 2016; Hanns W. Maull, The Politics of the EU: China's Relationship with Europe, *Asian Journal of Comparative Politics* (2016), available at http://journals.sagepub.com/doi/pdf/10.1177/2057891116662343 [accessed January 16, 2017]; Hanns W. Maull, European Policies Towards China and the United States: Can They Support a Strategic Triad? *European Foreign Affairs Review* 21, Special Issue (2016), pp. 29–46.

internal disarray, which at the time of this writing (early 2018) seems unlikely. India did not appear as an ordering power in any of our case studies, and seems unlikely to assume such a role anytime soon.[25] Finally, Russia is not a rising power, as China or India undoubtedly are, but a declining former superpower whose global importance lies in its nuclear and conventional military power, its diplomatic skills and resources, and its hydrocarbon potential, but which otherwise lacks economic and social resources to underwrite the role of a global ordering power.[26] In our case studies, it figures as a major actor only in the nuclear and the Middle Eastern regional orders, albeit not exactly in an ordering role.

The first part of our book analyzes functional partial order, or international regimes. We start with the *international trade and investment order (WTO order)*, perhaps the most effective part of international order we have: as Bernard Hoekman shows in his contribution, this functional order was significantly strengthened and widened with the conclusion of the Uruguay Round of trade negotiations and the establishment of the WTO in 1995. Albeit not successful in all its aspects, the international trade and investment regime functions are based on rule of law rather than power politics, and it has performed quite effectively so far. Yet there are now huge shadows hanging over its future.

The partial order to address man-made climate change has, as Joyeeta Gupta shows in Chapter 2, experienced a veritable transformation. An agreement between two of that partial order's most important actors, the US government and that of the People's Republic of China (PRC), in late 2014 cleared the way to the Paris Agreement on climate change in 2015, generally considered an important step forward in international efforts to combat global warming. Gupta's analysis shows a more complex picture, however. Iris Hunger's assessment of the functional partial order addressing international public health emergencies in Chapter 3 presents the reader with an international order that, over the last two decades, has registered important advances and thus offers a stark contrast to most other chapters in this book.

Turning from functional orders dealing with economic and welfare issues to security concerns, William Walker's assessment of the nuclear order in Chapter 4 presents a profoundly ambivalent picture. This ambivalence ultimately reflects divergent—and perhaps fundamentally incompatible—objectives, the abolition of the risks of nuclear war and the pursuit of civilian nuclear energy. The partial order for cyberspace, discussed by Myriam Dunn Cavelty in

[25] Christopher Coker, *The Improbable War: China, The United States and the Continuing Logic of Great Power Conflict*, Oxford: Oxford University Press, 2015, pp. 125–32.

[26] Hanns W. Maull, The Rise of New Powers: Implications for the Transatlantic World, in Daniel Hamilton and Kurt Volcker (eds.), *Transatlantic 2020: A Tale of Four Futures*, Washington, DC: Center for Transatlantic Relations, 2011, pp. 71–92.

Chapter 5, still has to be created: this realm probably comes closest to an absence of any order (and hence a high level of unpredictability) among all partial functional orders represented in this volume. In the realm of cyber-activities, it is the disjunction between national security considerations and the protection of individual rights that is both the most important driver behind efforts to create order and the most difficult to reconcile. Enhancing resilience thus may have to be the realistic alternative to a functioning partial order that could continue to elude political efforts.

In Part II of the book, we take a closer look at three particularly critical *regional* orders: greater Europe, the Middle East, and East Asia. The pan-European order, transformed in 1989/90, is again undergoing profound changes. In Chapter 6, Wolfgang Richter shows that the foundations of the new European order of 1990 were brittle from the beginning: much depended on the strategies and policies pursued by the principal actors and their respective definitions of their own national interests. The erosion and crisis of the pan-European order was driven by a lack of mutual trust and commitment to the underlying principle of mutual strategic restraint by both the United States (starting with the first administration of President G. W. Bush) and Russia (with the rise of Vladimir Putin to the Russian presidency in 2000).

The Middle Eastern regional order offers a stark picture of order disintegrating. As Volker Perthes and Hanns W. Maull show in Chapter 7, developments in that region almost provide a mirror image to the success of the state in East Asia: here, most states have failed to modernize their economies and societies successfully, and several states have fallen apart, transforming an already precarious and violence-prone regional order into one that functions largely on the principle of organized violence to achieve the actors' aspirations. What is more, inter-state and intra-state violence have become inextricably interlinked in ways that remind European observers of the Thirty Years War in the first half of the seventeenth century and Asians of the parallel collapse of the Chinese Ming dynasty.

The East Asian order, on the other hand, so far has shown remarkable resilience against the background of decades of dynamic socio-economic change; even the end of the Cold War did not produce major changes, suggesting an impressive capacity of this order to adapt. In their analyses, both Charles E. Morrison (Chapter 8) and Chaesung Chun (Chapter 9) underline that the successful drive for modernization (or "national rejuvenation," as Morrison calls it), which consolidated and strengthened national political orders, has been a crucial factor in securing regional stability—as much as, or perhaps even more than, the role of the United States as guarantor of regional stability and open markets.

The third empirical part deals with the two most important "ordering states," the United States and China. While Daniel Deudney (Chapter 10) emphasizes how much the USA has contributed to international disorder, thereby tragically helping to undermine the liberal democratic order at home, Marco Overhaus (Chapter 11) cautions against writing off America prematurely. The contributions by Zhongying Pang (Chapter 12) and Daniel Krahl (Chapter 13) both highlight the extraordinary ambivalence that characterizes China's conception of and policies toward international order, as well as its persistent search for ways to reconcile its quest for status with the benefits China derived from the US-dominated liberal international order.

The Conclusions summarize and evaluate our findings. They suggest that the post-Cold War international order has been undergoing a fundamental transformation that makes the significant achievements of this liberal international order look increasingly precarious. The decline of the post-Cold War order therefore portends not only a very different, but also a much weaker, international order.

Part I

Functional Partial Orders (International Regimes)

1

The International Trade Order—Performance and Challenges

Bernard Hoekman

1. INTRODUCTION

With the creation of the World Trade Organization (WTO) in 1995, the international trade order moved away from the treaty-based General Agreement on Tariffs and Trade (GATT) regime where implementation of many rules was voluntary and dispute resolution relied heavily on diplomacy and "pragmatic flexibility." Under the WTO all rules apply, in principle, to all members equally and dispute settlement is more formal and legally binding. The WTO provides a forum for negotiating enforceable agreements to constrain the use of trade distorting policies, as well as mechanisms through which countries monitor and enforce implementation of the agreed rules of the game. The effective dispute settlement system makes it an outlier among international organizations, but this is only one way through which members assure compliance with negotiated trade policy commitments.

The WTO is a partial realization of the original vision of the drafters of the stillborn International Trade Organization (ITO)—albeit some fifty years later. Despite being less ambitious than the ITO in terms of some policy areas, the creation of the WTO may prove to be a high-water mark for multilateral trade cooperation. Since 1995, attempts to expand the coverage of the WTO have proved very difficult. Initial efforts to complement the "built-in" negotiating agenda on agriculture and services embedded in the 1993 Uruguay Round agreements with a broader negotiating round were controversial. Many developing countries argued that their concerns regarding the benefits and costs of implementing existing WTO disciplines and provisions should be the priority. Other countries supported further expansion of the coverage of the WTO to new policy areas.

Following a failed Ministerial conference in Seattle in 1999, a broad round of negotiations was eventually launched in 2001: the Doha Development Agenda (DDA). Most of the "new" issues proposed for negotiation—procurement transparency, investment, and competition rules—were taken off the table at the 2003 Ministerial in Cancun. The only exception was trade facilitation. Only in 2013 was a first DDA result achieved: the "Bali package." This included the first ever multilateral agreement negotiated under WTO auspices—the Trade Facilitation Agreement (TFA). The TFA is significant both because it addresses a policy area that matters from an economic perspective and, perhaps more important, it demonstrates that WTO members are capable of crafting new multilateral policy disciplines. That said, it did not prove possible to agree on a broad "single undertaking" deal on the core DDA negotiating issues—additional disciplines on domestic agricultural support policies and market access commitments for trade in goods and services. The 10th Ministerial Conference in Nairobi in December 2015 effectively ended the DDA, although many developing countries continued to insist that progress in moving forward on new issues was conditional on DDA subjects being addressed. The resulting stalemate could not be resolved, leading to the 11th Ministerial Conference in Buenos Aires in December 2017 ending without any new agreements. Members were unable even to agree on a text of a joint ministerial declaration. Instead, a small number of initiatives were announced by subsets of WTO members to engage in discussions on subjects of interest to them, including e-commerce and investment facilitation. These proposed initiatives involve different groups of WTO members. The United States joined only one (on e-commerce).

Since the mid-2000s, most of the energy of WTO members has turned to preferential trade agreements (PTAs). Does this matter? And what does the post-1995 period imply for an assessment of the WTO's performance in establishing a framework for international cooperation, and, more generally, the international trade order? Does the current situation of stalemate represent a temporary plateau or a high-water mark for multilateral cooperation on trade matters? The answers to these questions depend on the view one takes of the role played by the trade order in supporting the very rapid growth realized by many countries since the mid-1980s and the importance of continuing to expand the ambit and scope of universally applicable rules to discipline national policies that generate negative international spillovers.

The stylized facts of the shifts that have occurred in world trade and development are well known: high sustained economic growth in many developing countries, especially China and East Asia, but also in Eastern Europe, parts of Latin America, and South Asia; a great increase in the global trade share of developing countries; ever more intra-industry trade and global value chains reflecting in part an explosion in two-way foreign direct investment (FDI) flows and stocks; and technological changes that supported ever finer specialization and rapid growth in trade in services, e-commerce, and cross-border digital transactions. All of these elements of the globalization process were supported by the GATT/WTO. In Europe and North America regional integration played a significant role in supporting the growth that occurred in international trade and investment flows, while in East Asia the process of trade-led growth mostly reflected autonomous policy reforms. However, in all cases the multilateral trade regime provided a supporting framework for the national policy reforms and investment decisions that were a precondition for trade expansion. The role of the WTO in this regard is perhaps most visible in the case of China, for which accession to the WTO was an important instrument to support reforms that led to the reintegration of China into the global economy. The inclusion of China in the WTO was also important for the international trade order because of its weight in global trade and thus the significance of China abiding by multilateral rules of the game for its trade policies and the ability of WTO members to initiate dispute settlement actions against perceived violations of those rules—which they did.

2. CHARACTERISTICS OF THE INTERNATIONAL TRADE ORDER

The WTO is a stand-alone international organization. It is independent of the United Nations system (i.e., it is not a UN specialized agency). It extends approaches and institutional features of the GATT, most notably the consensus principle, which helps to ensure legitimacy and ownership of decisions. The WTO secretariat is small (some 700 staff) and has little independent authority. The WTO is "member-driven." There are numerous WTO bodies, both standing and ad hoc, including committees and councils, working parties on accession, and dispute settlement panels. There are over 1,000 meetings a year. While day-to-day activities are undertaken by delegations based in Geneva, meetings frequently involve officials from capitals. The "hub-and-spoke" nature of the trade regime implies that WTO staff and member delegations are complemented by inputs from thousands of government officials in capitals, in turn informed by business associations and non-governmental organizations (NGOs) in member countries.

Only governments have standing in the WTO. The trade order is a state-to-state regime. No formal mechanisms exist for non-governmental groups, including businesses, to participate in negotiations or the deliberations of standing committees and other WTO bodies. Such groups must instead lobby their governments at home or exert pressure through the media and demonstrations. This is a feature of the two-level game that characterizes the functioning of the trading system: only governments play at the WTO level, but affected and interested groups determine the position and actions of these governments.

The Preamble of the GATT 1947 listed among its objectives raising standards of living, ensuring full employment and a large and steadily growing volume of real income and effective demand, developing the full use of the resources of the world, and expanding the production and exchange of goods. It goes on to say that reciprocal and mutually advantageous arrangements involving a substantial reduction of tariffs and other barriers to trade as well as the elimination of discriminatory treatment in international trade will contribute to the realization of these objectives.

The objectives of the WTO are essentially the same as those mentioned in the GATT Preamble. The main difference is that sustainable development was added as a goal and there is explicit recognition of the "need for positive efforts to ensure that developing countries, and especially the least developed among them, secure a share in the growth in international trade commensurate with the needs of their economic development." The broad goals listed in the WTO Preamble are complemented by more specific tasks. WTO Articles II and III charge the organization with facilitating the implementation and operation of the Multilateral Trade Agreements (GATT, General Agreement on Trade in Services (GATS), and Trade-Related Aspects of Intellectual Property Rights (TRIPS)), providing a forum for negotiations, administering the dispute settlement understanding, multilateral surveillance of trade policies, and cooperating with the World Bank and the International Monetary Fund (IMF) to achieve greater coherence in global economic policy-making.

There are nonetheless some major differences between GATT and WTO.

- Under the GATT, new disciplines that were negotiated took the form of "Codes" that parties could decide whether or not to participate in. This meant that like-minded countries could move forward in a given area even if some (or many) countries were not willing to do so. Under the WTO (almost) all agreements apply to all members. This arguably has impeded progress in developing new rules of the game.
- Under the GATT, establishment of a court (a dispute settlement panel) and adoption of its decisions required the consent of all parties to a dispute. This meant that a country alleged to violate a commitment could refuse either to allow a panel to be established or refuse to accept the findings of a panel. Under the WTO, it is not possible to block the formation of dispute settlement panels or the adoption of panel reports, or the authorization of retaliation in instances of non-implementation of rulings.
- The WTO Secretariat has a stronger mandate to pursue transparency and surveillance functions through the Trade Policy Review Mechanism. The WTO is also much more open than the GATT was as regards

its operations ("internal transparency"). Most documents discussed in committees and councils are available on the Internet. This contrasts with the GATT, where most documents were "restricted" and not made available to the public.

- For much of its history the GATT was a "club" of like-minded countries, dominated by a hegemon (the USA). Today, the WTO has almost universal membership. As a whole, the 160+ members are less like-minded than the core members of the GATT were. The WTO operates in a multi-polar global economy, one in which members have had to accommodate the rise of China as a trade power.[1]

3. PERFORMANCE OF THE REGIME

Assessing the performance of the international trade order requires establishing the counterfactual—what would have occurred in the absence of the WTO? The "formal" objectives of the WTO listed in the Preamble and in the various agreements are generally not suitable baselines for an assessment of performance because they are very broad in scope and not "under the control" of the WTO. As a result, performance assessment in much of the academic literature has tended to center on relatively narrow questions. Thus, legal scholars focus on the effectiveness of adjudication of disputes, while economists have assessed whether the WTO has led to more trade and enhanced welfare. In both instances, the general assessment in these literatures is positive—the dispute settlement system works relatively well (some 500 cases since 1995), with judgments mostly implemented by the losing party. There is consistent empirical evidence that the WTO has increased trade and, through trade, average real incomes.[2] The mechanisms that are at play here span various elements of the WTO, including the reduction in uncertainty associated with policy commitments and transparency.

Both international relations and trade policy researchers have focused on various systemic objectives attributed to WTO members. These include "macro goals" that revolve around the stability of the system, as well as a set of specific tasks or functions that are embodied in provisions of agreements.[3] Macro goals include:

[1] See R. Wolfe, First Diagnose, Then Treat: What Ails the Doha Round? *World Trade Review* 14:1 (2015), pp. 7–28.

[2] See, e.g., M. Tang and S. J. Wei, The Value of Making Commitments Externally: Evidence from WTO Accessions, *Journal of International Economics* 78:2 (2016), pp. 216–29.

[3] M. Elsig, B. Hoekman, and J. Pauwelyn, Thinking about the Performance of the World Trade Organization: A Multi-Disciplinary Perspective, in Elsig, Hoekman, and Pauwelyn (eds.),

- upholding of the "rule of law," reflected in disciplines that control the exercise of power;
- providing a system that is both robust and flexible enough to be capable of accommodating expansion of the trade order, in particular new members;
- the extent to which the regime addresses capacity differentials and effectively integrates and assists the poorest/weakest states so that they benefit from the regime;
- providing a system that is robust to exogenous shocks—the test being whether governments stick to their commitments not to use certain types of policies.

Specific tasks or functions that have been analyzed in the literature include:

- the provision of a negotiation platform to agree on new disciplines;
- regime management processes that support the implementation of the agreements, including operation of WTO Councils, Committees, informal groups, etc. and the numerous transparency and monitoring-related activities;
- the implementation and effects of specific provisions of WTO agreements, e.g., in the area of antidumping, product standards, and protection of intellectual property rights.

The performance of the trade order in achieving these various objectives and tasks has been mixed but on balance positive. On the "rule of law" front, the system has largely delivered. A key objective of many countries in moving to the WTO was to tame aggressive US unilateralism.[4] This was achieved—the USA has worked through the WTO in contesting foreign trade policies and small countries have successfully challenged US policies, which has complied with rulings against it. The available evidence suggests that small and weak states do make use of dispute settlement mechanisms in situations where they might otherwise have been dissuaded from invoking their rights due to, e.g., fear of retaliation. The track record of cases brought forward and compliance with rulings suggests that the system works reasonably well, although the United States in particular has been critical of how the Appellate Body—the WTO appeals court—functions. US dissatisfaction with elements of the working practices of the Appellate Body culminated in 2017, leading to refusal to approve new appointments of new judges, a situation that may result in the

Assessing the World Trade Organization: Fit for Purpose? Cambridge: Cambridge University Press, 2017, pp. 12–42.

[4] J. Bhagwati and H. Patrick (eds.), *Aggressive Unilateralism: America's Trade Policy and the World Trading System*, New York: Harvester-Wheatsheaf, 1990.

demise of the appeals function. This situation, ongoing at the time of writing, represents a serious threat to the operation of the WTO.[5]

The system has also proven capable of accommodating new states. The WTO had 164 members as of December 2017, as compared to 128 "original members" in 1995. The successful accession of China was both a landmark test and a signal development for the trade order.[6] In contrast to the GATT years, when the trade regimes of newly acceding countries were often not subjected to serious scrutiny, under the WTO, the thirty-six members that joined after 1995 were required to bring their policies into compliance with WTO requirements. Accession to the WTO is a lengthy and serious process, one that substantially improves the quality of trade institutions in the countries concerned.

A pertinent question here is not just whether the system could accommodate large new members such as China, but whether new entrants are responsible stakeholders—i.e., constructive players, following the rules of the game, complying with dispute settlement rulings, participating in negotiations, etc. Here, the evidence is also mostly positive—some new members are very active users of the dispute settlement mechanism, and many participate actively in the day-to-day activities of the WTO, including negotiating processes.[7]

The heterogeneity of the organization's membership is enormous, even within the group of so-called developing countries. In 2013, Malawi had a per capita income of around US$270 per year, and Brazil US$11,700.[8] The traditional response to capacity and income differentials in the GATT/WTO has been "special and differential treatment" (SDT) for developing countries. SDT involves promises by rich countries to provide preferential market access, allow for "less than full reciprocity" in trade negotiations, and permit developing countries greater leeway ("policy space") to use trade restrictions. SDT in the WTO has increasingly been targeted on least developed countries (LDCs). Many Organization for Economic Co-operation and Development (OECD) countries insist that large emerging economies like Brazil, China, and India no longer should be eligible for SDT and need to do more to liberalize access to their markets given that these countries are competitive in global markets. An inability of the WTO membership to agree on a narrower

[5] See G. Sacerdoti, The Future of the WTO Dispute Settlement System: Confronting Challenges to Consolidate a Success Story, in C. Braga and B. Hoekman (eds.), *Future of the Global Trade Order*, 2nd edn. Florence: European University Institute. Available at: http://cadmus.eui.eu/handle/1814/49384 [accessed December 20, 2017].

[6] L. A. Winters, China and the World Trading System: Will "In and Up" be replaced by "Down and Out"? RSCAS Working Paper 2015/82, Florence: European University Institute, 2015. Available at http://cadmus.eui.eu/handle/1814/37823 [accessed December 10, 2017].

[7] L. Li and M. Yu, Impact of the WTO on China's Rule of Law in Trade: Twentieth Anniversary of the WTO, *Journal of World Trade* 49:5 (2015), pp. 837–72.

[8] Data from the World Bank, Gross National Income per capita. Available at http://data.worldbank.org/indicator/NY.GNP.PCAP.CD/countries?display=default.

targeting of SDT on the countries that need it most has been one driver behind the shift to PTAs by OECD nations, as these allow emerging economies to be excluded from market access liberalization commitments.

A significant innovation that occurred under WTO auspices to recognize the heterogeneity of the membership is the 2013 Trade Facilitation Agreement (TFA). The TFA breaks new ground in the approach taken to recognize differences in implementation capacity across countries by letting governments determine themselves which elements will be implemented with a time lag. The TFA also recognizes that some of its provisions will require resources to implement, and that some countries will need assistance. An innovation in this regard was to link implementation of such provisions to the supply of technical assistance and aid for trade. This approach helps to address differences in views as to who should be eligible for SDT by putting the onus on emerging economies to request technical assistance for implementation, which brings with it an embarrassment factor if the country clearly has the capacity to implement.

The WTO has done much more than the GATT did in supporting LDCs to use the trading system—one of the goals explicitly mentioned in the WTO Preamble. Assessing performance in this area requires measuring the change in both the level of integration in narrow trade terms and the extent to which LDCs make use of the WTO—e.g., dispute settlement, or putting forward negotiating proposals. Another relevant metric is the extent to which richer countries have taken actions to assist LDCs to address capacity constraints. A significant development in this regard was achieved in 2005 with the agreement of developed WTO member countries to provide duty- and quota-free access to merchandise exports from LDCs and to launch an "aid for trade" (AFT) program, including the establishment of a specific mechanism, the Enhanced Integrated Framework, to assist LDCs to define trade and capacity-building priorities that can be supported through development aid programs. These initiatives constitute a move by WTO members to increase policy coherence by linking trade and development assistance. Significant amounts of funding have been mobilized.[9] More important than the funding, however, is that the aid for trade program increased the attention for trade policy matters at national level. AFT has become a mechanism to engage development agencies (bilateral and multilateral) more in the trade integration agenda and helps to raise the profile of trade issues in the process of determining priorities for investment and policy reform at the country level.

[9] According to OECD data, using a narrow measure of trade assistance that excludes infrastructure projects and sector-specific projects, between 2002 and 2012 assistance increased from US$660 million to US$1,260 million. If a broad measure of aid for trade is used, including all trade-related sectoral projects, total disbursements rose from some $25–$30 billion in the early 2000s to around $45 billion a decade later. See http://www.oecd.org/dac/aft/aid-fortradestatisticalqueries.htm.

Another measure of the performance of the WTO is how well the trade order works in times of crisis, whether at national or global level. Here the stylized facts are that the system works relatively well, and certainly better than was the case in the GATT years. The WTO appears to have been more effective than the GATT in helping governments to manage and respond to pressures by domestic actors for protection of national markets. Research suggests there is some evidence of a positive effect of the WTO on the "quality" of trade policy, e.g., case studies of specific countries[10] showing how WTO disciplines can be and have been used to manage and deflect pressures for protection by powerful interest groups. However, monitoring efforts have also demonstrated that many Group of Twenty (G20) countries have made active use of trade-distorting policies after the 2008 financial crisis and often have employed policy instruments that are not well covered, if at all, by WTO disciplines.[11]

One major area in which WTO performance unambiguously gets a failing grade is in providing an effective platform for multilateral negotiations to agree on additional trade policy disciplines and new rules of the game. Although cooperation certainly has not broken down—the daily business of the WTO, including activities aimed at ensuring transparency of trade policy and settlement of disputes, has worked well—it has not proven possible to successfully conclude the long-running Doha Round. Moreover, the recent refusal by the USA to accept new appointments to the DSB Appellate Body poses a serious threat to dispute resolution in the future. This is not the place to explain this failure but even here the picture is not all negative.[12] The conclusion of a new agreement on trade facilitation in 2013 is a counter-example, as is a 2015 agreement to ban agricultural export subsidies. Moreover, there have been efforts to negotiate market access liberalization on a "critical mass" basis, between only a subset of the WTO membership that accounts for most of the trade in a given product. Such agreements (will) apply on a most-favored-nation basis because that is required by the WTO. Examples of such critical mass initiatives include the Information Technology Agreement (ITA), the coverage of which was expanded in 2015, another illustration that WTO members can get to "yes." Initiatives launched at the 11th WTO Ministerial Conference in Buenos Aires in December 2017 to explore potential cooperation between groups of WTO members on issues such as rules for e-commerce and investment facilitation may eventually lead to additional agreements between like-minded countries that are open to all WTO members.

[10] E. J. M. Baracat, P. Finger, L. Raul Thorne, and J. Nogues, *Sustaining Trade Reform: Institutional Lessons from Peru and Argentina*, Washington, DC: World Bank, 2013.

[11] See the monitoring reports and analysis of the Global Trade Alert at http://www.globaltradealert.org/ [accessed December 20, 2017].

[12] See, e.g., Wolfe, First Diagnose, Then Treat.

4. CHALLENGES AND PROSPECTS FOR THE INTERNATIONAL TRADE ORDER

Notwithstanding these examples of continued efforts to work through the WTO, the focus of policymakers increasingly has turned to PTAs. This raises numerous questions regarding the possible consequences for developing (and other) countries that are either excluded or are “price takers.” The WTO as a multilateral institution is particularly important to small countries that do not have market power. A breakdown in the ability of the WTO to agree to new disciplines on policy areas that generate negative spillovers may affect mostly the many countries that are not part of most PTAs. While there are strong economic forces that are likely to keep markets open,[13] rules of origin, regulatory convergence, and mutual recognition agreements of countries that join PTAs may create incentives for companies to locate in a bloc, or to source from firms located within a bloc, to the detriment of outside firms.

Two factors arguably have played an important role in inducing the shift to a preferential trade agreement-centered trade strategy and away from the WTO: (i) the difficulties that have been experienced in getting to “yes” on the DDA, reflecting the increasing economic size of emerging economies and differences in views regarding the continued salience and appropriateness of special and differential treatment for such countries; and (ii) the increasing complexity of dealing with the international spillover effects of domestic policies and the impacts of technology in driving a rapid increase in trade in services and associated cross-border data flows.

The structural changes and power shifts since 1990, most notably the growth of China, underlie the first factor.[14] The launch of the DDA and China’s accession to the WTO both occurred at the Doha Ministerial meeting in 2001. Little thought was given at the time to the implications of the latter for the former given the stated goal of concluding the round within four years. As the DDA headed into its second decade, it became clear that the initial implicit understanding that China had “already paid its admission fee” in 2001 and would not be expected to make significant additional commitments in the DDA was no longer tenable. The resistance by China (and other emerging economies) to make more commitments led the USA to launch the Transpacific Partnership (TPP) negotiations with like-minded Asia-Pacific countries. This initiative excluded China. This shift in policy was only in part the result of

[13] For example, the increasing role of global value chains and international production networks creates political economy incentives to oppose/refrain from import protectionism. See K. Gawande, B. Hoekman, and Y. Cui, Determinants of Trade Policy Responses to the 2008 Financial Crisis, *World Bank Economic Review* 29:1 (2015), pp. 102–28.

[14] Wolfe, First Diagnose, Then Treat; Winters, China and the World Trading System.

deadlock at the WTO and more generally reflected rising geo-political rivalry between the USA and China.[15]

Also important is the second factor: the agenda that was the focus of the DDA did not address many of the concerns of businesses that produce goods and services or the households that consume them. The predominant focus of the DDA was on agriculture and tariffs on manufactured products, not on industrial policies, trade and investment in services, and digital trade and e-commerce—areas of interest and concern to large numbers of firms in both developed and developing economies. Mega-regional trade initiatives such as the TPP and the effort to conclude a plurilateral Trade in Services Agreement (TiSA) put these types of policies at center stage.[16]

The mega-regional approach to new rule-making turned out to be more difficult than envisaged by proponents. Although the TPP talks were concluded successfully at the end of 2016, one of the first acts of the Trump administration in early 2017 was to withdraw from the TPP. EU-led efforts to negotiate deep trade agreements with Canada and the USA confronted widespread opposition by civil society in the EU. Talks between the EU and the USA have been on hold since 2017 following the election of Donald Trump as US president. The same is true for the TiSA negotiations. The Trump administration is not a proponent of multilateral trade agreements and skeptical towards the value of existing bilateral trade agreements. More generally, trade agreements have become a focal point for opposition by many voters in developed countries as they are concerned they are not benefitting from an open world economy and that the gains from globalization have primarily accrued to those who are highly skilled and to workers in emerging economies.

The trade order has played a major role in helping to raise large numbers of households in developing economies out of poverty. As a group, developing nations today account for 43 percent of global trade, up from a little over 20 percent in the late 1980s. Since 1990, per capita incomes in East Asia have increased six-fold; those in South Asian countries have tripled. While cross-country average income inequality has fallen as a result, intra-national inequality has risen in many countries, both developed and developing, as a result of trade integration, skill-biased technical change, and an increasing share of national income growth accruing to the richest households in societies. Concurrently, voters and consumers have become more concerned with global climate change, migration pressures and management of refugee flows,

[15] See the discussion by Charles Morrison in Chapter 8 in this volume.

[16] The TiSA talks occurred outside the ambit of the WTO and were launched by a group of like-minded countries, including the EU and the USA, interested in establishing new rules on domestic regulation of services and additional disciplines on policies affecting trade in services.

and matters such as safeguarding their data privacy (see Chapter 5 of this book by Myriam Dunn Cavelty) and the protection of human and social rights.

The challenge confronting the WTO as an institution goes beyond moving on from the failed Doha Round of negotiations and beginning to address the types of issues that are on the table in the mega-regional discussions. More important is to demonstrate that sustaining multilateral trade cooperation is critical for future growth of all countries and that deeper cooperation is part of the solution to the concerns that large segments of civil society and polities have regarding trade agreements. In the post-2009 period following the global financial crisis there has been a steady increase in the use of trade-distorting policies by major economies, including by the United States. Reversal of trade openness will not address the underlying drivers of technological change and the adjustment costs that have been incurred as a result of the growth of developing countries. The policies needed are largely domestic—pertaining to the labor market, tax regimes, and the education system.

Deepening trade cooperation can help address some of the negative spill-overs of policies that are not effectively covered by the global trade order. Pursuit of such cooperation will arguably have to entail greater moves to variable geometry—cooperation between clubs of countries as opposed to all of the WTO membership. The revealed preference for PTAs illustrates that this is inevitable. The challenge for the WTO is to channel more of the energy that has been—and continues to be—invested in PTAs towards plurilateral rule-making under the WTO umbrella. Necessary conditions for moving down this path include: (i) pursuit of deliberative mechanisms to discuss the substance of international cooperation and how this can promote common objectives—such as sustainable development; and (ii) becoming more open to engage in cooperation on a plurilateral basis in the WTO.

4.1. Fostering More Deliberation in the WTO

The trade order has gone from strong North–South disagreement on basic norms ("free trade" as an ideal vs. import substitution and infant industry protection as a central feature of development policy) to a situation where there is greater agreement on the value of a liberal rules-based trade order, but the substance of (required) rules has become more contested in the North as a result of the economic success of the South. There has been substantial convergence in views on the benefits of an open trade regime. This is reflected in the low average tariffs that prevail today and the more limited use of barriers to trade than was the case as recently as the mid-1980s.

Looking forward, the "2nd generation" agenda confronting the WTO centers on "behind the border" nontariff policies, including differences in product regulation that create excess transaction costs for businesses and the use of industrial policies that favor domestic production. Reducing the market-segmenting effects of differences in regulations is difficult because of concerns that it may compromise the attainment of regulatory objectives ("race to the bottom"). Agreeing on new rules regarding the use of industrial policies that support domestic firms and discriminate against foreign companies—such as local content or transfer of technology requirements for foreign investors—is difficult as it is seen by the countries that have successfully used such policies as a driver of industrial development.

There is great potential in this regard to learn from the experience of PTAs, as these may serve as laboratories in which countries experiment with approaches to address differences in regulatory regimes and agree to disciplines on the use of specific industrial policies. A precondition for such learning is that countries that are not members of a preferential trade agreement have information on what is being done in the preferential trade agreement context. Ideally, signatories to the PTAs would agree to provide information and share their experiences with implementation with all WTO members, and the WTO secretariat could be mandated to analyze and report on the approaches that have been implemented in PTAs and their impacts on economic outcomes. Here there is much scope for the WTO to cooperate with other organizations, including the secretariats of regional economic communities, multilateral development banks, and other international agencies, to harness complementarities in dealing with matters that impact on trade and investment flows.

Many international organizations and partial orders contribute to the global governance of trade and investment. The WTO is in many respects a very weak organization in comparison with the Multilateral Development Banks (MDBs) and the IMF, etc., all of which have greater resources and a larger footprint than does the WTO in, for example, capacity-building, research and analysis, deliberation, policy dialog, and advisory services. There are many linkages, overlaps, and interdependencies between the domain of the WTO and the areas and activities of other institutions. Examples include sectoral regulation and associated international efforts and networks through which regulatory cooperation is pursued; governance of (multinational) business and associated global value chain-based production and trade (including private product and production standards, labeling and traceability requirements, corporate social responsibility initiatives, etc.); preferential trade agreement-based initiatives in areas of direct relevance to the trade order (e.g., moves to establish investment courts as part of new EU trade agreements); and the international regimes governing international financial flows, and monetary and exchange rate policies (i.e., IMF and Bank for International Settlements (BIS)).

As mentioned, a major challenge for the international trade order is to confront and address the concerns by stakeholders regarding the effects of trade agreements. One element of addressing this challenge is to demonstrate that the WTO adds value by helping to achieve common objectives that have been established at the international level such as those that are reflected in the Preamble to the WTO agreement. The most comprehensive set of such objectives are the sustainable development goals (SDGs).[17] Trade is referenced as an instrument in five of the seventeen goals: (i) in goal 2 (end hunger), which includes a call to correct and prevent trade restrictions and distortions in world agricultural markets, including through the parallel elimination of all forms of agricultural export subsidies and all export measures with equivalent effect; (ii) in goal 8 (decent work and economic growth), through a call to improve AFT support for developing countries, in particular through the Enhanced Integrated Framework for LDCs (8.a); (iii) in goal 9 (industry, innovation and infrastructure), which includes calls for development of quality, reliable, sustainable, and resilient infrastructure, including regional and trans-border infrastructure (9.1) and increasing the integration of small-scale industrial and other enterprises, in particular in developing countries, into value chains and markets (9.3); (iv) in goal 10 (reduce inequality), through implementation of the principle of special and differential treatment for developing countries, in particular LDCs, in accordance with WTO agreements; and (v) in goal 17 (partnerships for the goals), as a means of implementation, through promotion of a universal, rules-based, open, non-discriminatory, and equitable multilateral trading system, including through conclusion of the DDA (17.10); significantly increasing exports of developing countries, including doubling the LDC share by 2020 (17.11); and timely implementation on a lasting basis of duty-free, quota-free market access for all LDCs (17.12).

The SDGs entail little new relative to what was the focus in the context of the Millennium Development Goals that guided international development programs in the 2000 to 2015 period. The mercantilist bias implied by the focus on developing country exports disregards that in practice lack of competitiveness and limited diversification of low-income economies is a result of domestic policies, including import policies. The definition of the SDGs was driven by a very broad set of actors, including a large number of civil society groups and development organizations at local and global level. These groups often are skeptical about whether trade can help to generate inclusive and sustainable growth. Arguably the government representatives of WTO members in Geneva did too little to engage in the SDG process, missing an opportunity to illustrate the potential role that trade and trade-related policies can play to realize the goals.[18]

[17] UN General Assembly: *Transforming our World: The 2030 Agenda for Sustainable Development*, Resolution A/Res/70/01 of September 25, New York: United Nations, 2015.

[18] See, e.g., M. Fiorini and B. Hoekman, Services Trade Policy and Sustainable Development, European University Institute RSCAS Working Paper 2017/41. Florence: European University

The limited focus on the role that trade can—and should—play in achieving the SDGs is one illustration of the downside of the basis of cooperation in the WTO being restricted to central government, state-to-state interactions. Governments at different levels (central, sub-central, municipal), regulators, multinational companies, and NGOs are all engaged on trade issues and interact with counterparts across borders (other jurisdictions). Municipal and state/provincial governments increasingly pursue distinct trade strategies that revolve around attracting and retaining trade-intensive investment (investors), including public–private partnerships. Such "sub-central" activity is set to increase further, in part because of increasing urbanization and the rise of "mega cities" and in part because relevant policies are implemented at the "local" level. Companies set standards for quality, health, and safety for both products and processes that occur in their supply chains. They increasingly cooperate in private standards-setting activities that have as a goal achievement of inter-operability and minimum standards across supply chains—sometimes in cooperation with NGOs and governments (e.g., the Global Food Safety Initiative). NGOs do the same—there is a plethora of private standards-setting bodies that develop norms and offer certification services to companies that engage in international trade. Regulators frequently have their own mechanisms through which they interact with each other internationally.

The WTO will need to find ways to connect to these networks and communities of practice if it is to play a complementary role in efforts to reduce the trade-impeding effects of differences in regulation—public and private—across jurisdictions. A first step would be to do more to learn from what is being done in other forums. Pursuit of a strategy of engagement with these various stakeholders in the global trade order would appear to be a necessary condition for identifying priority areas for cooperation to facilitate trade and investment in ways that do not detract from the realization of national economic development and regulatory goals but conversely will help to attain such goals more efficiently and effectively.[19]

4.2. Facilitating Plurilateral Cooperation in the WTO

Numerous observers have argued that cooperation on regulatory "behind-the-border" policies cannot occur between 160+ countries and that this helps explain the increased recourse to PTAs. An implication is that the WTO membership should do more to pursue small group cooperation *inside* the

Institute, 2017. Available at http://cadmus.eui.eu/handle/1814/47684 [accessed December 10, 2017].

[19] B. Hoekman, Fostering Transatlantic Regulatory Cooperation and Gradual Multilateralization, *Journal of International Economic Law* 18:3 (2015), pp. 609–24.

organization as opposed to leaving the field to PTAs, given that the latter are explicitly discriminatory and often nontransparent for third countries. The WTO offers two alternative mechanisms for members to form "clubs" on an issue of common interest without necessarily involving all WTO members. The first is conclusion of a so-called Plurilateral Agreement under Art. II.3 WTO;[20] the second are so-called critical mass agreements. Both involve initiatives where negotiated disciplines bind only those countries that participate in them. They differ in that in the latter the benefits of agreement are applied on a nondiscriminatory, most favored nation (MFN) basis to all WTO members, whereas in a Plurilateral Agreement they need not. Examples of critical mass agreements include the Information Technology Agreement and agreements on basic telecommunications and financial services under the GATS. From the perspective of the trade order both types of agreements are superior to an ever expanding number of PTAs—they are more transparent, imply less dispersion in rules, and thus lower transactions costs for firms and they offer a way to multilateralize elements of what has been agreed by countries in PTAs.[21]

There is little to prevent more use of agreements between groups of WTO members that are applied on a nondiscriminatory basis. The initiatives on e-commerce or investment facilitation that were announced by groups of WTO members at the December 2017 WTO Ministerial Conference are potential examples. However, negotiation of new Plurilateral Agreements under which non-signatories do not benefit from what has been agreed confronts greater difficulties. Because such agreements limit the benefits to signatories, current WTO rules impose a consensus requirement on incorporation of new Plurilateral Agreements into the WTO, so that nonparticipants can prevent a subset of WTO members from implementing a proposed Plurilateral Agreement. In practice, this is a major disincentive for countries to attempt to negotiate Plurilateral Agreements in the first place. If the WTO is to accommodate more variable geometry-based agreements, this constraint needs to be reconsidered. Doing so will be difficult. A first step might be to seek to establish a code of conduct that provides assurances that non-signatories will not be adversely affected, are kept fully informed, and are able to participate in the future if they wish to on the same terms that apply to incumbents.[22]

Moving in these directions can help to ensure that the international trade order remains a relevant pillar of the international order more broadly conceived and plays a constructive role in addressing rising geo-political

[20] There are currently two such Plurilateral Agreements: the Agreement on Civil Aircraft and the Agreement on Government Procurement.

[21] B. Hoekman and P. C. Mavroidis, Embracing Diversity: Plurilateral Agreements and the Trading System, *World Trade Review* 14:1 (2015), pp. 101–16.

[22] Ibid.

tensions, the national security concerns of states, and increasing questioning by polities regarding the distribution of the benefits of globalization. Active pursuit of more bottom-up, plurilateral forms of engagement on trade policy matters in the WTO may permit more cooperation between the USA and China on trade and investment matters and thereby help to attenuate the geo-economic and geo-political tensions that have been created by the very rapid growth of the Chinese economy. As noted by Joyeeta Gupta in Chapter 2 in this volume, one lesson from the UN Framework Convention on Climate Change (UNFCCC) negotiations that led to the 2015 Paris Agreement is that a bottom-up process that revolves around countries defining and committing to national targets and associated carbon reduction strategies and agreeing to pursue a concerted effort on a voluntary basis could be a more effective approach to international cooperation than a top-down one where nations seek to negotiate binding commitments. Similar approaches will need to be pursued in the trade context. The December 2017 WTO Ministerial Conference in Buenos Aires suggests that many countries are ready to move down this path. However, it should be noted that China did not join the e-commerce initiative that was launched (the USA did) while the USA did not join the initiative on investment facilitation for development (China did). Very few African nations joined either initiative (Nigeria being the only African state to participate in both). Ensuring that such initiatives remain open and transparent is critical, as are efforts to engage with many developing nations that abstained from supporting them. While the launch of small group initiatives in the WTO is a positive development, the core need is an accommodation between China and other large emerging economies on the one hand and the United States and other OECD nations on the other as regards rules of the road for industrial development policies that are perceived to generate negative international spillover effects.

5. CONCLUSION

The WTO, the keystone of the rules-based multilateral trading system, is under significant pressure. Increasing recourse to trade-distorting policies in conjunction with the decision by the USA to block new Appellate Body appointments is compounding the negative impact on the credibility of the WTO created by the inability of WTO members "to get to yes" in the Doha Round. These developments should not be taken to imply a lack of relevance of the WTO. Multilateral negotiations have become more complex because developing countries have interests that they are pursuing and objectives they want to achieve. The trade tensions between the USA and China, and to a lesser extent, other emerging economies, are a reflection of the success of the latter and the policies they have put in place. Sustaining and enhancing cooperation is also more complex because the issues increasingly involve national "behind-the-border" regulatory and development policies. PTAs may well be more effective mechanisms to address matters of a regulatory nature, or that involve the liberalization of politically sensitive areas such as the movement of people. It is noteworthy that the interface between the trade order—if defined to comprise the WTO—and other partial orders is more limited in scope than many PTAs in terms of coverage of policy areas. Many PTAs address matters such as labor and environmental standards, may cover temporary cross-border movement of natural persons (e.g., service suppliers), while deeper integration arrangements may include a focus on human rights, rule of law, and political regimes. These areas of policy are covered by the WTO only tangentially, if at all. As discussed above, that may change, insofar as more WTO members decide to push into "behind-the-border" issues, but many nations have objections to going down this path.

In some policy domains there already is a substantial interference between the WTO and other orders—one example is in the area of product standards (health and safety norms for food and animal products); another is the protection of intellectual property rights. In both of these areas, other partial orders take the lead in setting substantive norms (International Organization for Standardization (ISO), Food and Agriculture Organization (FAO)/Codex Alimentarius for product standards; World Intellectual Property Organization for intellectual property). Another area where the interface has been growing is development assistance, where the WTO today interacts much more with the multilateral development banks. Mention can also be made of linkages between the trade and financial orders, illustrated by pressure in recent years by some countries for the WTO to address situations of alleged manipulation of exchange rates, and to become involved in the process of standard setting in areas that directly impact on trade. An example was the treatment of trade finance in the revision of the Basel capital adequacy regulations for banks, which were of great concern to traders as they were argued to be excessive given the very low historic default risk associated with trade finance.

These are all areas where PTAs have little role. PTAs also generally do not address subjects that have been the source of disagreement in WTO negotiations such as agricultural support policies, which are important to many developing countries, and industrial and innovation-related policies that involve subsidies of different types. Moreover, as the world economy becomes even more interconnected as a result of the "Internet of things," e-commerce, and the associated increase in cross-border service flows, policies that limit or raise the cost of digital trade and data flows will become ever more important. PTAs may include provisions on such matters, but from a global efficiency perspective what is needed are rules of the game that span all major economies.

Given that it will be difficult to obtain agreement on industrial policies or regulatory cooperation among 160+ countries, the continued relevance of the trade order may well depend on the use of open plurilateralism and variable geometry forms of cooperation. In practice, this may well be the most feasible mechanism for subsets of countries to cooperate and engage in rule-making that goes beyond current WTO disciplines. Deeper integration will inevitably occur within clubs—what is needed from the perspective of an effective and efficient international trade order is to ensure that such variable geometry can be accommodated under the umbrella of the WTO as opposed to being pursued through PTAs.

2

Climate Change and the Future of International Order

Joyeeta Gupta

1. INTRODUCTION

The Paris Agreement (PA) of 2015 has given a new lease of life to international efforts to limit climate change and pushed negotiations into a new direction. It obliges all participating countries to ratchet up their national climate policy targets (called Intended Nationally Determined Commitments (INDCs)) every five years with the objective of bringing down global concentrations of greenhouse gases (GHGs) to a level consistent with a 1.5–2°C rise in global temperatures as compared to pre-industrial era levels.[1] The Agreement breaks with past climate policy agreements (such as the Kyoto Protocol) by requiring all countries to adopt targets. This is a significant step forward, not least because developing countries like China and India have now accepted this common approach.[2]

While the Paris Agreement is legally binding, it does not specify by when GHG emissions would have to reach zero. The actual national targets (INDCs) are not included in the PA, nor are the responsibilities of rich countries in terms of technology transfer and financial commitments to developing countries specified in ways that would allow measurement and thus verification. Moreover, the INDCs submitted to the Secretariat (which may vary from the NDCs submitted upon ratification), while ambitious, fall significantly short of what will be needed to achieve the long-term climate policy objective.[3]

[1] UNFCCC, Paris Agreement, December 12, 2015, available at http://unfccc.int/files/home/application/pdf/paris_agreement.pdf [accessed 15 February 2016].

[2] G. Ananthakrishnan, China, Russia, Venezuela and Arab states support Paris Agreement, in *The Hindu* online, December 13, 2015, available at http://www.thehindu.com/sci-tech/energy-and-environment/cop21-climate-change-summit-at-paris-china-russia-venezuela-and-arab-states-support-paris-agreement/article7983278.ece [accessed February 15, 2016].

[3] UNFCCC, COP 21 Decision, FCCC/CP/2015/L.9/Rev.1/III (22).

Still, despite its shortcomings the Paris Agreement launches the global community onto a transition to a GHG-free world.[4] This transition will be fraught with difficulties: at present, the world economy runs largely on fossil fuels, vested interests oppose change, and the current low oil prices also stand in the way of real progress.

This chapter addresses the following questions: How has the climate change regime evolved since the 1970s? How has it contributed to, and built upon, the present international order? What are major identifiable trends in this order? How does the climate change order relate to the Sustainable Development Goals[5] and the dominant neoliberal capitalist order?

2. THE EVOLUTION OF THE INTERNATIONAL CLIMATE CHANGE POLICY ORDER

The climate change negotiations can be divided into five phases.[6] In the first, pre-1990 phase, a broad scientific consensus on the dangers of global warming emerged through the work of the Intergovernmental Panel on Climate Change (IPCC). In the second phase (1990–6), international negotiations led to the adoption of the United Nations Framework Convention on Climate Change (UNFCCC 1992)[7] and the first two meetings of the Conference of the Parties (COP) to the Convention. The Convention was based on the *leadership paradigm*. This meant that rich countries would reduce their emissions first (because they had polluted more in the past and were better placed to do so with respect to their resources and capacities) and assist developing countries with technology and finance to modify their development paths to both mitigate and adapt to climate change.[8]

The Framework Convention lacked legally binding targets for the developed countries. The third phase (1997–2001) led to the adoption of the Kyoto Protocol (KP)[9] in 1997, which stipulated GHG reduction and limitation targets for industrialized countries for the period 2008–12. The top-down nature of the targets was

[4] IPCC-III, *Climate Change: Mitigation*, Cambridge: Cambridge University Press, 2014.

[5] UN General Assembly, *Transforming our World: The 2030 Agenda for Sustainable Development*, United Nations General Assembly Resolution A/Res/70/01 of September 25, 2015.

[6] J. Gupta, *The History of Global Climate Governance*, Cambridge: Cambridge University Press 2014; J. Gupta, Climate Change: Governance History, Future Implications, Towards Triple Loop Learning?, *WIRES Climate Change*, Wiley 2016, doi.10.1002/wcc.388.

[7] UNFCCC, *United Nations Framework Convention on Climate Change*, New York: UNFCCC, 1992.

[8] J. Gupta, Leadership in the Climate Regime: Inspiring the Commitment of Developing Countries in the Post-Kyoto Phase, *Review of European Community and International Environmental Law* 7:2 (1998), pp. 178–88.

[9] UNFCCC, *Kyoto Protocol to the United Nations Framework Convention on Climate Change*, New York: UNFCCC, 1997.

softened through the introduction of market-based instruments that were elaborated in the Marrakesh Accords in 2000. This approach to slow global warming was derailed, however, by the United States when the US Senate refused to ratify the KP.[10]

In the fourth phase of the regime (2001–8), the departure of the USA ironically speeded up the ratification by other countries, and so the KP entered into force in 2005. However, the time lapse delayed the introduction of market mechanisms.[11]

The fifth phase (2008–15) began with the start of the recession in industrialized countries and increased economic growth in key developing countries. This fundamentally changed the geo-political context for the negotiations;[12] the hopes that new GHG reduction targets for 2012–17 would be adopted at the Copenhagen COP in 2009 evaporated. Voluntary targets for developed countries, except the USA, Canada, Russia, Japan, and New Zealand, were included in the Doha amendment for 2012–20; these will become legally binding once 144 countries have ratified this amendment. So far, however, only 91 ratifications have been received; the EU has not yet ratified as a whole. This is disappointing as it shows that developed countries are hesitant in keeping their commitments for the period 2012–20.[13] INDCs for all countries for the period beyond 2020 were taken up by the Paris Agreement of 2015. A history of the reduction targets is presented in Table 2.1.

The following sections explain the climate change order in terms of the actors and coalitions; its principles, norms, and rules; its organization and procedures; and its instruments, and then assess the order in terms of some aspects of good governance—namely predictability (of process and actors); legitimacy (countries and non-governmental organization (NGOs) participating); equity (distributive justice); efficiency (use of market mechanisms and compliance mechanisms) and effectiveness (measured in changing social structures rather than just reducing emissions); and learning. Predictability helps countries and social actors to make assessments regarding whether they need to change their short- to long-term investment, production, and consumption strategies; legitimacy ensures commitment; equity enhances distributive justice; efficiency helps keep costs within limits, and effectiveness helps with ensuring long-term change. Learning refers to how institutions learn: single-loop learning implies improving routines, double-loop learning implies questioning assumptions, and triple-loop learning calls for re-examining underlying discourses.[14]

[10] US Senate Resolution 98 on Global Warming, Congressional Record, Senate, pp. S10308–S10311, October 3, 1997 ("Byrd/Hagel Resolution").

[11] The one exception was the Clean Development Mechanism (CDM), which was operationalized in 2000.

[12] J. Gupta, A History of International Climate Change Policy, *WIRES Climate Change*, Wiley Interdisciplinary Reviews 1:5 (2010), pp. 636–53, doi.10.1002/wcc.67.

[13] See UNFCCC website, http://unfccc.int/kyoto_protocol/doha_amendment/items/7362.php.

[14] Gupta, Climate Change.

Table 2.1. The history of targets and timetables in the climate regime

Agreement	For	Target	Comment
UNFCCC 1992	2000, w.r.t. ±1990 levels	Stabilization of GHG emissions by all developed countries	Target worded ambiguously although in legally binding document
	2000–8	No target	
KP 1997	2008–12 w.r.t. ±1990 levels	Reduce emissions by 5.2% for all developed countries	Target allows some countries to increase emissions; USA did not ratify at all; Australia delayed ratification till 2007; Canada withdrew its ratification in 2011
Doha Amendment to KP 2012	2012–20 w.r.t. ±1990 levels	Reduce emissions based on bottom-up commitments	USA, Canada, Russia, Japan, and New Zealand do not participate; 112 ratifications received out of the 144 needed to make this legally binding
Paris Agreement 2015	2020–	Proposed commitments for *all* countries—INDCs; these are not included in the Paris Agreement and are thus not legally binding. When countries ratify the Agreement they need to specify their INDCs. Parties must regularly submit new INDCs for following periods	Developed countries use different base years (e.g. USA/Canada use 2005, EU uses 1990) and have different targets. Developing countries have also come up with a range of targets

Source: Compiled from the texts of the treaties shown in the table

3. CLIMATE CHANGE AND PAST INTERNATIONAL ORDER

3.1. The Climate Regime and International Order (pre-1990–2007)

Actors: The early scientific discussions led to global negotiations involving five categories of actors—scholars organized within IPCC; nation-states and the European Community/Union (EU) that initiated the negotiations on the UNFCCC; the new international secretariat and other subsidiary bodies of the Convention that executed work between negotiating sessions; and concerned NGOs including business organizations, intergovernmental organizations, and city governments that were meeting as far back as 1990 to discuss climate policy at the local community level.

Prior to the UNFCCC, these five groups of actors were fairly united; thereafter, the divisions between and within these groups began to emerge. Although the scientific consensus in the IPCC reports deepened, climate skeptics began to question the science behind the reports. While the leadership paradigm had secured the agreement between developed and developing countries in 1992, US reluctance to accept its leadership role also affected other developed countries. By 2007, the neat North–South divide evident in the past had given way to several coalitions, most of them dividing the South. Similarly, the NGO community that had initially been quite united, by 2007 was sharply divided by differences between environmental, developmental, Northern, Southern, and business NGOs. Moreover, the ability of governments to negotiate was sometimes compromised by vested interests whose fossil fuel investments led them to object to strong greenhouse gas limitation targets.

Principles and norms: Negotiators developed a legally binding international climate change law with follow-up meetings that allow for a dynamic global administrative law system.[15] The 1992 Climate Treaty explicitly stipulates five principles: (1) the precautionary principle; (2) the principle of common but differentiated responsibilities and respective capabilities; (3) the right to *promote* sustainable development; (4) the principle of promoting "a supportive and open international economic system" and that "measures taken to combat climate change should not constitute a means of arbitrary or unjustifiable discrimination or a disguised restriction on international trade," and (5) addressing the special vulnerabilities of specific countries. The relationship between these principles contains tensions, possibly even contradictions. For example, sustainable development and free trade are treated as equally important and fully compatible, which will certainly not always be the case. The precautionary principle is made subject to considerations of cost-effectiveness, and the right to development as articulated in the UN General Assembly Resolution of 1986 was re-worded during the negotiation as "The Parties have a right to, and should, promote sustainable development," implying that developing (and industrialized) countries have a right to promote sustainable development.[16] Moreover, these five principles represent only a subset of the twenty-seven principles listed in the Rio Principles on Environment and Development.[17] For example, the principle

[15] E. Hey, The Climate Change Regime: An Enviro-Economic Problem and International Administrative Law in the Making, *International Environmental Agreements, Politics, Law and Economics* 75 (2001), p. 100.

[16] For more details, see J. Gupta and K. Arts (2018), Achieving the 1.5°C Objective: Just Implementation through a Right to (Sustainable) Development, *INEA*, https://doi.org/10.1007/s10784-017-9376-7.

[17] Rio Declaration and Agenda 21, Report on the UN Conference on Environment and Development, Rio de Janeiro, June 3–14, 1992, New York: United Nations 1992 (= A/CONF.151/26/Rev.1 (Vols.1–III)).

that states have the sovereign right to pursue their own environmental and development policies, and the responsibility to ensure that activities within their jurisdiction do not cause damage to others are included in the Preamble to the Convention but not in its operational part. One could read this as implying either that the principle of sovereignty is not given its due importance or that the "no harm" component of the principle is watered down. Moreover, the principle that states that cause harm to other states should compensate them is missing. Still, the particular combination of norms included in the climate change order indicates that climate policies need to take the precautionary and equity approach, and that they should promote sustainable development.

Organization and procedures: The climate change order has five main bodies (the Secretariat, the Conference of the Parties, the Subsidiary Body for Implementation, the Subsidiary Body for Scientific and Technological Advice, and the Financial Mechanism) and has continually established new bodies. Its procedures promote rule-based interactions at regular intervals to ensure that policies are in line with the latest scientific knowledge and that the negotiations move forward: every year, the COP meets to assess actions taken and improve the administrative rules in the system.

The instruments: The operational tools of the climate change order include (a) targets and timetables (see Table 2.1); (b) mechanisms to promote compliance; (c) market mechanisms such as emissions trading, joint implementation, and the Clean Development Mechanism (CDM) to promote cost-effective achievement of the targets of the developed countries; (d) a financial mechanism to help trigger policy change in the South especially with respect to mitigating GHGs; and (e) the requirement that all countries should regularly report on their measures. Since this pre-2008 period ended before the first commitment period or the period during which the targets were operational, i.e., 2008–12, many of these instruments were still in the design stage by 2008 when that climate change order began to fall apart.

3.2. Assessing the Order (pre-1997–2007)

In 1987, the global population was around 5 billion and CO_2 emissions were about 20.4 billion tonnes. By 2007, world population had increased—by about 30 percent—to 6.5 billion, while emissions had grown—by 54 percent—to 31.4 billion tonnes.[18]

[18] Plan Bureau Nederland: Are Global Emissions Still Rising? The Hague: Plan Bureau Nederland 2015, available at http://infographics.pbl.nl/website/globalco2-2015/[accessed February 15, 2016].

The KP climate change order created considerable predictability. First, although substantive progress was slow, all countries regularly submitted their "National Communications," showing the measures taken. Second, although the Convention's principles were inadequately implemented, they did shape discussions on who should take action first and what sort of action that should be. Third, since the Noordwijk Conference on Climate Change the US position has been predictable: Washington would not accept any special "developed country" responsibility. It prevented the adoption of a clear target in the Climate Change Convention of 1992, and refused to ratify the Kyoto Protocol of 1997.[19] Fourth, the reluctance to include the no harm, liability, and compensation principles, along with the lack of clear commitments regarding financial transfers at the start of the regime, was a sign that financial and technological resource transfers would be insufficient.

The regime enjoyed considerable *legitimacy*. Most UN states became party to the Climate Convention and its Kyoto Protocol. There was large-scale participation by NGOs (including business) and UN agencies as observers, and negotiations reflected the diversity of positions in the public domain. The UNFCCC also includes *equity* among its core principles.

The regime also scored well on *efficiency* by developing market mechanisms (Activities Implemented Jointly Concept in 1995; Clean Development Mechanism (CDM); Joint Implementation and Emissions Trading in 1997; and proposals for Reducing Emissions by Deforestation and Forest Degradation in 2005). The CDM, in particular, has been quite effective in addressing climate change globally through promoting emission reduction projects in developing countries.

Overall, the order was—contrary to a widespread perception—remarkably effective, if one considers the dimensions of the problem realistically. Limiting global warming ultimately calls for the wholesale restructuring of production, consumption, and distribution patterns worldwide. The fact that the UNFCCC order instigated a serious debate within an orderly legal framework and that its procedures are being followed by 195 countries, no matter how imperfectly, underlines its important contribution in launching the world onto an irreversible path towards a low-GHG world.

The order scored well on *single-loop learning* (i.e., improving routines). Thus, it managed to exclude issues of deforestation and desertification from the UNFCCC, and it developed new, innovative institutional methods for continuing the negotiations prior to the enactment of the Convention in 1994, and for launching the CDM prior to the KP's adoption. The climate change order in this period also scored quite well on *double-loop learning* (i.e., reflecting and modifying one's assumptions), notably by recognizing the

[19] D. Bodansky, The United Nations Framework Convention on Climate Change: A Commentary, *Yale Journal of International Law* 18 (2003), pp. 451–558.

voluntary Nationally Appropriate Mitigation Actions of developing countries. In doing so, it accepted that developing countries do not always have the ability to implement legally binding mitigation targets and recognized the diversity of their efforts to reshape their economies.

3.3. Implications

In its first twenty years, the dominant mode of interaction in this order for collective climate security was cooperation. The fact that the USA, then still the unchallenged number one great power, acted as a laggard represented a significant challenge, however, as the USA was free-riding on the policies of the other developed countries. At the same time, levels of economic interdependence and social interconnectedness between countries and societies continued to rise, further strengthening the need for global cooperation. In this cooperation, nation-states were called upon to play the critical role, but where national governments failed to ratify the Kyoto Protocol (e.g., the USA, and Australia until 2007), sub-national and municipal authorities tried to fill in by pushing for policy implementation at sub-national levels (Table 2.2).

4. CLIMATE CHANGE AND INTERNATIONAL ORDER, 2008 TO 2014

4.1. Towards a Different Kind of Climate Order

Actors: Although IPCC reports continued to provide evidence of climate change, climate skeptics and politicians for whom climate change was inconvenient[20] continued to argue that climate change was a mere hypothesis. Moreover, the financial crises in the developed world and the rise of the emerging economies made rich countries increasingly reluctant to reduce their GHG emissions unilaterally and Canada withdrew from the Kyoto Protocol in 2011. The USA, Canada, Russia, New Zealand, and Japan refused to participate in the second Kyoto period (2012–20; see Table 2.1) in the Doha Amendment, which poor countries perceived as a breach of trust. At the same time, the window for addressing climate change continued to narrow. Thus, the leadership paradigm effectively broke down, with only the EU

[20] A. Gore, An Inconvenient Truth, documentary directed by Davis Guggenheim, produced by Lawrence Bender Productions and Participant Productions, 2006.

Table 2.2. Assessing the climate change regime (pre-1990–2007)

	Environment	Economic welfare	Social issues/culture	Security	Politics
Global	Strong legal order (only USA/Australia not participating in KP)	Focus on sustainable development	Common but differentiated responsibilities (CBDR) principle aims to address equity issues	End of Cold War may bring investment for environment; reversal since 9/11	Climate change being addressed through political cooperation order; state is dominant actor
Regional (EU)	Strong leadership by EU	EU is able to avoid climate–growth trade-offs	EU is able to address internal equity issues	Stress in some EU neighboring countries does not affect climate change policy	EU political order is effective; although it does affect its negotiating ability
National	All 195 countries participating in negotiations	Growth everywhere	Lives improve	Security challenges simmer in the post 9/11 world; does not prevent countries in crises from ratifying the KP	Democracies, communist countries, dictatorships—all commit to climate policy
Local	City governments active in many countries, but esp. in USA and Australia; rural areas less active, more vulnerable	Extreme events affect local livelihoods in some places	Rise of peri-urban challenges; greater vulnerability to climate change	n/a	City actors more powerful than rural actors/farmers

Source: Compiled from descriptions and analysis in J. Gupta, *The History of Global Climate Governance*, Cambridge: Cambridge University Press, 2014

(and Australia, which ratified the Kyoto Protocol in 2007) trying to maintain the leadership role of the developed countries. The global South splintered into several coalitions (e.g., Bolivarian Alliance for the Peoples of our America (ALBA, in Spanish); Rainforest coalition, Central Asia, Caucasus, and Moldova (CACAM); Brazil, South Africa, India, China (BASIC); Central American Integration System (SICA)), and its collective power to demand substantial long-term emission reductions from the North weakened in the process.

Principles, norms, rules: The principles of the climate change order and its legal regime in theory remained valid, although they were increasingly challenged in practice. The precautionary principle has been scarcely implemented as the targets were weakened over time, and the common but differentiated responsibilities principle was continually questioned by the developed countries. Thus, the period 2008 to 2012 saw almost all developed countries with the exception of the USA and Canada participating in legally binding emission limitation and reduction targets. For the period 2012 to 2020, however, targets exist in the Doha Amendment only for the EU and Australia, while the USA, Canada, New Zealand, Russia, and Japan are not participating. Moreover, since only 112 countries have ratified the Doha Amendment as of June 2018, this has still had not entered into force. Thus, there has been no clear leadership by the developed countries as a whole to demonstrate that they can reduce their emissions—a clear requirement for effective implementation of both the precautionary principle and the common but differentiated responsibilities principle.

Organizations and procedures: The key Convention bodies have continued to push for rule-based interactions. Other agencies within the UN system have also become active, e.g., through the global promotion of bio-fuels, the establishment of the International Renewable Energy Development Agency (IREDA) to promote renewable energy, and through the United Nations Programme on Reducing Emissions from Deforestation and Forest Degradation, which shifted climate-related forest negotiations to other forums. Some authors argue that the regime was gradually fragmenting;[21] others saw it becoming dependent on related regimes or regime complexes;[22] and still others that climate change is being mainstreamed into the other agencies of the UN.[23]

[21] H. Van Asselt, *The Fragmentation of Global Climate Governance: Consequences and Management of Regime Interactions*, Cheltenham, UK/Northampton, MA: Edward Elgar, 2013.

[22] R. Keohane and D. Victor, The Regime Complex for Climate Change, Kennedy School Discussion Paper, Harvard University, 2010, pp. 10–33.

[23] Gupta, *Global Climate Governance*.

The instruments: It was critical for the climate change order that most developed countries actually managed to reduce their emissions. While implementation difficulties led Canada to withdraw from the KP, the EU and some other developed countries have remained on track. Although the CDM took off successfully, emissions trading and joint implementation were affected by the low price of carbon, due largely to the absence of the USA from the regime. New funding mechanisms were created, each with different rules but not necessarily with new money. The Adaptation Fund, born in 1997 and operationalized in 2008, receives the bulk of its resources from a levy on the CDM and is thus funded de facto by a tax on North–South cooperation. With reduced incentives to participate in the CDM, as there are no operational targets yet in the post-2012 period, the resources are dwindling. The new Green Climate Fund is supposed to generate an additional US$100 billion per year for climate funding from 2020 onwards. It is unclear, however, who exactly is to pay into this fund, whether these resources are additional or simply to be taken from Official Development Assistance, and whether the money will be in aid or loans. If it were to be the latter this could initiate a new era of exploding developing country debts. The regular national reporting requirement is perhaps the most important and reliable instrument of the regime as it obliges all countries to revisit their policies at regular intervals.

4.2. Evaluating the Order

During the period 2008–14, global emissions increased—by about another 8 percent—to 33.3 billion tonnes in 2014, but the rate of growth appeared to be slowing down in comparison to the previous period.[24] The global 2008 recession affected the predictability, legitimacy, equity, efficiency, and effectiveness of the order, which came to be increasingly influenced by power politics. In terms of *predictability*, the member countries seem to take their homework seriously: as many as 168 countries submitted their INDCs prior to the 2015 Paris COP. Unfortunately, financial flows also remain predictably unpredictable. The leadership paradigm is losing its relevance, since—with the exception of the EU—the West has failed to lead, due to both a lack of political will and technological difficulties. The responsibility for successful transformation now lies with the South, which may be less constrained by existing (and therefore confining) technological, political, and institutional structures and therefore better placed to show the way forward.

The *legitimacy* of the order remains unchallenged, as all UN member states and many NGOs continue to participate, and can therefore be considered

[24] Plan Bureau Nederland, Are Global Emissions Still Rising?; see also Gore, An Inconvenient Truth.

high. In terms of *equity* and distributive justice, however, as expressed in the common but differentiated responsibilities and respective capabilities principle, there has been considerable deterioration. Some rich countries refused to accept quantitative reduction measures and used Chinese growth in emissions as an excuse for not taking action, while small island states and other vulnerable countries felt that their vulnerability was ignored. Ironically, the recession further contributed to inequality, concentrating wealth even further in the hands of the few: by 2016, 1 percent of the global population possessed more than the remaining 99 percent.[25]

Efficiency has been affected by the limited successes of Joint Implementation and Emissions Trading, as these mechanisms depend on legally binding targets to provide incentives for market mechanisms. Regime *effectiveness* has become increasingly dubious, as the developed countries as a group were unable to reduce their emissions by the promised 5.2 percent by 2012 over the levels prevailing in 1990. *Non-compliance mechanisms* for the climate change order were developed in 2001 in the Marrakesh Accords, and there have been efforts to implement these as some developed countries like Greece, Croatia, and Bulgaria went into non-compliance in the period 2008–12. The Enforcement Branch of the Marrakesh Accords has been dealing with these issues.[26]

In this phase, while there was continued evidence of *single- and double-loop learning*, there clearly was not enough of it to address climate change.

4.3. Implications

Although the climate change order governance continued to function along the expected lines, its outputs deteriorated: the need to provide jobs during the recession distracted from efforts to reduce emissions. While recessions lead to a temporary dip in emissions, they also—and more importantly—offer opportunities for restructuring economies towards a green and inclusive future. These opportunities were largely missed, however, in this recession, as policies focused almost exclusively on creating jobs. Learning was thus avoided.[27] Cooperation remained the principal mode of interaction to develop the order further, but power politics increasingly intruded (Table 2.3).

[25] Oxfam, Wealth, Wanting it all and wanting more, Oxfam Issue Briefing, January 2015, available at https://www.oxfam.org/sites/www.oxfam.org/files/file_attachments/ib-wealth-having-all-wanting-more-190115-en.pdf [accessed February 15, 2016].

[26] J. Brunnee, M. Doelle, and L. Rajamani, *Promoting Compliance in an Evolving Climate Regime*, Cambridge: Cambridge University Press, 2012.

[27] P. Obani and J. Gupta, The Impact of Economic Recession on Climate Change: Eight Trends, *Climate and Development* 8:33 (2015), pp. 211–23.

Table 2.3. Assessing the climate change order (2008–14)

	Environment	Economic welfare	Social issues/ culture	Security	Politics
Global	Legal order affected by non-participation of USA, Canada, Japan, Russia, NZ in KP-2 targets (Doha Amendment)	Focus on green economy/ ecological modernization; new sources of oil/petroleum and new energy in extraction; oil prices fluctuate	CBDR under attack	Rise of IS and new security challenges lead to more defense activity and hence more GHGs. Climate change may have security impact	Rise of alternative regimes—fragmentation/ regime complexes; order through competition and power
Regional (EU)	Strong leadership by EU	EU continues to be able to avoid climate–growth trade-offs	EU addresses internal and external equity issues	Increasing stress from refugee and terrorism crises	EU political order is effective, but affected by recession
National	All countries are taking measures	Recession in the North; some growth in South	Recession and loss of jobs	Security issues become important	n/a
Local	Sub-national governments active in some places	n/a	Loss of jobs in cities, as well	n/a	n/a

Source: Compiled from analysis in J. Gupta, *The History of Global Climate Governance*, Cambridge: Cambridge University Press, 2014.

5. CLIMATE CHANGE AND FUTURE INTERNATIONAL ORDER

5.1. The Climate Regime and International Order (2015–)

Actors: In 2015, all states adopted the 2030 Agenda for Sustainable Development with its seventeen goals, including one on climate change. With the adoption of the Paris Agreement in December 2015 and its implementation the following year, all countries are now committed to long-term objectives and to reducing their (rate of growth of) emissions in the period after 2020. They have also agreed to increase their targets every five years, in line with the long-term objective of containing global warming. However, although member countries of the Paris

Agreement are legally bound to make commitments, the targets themselves are not included in the legally binding components of the agreement.

The original leadership norm required that rich countries would reduce their emissions first and move to a low-carbon future that would then be followed by the developing countries; this has been replaced by the new norm pushed by the USA: the rich countries now will only accept legally binding commitments if key developing countries do so as well. Developing countries perceive this as a breach of an international social contract by some rich countries. Furthermore, they argue that if economically, technologically, and institutionally rich countries cannot structurally decouple emissions from economic growth, then this will be even more difficult for the poorer countries.[28]

At the local level, many cities have been taking climate action since 1990, but although their support is certainly needed, they so far have been unable to make significant dents in global emissions. NGOs and social movements are mobilizing globally for action on climate change, however, and many corporations are beginning to respond to this pressure.

Looking into the future, it is increasingly evident that although all kinds of actors must support climate governance, it is states that need to play the key role. They must assume that responsibility and be held accountable for failures, both domestically and internationally. The state cannot only represent domestic interests; it must also take responsibility for costs and damage that it imposes on others—the "no harm" principle. This principle of international law, which has existed since the 1940s Trail Smelter case between the USA and Canada[29] has yet to be fully implemented in the climate change order. A stable climate is a global public good. States therefore need to take the lead in ensuring that global GHG emissions peak soon, and no state must be allowed to opt out of its responsibilities, least of all powerful and rich countries. None of this means that other actors do not have responsibilities, but the key to maintaining a habitable global climate order rests with the state. After all, all other actors will usually be acting within specific national jurisdictions, and therefore can only be made to comply, and be held accountable, by their respective states.

Principles, norms, rules: With the Paris Agreement, the important precautionary principle has now been taken up through the adoption of the long-term objective to contain global warming within a range of 1.5–2°C, and through the requirement to revisit national commitments every five years in the light

[28] Z. Ji and F. Sha, The Challenges of the Post-COP21 Regime: Interpreting CBDR in the INDC Context, *International Environmental Agreements: Politics, Law and Economics* 15:4 (2015), pp. 421–30.

[29] Trail Smelter Arbitration (United States vs. Canada), April 16, 1938, March 11, 1941: *Reports of International Arbitration Awards, Volume III* (2006), pp. 1905–82, available at http://legal.un.org/riaa/cases/vol_III/1905-1982.pdf.

of that objective. Most countries, including developing countries, submitted their INDCs prior to the Paris negotiations, and the Conference of the Parties adopted a series of decisions in the Paris Agreement in 2015. The common but differentiated responsibilities principle, however, has largely been pushed aside, since all countries now have to make commitments on emissions reduction.

While the bottom-up approach of the Paris Agreement fits the anarchic nature of the international order, it ignores the evidence from climate change science and its equity implications for the South. As such, it reflects a broader pattern in global politics: a shift from legally binding treaties to soft language that appears in a seemingly hard law text. Much of the literature tends to see these kinds of treaties as ineffective.[30] Good-faith implementation of national commitments may ensure that we are indeed launched onto an irreversible path to zero carbon emissions; but a poor-faith implementation by some important states could lead to the disintegration of the climate change regime. While legally binding targets could allocate responsibilities fairly and hold countries accountable, the present, legally non-binding target system does not address climate change with the urgency with which it needs to be tackled.

Moreover, phasing out fossil fuels might risk the collapse of the global financial system, as so much capital is locked into the fossil fuel industry. Each country and each company with such assets now has to take decisions that will affect the overall future of the international order. Should they first divest themselves of their oil resources at a high price (to other countries and actors) and then demand legally binding commitments; or should there never be legally binding commitments? Chinese companies are buying fossil fuel resources abroad—will they be left stranded with those resources once these assets have been sold to them?[31]

Despite its light touch and bottom-up characteristics that bow deeply to the principle of national sovereignty, and despite its weaknesses, US President Trump decided to leave the Paris Agreement. This may encourage others to abandon their obligations for short-sighted domestic reasons. However, the good news is that Canada is back in the Paris Agreement.

Organization and procedures: The organizational bodies of the UNFCCC are by now fully consolidated and able to move forward. Climate change is also entering the mainstream activities of other UN agencies, with the effect that many of these agencies are now also pushing the climate change agenda. From

[30] P. Pattberg, F. Biermann, S. Chan, and A. Mert, *Public–Private Partnerships for Sustainable Development: Emergence, Influence and Legitimacy*, Cheltenham, UK/Northampton, MA: Edward Elgar, 2012.

[31] J. Gupta, E. Chu, K. Bos, and T. Kuijten, The Geo-Ecological Risks of Oil Investments by China and the Global South: The Right to Development Revisited, in M. P. Amineh and L. Guang (eds.), *Geopolitical Economy of Energy and Environment: China and the European Union*, Leiden: Brill, 2017.

an emissions standpoint, the climate change order is an energy and forest regime, while from an adaptation standpoint, it is mostly about water. However, since there is no effective global energy order, merging and reconciling climate and environmental policies with energy and oil extraction policies will be extremely difficult. Furthermore, global water law, trans-boundary water regimes and national water laws so far have not yet integrated the expected climate change impacts of melting glaciers, rising sea levels, changing rainfall patterns, extreme weather events, and increasing evaporation. The emissions from international shipping, air transport, and the defense sector are also still outside the purview of the climate change order, although the air transport sector now seems to be moving towards targets. Deforestation receives considerable attention now in the climate change and other partial orders, but it is not always clear whether those efforts will make a significant dent in global deforestation rates.

Instruments: While the reporting instruments clearly will keep up the pressure on states to take action, financial resources from the North will likely be insufficient. The South would therefore do better to focus on ensuring that the North mitigates without allowing the limited financial resources available to be used as a way to divide and rule them. If the Green Climate Fund would indeed only provide loans in hard currency, as rumors have it, experience with debt should make the South cautious about accepting such loans. As for technology transfer, the North appears to be so locked into a fossil fuel world that it would seem much better if the Greenfield economies of the South tried to find alternative routes to sustainable development than to buy old Western ideas, infrastructure, and technologies. Nor should it buy oil and gas fields from the North, as Chinese companies are presently doing.[32] These are destined to become stranded assets.

5.2. Prospects for the Climate Change Order

With the Paris Agreement, the climate change order has adopted a long-term objective and now requires parties to ratchet up their commitments and report on these regularly. The order functions without recourse to force and remains cooperative. The leadership paradigm it used initially has been compromised, but there is not enough time to wait for alternatives (such as the developed

[32] S. Hardus, Chinese National Oil Companies in Ghana: The Cases of CNOOC and Sinopec, *Perspectives on Global Development and Technology* 13 (2014), pp. 588–612; J. Holslag, China's New Mercantilism in Central Africa, *African and Asian Studies* 5:2 (2006), pp. 133–69; B. Hoogenboom, Latin America and China's Transnationalizing Oil Industry: A Political Economy Assessment of New Relations, *Perspectives on Global Development and Technology* 13 (2014), pp. 626–47.

countries as a group assuming the lead), as the climate problem becomes increasingly serious.[33]

The order has lost its *predictability*. Developing and developed countries have agreed to targets, but these targets are not legally binding. The Paris Agreement is an Agreement and not a Protocol or Treaty that would have allowed the then US President Obama to enter into it without having to submit it for ratification to the US Senate (which would almost certainly reject it if it were even asked). This backfired, as President Trump has decided to take the United States out of the Paris Agreement by an administrative decision. This helped the Obama administration to circumvent Congress, but it also enabled Trump to leave the agreement without consulting the Senate.[34] Moreover, a recent Supreme Court case in the USA has questioned the use of presidential executive power on climate-related measures.[35]

The order retains its *legitimacy*, though at a lower level, as its *equity* has largely been sacrificed; the order would need to develop new tools, such as litigation to demand compensation, to recover its claim to a just order. *Efficiency* also has become problematic in a world of unclear targets that makes it very difficult to support either the market mechanisms by setting a price on greenhouse gas emission reductions or signaling the end of the fossil fuel era. The *effectiveness* of the order appears increasingly doubtful: even if all the INDCs were implemented in good faith, the world would still be moving towards a 2.7–4.0°C rise in average global temperatures.[36]

The regime is also struggling with *learning*. The current phase needs to experience triple-loop learning, which would require questioning deeply held underlying assumptions and ideologies. Although the neoliberal capitalist order was not questioned in Paris, the North–South divide was tackled head-on in terms of respective quantitative responsibilities. In recognizing multiple speeds of development within a legally binding framework, the order also accepts that countries face different political and economic constraints that need to be acknowledged. However, effective triple-loop learning would also require:

[33] IPCC-III, *Climate Change*.

[34] On the other hand, a court in the Netherlands found that no matter who else fails to meet its commitments, the Netherlands must reduce its emissions in line with its responsibilities. See District Court, The Hague: Case number C/09/456689/HA ZA 13–1396, June 24, 2015, available at http://deeplink.rechtspraak.nl/uitspraak?id=ECLI:NL:RBDHA:2015:7145 [accessed February 15, 2016].

[35] A. Liptak and C. Davenport, Supreme Court Deals Blow to Obama's Efforts to Regulate Coal Emissions, *The New York Times* online, February 2016, available at http://www.nytimes.com/2016/02/10/us/politics/supreme-court-blocks-obama-epa-coal-emissions-regulations.html?_r=0 [accessed February 15, 2016].

[36] See UNFCCC, Synthesis Report on the Aggregate Effect of Intended Nationally Determined Contributions, UNFCCC 2015, available at http://unfccc.int/files/focus/indc_portal/application/pdf/synthesis_report_-_overview.pdf; see also Climate Action Tracker, http://climateactiontracker.org/ [accessed February 15, 2016].

- An examination of whether neoliberal capitalism and free trade are consistent with planetary resource boundaries. Neoliberal capitalism aims at short-term profit maximization while externalizing its impact. If it were possible, however, to embed it within a framework of principles and rules that aim to protect the global ecology and global public goods while enhancing human well-being, the conflict potential could be minimized. This would require a hierarchy of principles that subordinates the free trade paradigm to that of sustainable development.
- Constitutionalism and rule of law, which could guarantee such a hierarchy in paradigms and ensure that no power, no organization would act in violation of the constitution. There is evidence of growing environmental constitutionalism at national levels,[37] but there is also a need for constitutionalism at the global level. This would work only, however, if all nation-states were to submit voluntarily to this order. Clearly, this is an idealistic notion, but it is becoming increasingly urgent to think and act in terms of the collective well-being of people and the planet. We need responsible, accountable, legitimate, and effectively equipped states which, through proper tax laws, are able to both ensure that they are able to provide "glocal" public goods as well as engage in the necessary redistribution needed to deal with the impacts of climate change.

6. CONCLUSION

The partial order to limit climate change initially tried to use international law to address an environmental problem. It soon became clear, however, that this problem could only be addressed by restructuring our societies and that societies locked into dependence on fossil fuels would find it very difficult to challenge the existing socio-economic paradigm. Thus, the United States failed to sign on to any legally binding targets under the climate change order, although the EU notably was able both to accept the Kyoto targets and to meet them. Since about 2010, the KP climate change order began to erode seriously, as Canada, Russia, Japan, and New Zealand followed in the wake of the US refusal to make binding commitments. Should the EU, which is creaking under the weight of the Greek debt issues, a huge rise in immigration from the South, and a proliferation of terrorist attacks by ISIS, now also fail to deliver on its commitments, the entire regime could disintegrate.

[37] J. R. May and E. Daly, *Global Environmental Constitutionalism*, Cambridge: Cambridge University Press, 2014.

At the same time, the Paris Agreement and the adoption of the Sustainable Development Goals[38] sent strong political signals for change. Although the SDGs do not explicitly address the dominant capitalist paradigm, they include targets that circumscribe the use of natural resources and make clear the need to address social issues.[39] The two partial orders thus are in principle mutually supportive.

However, the combination of globalization, neoliberal capitalism, and the rise in global inequality comes at a huge price for international order. World trade has grown more or less unchecked by environmental concerns,[40] while financial flows signal the offshoring of wealth and the hollowing-out of national tax regimes.[41] This has left states with limited power and resources to manage the governance of partial orders such as the one on climate change. The dominance of the present capitalist paradigm in trade, investment, and development, which is deeply embedded in contracts and financial arrangements, demands perpetual growth. This clashes with the sustainable development paradigm, with its calls for global well-being, as well as with soft law goals (such as the SDGs) or hard law objectives combined with soft law targets, as is the case in the Paris Agreement. Unless a new hierarchy in norms and values becomes globally dominant and enshrined in a new Constitutional order, the future of climate politics will remain highly uncertain.

Other partial orders are affected by comparable challenges. The partial order addressing global migration issues is collapsing under the weight of political indifference. The pervasive aspiration to high economic growth rates is unrealistic and environmentally irresponsible. Security challenges appear to have multiplied, and these high politics issues seem to have pushed climate change into the background.

All these crises underline the importance of strong, reliable, and responsible states. Private sector actors do not care sufficiently about (global) public goods, and in any case will find it difficult to ensure their protection. Non-state actors can contribute but do not have an overarching mandate nor the power and the resources to resolve the problems; only states can ensure that they are effectively addressed. What seems most urgently needed are good, strong, and

[38] The SDGs deal with seventeen issues (including climate change) and 169 targets that together attempt to change the way we produce and consume to live within planetary resource boundaries while meeting the basic needs of people. See UN General Assembly, *Transforming our World.*

[39] J. Gupta and C. Vegelin, Sustainable Development Goals and Inclusive Development, *International Environmental Agreements: Politics, Law and Economics* 16:3 (2016), pp. 433–48.

[40] M. Pelling, D. Manuel-Navarrete, and M. Redclift, *Climate Change and the Crisis of Capitalism*, London: Routledge, 2012.

[41] B. Quinn and J. Ball, UK's top companies condemned for prolific use of tax havens, *The Guardian* online, May 12, 2013, available at http://www.theguardian.com/uk/2013/may/12/uk-companies-condemned-tax-havens [accessed November 19, 2015].

accountable governments—governments that are accountable to both their own people and the global community.

Perhaps this will require revisiting our present paradigms of democracy. At the local level, communities are not necessarily willing to dispense with driving big cars because of global climate change. Communities may want to externalize the negative impacts of their behavior without incurring any costs, and they may not wish to take responsibility for global challenges. The question then is whether the "public good" is something that the state has to decide on, on behalf of its people. That would involve redefining the meaning of democracy and require that we invest much more in the *trias politica*, from the local through the national to the global level. In the last analysis, climate change and sustainable development can only be achieved through transforming the present into a more just and equitable international order. The use of human rights litigation from the national through to the global level may be one promising way to ensure that the rights of the minorities and those who are vulnerable are not ignored.

3

Coping with Public Health Emergencies of International Concern

Iris Hunger

1. INTRODUCTION

During the last quarter century, health has continually moved up the international governance agenda. States increasingly have come to recognize that they need to invest in health not only nationally but also globally in order to promote their own economic and social development and sustain their very ability to function as states in an environment of globalization.

Thus, health has become a key economic and political resource. The immense potential costs of global epidemics (pandemics) corroborate that perspective. In 2008, the World Bank estimated that a severe flu pandemic could result in US$3 trillion in global economic losses, equivalent to 4.8 percent of gross domestic product.[1] Following the 2014–15 Ebola virus disease outbreak in West Africa, the World Bank argued that "the annual global cost of moderately severe to severe pandemics is roughly $570 billion, or 0.7 percent of global income."[2]

Not surprisingly, health issues therefore have also attracted the attention of security analysts and the military. They have redefined disease as a security challenge, particularly infectious diseases that have the potential to spread rapidly around the globe. In the mid-1990s, a number of US think tanks started to describe infectious diseases—in particular the HIV/AIDS pandemic in Africa—as a threat to peace and security.[3] Growing concern over the use of

[1] World Bank, Topics, pandemic: Overview, 2015, available at http://www.worldbank.org/en/topic/pandemics/overview [accessed August 31, 2016].

[2] World Bank, Pandemic Emergency Facility: Frequently Asked Questions, available at http://www.worldbank.org/en/topic/pandemics/brief/pandemic-emergency-facility-frequently-asked-questions [accessed August 31, 2016].

[3] Center for Strategic and International Studies (CSIS), *Global HIV/AIDS: A Strategy for U.S. Leadership*, Washington, DC: CSIS, 1994; S. Elbe, *Virus Alert: Security, Governmentality, and the AIDS Pandemic*, New York: Columbia University Press, 2009.

pathogens by terrorists after the anthrax letter attacks in the USA immediately following 9/11 added to the securitization of health.

This chapter focuses on the part of international order relating to surveillance and response to public health emergencies of international concern, i.e., extraordinary, unusual, or unexpected disease events with serious public health impacts that constitute a public health risk to other states through the international spread of disease and potentially require a coordinated international response.[4] This particular international order in turn forms part of the broader partial international order on global health; it has been chosen for several reasons: (1) it has a comparatively high level of regulation; (2) it represents an area of health governance with a very long tradition (the first international sanitary conference took place in 1851); (3) it deals with a topic of truly global concern; and (4) it represents a part of international order in which immense changes have taken place over the past twenty years. Remarkably, many of these changes can be seen as a deepening of international order at times when many other parts of the international order have been fraying and disintegrating. I will look at the major changes in the international health emergencies regime since 1995; assess its effectiveness, legitimacy, and interdependence with partial orders in other subject areas; and conclude with a few thoughts on why the international health emergencies regime seems to have been remarkably robust if compared to other issue areas.

2. RECENT DEVELOPMENTS AND THE CURRENT STATE OF THE INTERNATIONAL HEALTH EMERGENCIES ORDER

The main actor on international disease outbreak control is the World Health Organization (WHO), in particular its Global Outbreak Alert and Response Network (GOARN), with the International Health Regulations (IHR) being the applicable legally binding document.

The establishment of a global health organization was discussed already during the negotiations in San Francisco that prepared the establishment of the United Nations (UN) in 1945. At the request of Brazil, health appeared in the UN Charter, and Brazil and China co-authored a resolution on setting up a global health agency.[5] The Constitution of the WHO came into force on April 7, 1948.[6]

[4] World Health Organization, International Health Regulations (2005), available at http://www.who.int/ihr/9789241596664/en/ [accessed August 31, 2016]: see especially Art.1.1, 7, and Annex 2.

[5] M. B. Shimkin, The World Health Organization, *Science* 104:2700 (1946), pp. 281–3, doi.10.1126/science.104.2700.281.

[6] World Health Organization, Constitution, available at http://www.who.int/governance/eb/who_constitution_en.pdf [accessed August 31, 2016].

2.1. WHO and IHR as Central Elements of the International Health Emergencies Order

WHO has been the central international actor in the health field since its foundation. In contrast to other issue areas such as the non-proliferation regime for weapons of mass destruction, WHO was established with a very general objective—the attainment "by all peoples of the highest possible level of health" (Article I of the Constitution)—but no detailed specifics were included in the Constitution on how this was to be done. Instead, activities and programs were to be developed by the WHO Secretariat and approved by the annual World Health Assembly (WHA), with "opt-out" possibilities for WHO member states. The only area where international regulations existed before the establishment of WHO was in international sanitary rules. Those rules were to prevent the international spread of selected infectious diseases (cholera, plague, relapsing fever, smallpox, typhus, and yellow fever) without unduly interfering with trade. As a result of the establishment of WHO, the twelve pre-existing international sanitary conventions and related agreements were in 1951 replaced by one consolidated text. This text became the primary set of regulations on international infectious disease control; in 1969, it was renamed International Health Regulations (IHR).

Those regulations remained basically unchanged for the next forty-five years. They required states to notify disease outbreaks on their territories and to limit disease prevention measures that restrict trade and travel to those deemed scientifically sound and necessary on public health grounds.[7] By 1995, however, the IHR had become marginalized and outdated for mainly two reasons. First, there were only three remaining diseases that were covered by the IHR (cholera, plague, and yellow fever). Second, compliance with the rules was unsatisfactory, both with regard to notification but also to limits on trade and travel restrictions.[8]

In May 1995, the World Health Assembly requested the WHO Secretariat to revise the IHR.[9] The first draft of the revised IHR was issued by the WHO Secretariat in January 1998. After further drafts in January 2004 and January 2005—considerably pushed along by the international concern over the 2003 SARS (severe acute respiratory syndrome) outbreak—the new IHR were approved in May 2005 and entered into force in 2007. They were widely considered remarkably different:

[7] World Health Organization, International Health Regulations (1969), available at http://apps.who.int/iris/bitstream/10665/96616/1/9241580070.pdf [accessed August 31, 2016].

[8] D. P. Fidler, From International Sanitary Convention to Global Health Security: The New International Health Regulations, *Chinese Journal of International Law* 4:2 (2005), pp. 325–92 (335–6, 339).

[9] World Health Assembly: Revision and updating of the International Health Regulations, WHA48.7 (1995), available at http://apps.who.int/iris/bitstream/10665/178403/1/WHA48_R7_eng.pdf [accessed September 21, 2016].

> [T]he new IHR constitute one of the most radical and far-reaching changes in international law on public health since the beginning of international health co-operation in the mid-nineteenth century.[10]

The "radical and far-reaching changes" concerned four major points. *First*, instead of defining which diseases would be notifiable (as under the old IHR), the new IHR covers all disease events that constitute an urgent international public health concern, be they communicable (e.g., influenza, plague, hemorrhagic fevers) or non-communicable (e.g., chemical accidents, radiological exposures), naturally occurring or intentionally caused (e.g., bioterrorism). This ensures that a wide range of known but also unknown disease threats are covered. *Second*, the WHO Secretariat is empowered to use not just reports from states (as under the old IHR), but also from other sources, such as non-governmental organizations (NGOs). This allows WHO to look into disease threats even if the state where the outbreak occurs chooses not to notify it. The new IHR also react to the changing technological possibilities by making use of new methods of disease surveillance and information sharing.[11] *Third*, instead of defining maximum control measures (as under the old IHR) WHO is granted the authority to declare the existence of a "public health emergency of international concern" (PHEIC) and to issue recommendations to states on how to respond to it. (In the past, when a state did not declare an emergency and refused to cooperate, WHO was essentially helpless, as it was legally barred from taking further action.) *Fourth*, the new IHR define core capacities that a state is required to set up in order to detect and respond to a disease outbreak.

During the revision process, two other important developments took place. *First*, the WHO set up the Global Outbreak Alert and Response Network (GOARN) to strengthen global surveillance of and response to infectious disease events. For event detection, this network relies not just on government information, but open sources as well. It was informally established in 1997, then formalized in 2000 and approved by the WHA in May 2001.[12] Remarkably, GOARN tried the first two features of the new IHR—broad disease coverage and use of open sources—long before the new IHR entered into

[10] Fidler, International Sanitary Convention, p. 326.

[11] ProMEDmail, HealthMap, and Google Flu Trends (the latter discontinued in 2015) are prominent examples of non-governmental global disease surveillance efforts that use instant electronic communication. See D. Butler, Web Data Predict Flu, *Nature* 456 (November 20, 2008), pp. 287–8; L. C. Madoff and J. P. Woodall, The Internet and the Global Monitoring of Emerging Diseases: Lessons from the First 10 Years of ProMED-mail, *ARCMED* 36:6 (2005), pp. 724–30, doi: http://dx.doi.org/10.1016/j.arcmed.2005.06.005. The Global Public Health Intelligence Network is an important example of a government-run media-based surveillance system (http://www.phac-aspc.gc.ca/cphorsphc-respcacsp/2014/tech-eng.php).

[12] T. Brookes, *Behind the Mask: How the World Survived SARS*, Washington, DC: American Public Health Association, 2005, pp. 21–6; World Health Organization, Global Outbreak Alert and Response. Report of a WHO meeting (2000), WHO/CDS/CSR/2000.3; World Health Assembly, Global health security: Epidemic alert and response (2001), A54/9.

force in 2007. Today, more than 60 percent of the initial outbreak reports come from open sources.[13] GOARN has grown into a multidisciplinary collaboration effort of over 200 technical institutions and networks that can draw on over 600 partners worldwide.

> [It] provides a global operational framework linking a broad range of public health capacities and expertise to keep the international community alert to the threat of outbreaks, and ready to coordinate support to countries and effectively deploy emergency response teams.[14]

Second, when SARS appeared in 2003, the WHO's "effective handling"[15] along the lines of the new but still not formally accepted IHR, illustrated the feasibility and promise of the envisaged IHR reforms. In the context of the SARS outbreak, the WHO used, for the first time, non-governmental information for surveillance and issued recommendations, including on travel restrictions, without waiting for action from the states concerned (mainly China).[16]

2.2. Supplementary Elements of the International Health Emergencies Order

Morse and Keohane describe some developments in global health governance as examples of "contested multilateralism." Contested multilateralism "occurs when states and/or non-state actors either shift their focus from one existing institution to another or create an alternative multilateral institution to compete with existing ones," leading to a fragmentation of the overall regime. Two often cited examples of fragmentation in the global health arena are the Joint United Nations Programme on HIV/AIDS (UNAIDS)—a group of ten UN organizations established in 1996 to strengthen coherent international response to AIDS—and the Global Alliance for Vaccines and Immunization (GAVI)—an international organization that was created in 2000 to improve access to new and underused vaccines for children living in the world's poorest countries.[17]

[13] World Health Organization, Emergency Preparedness: Response, available at http://www.who.int/csr/alertresponse/epidemicintelligence/en/ [accessed August 31, 2016].

[14] World Health Organization, International Health Regulations: Global Outbreak Alert and Response Network.

[15] Fidler, International Sanitary Convention, p. 354.

[16] World Health Organization, World Health Organization issues emergency travel advisory, March 15, 2003, available at http://www.who.int/csr/sars/archive/2003_03_15/en/ [accessed August 31, 2016]; World Health Organization, Update 19—China deepens its collaboration to contain SARS, WHO revises its advice to international travellers as new data come in, April 2, 2003, available at http://www.who.int/csr/sars/archive/2003_02_02b/en/ [accessed August 31, 2016].

[17] C. Morse and R. O. Keohane, Contested Multilateralism, *Review of International Organizations* 9 (2014), pp. 385–412 (387).

Fortunately, fragmentation does not seem to have taken place with regard to surveillance and response to international health emergencies. While the regime has not become fragmented in any serious way, it has been getting more complex in recent decades, with a number of new initiatives and programs supporting global disease outbreak surveillance and response that work in cooperation with WHO. Examples are the Global Health Security Initiative (GHSI), the Global Health Security Agenda (GHSA), various non-governmental surveillance initiatives such as ProMEDmail and Connecting Organizations for Regional Disease Surveillance (CORDS), the US Department of Defense Global Emerging Infections Surveillance and Response System (GEIS), the World Bank's Pandemic Emergency Facility (recently established in response to the Ebola virus disease outbreak in West Africa), numerous NGOs involved in disease outbreak response such as Médecins Sans Frontières (MSF),[18] and national and international Red Cross/Red Crescent societies.

An interesting question is whether the six regional offices of WHO amount to fragmentation of order. Coordination and coherence of regional office activities with headquarter priorities have been a concern, in particular in relation to fundraising and allocation of resources. The African regional office in particular has been strongly criticized, most recently because of its management of the polio re-emergence and the Ebola virus disease outbreak.[19] On the other hand, the comparatively smooth management of the Zika virus outbreak, which mostly affects the Americas, has been attributed to the strength and effectiveness of the pan-American regional office.

The Global Health Security Agenda is one example of supplementary elements of order. It was launched in February 2014 by twenty-nine countries and the WHO, the Food and Agriculture Organization (FAO), and the World Organization for Animal Health (OIE). It was initiated by the USA and has a security focus.[20] GHSA "is an effort between the U.S. government, other

[18] During the first five months of the Ebola virus disease outbreak in West Africa, MSF handled more than 85% of all hospitalized cases. Fourteen Ebola treatment centers were run by MSF between March 2014 and December 2015. See Médecins Sans Frontières, Ebola 2014–2015 Facts and Figures, available at http://www.msf.org/sites/msf.org/files/ebola_accountability_report_low_res.pdf [accessed August 31, 2016].

[19] L. van Schaik and R. van de Pas, *Transnational Governance and Democratic Legitimacy: The Case of Global Health*, Clingendael, Netherlands Institute of International Relations, July 2014, https://www.clingendael.nl/sites/default/files/Transnational%20Governance%20and%20Democratic%20Legitimacy%20-%20Global%20Health.pdf [accessed September 28, 2016], p. 54.

[20] The affiliations of the participants in the tele-briefing on the GHSA ahead of its launch in February 2014 clearly demonstrate the security focus: Laura Holgate (Senior Director for Weapons of Mass Destruction, Terrorism, and Threat Reduction at the National Security Council), Tom Frieden (Director of the CDC), and Andrew Weber (Assistant Secretary of Defense for Nuclear, Chemical and Biological Defense Programs). See Center for Disease Control and Prevention, Telebriefing on launch of global health security agenda, Press Briefing

nations, international organizations and public and private stakeholders, to accelerate progress toward a world safe and secure from infectious disease threats and to promote global health security as an international security priority."[21] Three additional meetings took place in 2014 after the launch. A meeting in Helsinki in May discussed "…strategic, measurable actions that nations can take to advance the…objectives of the GHSA." In Jakarta in August, the objective was to "…solidify plans for advancing the GHSA." And a meeting in Washington, DC in September focused on making "…specific commitments to implement the GHSA and to work toward a commitment to assist West Africa."[22] No lists of participating countries and no consensus outcome documents are available for the 2014 GHSA meetings.

This changed in the following year. In September 2015 in Seoul, a "Ministerial Meeting for all participating countries and international organizations" was organized "…to share [the] collective commitment and leadership and to make enhanced common ground for GHSA."[23] For the first time, a list of the forty-four participating countries was made available.[24] In the declaration adopted, members call on "all countries to make an effort to strengthen their existing national health systems and to fully and rapidly comply with health security responsibilities required by the World Health Organization's International Health Regulations."[25] An explosion of GHSA activity followed in 2016, with numerous meetings on a number of the action package topics all over the world.[26] Currently, GHSA membership stands at fifty-three countries;

Transcript, February 12, 2014, available at http://www.cdc.gov/media/releases/2014/t0213-global-health-security.html [accessed August 31, 2016].

[21] Topics currently under discussion—the "action packages"—are (1) antimicrobial resistance, (2) zoonotic disease, (3) biosafety and biosecurity, (4) immunization, (5) national laboratory system, (6) real-time surveillance, (7) reporting, (8) workforce development, (9) emergency operations centers, (10) linking public health with law and multisectoral rapid response, and (11) medical countermeasures and personnel deployment. See https://ghsagenda.org/packages.html [accessed September 21, 2016] and T. Inglesby and J. E. Fischer, Moving Ahead on the Global Health Security Agenda, *Biosecurity and Bioterrorism* 12:2 (2014), pp. 63–5.

[22] Centers for Disease Control and Prevention (CDC) and the Global Health Security Agenda, Meeting in Seoul, Korea, September 7–9, 2015, available at http://www.cdc.gov/globalhealth/security/events/default.html [accessed August 31, 2016].

[23] Ibid.

[24] Those forty-four countries were: Australia, Azerbaijan, Canada, Chile, China, Denmark, Ethiopia, Finland, France, Georgia, Germany, Guinea, India, Indonesia, Israel, Italy, Japan, Jordan, Kenya, Liberia, Malaysia, Mexico, Netherlands, Norway, Pakistan, Peru, Portugal, Republic of Korea, Saudi Arabia, Sierra Leone, Singapore, South Africa, Spain, Sweden, Switzerland, Thailand, Turkey, Uganda, Ukraine, United Arab Emirates, United Kingdom, United States, Vietnam, Yemen.

[25] Global Health Security Agenda, Seoul Declaration, 2015, available at http://www.ghsa2015seoul.kr/SeoulDeclaration.pdf [accessed August 31, 2016].

[26] Global Health Security Agenda, Events and Updates, available at https://ghsagenda.org/events.html [accessed September 26, 2016].

WHO, FAO, OIE, and other international organizations are involved as advisors.[27] It remains to be seen how GHSA activities will relate to WHO activities in terms of international health emergencies response; at the moment it is still unclear whether GHSA is adding to WHO programs or setting up separate ones.

2.3. Effectiveness, Legitimacy, and Interdependence of the Regime

2.3.1. Effectiveness

Any political order is considered effective if actors behave according to the rules and the stated aim of the order is achieved.[28] There is convincing evidence that the international health emergencies order has become more effective since 1995. *First*, the surveillance system has become more sensitive, reporting on not just three diseases as was the case prior to 2000, and more rapid, thanks to dedicated staff at the WHO, the use of informal data sources, and the right of the WHO to investigate indications of disease outbreaks. In 2003, the WHO reported that under its new GOARN program, it had identified and investigated 538 outbreaks of international concern in 132 countries between January 1998 and March 2002.[29] Between September 2015 and August 2016, 167 outbreak news reports were published by WHO.[30] *Second*, international response to disease outbreaks has been strengthened. Since its inception in 2000,

> GOARN has responded to over 120 deployments in 85 countries deploying more than 2300 experts in the field to assist Member States [to] characterise and control disease outbreaks and respond to natural disasters and humanitarian emergencies... Since the start of the [Ebola virus disease] outbreak in March 2014, the GOARN network has identified and deployed a multidisciplinary workforce of 895 experts in the Ebola virus disease outbreak response operation in West Africa.[31]

As Giorgetti wrote in 2010:

[27] Global Health Security Agenda, Membership, available at https://ghsagenda.org/members.html [accessed September 26, 2016].

[28] See the Introduction to this volume.

[29] World Health Organization, *Severe Acute Respiratory Syndrome (SARS): Status of the Outbreak and Lessons for the Immediate Future*, Geneva: WHO, 2003, available at http://www.who.int/csr/media/sars_wha.pdf [accessed August 31, 2016].

[30] World Health Organization, Disease outbreak news, available at http://www.who.int/csr/don/en/ [accessed September 25, 2016].

[31] World Health Organization, Emergencies preparedness, response. Partners: Global Outbreak Alert and Response Network (GOARN) (2016), available at http://www.who.int/csr/disease/ebola/partners/en/ [accessed August 31, 2016].

> [I]t seems that GOARN is able to provide effective assistance in cases of a disease outbreak and to control the spread of disease... GOARN is effective in reporting, managing and—to a certain extent—controlling the spreading of disease even in failed states, where health systems do not exist or do not properly function.[32]

A *further* indication that the WHO is rather effectively detecting and responding to international health emergencies is the noticeable absence of calls for alternative global disease surveillance and response mechanisms. This does not at all, however, preclude calls for WHO reform to improve its performance.[33]

An obvious way to assess the effectiveness of the partial order relating to international health emergency management in more detail is an analysis of WHO's performance in the four Public Health Emergencies of International Concern (PHEIC) declared so far[34]—pandemic influenza ("swine flu") 2009, polio 2014, Ebola 2014, and Zika 2016—which is presented in the following.

2.3.1.1. Influenza A (H1N1) ("swine flu") 2009

Influenza pandemics are rare global events. An influenza pandemic is always triggered by a new subtype of the influenza virus with three necessary characteristics: (1) the population has no immunity against the virus; (2) the virus causes human illness (i.e., infection is not completely asymptomatic); and (3) the virus is easily transmitted from person to person.[35] After a pandemic has run its course, the respective subtype circulates as seasonal influenza until a new subtype appears. There have been four influenza pandemics over the last one hundred years: (1) the 1918 "Spanish flu" (an H1N1 subtype), affecting approximately one third of the global population, of unusual severity and causing approximately fifty million deaths; (2) the 1957 Asian influenza (an H2N2 subtype), the first pandemic that could be thoroughly studied in laboratories; (3) the Hong Kong influenza 1968 (an H3N2 subtype); and (4) the 2009 "swine flu" (an influenza H1N1 subtype).[36]

[32] C. Giorgetti, *A Principled Approach to State Failure: International Community Actions in Emergency Situations*, Leiden: Koninklijke Brill NV, 2010, p. 100.

[33] See section 2.3.1.3, Ebola 2014.

[34] Two more outbreaks have been considered by Emergency Committees under the IHR but were not considered to be PHEICs: MERS since July 2013, and yellow fever since May 2016. See http://www.who.int/ihr/procedures/ihr_committees/en/ [accessed August 31, 2016].

[35] Robert Koch Institut, Nationaler Pandemieplan II, RKI: 2016, p. 15, available at http://www.rki.de/DE/Content/InfAZ/I/Influenza/Pandemieplanung/Downloads/Pandemieplan_Teil_II_gesamt.pdf?__blob=publicationFile [accessed August 31, 2016].

[36] E. D. Kilbourne, Influenza Pandemics of the 20th Century, *Emerging Infectious Diseases* 12:1 (January 2006), pp. 9–14, available at http://wwwnc.cdc.gov/eid/article/12/1/pdfs/05-1254.pdf [accessed August 31, 2016]; J. Taubenberger and D. M. Morens, 1918 Influenza: The Mother of all Diseases, *Emerging Infectious Diseases* 12:1 (January 2006), pp. 15–22, available at http://wwwnc.cdc.gov/eid/article/12/1/05-0979_article [accessed August 31, 2016].

Outbreaks of influenza-like illnesses were noted in Mexico in March and April 2009. These—it was later shown—were caused by a new influenza subtype never before seen in animals or humans and recognized first in the USA in mid-April 2009. Already ten days later, on April 25, 2009, the WHO declared the H1N1 influenza outbreak to be a PHEIC. On June 11, 2009, the WHO announced to the world that an influenza pandemic was underway and raised the worldwide pandemic alert level to six, the highest level possible. By that time, seventy-four countries had reported a total of 28,774 cases.[37] Massive vaccination campaigns were initiated once the vaccine for the 2009 H1N1 influenza strain became available in October 2009. The pandemic ran its course, and on August 10, 2010—by then, "more than 214 countries and overseas territories or communities [had] reported laboratory confirmed cases of pandemic influenza H1N1 2009, including over 18449 deaths"—the WHO declared that the pandemic had ended, with the pandemic strain moving towards behavior like a seasonal influenza strain.[38] The 2009 flu pandemic thus fortunately was less severe than had been feared initially,[39] as the virus did not mutate during the pandemic into a more lethal form. Nor did resistance to antiviral drugs become a problem. And lastly, the vaccine proved to provide good protection against the new influenza virus and showed an excellent safety profile (i.e., had no serious side-effect).[40]

There were numerous accusations of "overreaction" against the WHO, mostly from outside expert circles. The guidelines issued by the WHO were criticized for evoking "unjustified scares and fears about the health risks" faced by the public; it was also alleged that some of the experts advising WHO on the pandemic had financial ties with drug companies that were producing antiviral drugs and influenza vaccines, and that as a result, the WHO was unduly influenced to declare a pandemic and to exaggerate its potential severity.[41]

[37] World Health Organization, Emergencies preparedness, response: Influenza A(H1N1)—update 47 (2009), available at http://www.who.int/csr/don/2009_06_11/en/ [accessed August 31, 2016].

[38] World Health Organization, Emergencies preparedness, response: Pandemic (H1N1)—update 112 (2010), available at: http://www.who.int/csr/don/2010_08_06/en/; World Health Organization, Emergencies preparedness, response: Director-General statement following the ninth meeting of the emergency committee (2010), available at http://www.who.int/csr/disease/swineflu/9th_meeting_ihr/en/ [accessed August 31, 2016].

[39] D. E. Low and A. McGeer, Pandemic (H1N1) 2009: Assessing the Response, *Canadian Medical Association Journal* 182:17 (2010), pp. 1874–8.

[40] Centers for Disease Control and Prevention, The 2009 H1N1 Pandemic: Summary Highlights. April 2009–April 2010, updated June 16, 2010, available at http://www.cdc.gov/h1n1flu/cdcresponse.htm [accessed August 31, 2016]; World Health Organization, Global Advisory Committee on Vaccine Safety, June 16–17, 2010, available at http://www.who.int/vaccine_safety/committee/reports/Jun_2010/en/ [accessed September 28, 2016].

[41] F. Godlee, Conflicts of Interest and Pandemic Flu, *British Medical Journal* 340 (June 2010), p. c2947; A. O'Dowd, Council of Europe Condemns "Unjustified Scare" Over Swine Flu, *British Medical Journal* 340 (June 2010), p. c3033.

However, an independent panel assessing WHO performance found among other things, that:

> WHO performed well in many ways during the pandemic, confronted systemic difficulties and demonstrated some shortcomings. The Committee found no evidence of malfeasance.... WHO provided welcome leadership in coordinating the global response throughout the pandemic. WHO's epidemic intelligence functions have strengthened in recent years [...] Although confidentiality represented an understandable effort to protect the members from external pressures, this paradoxically fed suspicions that the Organization had something to hide.[42]

Leung and Nicoll also refute accusations of overreaction, arguing that given the uncertainty around influenza viruses and pandemics, "reasonable application of the precautionary principle should prevail in the responses."[43]

2.3.1.2. Polio 2014

In 1988, the WHA decided to work towards the global eradication of polio. At that time, polio was endemic in more than 125 countries and paralyzed 350,000 children every year. In 2012, those horrendous numbers had fallen to 223 wild-type polio cases that were reported from five countries (Afghanistan, Chad, Niger, Nigeria, and Pakistan). In 2013–14, the Pakistan polio virus spread into Syria and Iraq. Five previously polio-free countries in Africa also registered polio cases. On May 5, 2014, the WHO declared the continuing international spread of polio from the remaining endemic countries to polio-free countries a PHEIC.[44] Currently, there are three countries left with endemic transmission of wild-type polio: Afghanistan, Nigeria, and Pakistan, from which seventy-four cases were reported in 2015, and thirty-seven in 2016.[45] Wild-type polio transmission is currently lower than at almost any time in the past, opening up the very real possibility of eradicating polio globally—the second disease after smallpox.

[42] H. V. Fineberg et al., Strengthening response to pandemics and other public health emergencies, Report of the Review Committee on the Functioning of the International Health Regulations (2005) and on Pandemic Influenza (H1N1) 2009 (2010), available at http://apps.who.int/iris/bitstream/10665/75235/1/9789241564335_eng.pdf?ua=1 [accessed August 31, 2016].

[43] G. M. Leung and A. Nicoll, Reflections on Pandemic (H1N1) 2009 and the International Response, *Public Library of Science Medicine* 7:10 (2010), e1000346.

[44] Global Polio Eradication Initiative, Public Health Emergency status, available at http://polioeradication.org/polio-today/polio-now/public-health-emergency-status/ [accessed November 28, 2017].

[45] Polio Global Eradication Initiative, list of wild poliovirus by country and year as of November 28, 2017, available at http://polioeradication.org/wp-content/uploads/2017/11/global-wild-poliovirus-2012-2017-29112017.pdf [accessed November 28, 2017].

There is almost no assessment of the effectiveness of the WHO's polio work available in the literature. The Independent Monitoring Board of the Global Polio Eradication Initiative[46] has criticized WHO Africa in relation to polio being exported from Nigeria:

> The WHO African Regional Office failed to mount a strong sub-regional outbreak response, and is now [2014] (understandably) impeded in doing so by its need to focus on Ebola.[47]

In its report from October 2015, the Independent Monitoring Board notes that the Global Polio Eradication Initiative's "[d]ecision-making, partnership working, overall leadership, financial transparency, and the cohesiveness of the programme have steadily improved since [2014] but the level of coordination across partners necessary to assure high within-country performance remains problematic."[48]

2.3.1.3. Ebola 2014

The Ebola virus disease outbreak, which started late in 2013 and mainly affected the West African countries Guinea, Liberia, and Sierra Leone, has been unprecedented in length, severity, complexity of response, and loss of life. By August 2015, when the outbreak was down to occasional cases, it had caused close to 29,000 cases and more than 11,000 deaths. Previous Ebola virus disease outbreaks never took place in West Africa, and the number of cases had always been between a few dozens and a few hundreds.

The 2014 outbreak was declared a PHEIC on August 8, 2014. On September 18, 2014, the UN Security Council adopted Resolution 2177, calling the outbreak "a threat to international peace and security." One day later, the UN General Assembly adopted Resolution 69/1 establishing the UN Mission for Ebola Emergency Response (UNMEER), the first ever emergency health mission.

[46] The Global Polio Eradication Initiative is a public–private partnership led by national governments and spearheaded by the World Health Organization, Rotary International, the US Centers for Disease Control and Prevention (CDC), and the United Nations Children's Fund (UNICEF). See www.polioeradication.org.

[47] Independent Monitoring Board of the Global Polio Eradication Initiative, Tenth report, October 2014, available at http://www.polioeradication.org/Portals/0/Document/Aboutus/Governance/IMB/11IMBMeeting/11IMB_Report_EN.pdf [accessed September 28, 2016]. WHO's African Regional Office has also been harshly criticized in connection with the Ebola virus disease outbreak in West Africa in 2014/15; a new head was appointed in January 2015. See L. Schlein, New Africa Regional Chief Aims to Shake Up Maligned WHO Office, *Voice of America*, January 31, 2015, available at http://www.voanews.com/a/ebola-who-africa-director/2622985.html [accessed September 28, 2016].

[48] Independent Monitoring Board of the Global Polio Eradication Initiative, Twelfth report, October 2015, available at: http://www.polioeradication.org/Portals/0/Document/Aboutus/Governance/IMB/13IMBMeeting/13IMB_Report_EN.pdf [accessed September 28, 2016].

WHO has been harshly criticized for its handling of the Ebola crisis—Fidler speaks of "epic failure"[49]—in particular for the late declaration of the PHEIC and the delayed and insufficient outbreak response. For instance, the International Crisis Group wrote in October 2015:

> The World Health Organization (WHO), which had stalled for far too long on declaring an international health emergency, then proved incapable of mounting an effective response.[50]

Médecins Sans Frontières voiced similar criticism in March 2015:

> [T]here was a clear lack of leadership from the WHO: decisions on setting priorities, attributing roles and responsibilities, ensuring accountability for the quality of activities, and mobilising the resources necessary were not taken on the necessary scale.[51]

So did the Harvard/LSHTM (London School of Hygiene & Tropical Medicine) panel, which noted:

> Ebola exposed WHO as unable to meet its responsibility for responding to such situations and alerting the global community.[52]

Save the Children was a little more nuanced in its criticism:

> The international system did not respond rapidly enough nor function as required in the early part of the outbreak.[53]

Interestingly, most WHO critics assign responsibility for the WHO's failures not only to the WHO Secretariat, but also to political developments and by extension to member states. The International Crisis Group attributed the lack of response to "...WHO's weak leadership and funding mechanism."[54] Save the Children referred to "autonomy of [WHO's] regions and the political nature of elections of officials," as well as to severe budget reductions as part of

[49] D. P. Fidler, Epic Failure of Ebola and Global Health Security, *The Brown Journal of World Affairs* 21:2 (2015), available at https://www.brown.edu/initiatives/journal-world-affairs/sites/brown.edu.initiatives.journal-world-affairs/files/private/articles/Fidler.pdf [accessed September 24, 2016].

[50] International Crisis Group, The Politics Behind the Ebola Crisis, Africa Report No. 232 (October 28, 2015), p. ii, available at http://www.crisisgroup.org/~/media/Files/africa/west-africa/232-the-politics-behind-the-ebola-crisis.pdf [accessed August 31, 2016].

[51] Médecins Sans Frontières, *Pushed to the Limit and Beyond: A Year into the Largest Ever Ebola Outbreak*, March 2015, p. 9, available at https://www.doctorswithoutborders.org/sites/usa/files/msf143061.pdf [accessed August 31, 2016].

[52] S. Moon et al., Will Ebola Change the Game? Ten Essential Reforms before the Next Pandemic, The Report of the Harvard–LSHTM Independent Panel on the Global Response to Ebola, *The Lancet* 386:10009 (2015), pp. 2204–21 (2204), available at http://www.thelancet.com/pdfs/journals/lancet/PIIS0140-6736%2815%2900946-0.pdf [accessed August 31, 2016].

[53] Save the Children, *A Wake-up Call: Lessons from Ebola for the World's Health System*, London: Save the Children, 2015, available at http://www.savethechildren.org.uk/resources/online-library/wake-call-0 [accessed August 31, 2016].

[54] International Crisis Group, The Politics Behind the Ebola Crisis, p. 21.

the explanation for failure to respond effectively.[55] Accordingly, there have been no calls for the establishment of alternative regimes for dealing with international health emergencies; instead, there is virtual unanimity in calling for investments to strengthen the operational capacity of the WHO for health emergency responses. The Ebola Interim Assessment Panel, an independent expert panel put in place in March 2015 to assess "...all aspects of WHO's response to the Ebola outbreak," wrote in its final report in July 2015:

> Having reviewed all the options, the Panel has concluded that WHO should be the lead health emergency response agency. This requires that a number of organizational and financial issues be addressed urgently.... WHO must re-establish its pre-eminence as the guardian of global public health; this will require significant changes throughout WHO with the understanding that this includes both the Secretariat and the Member States.... The Ebola crisis not only exposed organizational failings in the functioning of WHO, but it also demonstrated shortcomings in the International Health Regulations (2005).[56]

The Ebola crisis also demonstrated that UNMEER—and the EU Ebola response coordination structures—added an additional layer of a coordination bureaucracy but did not effectively solve problems of missing capacities and capabilities either at the national or at the international level. The Ebola Interim Assessment Panel "...strongly recommended against the establishment of a United Nations mission for future emergencies with health consequences."[57]

2.3.1.4. Zika 2016

In October 2015, Brazil reported an unusual increase in microcephaly in newborns in regions where a Zika virus outbreak had been ongoing since late 2014. The Zika virus was first identified in Uganda in 1947; it is transmitted primarily through mosquitoes. Infection with the Zika virus usually causes a fairly mild illness; many people infected remain free of symptoms. However, a Zika virus infection is particularly dangerous for pregnant women, as scientific consensus emerged in early 2016 that it leads to microcephaly in newborns. In addition, neurological disorders—in particular the disabling Guillain–Barré syndrome—are medical complications associated with Zika virus infections.[58]

The WHO declared the Zika virus outbreak a PHEIC on February 1, 2016. According to the Emergency Committee convened by WHO to decide on the

[55] Save the Children, *A Wake-up Call*, p. 6.

[56] World Health Organization, Final report of the Ebola Interim Assessment panel, July 2015, available at http://www.who.int/csr/resources/publications/ebola/report-by-panel.pdf?ua=1 [accessed August 31, 2016]. The shortcomings in the IHR (2005), that the Panel identified, relate mostly to the implementation of the IHR, not their substance.

[57] World Health Organization, Final report of the Ebola Interim Assessment panel, p. 24.

[58] World Health Organization, The history of Zika virus, available at http://www.who.int/emergencies/zika-virus/history/en/ [accessed September 24, 2016].

issue, the decision was based on "what is not known about the clusters of microcephaly, Guillain–Barré syndrome, and possibly other neurological defects reported . . . that are associated in time and place with outbreaks of Zika infection."[59] By November 2016, sixty-nine countries had reported an outbreak of Zika virus since 2015 with no previous evidence of circulation. Brazil had reported 2,189 cases of microcephaly and central nervous system malformation by that time.[60]

The WHO has not been criticized for declaring the Zika virus spread a PHEIC, nor for being too slow, as was the case with the PHEIC declaration relating to the Ebola virus disease outbreak in West Africa. Shortly after the declaration of PHEIC, WHO launched a global Strategic Response Framework and Joint Operations Plan to guide the international response to the Zika virus outbreak. Besides coordinating and supporting surveillance and response, the focus of WHO is on coordinating research, because little was known about the resulting disease and the connection to congenital malformations and other neurological complications. The declaration of a PHEIC did not automatically lead to comprehensive global action as illustrated by the fact that as of mid-2016 all Zika-related international "funding needs have been largely unmet, both for WHO and for its partners."[61] WHO's coordination of efforts to manage the Zika virus-related outbreak of health complications has been described as "commendable."[62]

2.3.2. *Legitimacy*

The legitimacy of any political order is based on the appeal of its normative foundations, the possibilities for participation in decision-making, its representativeness and transparency, and its results.[63] Beyond that, other characteristics such as expertise can also be a source of legitimacy.[64] The legitimacy of the WHO in general appears to be comparatively high. *First*, all states can

[59] D. L. Heymann et al., Zika Virus and Microcephaly: Why is this Situation a PHEIC? *The Lancet*, published online February 10, 2016, available at http://www.thelancet.com/pb/assets/raw/Lancet/pdfs/S0140673616003202.pdf [accessed August 31, 2016].

[60] World Health Organization, Situation Report, Zika-Virus, Microcephaly, Guillain–Barré Syndrome, December 1, 2016, available at http://apps.who.int/iris/bitstream/10665/251811/1/zikasitrep1Dec2016-eng.pdf?ua=1 [accessed November 28, 2017].

[61] World Health Organization, Zika strategic response plan, p. 13, June 2016, available at http://apps.who.int/iris/bitstream/10665/246091/1/WHO-ZIKV-SRF-16.3-eng.pdf?ua=1&ua=1&ua=1 [accessed September 24, 2016].

[62] Another Kind of Zika Public Health Emergency (editorial), *The Lancet* 389:10069, p. 573, February 11, 2017, available at http://www.thelancet.com/pdfs/journals/lancet/PIIS0140-6736(17)30325-2.pdf [accessed 28 November, 2017].

[63] See the Introduction to this volume.

[64] D. Bodansky, Legitimacy in International Law and International Relations, APSA 2011 Annual meeting paper, available at http://papers.ssrn.com/sol3/papers.cfm?abstract_id=1900289 [accessed August 31, 2016].

become member states and all member states have the same rights and responsibilities. *Second*, decisions on major issues are taken by a two-thirds majority vote, decisions on other questions by a simple majority vote in the World Health Assembly, the decision-making body of the WHO. In contrast to other international forums governed in accordance with the consensus rule, this prevents individual states from blocking action. It should also, in theory at least, guarantee that the interests of all members are adequately represented.

Yet legitimacy based on representativeness has been somewhat undermined by two trends. *First*, more and more of the WHO's financial resources have come as project-specific funding:

> At present, less than 25 per cent of WHO's biennial programme budget comes from assessed contributions; the remainder comes from voluntary funds that are largely restricted for purposes specified by donors.[65]

Such contributions limit the WHO in prioritizing activities independently. *Second*, donor countries make ever more funds available outside the WHO for specific health purposes, such as the GHSA mentioned in section 2.2. While this does not directly affect the WHO budget, it is counted nationally as international health investment and therefore may draw funding away from the WHO. This problem has been widely recognized by major WHO evaluations. Thus, the Harvard/LSHTM panel is demanding a new deal for an "appropriately financed WHO."[66] The UN Secretary General High Level Panel similarly recommends that "... WHO Member States increase their assessed contributions to the WHO budget by at least 10 per cent" and that "10 per cent of all voluntary contributions to the WHO—beyond programme support costs—are mandatorily directed to support the Centre for Emergency Preparedness and Response."[67]

Expertise as a source of legitimacy is particularly relevant in highly technical and scientific issue areas. Disease outbreak response is such an issue area, and the WHO's legitimacy undoubtedly also rests on its medical expertise that is reflected in its norm-setting and guidance-generating initiatives. Frequently, WHO guidance is considered either gold standard—e.g., for clinical management of diseases—or it is an important point of reference.

[65] World Health Organization, Final report of the Ebola Interim Assessment panel, July 2015, p. 16, available at http://www.who.int/csr/resources/publications/ebola/report-by-panel.pdf?ua=1 [accessed August 31, 2016].

[66] Moon et al., Will Ebola change the game?, p. 2216.

[67] United Nations, High-Level Panel on the Global Response to Health Crises: Protecting Humanity from Future Health Crises (advance unedited copy), pp. 64–5, January 25, 2016, available at http://www.un.org/News/dh/infocus/HLP/2016-02-05_Final_Report_Global_Response_to_Health_Crises.pdf [accessed August 31, 2016].

2.3.3. Interdependence with Other Partial Orders

What happens in the regime to cope with international health emergencies foremost affects—and is affected by—what happens in the regimes on development cooperation, humanitarian aid, and world trade. A strong interdependence also exists with scientific research and development (R&D), an area for which almost no international governance mechanisms exist. There are also connections with global environmental, intellectual property, and weapons of mass destruction proliferation issues.

The effectiveness and sustainability of the international health emergency order largely depends on primary healthcare and health emergency response capabilities at the national level. In cases where these capabilities are limited or non-existent, development cooperation is crucial to close gaps in national capabilities. Only if basic national capabilities are in place, is effective international health emergency response possible. There are numerous reasons why a focus on primary healthcare is important. In our context, it is (1) because healthy people are less vulnerable to disease, making it less likely that illness leads to major epidemics; (2) because a functioning health system catering to people's needs builds trust in national healthcare and its personnel and more generally in the functioning of state structures, making it more likely that people will follow health recommendations during times of crisis; and (3) because a sufficient and well-trained national health workforce is indispensable to make good use of international health emergency support (both in terms of materials such as distributing and administering vaccines and in terms of personnel such as epidemiologists and contact tracers). A focus on health emergency response is important to recognize disease outbreaks early and move quickly to contain their spread. National core capacities are written down in the International Health Regulations (2005): "There is a close relationship between compliance with IHR Core Capacity requirements and the wider improvement of health systems."[68]

During major health emergencies, national and international health actors need support from non-health humanitarian actors, for example to provide logistics (long haul as well as local transportation); sanitation, water, and hygiene; education and community engagement; housing and camp management; and food security. Moreover, in such a crisis, states are quick to implement travel and trade restrictions, even if the usefulness for control of disease spread is limited or even non-existent.[69] This has the unfortunate effect that states in which outbreaks occur hesitate to notify the WHO. Incentives may therefore

[68] United Nations, High-Level Panel on the Global Response to Health Crises, p. 45.

[69] Recent examples include shutting down commercial flights to West Africa during the Ebola virus disease outbreak although exit screening of passengers was in force in the affected countries, and calls to cancel the Olympic Games in Brazil although the mostly insect-transmitted Zika virus was already circulating globally and insect control measures had been put in place in Brazil.

be needed for such states to notify early, as well as disincentives for states that wrongfully implement travel and trade restrictions.

The capability to detect and respond to disease outbreaks globally would be strengthened if medical countermeasures (MCM) existed for all diseases with epidemic potential. For lack of market incentives, development of MCM for diseases that do not affect Western countries is often not sufficiently funded. Ebola is a case in point: vaccine candidates had been developed by the time the outbreak in West Africa was detected (mostly because of Western fears over Ebola virus as a potential bioterrorism or bioweapons agent), but testing and approval of a vaccine for public use—which is costly, legally challenging, and usually done by private companies—had not been conducted. Recognizing this problem, WHO in 2015 initiated a global strategy and preparedness plan (known as WHO's R&D Blueprint) to ensure that targeted research and development "can strengthen the emergency response by bringing medical technologies to patients during epidemics."[70]

3. CONCLUDING THOUGHTS

In contrast to numerous other partial orders, the partial order on international health emergencies has proved remarkably robust over the past twenty years, and even evolved towards more cooperation and stronger international governance.

Two major external factors profoundly shaped the evolution of the regime for international disease outbreak surveillance and response from 1995 onwards. *First*, the regime as of 1995 could not even hope to address successfully the rapidly growing number of emerging and re-emerging infectious diseases; examples include HIV/AIDS, tuberculosis, malaria, dengue, classic and new forms of cholera, Rift Valley fever, hantavirus pulmonary syndrome, Lyme disease, and different hemorrhagic fevers. The *second* major external driver of change was a growing concern about bioweapons and bioterrorism, particularly in the USA; the possibility of intentional use of pathogens by states or terrorists opened up the theoretical prospect of dangerous diseases such as plague, anthrax, or hemorrhagic fevers suddenly affecting Western states where they had become virtually unknown. These two external factors were the driving force for major changes in the regime.

In addition, there were also factors internal to the regime that made change possible, foremost the constitutional ability of the WHO to take initiatives that

[70] World Health Organization, A research and development Blueprint for action to prevent epidemics, available at http://www.who.int/csr/research-and-development/en/ [accessed September 29, 2016].

the leadership of the organization was willing to exploit at the time, as illustrated by the establishment of GOARN and the handling of SARS in 2003. As Fidler observed, "[t]he absence of an international legal framework was not, apparently, seriously restraining WHO's development and implementation of the [new] approach."[71]

Further facilitating the robustness and evolution of the regime is the existing broad international acceptance of the norm that disease outbreaks need to be effectively countered, independent of where they occur. Of particular importance here is the repeatedly expressed interest of powerful states to strengthen international disease outbreak responses; the statements at the Group of Seven (G7) summits in 2015 and 2016 are powerful examples.[72] Supporting the norm of strong international health emergency response can be the result of humanitarian considerations, but is often also or even primarily motivated by national self-interest. As an Indian newspaper commentator observed in early 2016:

> [W]hen a disease has potentially strong impacts on North America and Europe the political calculations change very quickly. That drives the media and pushes WHO to act.[73]

In summary, the following observations are offered on why the partial order on international health emergencies has been comparatively robust and has become stronger over the last two decades:

- Cooperative international order is more likely if individual nation-states cannot cope alone and are therefore negatively affected by absence of order, i.e., if there is a common goal.
- Cooperative international order is more likely if scientific and technical issues are largely uncontested and not politicized, i.e., if there is a commonly agreed way to reach the common goal.
- Order is more likely if powerful states support it.
- Crises can be conducive to an evolution of order.
- Evolution of order is more likely if actors have already "pre-thought" necessary reforms and—even better—tested individual elements of the

[71] Fidler, International Sanitary Convention, p. 349.

[72] See statements of the G7 summits in Elmau, Germany, 2015, available at https://sustainabledevelopment.un.org/content/documents/7320LEADERS%20STATEMENT_FINAL_CLEAN.pdf [accessed September 26, 2016], and in Ise-shima, Japan, 2016, available at http://www.mofa.go.jp/files/000160266.pdf [accessed September 26, 2016].

[73] R. Prasad, I Think WHO Should Declare an Emergency, *The Hindu*, January 31, 2016, available at http://www.thehindu.com/sci-tech/health/zika-i-think-who-should-declare-an-emergency/article8172249.ece [accessed August 31, 2016].

> reformed order. If international organizations are involved, they should therefore be supported in their ability to work proactively, which includes decision-making procedures that avoid the need for consensus.

There is little reason to expect a weakening of the international health emergencies order any time soon. Political interest in international health governance remains strong and there is continuous support for WHO as lead agency for surveillance and response to international health emergencies. As WHO Director-General Chan expressed it in her closing remarks to the 69th World Health Assembly in May 2016:

> You want WHO, as the single agency with universal legitimacy in matters of international health, to lead and coordinate the response to emergencies. This function stays at WHO. Thank you.[74]

In addition, WHO has embarked on a reform to complement its "traditional technical and normative role with new operational capacities and capabilities for its work in outbreaks and humanitarian emergencies."[75] And further, establishing and strengthening IHR core capacities and capabilities at the nation-state level has received increased attention with the development of the so-called Joint External Evaluation tool that signals a "move from 'exclusive self-evaluation' to external evaluation [because of] the recognition that transparency and mutual accountability in the international community are essential in implementing IHR collectively."[76]

A strong indication that the international health emergencies partial order is not likely to follow other partial orders into decline from neglect or demolition is the taking up of global health issues for the first time in detail by the Group of Twenty (G20) in 2017, with a separate meeting of G20 health ministers—the first ever—in May 2017. The G20 emphasized in their 2017 declaration the importance of safeguarding against health crises and "WHO's central coordinating role, especially for capacity building and response to health emergencies."[77] While in the current political climate Ebola 2014/15 might not generate the long-term, large-scale changes towards stronger global

[74] World Health Organization, Closing Remarks at the Sixty-Ninth World Health Assembly, Dr Margaret Chan, Director-General of the World Health Organization, Geneva, Switzerland, May 28, 2016, available at http://www.who.int/dg/speeches/2016/wha69-closing-remarks/en/ [accessed September 29, 2016].

[75] World Health Organization, Reform of WHO's work in health emergency management, document A69/30, May 5, 2016, available at http://apps.who.int/gb/ebwha/pdf_files/WHA69/A69_30-en.pdf [accessed September 29, 2016].

[76] World Health Organization, Joint External Evaluation Tool: International Health Regulations (2005), 2016, available at http://apps.who.int/iris/bitstream/10665/204368/1/9789241510172_eng.pdf [accessed September 29, 2016].

[77] G20, G20 Leaders' Declaration: Shaping an interconnected world, Hamburg, July 7–8, 2017, available at: https://www.g20.org/en/g20/timeline [accessed November 28, 2017].

health governance hoped for by health advocates—similar to SARS 2003 being a turning point towards progress of the international health emergencies order—there is equally no reason to fear excessively for this particular partial order just yet.[78]

[78] I would like to thank colleagues at the Robert Koch Institute, the German section of Médicins Sans Frontières and the German Institute for International and Security Affairs (SWP), all in Berlin, for insightful discussions and helpful comments.

4

The International Nuclear Order after the Cold War—Progress and Regress

William Walker

1. INTRODUCTION

The Absolute Weapon: Atomic Power and World Order was the first important book on the political and military implications of nuclear weapons.[1] Published in the year after Hiroshima, its title implied that this was a weapon that surpassed all others and was absolute in its destructiveness and effect on the human condition. It also implied that the weapon's arrival had fundamental consequences for the arrangement, exercise, and regulation of power within the international system, and that the consequences were global.

The book's preparation had accompanied an intense debate in 1946 on whether the atomic bomb's adoption as an instrument of war should be avoided, or whether its development and deployment should be accepted as primary means of balancing power and discouraging further great wars. The latter view prevailed in Washington and Moscow. As Bernard Brodie famously asserted, "Thus far the chief purpose of our military establishment has been to win wars. From now on its chief purpose must be to avert them."[2] This sentiment underpinned the US policy of containment elaborated in the seminal NSC-68 of 1950.[3] Especially after the thermonuclear weapon's invention, the USA, Soviet Union, and their alliances were committed to the avoidance of nuclear war, whilst actively using its threat to project power and constrain the opponent.

[1] Bernard Brodie (ed.), *The Absolute Weapon: Atomic Power and World Order*, New York: Harcourt, Brace, and Company, 1946.

[2] Bernard Brodie, Implications for Military Policy, in Brodie (ed.), *Absolute Weapon*, p. 76.

[3] United States Objectives and Programs for National Security, *National Security Council Report 68*, April 1950, https://www.trumanlibrary.org/whistlestop/study_collections/coldwar/documents/pdf/10-1.pdf.

An intense arms race and jockeying for strategic advantage followed, abetted by rapid technological advances in warhead design and delivery systems, the move to mass production, and organizational entrenchment. In no sense was an order deserving that description established during the Cold War's early years. Nevertheless, it was increasingly realized that the sphere of nuclear armament would have to be regulated if nuclear war were to be avoided and the arms race dampened. Attention was given to constraining innovation (through test bans) and the production and deployment of weaponry (through arms limitation treaties), and to improving crisis management by facilitating communication between opposing sides (through dialog and hot-line agreements).

It was also recognized that the possession of nuclear weaponry could not be confined to the USA and USSR indefinitely. Many states and industries had become excited by the prospect of using nuclear fission to produce heat and electricity ("nuclear power"). A tension therefore developed between limiting access to nuclear arms and fostering access to nuclear power, the technologies of which overlapped. Agreement on norms and rules of engagement with nuclear technology would be required to constrain nuclear proliferation.

This chapter considers how an international nuclear order, with special characteristics, was established during the Cold War and consolidated in the decade that followed its end. Although retaining considerable resilience, it has suffered a loss of legitimacy, coherence, and direction since the mid-1990s for reasons that will be discussed. Besides being prey to renewed inter-state rivalry and posturing, the order is being challenged simultaneously by actors that are skeptical of international institutions, and by actors that refuse to accept that an order tolerating the existence of nuclear weapons deserves to be valued. Technological change is also raising fresh questions about the reliability and risks of nuclear deterrence. Across the board, the political volatility and apparent decline of the United States, historically the nuclear order's main shaper and steward, has become a serious complication.

2. TWO SITES OF NUCLEAR ORDERING AND THEIR INTERCONNECTION

Understanding nuclear order is best approached through recognition that there have been two distinct, albeit interconnected, sites of nuclear ordering, depicted in stylized form in Figure 4.1.[4] One site has entailed politico-military engagement with nuclear technology. It has involved inter alia production,

[4] William Walker, *A Perpetual Menace: Nuclear Weapons and International Order*, London: Routledge, 2012.

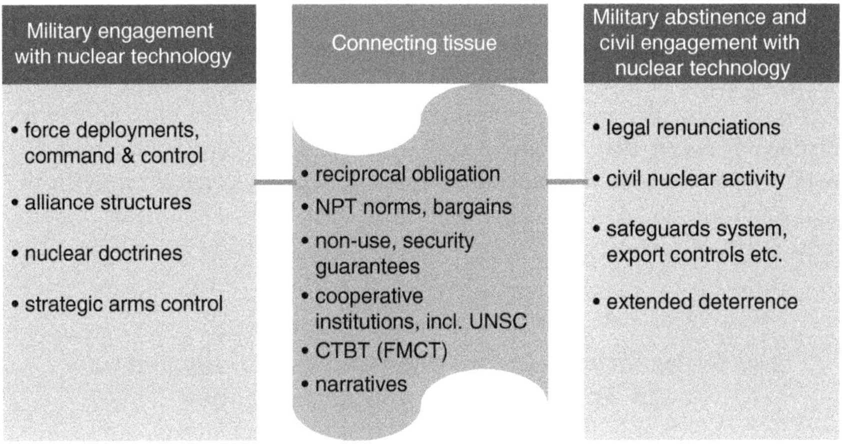

Figure 4.1 Sites of international nuclear ordering
Source: own design

testing, and deployment of nuclear weapons; command and control; deterrence theory and nuclear doctrines; and arms control agreements and practices. The main actors have been nuclear weapon states and their allies. The other site has entailed abstinence from military nuclear activity even as nuclear technology is being used for energy and industrial purposes. Forgoing the possession of nuclear weapons became a precondition for assistance with the development of nuclear power systems. The practice of non-proliferation has also involved regulatory instruments (notably international safeguards and trade controls); regional nuclear weapon-free zones; and extended deterrence ("nuclear umbrellas") giving protection to non-nuclear members of alliances.

These two sites of ordering have been connected, always controversially, by normative and instrumental tissue expressed especially through the norms, rules, and bargains contained in the Nuclear Non-Proliferation Treaty (NPT) of 1970. The NPT took the form of a contract. In return for the majority of states' renunciation of rights to possess nuclear weapons (waiving the UN Charter's right to self-defense by nuclear means), the nuclear weapon states Parties pledged—with several caveats—to pursue disarmament "in good faith" (Article VI) and to provide non-nuclear weapon states Parties with access to nuclear technology for civil purposes (Article IV) under international safeguards (Article III).[5]

[5] Article IV states that "Nothing in this Treaty shall be interpreted as affecting the inalienable right of all the [compliant] Parties to the Treaty to develop research, production and use of nuclear energy for peaceful purposes without discrimination...." Article VI states that "Each of the Parties to the Treaty undertakes to pursue negotiations in good faith on effective measures relating to cessation of the nuclear arms race at an early date and to nuclear disarmament...."

Although it was a "partial order" as described in Hanns Maull's Introduction to this volume, the nuclear order occupied a special position within, and was integral to, *the* international order during the Cold War. Nuclear weapons became a principal medium through which competitive *and* cooperative relations between the two dominant world powers were conducted. The weapons and associated strategies became their common currency when the rigid economic and ideological separation of their imperial domains disabled other forms of interaction.

2.1. Order through Competition and Power, Cooperation and Transformation, and Reconciliation

The emergent nuclear order exhibited all three of Muthiah Alagappa's "arrangements of order."[6] It exhibited "order through competition and power," in line with realist understandings of the behavior of sovereign states within the international system. Each site of ordering in Figure 4.1 entailed power balancing and projection, along with the self-interested promotion of norms and rules by hegemons acting in concert when it suited them, notably in the non-proliferation regime's formation. For many non-nuclear weapon states, mutual abstinence was a means of avoiding power imbalances, security dilemmas, and arms races in their neighborhoods. In addition, the nuclear order exhibited Alagappa's "order through cooperation" by incorporating ideas of collective security, the fostering of global and regional regimes, mutual assistance in regard to nuclear power, and participation in joint problem solving. And it exhibited his "order through transformation," especially by embodying progressive ideas about escape from the threat of nuclear catastrophe accompanied by a deepening habit and institutionalization of restraint.

The nuclear order featured another arrangement, here termed "order through reconciliation," that had a particular bearing on the NPT-centered order's struggle for global legitimacy. It is implicit in this definition of the international nuclear order:

> Given the existence of nuclear technology, the international nuclear order entails evolving patterns of thought and activity that serve primary goals of world survival, war avoidance and economic development; and the quest for a tolerable accommodation of pronounced differences in the capabilities, practices, rights and obligations of states.[7]

[6] Muthiah Alagappa, The Study of International Order: An Analytical Framework, in Alagappa (ed.), *Asian Security Order: Instrumental and Normative Features*, Stanford, CA: Stanford University Press, 2002, p. 52 and *passim*.

[7] Walker, *Perpetual Menace*, p. 12. My definition draws upon Hedley Bull's classic definition of international order: "a pattern of activity that sustains elementary or primary goals of the

"Order through reconciliation" has two facets: the reconciliation *of* clashing norms, rules, and interests so that they can coexist without ruinous discord; and states'—and peoples'—reconciliation *to* the above pronounced differences and to the very existence of nuclear weapons given their huge dangers and costs. The problem of reconciliation has haunted the politics of nuclear ordering in two particular respects. Firstly, the primary goal of war avoidance through nuclear deterrence conflicts with the primary goal of world survival if one accepts that deterrence can fail and nuclear war can happen by accident or design. In addition, the NPT rests upon denial of nuclear deterrence's contribution to the avoidance of war since ascribing value to deterrence confounds the non-proliferation norm. However appropriate it may be, a conception of nuclear order that embraces deterrence is inherently problematic in the NPT's context. Furthermore, ethical reasoning to justify nuclear deterrence on grounds of war prevention readily produces the disconcerting conclusion that non-proliferation is unethical.[8]

Thus, the nuclear order here described could not have taken shape without an accumulating taboo on the use of nuclear weapons during the Cold War's first decades.[9] Although the practice of nuclear deterrence rested on the taboo's persistent denial, decisions not to use nuclear weapons in the Korean, Vietnam, and other wars fostered a norm of restraint that came to permeate the nuclear order. Societies, including international society, reluctantly tolerated nuclear deterrence because they had sufficient trust that nuclear weapons would never be used in war. In a paradoxical way, the threat of absolute violence caused the nuclear order to rely upon denial of that violence's plausibility, a denial antithetical to the practice of nuclear deterrence. Quite a conundrum!

It may be more appropriate to speak of states and peoples being resigned to, rather than reconciled to, the existence of nuclear weapons. But resignation has not entailed inaction. Indeed the politics of reconciliation have long involved collective efforts—however inadequate—to persuade nuclear weapon states to exercise constraint and move in the direction of disarmament, especially through diplomatic horse-trading at the five-yearly NPT Review Conferences. As discussed later, refusal to be so resigned and accept the nuclear weapon states' political utterances at Review Conferences encouraged

society of states, or international society." Hedley Bull, *The Anarchical Society: A Study of Order in World Politics*, London: Macmillan, 1977, p. 8.

[8] The voluminous literature on non-proliferation pays little attention to this conclusion. Advocates of both deterrence and non-proliferation usually avert the ethical double standard by asserting that nuclear deterrence is a necessary evil and that a world without nuclear weapons could only be attained if proliferation were constrained. Or they assert that ethical judgment should play no part in realpolitik.

[9] See Nina Tannenwald, *The Nuclear Taboo: The United States and the Non-Use of Nuclear Weapons since 1945*, Cambridge: Cambridge University Press, 2007.

the Humanitarian Initiative's launch and Nuclear Weapon Ban Treaty's negotiation of recent years.

The second problem of reconciliation in nuclear politics arises in nuclear power's civil usage. Until the 1970s, the USA and USSR dominated the commercialization of nuclear power through their monopolies in the supply of enriched uranium. Confidence that exported items would not be put to military use was strengthened by development of the International Atomic Energy Agency (IAEA) safeguards system enabling inspection and material accountancy to be carried out by an independent, multilateral organization based in Vienna. The need for stronger rules on trade and development was revealed by the entry of ambitious new suppliers, India's use of civil plutonium to conduct a nuclear test explosion in 1974, and forecasts of a great post-oil-crisis expansion of nuclear power requiring adoption of fast breeder reactors that would widen access to plutonium.

In response, the USA persuaded other major exporters, including the Soviet Union, France, and Germany, to join it in the cooperative regulation of supply, achieved through agreement on the Nuclear Suppliers' Guidelines. This provoked a furious response from states claiming that Article IV's "inalienable right" to engage in civil nuclear activity was being violated. However, the main objectors (India and Pakistan among them) were not members of the NPT. The argument became entangled with the North–South disputes of the mid-1970s. It only died down when the export market for nuclear reactors collapsed as world energy prices fell and safety became an overriding concern following the Three Mile Island and Chernobyl accidents.

3. FROM CRISIS TO CONSOLIDATION (MID-1980s TO MID-1990s)

The NPT's negotiation was concluded in 1968 and the Treaty entered into force in 1970. The first Strategic Arms Limitation Treaty (SALT I) and the Anti-Ballistic Missile (ABM) Treaty were signed by the USA and Soviet governments in 1972. Through these and other developments, the late 1960s and early 1970s brought substantial institutionalization of restraint in the nuclear domain of world politics.

A decade later, a mood of crisis enveloped each site of nuclear ordering in Figure 4.1. A non-proliferation regime had taken shape, but it was wracked by disputes over terms of nuclear trade. Several important states, including China and France and the "threshold states" Argentina, Brazil, India, Israel, Pakistan, and South Africa refused to join the NPT. Worst of all, Soviet–American détente gave way to "the second" Cold War's dangerous confrontation. It was sparked partly by election of a US president scornful of international institutions, including arms control. Rather than stabilize nuclear relations with the Soviet Union, the Reagan administration sought superiority through a return to arms racing supported by levels of military spending and technological innovation that the Soviet Union could not match.

Despite his military assertion, Reagan had a disdain for nuclear weapons and fear of the apocalypse.[10] The Reagan administration was "counter-order," in the sense that it was instinctively opposed to the attitudes and policies—including arms control—that, in its perception, had locked states into behaviors that endangered survival whilst preventing the USA from exerting its full authority. One manifestation was Reagan's dream of a missile shield, termed the Strategic Defense Initiative or Star Wars that would protect the USA from attack. Ironically, attachment to this idea caused him to back away from the proposal to eliminate all nuclear weapons that he and Gorbachev discussed at the Reykjavik summit in 1986.

Nevertheless, the shifts in foreign and security policy that accompanied the summit ushered in a "golden age" in arms control. It included:

- Arms reduction treaties (INF, START I and II) involving dismantlement of around two-thirds of Cold War arsenals; US–Russia agreement in 1994 to de-target strategic nuclear weapons.
- The Soviet Union's "nuclear reconstitution" entailing removal of all nuclear weapons to the Russian Federation from other new-founding states; their accession to the NPT as non-nuclear weapon states (Russia alone remained a nuclear weapon state under the Treaty).
- Conclusion by the Conference on Disarmament (CD) of the Comprehensive Nuclear Test Ban Treaty (CTBT) (1996) and agreement in 1993 on a mandate to negotiate the Fissile Material Cut-off Treaty (FMCT).
- China, France, Argentina, Brazil, Spain, South Africa, and several other states' accession to the NPT, leaving only India, Israel, and Pakistan outside; the Treaty's indefinite extension in 1995 (it had been granted a twenty-five-year lifetime).
- Creation by treaty of nuclear weapon-free zones covering Africa (Pelindaba), South Pacific (Raratonga), and Southeast Asia (Bangkok).
- Elimination, mandated by UN Security Council Resolutions after the 1991 Persian Gulf War, of Iraq's weapons of mass destruction (WMD) capabilities by the IAEA and the UN Special Commission on Iraq.

[10] Frances Fitzgerald, *Way Out There in the Blue: Reagan, Star Wars and the End of the Cold War*, New York: Simon & Schuster, 2008.

- Reform of the IAEA safeguards system, culminating in agreement on the Additional Protocol (1997) to INFCIRC/153, the standard NPT safeguards document; strengthening of the Nuclear Suppliers' Guidelines on trade.

This was a remarkable set of achievements. It resulted partly from contemporaneous political and economic transformations including the former Soviet Union's abandonment of communism and rapprochement with the West, democratization in Latin America, and the end of apartheid in South Africa. Nuclear deterrence appeared to have lost relevance. Progress was assisted by the US use of its supremacy in the early post-Cold War period to foster international institutions. Aided by Russia's weakness and China's preoccupation with economic development, the UN Security Council's permanent members cooperated effectively for the first time in the nuclear field. The need to extend the NPT's lifetime in 1995 also encouraged cooperation and the expansion of membership.

4. RESPONDING TO IRREGULARITY WITH IRREGULARITY (MID-1990s TO MID-2000s)

The Indian and Pakistani test explosions in May 1998 were the most obvious setbacks in the second half of the 1990s. They have had lasting consequences. They brought arms racing and the threat of nuclear war into a volatile region, and the presence of three nuclear-armed states (including Israel) outside the NPT caused serious problems for the non-proliferation regime, its universalist ambition, and its regulatory apparatus. India's emergence as a nuclear power was accommodated to a fashion by the US–India nuclear deal of 2006. With most states' reluctant backing, it created an exception of India by treating it as a *de facto* nuclear weapon state enjoying many of the privileges of the NPT's *de jure* nuclear weapon states. From an Indian perspective, the revision of its status ended a long injustice. For many others, it aggravated perceptions of the nuclear order's engrained injustice and hypocrisy, not least because India was now basking in the inequality—in the "nuclear apartheid"—that it had previously deplored.

Within the United States, a change in attitude towards the nuclear order and problem of order came mainly from another direction. It may be illuminated with reference to Figure 4.2. Hitherto, nuclear ordering had been preoccupied within the Figure's top half—the "regular" domains of interaction among sovereign states and their governments and agencies. Although extreme in its effects, nuclear warfare was regarded as part of regular warfare. During the 1990s, concern grew about the behavior of states that defied international norms and rules and were acquiring the technologies for manufacturing weapons of mass destruction by irregular means (especially through A. Q. Khan's criminal network of suppliers). This became the category of "rogue state" in US parlance, with Iraq, Iran, Libya, and North Korea its principal members.

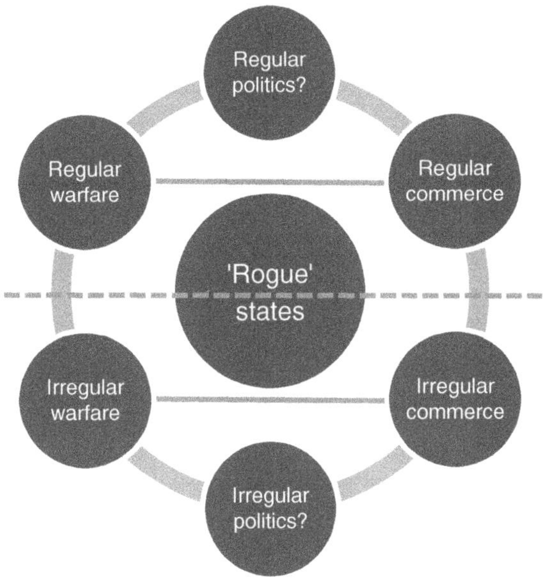

Figure 4.2 Regular and irregular domains of politics, commerce, and warfare
Source: own design

The behavior of these states, each a member of the NPT, suggested that traditional non-proliferation policy was inadequate. In particular, the NPT contained no rules guiding responses to acts of non-compliance beyond the IAEA's right-in-principle to refer breaches of safeguards to the UN Security Council. Gradually, non-proliferation gave way in the USA to counter-proliferation as the enforcement of compliance attained priority. This coincided with mounting anxiety about the emergence of terrorist groups, prominently al-Qaida, willing to commit mass murder. What would happen if technologies of mass destruction infiltrated Figure 4.2's irregular domains, domains that were intrinsically beyond normal regulation? The attacks on the World Trade Center and Pentagon on September 11, 2001 turned these anxieties into "present dangers" and existential threats to the USA in perception if not actuality.

There followed a fusion of the problems of rogue states and international terrorism, the former states allegedly being supporters of terrorism and channels through which terrorist groups would gain access to technology and expertise (a justification for the Iraq War of 2003). The result was a pronounced revision of the nuclear ordering strategy pursued by the United States. Informed by neoconservative ideas and steeped in a cosmology of good and evil, its defining document was the National Security Strategy of 2002 (NSS2002).[11]

[11] President George W. Bush famously called Iran, Iraq, and North Korea an "Axis of Evil" in his State of the Union Address of January 2002.

Four of its suppositions deserve notice, each of which turned out to be invalid or highly flawed. Firstly, a century of great power conflict had ended. China, India, and Russia had embarked on internal economic reforms that would bring greater convergence of politico-economic systems and values. Even if that did not happen, no state would be strong enough to compete militarily with the United States. Arms control was less relevant in this circumstance, and was injurious to American interests when it hindered technological development (US abrogation of the ABM Treaty in 2002 was one consequence).

Secondly, NSS2002 assumed that a policy of containment could not suffice in regard to rogue states. They were aggressive, revisionist, irrational, and amoral actors. The USA had a right and responsibility to wage preventive war against such recalcitrant states and enforce regime change if they did not change their ways. Its actions should not hang on the UN Security Council's consent. The American presumption that preventive war should play no part in non-proliferation policy, a presumption that had held since the early 1950s, was discarded.

Thirdly, international institutions did not contribute significantly to security. Remarkably, NSS2002 contained no reference to the UN Security Council, NPT, or international law. Although inherited multilateral treaties and regimes still had value as disciplinary measures, they should not be regarded as primary frameworks for the development of rules, norms, and practices. George W. Bush's administration showed its disdain for multilateral processes through, amongst other things, its withdrawal from negotiations to strengthen the Biological Weapons Convention and disinterest in the 2005 NPT Review Conference.

Fourthly, an assumption that democratization and economic globalization provided the surest route to peace and security permeated NSS2002. Appetites to acquire weapons of mass destruction would be diminished most effectively and durably by an American-led drive to extend democracy and free-market capitalism.

Taken together, these ideas and associated policies marked a departure from the concept of international nuclear order depicted in Figure 4.1. Non-proliferation was displaced by the interventionist and militaristic counter-proliferation, now run in Washington from the Department of Defense and intelligence agencies. The NPT and other multilateral institutions and processes had marginal significance. The problem of reconciliation did not and should not exist within the nuclear order.

The new strategy also marked a step away from the realist and institutionalist approaches to international relations that had dominated American thought and practice since World War II. This was an idealist, transformative project that sought global peace and prosperity—in the Middle East and elsewhere—through the spread of liberal democracy and market economics, hastened by the exercise of the United States' hegemonic power.[12]

5. BACK TO THE NPT AND DISARMAMENT (FROM THE MID-2000s)

Within a few years of NSS2002, the Bush administration found itself re-engaging, unenthusiastically, with multilateralism and policies of containment. As the deceit and folly of the Iraq War of 2003 became apparent, the policy of regime change was abandoned. Cooperative efforts to restrain Iran and North Korea were stepped up. Concerned about terrorist acquisition of weapon technologies and materials, international steps were taken to deny access and oblige all states to strengthen export controls and physical protection. Furthermore, renewed attention was given to power balancing and extended deterrence, especially in East Asia amidst concerns about North Korea and the rise of China.

In January 2007, four eminent American statesmen published an article in *The Wall Street Journal* in which they advocated "setting the goal of a world free of nuclear weapons and working energetically on the actions required to achieve that goal."[13] Like NSS2002, they were responding to fears of nuclear terrorism and a descent into irregularity. Although the objective was radical, especially coming from them, their recommendations were orthodox, including emphasis on the NPT and its members' obligations, invigoration of the START process, the CTBT's entry into force and FMCT's negotiation, and strengthened trade controls and physical protection.

The article was followed in June 2007 by the British Foreign Secretary's impassioned support of the NPT and multilateral disarmament in a speech given in Washington, DC.[14] Her words were echoed in President Obama's first major speech abroad, in Prague in April 2009, when he distanced himself from the policies of his predecessor by placing the NPT, multilateralism, and the goal of nuclear disarmament at the center of US policy. The International Institute for Strategic Studies in London had already published in 2008 a major study of complete nuclear disarmament—its ramifications for international

[12] See Michael Mazarr, George W. Bush, Idealist, *International Affairs* 79:3 (2003), pp. 503–22.

[13] George P. Shultz, William J. Perry, Henry A. Kissinger, and Sam Nunn, A World Free of Nuclear Weapons, *Wall Street Journal*, January 4, 2007.

[14] Margaret Beckett, A World Free of Nuclear Weapons, Keynote Address to the Carnegie Endowment's Non-Proliferation Conference, Washington, DC, June 25, 2007, https://carnegieendowment.org/2007/06/25/keynote-address-world-free-of-nuclear-weapons-event-1004.

security, whether a global consensus on means and ends could be achieved, and how the weapon's abolition might be made irreversible.[15]

There were some signs of movement. The US–Russian arms reduction process was revived, leading to conclusion of the New START Treaty in April 2010. Fresh life was injected into negotiations with Iran leading eventually to the Joint Comprehensive Plan of Action of July 2015. Summits were held on "nuclear security" aimed at preventing terrorist access to nuclear materials and technologies. Serious thought was given to extending multinational oversight of nuclear fuel-cycles in preparation for a possible "renaissance" of civil nuclear power. The period culminated in the 2010 NPT Review Conference and its concluding agreement on an "Action Plan" for honoring the Treaty's commitments on nuclear disarmament, non-proliferation, and peaceful uses. The Plan included commitment to hold a conference in 2012, under UN auspices, on creation of a WMD-free zone in the Middle East, involving all states in the region, implicitly including Israel.

However, the 2010 Conference's positive outcome could not mask widespread dismay over the lack of progress in nuclear arms control and disarmament, the absence of confidence that nuclear weapon states would honor the NPT's bargains and implement the 2010 Action Plan, and growing disbelief that disarmament could be achieved through consensual, step-by-step processes.

5.1. The Humanitarian Initiative and Nuclear Weapon Ban Treaty

A political movement therefore gathered steam to cut through the complexity and implausibility of multilateral disarmament. It was driven by a large group of non-nuclear weapon states in cooperation with the International Campaign to Abolish Nuclear Weapons, a coalition of non-governmental organizations founded in 2007. The movement's aim was to establish, drawing upon humanitarian law, a global legal ban on the possession and use of nuclear weapons. The consequent Humanitarian Initiative and Nuclear Weapon Ban Treaty drew inspiration from the International Court of Justice's Advisory Opinion of 1996 on the use and threat of use of nuclear weapons and from the Ottawa Treaty of 1999, negotiated outside the CD, which had banned antipersonnel mines in the teeth of resistance from great powers.[16]

[15] George Perkovich and James Acton, *Abolishing Nuclear Weapons*, London: IISS, 2008 (= Adelphi Paper 396).

[16] Whilst the International Court of Justice held back from asserting the illegality of the use and threat of use of nuclear weapons, it emphasized the legal responsibility of nuclear-armed states to negotiate their abolition.

The Humanitarian Initiative held international conferences in March 2013 (Oslo), February 2014 (Nayarit), and December 2014 (Vienna). The last was sponsored by the Austrian government which issued a document, subsequently called the Austrian or Humanitarian Pledge, expressing a commitment "to identify and pursue effective measures to fill the legal gap for the prohibition and elimination of nuclear weapons."[17] A total of 118 states had signed the Pledge by October 2015. With the UN General Assembly's backing, the Nuclear Weapon Ban Treaty's negotiation opened in New York in March 2017 and concluded on July 7, 2017. It was conceived as a stepping-stone towards a Nuclear Weapons Convention containing the provisions required for implementation of a universal and lasting abolition of nuclear weapons.

Two-thirds of UN member states expressed their support for the Nuclear Weapon Ban Treaty on its conclusion. However, their number included no nuclear-armed states and no states involved in nuclear alliances with the USA. It was telling that Japan, hitherto the most prominent advocate of nuclear disarmament, and Norway, an initiator of the Humanitarian Initiative, withheld their support for the ban treaty, the former preoccupied with the threats posed by North Korea and the rise of China, the latter responding to recent Russian belligerence and pressures to uphold the NATO nuclear alliance.

There is no predicting where the nuclear disarmament movement will go from here.[18] Of the 122 states that supported the Nuclear Weapon Ban Treaty's conclusion, only fifty-nine had signed and ten governments had ratified the Treaty in June 2018, approaching a year after the Treaty's opening for signature in September 2017. There is awareness that the initiative might wither away if the nuclear-armed states' and their allies' opposition remains unyielding. Diplomatic attention is shifting back to the NPT and its next Review Conference in 2020. The nuclear weapon States Parties and their allies can be expected to re-emphasize their support for the Treaty and its provisions. As yet, it is unclear whether such support will be forthcoming from states that have backed the Nuclear Weapon Ban Treaty, and whether some will tie attendance in 2020 to concessions on disarmament. Might the nuclear weapon states find the ability and willingness to compromise, for instance through the intensification of work on disarmament's verification? Questions abound.

[17] The Austrian or Humanitarian Pledge can be found at https://www.bmeia.gv.at/fileadmin/user_upload/Zentrale/Aussenpolitik/Abruestung/HINW14/HINW14vienna_Pledge_Document.pdf.

[18] For positive and skeptical views of the Nuclear Weapon Ban Treaty, see (respectively) Zia Mian, After the nuclear weapons ban treaty: A new disarmament politics, *Bulletin of the Atomic Scientists*, July 7, 2017, https://thebulletin.org/after-nuclear-weapons-ban-treaty-new-disarmament-politics10932; and George Perkovich, The Nuclear Weapon Ban Treaty: What would follow?, Carnegie Endowment for International Peace, Washington, DC, June 8, 2017, https://carnegieendowment.org/2017/05/31/nuclear-ban-treaty-what-would-follow-pub-70136.

In a statement issued jointly with France and the UK on July 7, 2017, the USA asserted that the new treaty "disregards the realities of the international security situation. Accession to the ban treaty is incompatible with the policy of nuclear deterrence." This is the nub of the matter. The Nuclear Weapon Ban Treaty has entered the frame at a time when those international realities are far from conducive to progress on nuclear disarmament, and when powerful states are unwilling to consider a security order stripped of nuclear deterrence.

6. THE LOSS OF ORDER AND ORDERING ABILITY

No substantial multilateral treaty affecting the development, production, deployment, or use of nuclear weapons has been negotiated since the mid-1990s. The last such treaty, the CTBT of 1996, has not entered into force, and negotiation of the FMCT has not begun. Nor has the conference on a WMD-free zone in the Middle East taken place. It was symptomatic that the 2015 NPT Review Conference ended in rancor without agreement on a final document. Stagnation has now given way to fears of a serious loss of order.

Underlying reasons may be encapsulated in Figure 4.3. During the Cold War, there was one dominant site of ordering of the military usage of nuclear technology—that involving the United States, Soviet Union, and their alliances. Although China, France, and the UK possessed nuclear forces, their

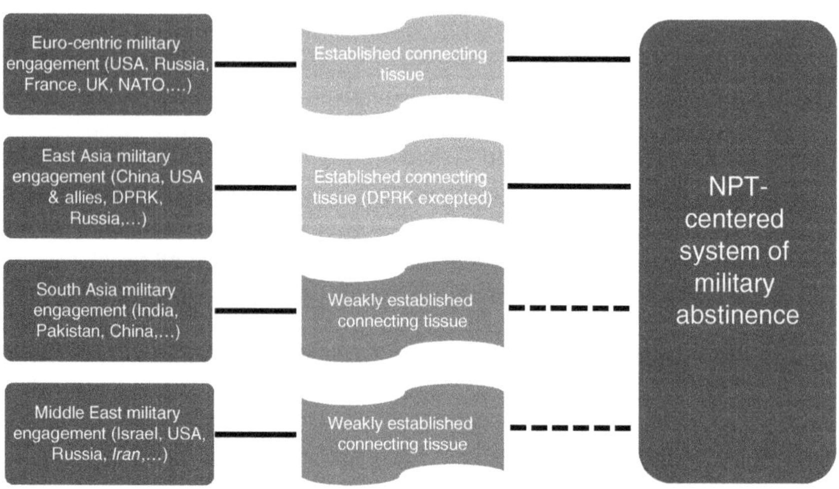

Figure 4.3 Contemporary sites of required nuclear ordering
Source: own design

policies were framed largely by the East–West conflict and the much greater scale and variety of Soviet and American capabilities.

For a decade after the Cold War ended, it seemed that the role of nuclear weapons in global affairs could still be addressed decisively through actions at this dominant site and through sustenance of a strong non-proliferation regime. This turned out to be incorrect. Today, nuclear deterrence is being practiced actively in four theaters. Within the long-standing Eurocentric theater, nuclear forces are being modernized, extended deterrence is being reactivated, and arms reduction processes have all but halted as US and NATO's relations with Russia have deteriorated. In South Asia, India and Pakistan are building extensive nuclear forces with little notion of sufficiency, whilst arms control and constructive dialog remain largely absent in their relations. In East Asia, North Korea's nuclear and missile capabilities, China's power and ambition, and Japanese and South Korean insecurity are giving nuclear deterrence fresh significance amidst many complications. Although the sudden rapprochement between Washington and Pyongyang in spring 2018 has given some hope, its outcome is very uncertain. In the Middle East, the Iran deal of 2014 has been upset by US withdrawal, Israel remains wedded to nuclear deterrence, and political relations are in turmoil across the region, to put it mildly.

Two consequences of this deterioration deserve highlighting. Firstly, the multiplication of "sites of military ordering" renders implausible an earlier notion of how nuclear arms reductions could be globalized and rendered irreversible. It foresaw successive arms reduction treaties in which the USA and Russia would be joined by China, France, and the UK as nuclear arsenals converged on a few hundred weapons apiece, combined with the CTBT, FMCT, and a constant strengthening of the non-proliferation regime and its regulatory instruments. Henceforth, the global institutionalization of restraint will have to be accompanied, and probably preceded, by the stabilization of relations and advance of arms control in each of the four theaters where deterrence is being practiced. Different political dynamics and various asymmetries in capabilities within and across them stand in its way.

Secondly, the narrative about the future that has long underpinned the non-proliferation regime's legitimacy is being confounded by political and military realities. That narrative regarded the possession of nuclear weapons as a temporary reality and trust: the reduction of nuclear forces to zero in the decades following the Cold War was an obligation and a desirable strategic move. A revised narrative today seems more realistic, in which nuclear weapons are again used to discourage wars in a dangerous period of power rivalry and transition, requiring postponement of the trend towards zero. Although pragmatism may draw governments towards this revised narrative, many would regard its acceptance as betrayal of the terms under which rights to possess nuclear weapons were renounced, and as a breach of the NPT's

Article VI and its subsequent elaborations.[19] The Nuclear Weapon Ban Treaty can be seen as their reaction to injustice, and as expression of refusal to accept prolongation of the world's dangerous experiment with nuclear weaponry.

In the medium- and long-term, however, the most significant challenge to nuclear order may come from various technological changes that are gathering pace. Singly and in combination, developments in cyber, robotics, remote sensing, drones, missile accuracy, and other fields are raising questions about, inter alia, the future reliability of the command, control, and communications upon which deterrence relies, the vulnerability of weapon systems (now including submarines) to disabling attack, and the relationship between nuclear weapons and rapidly advancing conventional military technologies. Although the cumulative effect of these changes is very uncertain, the rapid expansion of literature on them suggests that the consequences may be profound, affecting the politics and practice of nuclear deterrence in every region.[20]

If this is correct, the emphasis in nuclear ordering needs to shift, and rapidly, from a preoccupation with non-proliferation, counter-proliferation, and disarmament towards the reordering and re-regulation that is necessary within the politico-military domains in Figures 4.1 and 4.2. The technological changes may require re-conception of nuclear arms control (what should be controlled and how?) if belief in nuclear deterrence and its safety are to remain within government and the military.

Confidence that the many challenges facing the nuclear order will be addressed is being affected by the loss of authority of and trust in the USA, the order's principal shaper and guardian in history. Since the early 1980s, US policy has oscillated between the broad pro-institutionalism of the George H. W. Bush, Clinton, and Obama administrations and the anti-institutionalism of the Reagan, George W. Bush, and Trump administrations. Donald Trump's presidency has both exacerbated the divisions and confirmed foreign views of US unreliability and decline. Its reputation abroad has been seriously damaged by his ill-informed statements, threatening language, and erratic handling of foreign relations with, amongst others, Russia, China, and states in Europe (including allies) and the Middle East. Russia's encouragement and exploitation of America's troubles, probably against its long-term interest, have become an important part of the problem. It is disheartening that cooperation

[19] Among those elaborations, the 2010 NPT Review Conference's final document affirmed, by consensus, "the unequivocal undertaking of the nuclear weapon States to accomplish the total elimination of their arsenals."

[20] See, for instance, James M. Acton, *Silver Bullet: Asking the Right Questions about Conventional Prompt Global Strike*, New York: Carnegie Endowment for International Peace, 2013; Andrew Futter, *Cyber Threats and Nuclear Weapons: New Questions for Command and Control, Security and Strategy*, London: RUSI Occasional Papers, 2016; and Keir Lieber and Daryl G. Press, The New Era of Counterforce: Technological Change and the Future of Nuclear Deterrence, *International Security* 41:4 (Spring 2017), pp. 9–49.

between the USA and Russia, once so important to the nuclear order's development, is now in abeyance.

Come what may, the USA will remain a major player due to its alliances and huge capabilities, including possession of much the strongest and creative body of expertise on nuclear affairs outside government. There is today, however, lack of a central power or concert of powers able to bring coordination where there is fragmentation, uphold the rule-based order, and lead cooperative efforts to regulate where fresh regulation is needed. An important question is whether China will, as in the context of climate change, use its burgeoning power to become a norm entrepreneur and strong advocate of an institutionalist nuclear order, encouraged to an extent by the United States' vacation of leadership.[21] China's interest in an orderly international environment and vulnerability to arms racing and proliferation in Asia give it an incentive. Indeed, China's role is already pivotal due to its involvement in both East and South Asian sites of ordering (its relations with North Korea and Pakistan giving it potential leverage) and its strategic relations with Russia and the USA. Might Xi Jinping's assertion, at the UN in Geneva in January 2017, that "Nuclear weapons should be completely prohibited and destroyed over time to make the world free of nuclear weapons" signal China's willingness to take a lead in disarmament diplomacy, or is this wishful thinking?

7. CONCLUSION: ORDER AND THE RISK OF CATASTROPHE

The invention of nuclear weapons both aggravated and alleviated the problem of war in international relations. A nuclear war would bring death and devastation beyond any previous experience. However, that very prospect encouraged caution and war-avoidance. Fear of catastrophe gave life to the idea and practice of nuclear deterrence. The arrival of nuclear weapons also highlighted the problems of order and ordering at various levels in world politics. How could an effective, just, and legitimate order be constructed that would restrain the use and spread of nuclear weapons whilst leaving room for nuclear deterrence, accommodate inequalities among states, be rendered compatible with norms of state sovereignty, and reconcile the diffusion of nuclear technologies and materials for civil purposes with the need to avoid nuclear proliferation?

For a decade after the Cold War ended, there was hope that the problems of both nuclear war and nuclear order could find lasting solutions, realized

[21] On the evolution of China's nuclear policies, see Nicola Horsburgh, *China & Global Nuclear Order: From Estrangement to Active Engagement*, Oxford: Oxford University Press, 2015.

through the expansion of treaties and instruments that would bring permanent restraint. Encouraged by globalization, great power cooperation, and a raft of institutional achievements, talk of a "world free of nuclear weapons" no longer seemed fanciful. Twenty years on, nuclear weapons have still not been used, treaties remain in place and are being honored by and large, and there appears to be less appetite among states for acquiring nuclear weapons than in some earlier periods. In addition, the threat of nuclear terrorism has helped to strengthen non-proliferation norms, rules, and practices, the prospect of non-state actors acquiring nuclear technology being anathema.

Nevertheless, the hope that existed in the 1990s has largely evaporated. Nuclear arsenals are being modernized and expanded, treaty processes are frozen, threats of nuclear war have returned, and the nuclear order's central institution—the NPT—has suffered a loss of reputation. The Nuclear Weapon Ban Treaty is one response to regress. Although the order is not about to collapse, it is certainly troubled.

It is not easy to pin down why this has happened. The setbacks may be attributed partly to shifting power structures, strained relations among great powers, and the difficulty of fashioning global instruments when there is so much mistrust and so little consensus around. But regress may also be due to inattention. There has been a noticeable lowering of the priority that governments attach to nuclear diplomacy except in specific contexts, notably North Korea and East Asia at this time. Although still vital, the pursuit of nuclear order has lost its Cold War paramountcy. This is not surprising given the economic, environmental, regional, societal, and myriad other problems of order that are today pressing down on governments, as this book's other chapters attest. At a deeper level, however, the diminished attention given to nuclear ordering may stem from realization that the problem of war is itself changing, and that technological advances—especially in the cyber domain—are occurring that will influence strategic relations much more decisively than nuclear weapons in years ahead, albeit whilst adding to nuclear deterrence's dangers and complications.

Even if the role of nuclear weapons in world politics is diminishing—a contestable assertion—they retain their unique potency and capacity to do harm. It is on this note that the chapter should end. Two years before 9/11, Ashton Carter and William Perry wrote presciently that an incident of catastrophic terrorism "would divide our past and future into 'before' and 'after'. The effort and resources we have so far devoted to averting or containing this threat now, the period 'before', would seem woefully inadequate in hindsight."[22]

Hiroshima divided our common past and future into "before" and "after" seventy years ago. The project of nuclear ordering has been fundamentally

[22] Ashton B. Carter and William James Perry, *Preventive Defense: A New Security Strategy for America*, Washington, DC: Brookings Institution Press, 1999, p. 152. Carter and Perry have held the office of US Secretary of Defense in the Obama and Clinton administrations respectively.

about avoiding another "before" and "after." The depth of remorse that would be felt if nuclear weapons were used again—probably in greater numbers and involving thermonuclear weapons—can easily be imagined. Survivors' conclusion that the effort and resources devoted to avoiding this outcome had been "woefully inadequate" would be inescapable. It would seem an immense understatement.

Any assessment of the past and present performance of this partial order must therefore be colored by awareness of nuclear war's terrible aftermath. Even for supporters of nuclear deterrence, a positive verdict on the order's performance is contingent on the persistence of non-use. For its critics, such a verdict cannot be justified whilst the threat of use remains, however impressive the nuclear order's achievements may have been. But nuclear weapons are still being ascribed political and military value by powerful actors. They cannot be wished away. The task of nuclear ordering, at every site, must continue.

5

Aligning Security Needs for Order in Cyberspace

Myriam Dunn Cavelty

This chapter focuses on issues of order in the field of cyber-security. The literature defines cyber-security as the security one enjoys in and from cyber-space.[1] In a more narrow sense, cyber-security can also signify a set of technologies, policies, processes, and practices designed and implemented to protect networks, computers, programs, and data from attack, damage, or unauthorized access.[2] In security policy, cyberspace has a double role: it serves both as an attack vector through which objects and services of value for the state and society can be threatened (in peacetime and during conflict) and as a sphere of operations in which strategies and countermeasures against security threats are implemented and conducted. This way, cyber-security is not just about the security *of* cyberspace, but is also security created *through* cyberspace.[3]

A set of diverse threat forms have shaped the policy issue, ranging from hacktivism, to cyber-crime, cyber-espionage and cyber-war. After the hacking incidents during the US elections in 2016, the issue of strategic manipulation—also called information warfare—has recently been added to the threat spectrum.[4] These different threat forms are represented and treated in distinct ways in the political process since multiple actors employ differing political, private,

[1] For example, P. Cornish, R. Hughes, and D. Livingstone, *Cyberspace and the National Security of the United Kingdom: Threats and Responses*, A Chatham House Report, 2009, https://www.chathamhouse.org/sites/files/chathamhouse/public/Research/International%20Security/r0309cyberspace.pdf.

[2] T. Balzacq and M. Dunn Cavelty, A Theory of Actor-Network for Cyber-Security, *European Journal of International Security* 1:2 (2016), pp. 176–98.

[3] D. Betz and T. Stevens, *Cyberspace and the State: Toward a Strategy for Cyber-Power*, London: IISS, 2011.

[4] N. Inkster, Information Warfare and the US Presidential Election, *Survival* 58 (2016), pp. 23–32.

societal, and corporate notions of security.[5] Specifying whose security and what security is at stake and who should responsible for it thus becomes an intricate part of designing cyber-security policies—and lies at the very heart of the questions of order in cyberspace.

Given that cyberspace has been mainly shaped by the practices of companies and consumers over many years, a diverse set of non-state actors, including civil liberty organizations, tech companies, and technology aficionados see cyberspace as something in which states should have no (or at least very little) shaping power. More recently, however, a heightened sense of unease about the escalatory potential of cyber-conflict, fueled by the certainty that more and more states are using cyberspace for strategic ends, has led state actors to attempt to (re-)establish their authority in the virtual realm in the name of more security. This causes considerable resistance to the actions of governments, with high costs for all sides, signifying an ongoing struggle over the right to define the kind of order that is legitimate, efficient, and desirable.

To describe the characteristics and issues of establishing order in cyberspace via cyber-security, this chapter first characterizes the arrangements that evolved organically throughout the 1990s in many Western states (evolution of "1st order") (section 1). Cyber-security policy-responses were characterized mainly by a focus on the protection of critical infrastructures by technical means and a limited role of the state in general. Section 2 examines recent developments in cyber-aggression and the attempts by states to stabilize interaction in cyberspace due to these developments after 2010: in parallel to heightened threat perceptions, states feel that they need to invest in more order (evolution of "2nd order"). The chapter then describes intended and unintended effects of these new ordering efforts, pointing to the main sources of tension. Though those arrangements may create more predictability in state interaction, the changes are raising questions of legitimacy as national security concerns take precedence over other considerations. In the conclusion (section 3), the chapter looks at the policy implications of this and what it might mean for the future of order in cyberspace.

1. EVOLUTION OF NATIONAL CYBER-SECURITY ARRANGEMENTS (1990–2010)

We can trace the beginnings of cyber-security policy—and therefore attempts to create international order—back to the 1980s. Throughout the 1990s,

[5] T. Stevens and D. J. Betz, Analogical Reasoning and Cyber Security, *Security Dialogue* 44:2 (2013), pp. 147–64; M. Dunn Cavelty, *Cyber-Security and Threat Politics: US Efforts to Secure the Information Age*, London: Routledge, 2008.

a dispersed, not very efficient, but rather legitimate "arrangement" for cyber-security emerged, yet mainly organized on the national and not the international level.

1.1. Four Cyber-Security Discourses...

When focusing on the emergence of these policy arrangements, four different, but closely interrelated, sometimes overlapping, and often reinforcing "discourses"—understood here as distinct ways of imagining and talking about cyber-security issues in the form of threats and countermeasures—become apparent. The first discourse focuses on technical aspects of cyber-security, such as malware (viruses, worms, etc.) and system intrusions. The second is concerned with the phenomena of cyber-crime, the third with cyber-espionage. The fourth focuses on matters of cyber-terrorism and cyber-war, or more generally on cyber-incidents with very grave consequences. Each of them is shaped and dominated by specific actors/stakeholders and revolves around particular "referent objects"[6] and specific threats, as summarized in Table 5.1. Each viewpoint can be treated as an isolated sub-order; however, they all emerged at similar times, and threats in one influenced threat perceptions in the others. We therefore need to look at the interplay between them to understand what cyber-security order entails as a whole.

Table 5.1. Four alternative viewpoints on cyber-security

	Malware	Cyber-Crime	Cyber-Espionage	Cyber-war
Main actors	- Computer experts - Anti-virus industry	- Law enforcement - Police	- Intelligence community	- National security experts - Military - Civil defense/Homeland security
Main referent object	- Computers (machines) - Networked computers	- Individuals - Private sector (business) computers	- Classified information (government networks)	- Networked armed forces (military networks) - Critical (information) infrastructures
Main threat	- Hackers (all kinds) - Malware - Network disruptions	- Cyber criminals - Cyber mercenaries - APTs	- States (foreign intelligence) - Cyber mercenaries - APTs	- Catastrophic attacks on critical infrastructures - Cyber terrorists - States (cyber commands)

Source: compiled by the author

[6] That which is seen in need of protection: see B. Buzan, O. Wæver, and J. de Wilde, *Security: A New Framework for Analysis*, Boulder: Lynne Rienner, 1998, p. 36.

1.1.1. Malware

The technical discourse focuses on computer and networks disruptions caused by malware. At the very beginning of the cyber-threat story, we find the "Morris Worm" in 1988: the first major network incident that made the ARPANET—the precursor of today's Internet—unavailable. The devastating technical effect prompted the people in charge of the network to set up a center to coordinate communication among computer experts during computer emergencies and to help prevent future incidents: a Computer Emergency Response Team (CERT).[7] This center served as a role model for similar centers around the world. Around the same time, the anti-virus industry with its techniques and programs for virus recognition emerged, quickly gathering crucial expertise and power in the field.

The Morris Worm (and other cyber-incidents after it) also had a substantial psychological and subsequent political impact, by making policymakers aware just how insecure and unreliable the Internet was. While it had been acceptable in the 1960s that pioneering computer professionals were hacking and investigating computer systems, the situation had changed by the 1980s. Society had become dependent on computing in general for business practices and other basic functions. Tampering with computers suddenly meant potentially endangering people's careers and property; and some even said their lives.[8] Ever since, malware as "visible" proof of the pervasive insecurity of the information infrastructure has remained in the limelight of the cyber-security discourse.

1.1.2. Cyber-crime

The cyber-crime discourse and the technical discourse are very closely related. The development of legal tools to prosecute unauthorized entry into computer systems coincided with the first serious network incidents.[9] Tech-savvy individuals (often juveniles) with the goal of mischief or personal enrichment shaped the early history of cyber-crime. Today, professionals dominate the field. The Internet is a near ideal playground for organized crime for activities such as theft or fraud, forgery, extortion, and money laundering. Actors in the "cyber-crime black market" are highly organized regarding strategic and operational vision, logistics, and deployment. Like many real companies,

[7] W. L. Scherlis, S. L. Squires, and R. D. Pethis, Computer Emergency Response, in P. Denning (ed.), *Computers Under Attack: Intruders, Worms, and Viruses*, Reading: Addison-Wesley, pp. 495–504.

[8] E. H. Spafford, The Internet Worm: Crisis and Aftermath, *Communications of the ACM* 32:6 (1989), pp. 678–87.

[9] Cf. P. Mungo and B. Clough, *Approaching Zero: The Extraordinary Underworld of Hackers, Phreakers, Virus Writers, and Keyboard Criminals*, New York: Random House, 1993, pp. 52–70 and *passim*.

they operate across the globe.[10] Furthermore, experts suspect that state actors increasingly satisfy their need for cyber-capabilities in part by buying knowledge and skills on the black (or grey) market. Therefore, "cyber mercenaries" have emerged as a new threat-category.

1.1.3. *Cyber-espionage*

Network intrusions of unknown origin were important drivers in the cyber-threat story and its link to national security from the beginning.[11] Prominent hacking incidents in the 1990s led to a feeling in policy circles that there was a need for action. In quite a few of them, teenagers were the main culprits, which led to the conviction that if teenagers were able to penetrate computer networks that easily, better organized entities such as states would be far more equipped to do so. Other events that were hard or even impossible to attribute only supported the view that foreign nationals could acquire sensitive information relatively easily through hacking.

As time progressed, the West singled out China as the main culprit for high-level penetrations of government and business computer systems in Europe, North America, and Asia. Chinese authorities have stated repeatedly that they consider cyberspace a strategic domain and that they hope that mastering it will equalize the existing military imbalance between China and the USA more quickly.[12] However, the National Security Agency (NSA) revelations in 2013 by Edward Snowden have made clear how massive the data collection by the United States through cyberspace for strategic information gathering is and have given the cyber-espionage discourse a new twist. The threat perception has changed from a single-culprit discourse (China) to one in which all big intelligence organizations such as the American NSA or the UK-based Government Communications Headquarters (GCHQ) "spy" on friendly governments and their societies. Thus, the trade-off between privacy and security has become a new focal point in this debate in the West.

1.1.4. *Cyber-war*

Military strategists started to realize as early as the 1960s that networked computers would have a considerable impact on warfare.[13] Doctrine papers that emerged in the 1990s started to treat cyberspace as a "domain of warfare"

[10] European Police Office, Exploring Tomorrow's Organised Crime, March 2015, https://www.europol.europa.eu/content/massive-changes-criminal-landscape.

[11] Dunn Cavelty, *Cyber-Security and Threat Politics*, pp. 55, 80–4.

[12] D. C. Gompert and M. Libicki, Cyber Warfare and Sino-American Crisis Instability, *Survival* 56 (2014), pp. 7–22.

[13] B. D. Berkowitz, *The New Face of War: How War will be Fought in the 21st Century*, New York: Free Press, 2003, p. 57.

in theory and practice[14] and the Pentagon officially added it as the so-called "fifth" domain in 2011, next to land, sea, air, and space. From early on, this particular debate was characterized by a "double-edged sword" perspective: strategists saw great opportunities for winning wars through technology-aided "information dominance," but at the same time, there was an awareness of security-relevant vulnerabilities due to growing dependencies of the military on computers.[15] This notion was expanded from military networks to the whole society in the second half of the 1990s through a link to "critical infrastructures" as the backbone of modern societies.[16] The focus was on information as a weapon, method, or target to achieve strategic goals—in peace and in wartime.

1.2. . . . and the Respective Countermeasures

By the end of the 1990s, specific types of countermeasures at the national and the international level developed in respect of the four discourses (Table 5.2).

Table 5.2. Countermeasures at the end of the 1990s

	Malware	Cyber-crime	Cyber-espionage	Cyber-war
National Level	- Information Assurance Concepts (Risk Management) - CERTs	- Computer law	- Information Assurance Concepts (Risk Management) - Intrusion detection	- Critical (information) infrastructure protection - Resilience - Cyber defense (for military networks) - Cyber deterrence
International Level	- International CERTs - Information security standards	- Harmonization of law (i.e., Budapest Convention) - Mutual judicial assistance procedures	- Bilateral agreements - Diplomatic interventions	- Bilateral agreements - Diplomatic interventions - International regimes and norms - Arms control

Source: compiled by the author

[14] J. Arquilla and D. F. Ronfeldt (eds.), *In Athena's Camp: Preparing for Conflict in the Information Age*, Santa Monica, CA: RAND Corporation, 1997.

[15] G. Rattray, *Strategic Warfare in Cyberspace*, Cambridge, MA: MIT Press, 2001, pp. 10–14.

[16] M. Dunn Cavelty and K. S. Kristensen, Introduction: Securing the Homeland: Critical Infrastructure, Risk, and (In)Security?, in Dunn Cavelty and Kristensen (eds.), *The Politics of Securing the Homeland: Critical Infrastructure, Risk and Securitization*, New York: Routledge, 2008, pp. 1–14.

With relatively little variation across polities, the protection policies that emerged consisted of a three-pronged approach: A strong law enforcement pillar for countering cyber-crime, private–public partnerships for critical infrastructure protection, and private and public self-help for the rest of the networked infrastructure.[17] Importantly, it became a common (pragmatic) practice, one might even say *norm*, that everybody was responsible for "their own" assets as far as possible: governments protect government networks, militaries only military ones, companies protect theirs, and individual citizens are in charge of their own computer security. A measure proposed in almost all strategies at the time is better coordination and a more integrated approach on the domestic front, which would offer clear allocations of responsibilities and thus improve the efficiency of cyber-security measures.[18]

However, there are some assets in the hands of the private sector considered so crucial to the functioning of society that governments take additional measures to ensure an adequate level of protection. These efforts are subsumed under the label of critical (information) infrastructure protection. At the core of these practices, we find the preventive protection of critical infrastructures by technical means, namely information assurance practices, supplemented by the concept of resilience. Resilience accepts that disruptions are inevitable. The concept is commonly defined as the ability of a system to recover from a shock, returning either to its original state or to a new, adjusted state. Therefore, the concept promises an additional safety net also against large-scale, major, and unexpected events.[19]

Internationally, cooperation between different groups like technical experts, organized in CERTs, organically emerged as an important aspect of cyber-security practices, often without explicit state involvement. However, in the time period examined here (1990–2010), international efforts to curb cyber-espionage and cyber-war remained lackluster. Though there was a lot of talk about the potential risk of cyber-war in the form of "multi-dimensional cyber disaster scenarios,"[20] menacing scenarios of major disruptive occurrences in the cyber-domain triggered by either terrorists or state actors remained just

[17] M. Dunn Cavelty and M. Suter, Public–Private Partnerships are no Silver Bullet: An Expanded Governance Model for Critical Infrastructure Protection, *International Journal of Critical Infrastructure Protection* 2:4 (2009), pp. 179–87.

[18] M. Dunn Cavelty and M. Suter, The Art of CIIP Strategy: Taking Stock of Content and Processes, in J. Lopez, R. Setola, and S. D. Wolthusen (eds.), *Critical Infrastructure Protection: Information Infrastructure Models, Analysis, and Defense*, Berlin: Springer, 2012, pp. 15–38.

[19] L. J. Perelman, Shifting Security Paradigms: Toward Resilience, in J. A. McCarthy (ed.), *Critical Thinking: Moving from Infrastructure Protection to Infrastructure Resilience*, CIP Program Discussion Paper Series, Washington, DC: George Mason University, 2007, pp. 23–48; M. Dunn Cavelty, M. Kaufmann, and K. S. Kristensen, Resilience and (In)security: Practices, Subjects, Temporalities, *Security Dialogue* 46:1 (2015), pp. 3–14.

[20] L. Hansen and H. Nissenbaum, Digital Disaster, Cyber Security, and the Copenhagen School, *International Studies Quarterly* 53 (2009), pp. 1155–75 (1164).

and only that—scenarios. Even though we find the occasional attempt to tackle cyber-security issues at the level of the United Nations,[21] there was no great urgency to change the way cyber-security was dealt with at the national level.

1.3. Characteristics and Performance of Order: Distributed Security and the Risk Rationale

It is possible to see elements of an "order" in this web of highly diverse measures, if we are willing to understand the concept in a broad sense, as we do in this volume. It is not an international order: most solutions to counter this security issue are national measures, geared towards more security inside a territory by involving private sector actors and, to a lesser degree, citizens of a state. While there are some attempts like the Budapest Convention on Cybercrime to tackle "threat actors" transnationally, the majority of strategies attempt to reduce vulnerabilities in computer networks to lower the risks.

It is technically impossible and economically unfeasible to design and protect critical infrastructure to withstand all disruptions, intrusions, or attacks. Therefore, the traditional form of (national) security that is defined as "the absence of threats to acquired values and subjectively, the absence of fear that such values will be attacked"[22] has little meaning in the cyber-domain. In cyber-matters, security is approached through the rationale of risk management. In risk management processes, decisions are taken as to which insecurities (risks) to reduce to which degree and with what means, thereby always acknowledging that a certain level of risk remains. In this process, responsibility for creating security rests to a large degree on the shoulders of non-governmental actors, who are the only ones with the necessary access to and knowledge of computer systems and critical infrastructures to do the risk analysis, and the ones then called upon to spend money on security.

As a result, all Western states established an order based on "distributed security": The actor mainly in charge of security is not the state, but the private sector, which is urged to collaborate with national agencies on a voluntary basis. The role of the state is small, with a clear lack of coercive measures in the whole set-up (apart from an element of punishment in national law, related to crime). The overall approach is characterized by technical risk management strategies, standardization of methods and concepts, harmonization of law,

[21] C. Kavanagh, *The United Nations, Cyberspace and International Peace and Security: Responding to Complexity in the 21st Century*, UNIDIR Resources, 2017, http://www.unidir.org/publications/report-of-the-international-security-cyber-issues-workshop-series.

[22] A. Wolfers, National Security as an Ambiguous Symbol, *Political Science Quarterly* 67:4 (1952), pp. 481–502.

and attempts to achieve better coordination between different stakeholders, nationally and internationally. It is almost purely cooperative, with no instruments to enforce rules, apart from a different set of regulations that exist in different infrastructure sectors mainly to ensure safety.[23]

Evaluating the performance of such an order is not straightforward: some elements work to produce more security, others do not. The performance also differs over time and from country to country. However, if to produce more security overall is taken to be the optimal output of these governance arrangements, then in their totality they did not deliver what they should have: a plethora of reports show an upsurge in criminally motivated attacks and related costs for companies over the years.[24] The overall effectiveness of these arrangements is thus lacking. Arguably, however, due to the diversity of viewpoints that have shaped it—the non-coercive form of collaboration, and the non-hierarchical relationship between different partners/stakeholders—this type of arrangement enjoyed a high degree of legitimacy at the time.

2. EVOLUTION OF ORDER: A HEIGHTENED THREAT (2010–)

The set of practices described in section 1 were stable for more than a decade. More recently, however, the threat perception has changed—and with it the pressure for a new type of order that produces more security internationally. The decisive event is the discovery of Stuxnet, the computer worm that damaged Iranian nuclear centrifuges in 2010, commonly attributed to the United States government (developed in collaboration with Israel). This malware, which is seen by some observers as a "digital first strike," changed the overall tone and intensity of the debate.[25] With it came a shift of attention to so-called advanced persistent threats (APTs)—sophisticated malware that is written for a specific purpose or target (section 2.1). In conjunction, the certainty that states are using cyberspace for strategic purposes has led to activities aimed at regulating the behavior of state actors (section 2.2). Because

[23] N. Kshetri, *The Quest to Cyber Superiority: Cybersecurity Regulations, Frameworks, and Strategies of Major Economies*, Cham, Switzerland: Springer International Publishing, 2016, pp. 25–52.

[24] M. Dunn Cavelty and R. Van der Vlugt, A Tale of Two Cities: Or How the Wrong Metaphors Mess With Our Security, *Georgetown Journal for International Affairs, International Engagements on Cyber V* (2015), pp. 21–9.

[25] J. Farwell and R. Rohozinski, Stuxnet and the Future of Cyber-War, *Survival, Global Politics and Strategy* 53:1 (2011), pp. 23–40; M. Dunn Cavelty, Militarizing Cyberspace: Why Less May Be Better, in C. Czosseck, R. Ottis, and K. Ziolkowski (eds.), *Proceedings of the 4th International Conference on Cyber Conflict*, Talinn: NATO, 2012, pp. 141–53.

it is happening mainly under the heading of national security, this is creating a clash with the logic of the "old" order, which was based on cooperation with non-state actors. Even though we are still in a transformation process now, legitimacy issues are already undermining the new ordering attempts (section 2.3).

2.1. The Professionalization of Cyber-Aggression

APTs are stealthy and continuous cyber-operations targeting a specific entity's information or functionality. They are "advanced" because the malware that is used for these operations is sophisticated. They are "persistent" because there is constant monitoring of the activity of the malware, and constant extraction of data. Moreover, they are "threats," in line with information security vocabulary, since they are orchestrated by a human actor.

APTs stand for the increasing professionalization of attackers. This, in turn, is an indication for (a) a criminal market that has reached a certain maturity and (b) the efforts of state actors to build up cyber-capabilities in order to use cyberspace to achieve strategic ends. There is an assumed connection between (a) and (b), whereby state actors satisfy their need for cyber-capabilities in part by buying knowledge and skills on the black (or grey) market. This is a factor furthering professionalization, because of the heightened demand for higher levels of skill.[26]

Many experts call APTs cyber-*weapons* and regard the build-up of capabilities by state actors as part of an arms race in cyberspace. The uncertainty about the intentions of other states, and the practical inability to know whether such capabilities are offensive or defensive, leads to heightened feelings of insecurity. The reaction is that more and more states are opening up "cyber-commands," which are military units for cyber-war activities. Though consolidated numbers are unavailable, the amount of money spent on defense-related aspects of cyber-security is rising. The new cyber military–industrial complex that has emerged is estimated to make returns between US$80 billion and US$150 billion per year, with big defense companies like Boeing and Northrop Grumman repositioning themselves to service the cyber-security market.[27] Of course, having "weapons" does not automatically translate into using them, but cyberspace is different from other operating environments as it grants a high level of obscurity (or anonymity), which, as

[26] Michael N. Schmitt, Below the Threshold Cyber Operations: The Countermeasures Response Option and International Law, *Virginia Journal of International Law* 3 (2014), pp. 697–732.

[27] R. Deibert and R. Rohozinski, The new cyber military-industrial complex, *The Globe and Mail*, March 28, 2011, http://www.theglobeandmail.com/news/opinions/opinion/the-new-cyber-military-industrial-complex/article1957159/.

some observers like to point out, may influence cost–benefit analyses in favor of launching cyber-attacks since there is little fear of punishment.[28] However, recent analyses have shown that there is a high level of restraint in the use of cyber-tools in political conflict,[29] paired with the questionable coercive power of cyber-tools.[30] Nonetheless, politically, the pressure to build up cyber-capabilities is continuing, not least since globally, the security situation has become increasingly tense and cyber-tools appear to be a necessary addition to the conflict toolbox alongside more conventional capabilities.

2.2. An Increase in State Power

Because of the growing unease, many states are showing willingness to place security needs above other needs when tackling cyber-issues (felt, for example, in more traditional "Internet governance" settings, where issues of security are demanding and gaining more attention). Feelings of insecurity have also led to higher incentives for states to control the risk of escalation and conflict. As a result, the number of ministerial meetings and conferences has increased, and norms aiming to curb aggression in and through cyberspace are emerging. In particular, there are clear signs that powerful states like the USA are working to build a specific deterrence regime for cyberspace. The considerable involvement of US officials in many of the international cyber-security governance processes is linked to its strategic interest in shaping international norms for behavior in cyberspace,[31] which, together with more real-world evidence, will create more certainty about the costs (and benefits) of a cyber-attack.[32]

In the same vein, the applicability of international law to the cyber-domain has also been discussed and partially settled. In 2013, a consensus emerged among several states, and at the UN, EU, and NATO, that International Humanitarian Law fully applies in cyber-operations—an interesting example of interference between orders. In parallel, several intergovernmental bodies confirmed the applicability of state sovereignty and the international norms and principles that flow from sovereignty. The most important questions with regard to *jus ad bellum*, i.e., when a cyber-attack would be considered an

[28] J. B. Sheldon, Deciphering Cyberpower: Strategic Purpose in Peace and War, *Strategic Studies Quarterly* 5:2 (Summer 2011), pp. 95–112.

[29] B. Valeriano and R. C. Maness, The Dynamics of Cyber Conflict between Rival Antagonists, 2001–11, *Journal of Peace Research* 51:3 (2014), pp. 347–60.

[30] E. D. Borghard and S. W. Lonergan, The Logic of Coercion in Cyberspace, *Security Studies* 26:3 (2017), pp. 452–81.

[31] T. Stevens, A Cyberwar of Ideas? Deterrence and Norms in Cyberspace, *Contemporary Security Policy* 33:1 (2012), pp. 148–70.

[32] M. Dunn Cavelty, The Normalization of Cyber-International Relations, in O. Thränert and M. Zapfe (eds.), *Strategic Trends 2015: Key Developments in Global Affairs*, Zurich: Center for Security Studies, 2015, pp. 81–98.

armed attack by another state and how to react in that case, are discussed in the *Tallinn Manual on the International Law Applicable to Cyber Warfare*.[33]

Importantly, these developments do not happen at the cost of old solutions—they are extensions or add-ons to the more nationally oriented arrangements. However, more state power permeates old arrangements as well and could change or at least marginalize them. The beautiful utopia of cyber-libertarians like Barlow,[34] who saw cyberspace as a serious challenge to traditional state power, was never a reality. However, a changing threat landscape has accelerated tendencies for a "feudal power structure" that consolidates power in the hands of the few.[35] What has changed is that states are far more ready to assert their power positions,[36] mostly in the name of security, both nationally and internationally. This will lead to more regulation in the future, a fact which is already visible in the European Union.[37]

Furthermore, assertion of state power is linked to the possibility (and desirability) of creating borders in cyberspace[38] because of the link to the concept of sovereignty. Prominent concepts like "Cyber-Westphalia" tap into the founding myths of a stable political world order based on state power and invoke images of a delimited and thus defendable and securable place, newly reordered by the state as the real guarantor of security.[39] In this view, the process of re-establishing state control in cyberspace is both inevitable and desirable, because only that will allow the creation of a stable international order.

Of course, there is a certain appeal to a vision in which the unruly, anarchical, and dangerous side of cyberspace is kept "outside," and relative security can be established within and among states. However, this image simplifies the complex reality. Not only is it very difficult to divide cyberspace into "inside" and "outside," but state control also often means control over information flows, raising important issues of human rights, including privacy. Indeed, an increasing number of governments are already controlling what their citizens can and cannot do on the Internet. Authoritarian governments are embracing a growing "cyber-sovereignty" movement to consolidate

[33] M. N. Schmitt (ed.), *Tallinn Manual on the International Law Applicable to Cyber Warfare*, Cambridge: Cambridge University Press, 2013, http://www.ccdcoe.org/249.html.

[34] J. P. Barlow, A Declaration of the Independence of Cyberspace, 1996, http://homes.eff.org/~barlow/Declaration-Final.html [accessed December 7, 2017].

[35] B. Schneier, When It Comes to Security, We're Back to Feudalism, *Wired*, 2012, http://www.wired.com/opinion/2012/11/feudal-security/.

[36] B. Schneier, The Battle for Power on the Internet, *The Atlantic*, 2013, http://www.theatlantic.com/technology/archive/2013/10/the-battle-for-power-on-the-internet/280824.

[37] G. Christou, *Cybersecurity in the European Union: Resilience and Adaptability in Governance Policy*, London: Palgrave Macmillan, 2016, p. 102.

[38] M. Mueller, A. Schmidt, and B. Kuerbis, Internet Security and Networked Governance in International Relations, *International Studies Review* 15:19 (2013), pp. 86–104.

[39] C. Demchak and P. Dombrowski, Rise of a Cybered Westphalian Age, *Strategic Studies Quarterly* 5:1 (Spring 2011), pp. 32–61.

their hold on power. Overall, government cyber-security practices such as online censorship, curtailing of encryption, surveillance, deep packet inspection, and government hacking have become prevalent across regions.[40] For one prominent observer, these developments are of mounting concern since "in liberal democratic countries we are lowering the standards around basic rights to privacy just as the centre of cyberspace gravity is shifting to less democratic parts of the world."[41] Overall, while the jury is out on the issue of effectiveness of potentially new "ordering" mechanisms, we can already see that the additional role that states aspire to play in cyber-security has led to serious questions of legitimacy.

2.3. The New Cyber-Order: Will it Perform?

In the international realm, cyber-governance at this point in time is best defined as "loosely coupled norms and institutions that rank somewhere between an integrated institution that imposes regulation through hierarchical rules, and highly fragmented practices and institutions with no identifiable core and non-existent linkages."[42] Overall, it is too early to make any conclusive statements about the shape of a new cyber-security arrangement that is in the making. An evaluation of this new "order" is also not possible because it is presently unclear what it will ultimately look like.

What seems apparent though is this: On the one hand, the focus on regulating the behavior of (other) states promises to have positive effects for cyber-security mainly by reducing the risk of escalation. At the same time, however, this recent focus on state-to-state relations and on state intervention is partially contested. Because cyberspace is a realm used by different actors for highly diverse activities, the security-seeking actions by states often directly clash with other uses and conceptions of cyberspace, both social and economic. In particular, there are problems associated with the empowerment of intelligence and military establishments in matters of cyber-security. The military accumulation of cyber-capabilities also in Western states is outpacing civilian comprehension and control. Similar problems hold true for intelligence agencies: While they may have the budget and technological resources that are best suited to respond to cyber-threats, their role also elicits great public unease. Public disquiet over government surveillance and cyber-capabilities could

[40] AccessNow, A Human Rights Response to Government Hacking, 2016, https://www.accessnow.org/governmenthackingdoc/.

[41] R. J. Deibert, *Black Code: Inside the Battle for Cyberspace*, Toronto: McClelland & Stewart, 2013, p. 131.

[42] J. Nye, *The Regime Complex for Managing Global Cyber Activities*, Global Commission on Internet Governance Paper Series No. 1, 2014, p. 7, https://www.cigionline.org/sites/default/files/gcig_paper_no1.pdf.

prove to be difficult for cyber-security strategies (and by extension order) in the future.

Trust in the benign intent of states about civil liberties, most notably privacy, has taken a serious hit through Edward Snowden's NSA revelations. Currently, more and more user or system specific data is up for grabs—for anybody who is interested in it, ranging from businesses, to criminals, and the intelligence services. From a data protection perspective, these developments are daunting, particularly because the so-called commercialization of data is not done against the wishes of the user, but rather because it seems to make our lives so much more efficient and convenient. Here, the clash of different types of security becomes directly visible: From a human and political rights perspective, privacy and anonymity are not a threat to security; they are a crucial part of it. From a national security perspective, anonymity is the key problem for punitive action.

This also highlights an interesting shift in the discussion on cyber-security overall, with potential effects on international order. Whereas different types of cyber-attacks in the form of cyber-crime, -espionage, -terrorism, or -war were central in the 1990s, cyber-surveillance has been added more recently paradoxically as both a key solution for more security and a core concern for society. This takes cyber-security issues beyond what they were and links them to issues such as Islamic terrorism, opening up many possibilities for future interference between orders. Whereas the first phase described here was about the security *of* cyberspace, creating security *through* cyberspace has become more important in recent years.

This shift has also given the use of cyber-means to attack "enemies" more legitimacy in national security circles. For example, the NSA has bought and exploited so-called zero-day vulnerabilities in current operating systems and hardware to inject malware into numerous strategically opportune points of the Internet infrastructure,[43] ostensibly for surveillance purposes, but also (potentially) for disruptive operations. However, backdoors and unpatched vulnerabilities reduce the security of the entire system—for everyone. Nor is there any guarantee that an intelligence actor who has acquired knowledge about an exploitable vulnerability has full control over it and/or can keep it secret: they can be identified and exploited by criminal hackers or even "terrorists" as well. The paradox that emerges here is that security through cyberspace creates insecurity of cyberspace.

If the emerging order is measured against its ability to create more security, this development is not boding well for effectiveness. The quest for more national security with cyber-means will always mean less cyber-security,

[43] G. Greenwald and E. MacAskill, Obama orders US to draw up overseas target list for cyber-attacks, *The Guardian*, June 7, 2013, http://www.theguardian.com/world/2013/jun/07/obama-china-targets-cyber-overseas.

which will always mean less national security because of vulnerabilities in critical infrastructures. Such an arrangement will be neither efficient, nor legitimate. The new trends reveal that in the end, it will not be possible to have both a strategically exploitable cyberspace full of vulnerabilities and a secure and resilient cyberspace.

3. CONCLUSION

States are currently expanding their power in cyberspace in an attempt to gain more security. The trend is to invest in the old ways of stabilizing international relations, focusing mainly on transparency measures and attempts to create deterrence effects through norm-building, ultimately coveting more order in cyberspace. This is currently giving rise to hopes for more stability as the risk of escalation is reduced. Overall, indeed, it is clear that a secure, safe, and open cyberspace is not possible without the involvement and commitments of state actors. At the same time, however, states themselves remain the biggest threats to stability. State practices linked to cyber-exploitation are emerging as a major, if not the biggest part of the problem, constantly creating more insecurity and in fact also hindering the removal of known insecurities. The main issue is that normalization and stabilization efforts are geared towards a form of high-impact cyber-aggression that could indeed be devastating but that also has a low probability of occurrence. However, the biggest current issue, besides cyber-crime, is cyber-exploitation, which is done with the help of APTs: it is the world of intelligence communities, whose actions in home states are regulated by national law, but who are expected to act unfettered and without restraint in the international realm.

Because of many highly divergent interests, it is questionable whether we will ever have one "proper" and stable cyber-security order. Cyberspace is shaped and used by many different actors, and for more than two decades non-state actors have been in the driver's seat. The security arrangements that emerged in the 1990s were sensitive to this, with a high degree of legitimacy. The more recent attempts to stabilize the risk of cyber-conflict escalation are not sensitive to it, at least not in practice. Even though the importance of non-state actors in (co-)defining security standards is stressed repeatedly in policy documents, there is little substantial space for them in traditional diplomatic interactions. Here, a problem with the concept of "order" emerges: even though the world of states acknowledges the importance of non-state actors in any system or order, they cannot imagine an order in which they themselves might not play the defining role, which is directly related to how "order" is traditionally imagined. Yet, if we want cyberspace to be an inclusive place with value for many people and many activities, such new imaginations are crucial.

How, then, can this problem be overcome? Because cyberspace is shaped and used by many non-state actors, solutions cannot be found solely in the cooperation between states. Non-state actors need a voice, and not only a perfunctory one. While it seems indubitable that (democratic) states will have to be central pillars of an international security order because of their political authority, any future legitimate, effective, and efficient order will have to build on the strength of what was called "1st order" and extend this model into the international realm. What this leads to is that for security issues, a type of multi-stakeholder approach like the one practiced in Internet Governance for many years is needed as well. The open and currently unstudied question is at what level of the policy process multi-stakeholder input is necessary, desirable, and feasible and how such a process should be organized for maximum legitimacy. Most importantly, however, such a policy approach must adopt an anti-vulnerability approach. The choice between a strategically exploitable cyberspace full of vulnerabilities and a secure and resilient cyberspace is an easy one: only the second will ensure prosperity and security.

Part II

Regional Orders

6

The European Peace and Security Order at Risk

Wolfgang Richter

1. THE EUROPEAN SECURITY ORDER IN THE GLOBAL CONTEXT

What constitutes "Europe" in the context of political geography? Traditionally, Europe has been described geographically as the area between the Atlantic and the Urals. Political realities lead to a different conclusion: The security of Europe was shaped historically by the strength or weakness of Germany as its central power, the alliance politics of the United Kingdom and France with or against each other, and their relations to Russia. Since the end of World War II, the European security order has been inseparably linked with the regional presence and the geo-political rivalry of the "wing powers" United States and Russia (respectively the Soviet Union up to 1991).

The broadest and most persuasive political definition of the European security order coincides with the participation in the Organization for Security and Cooperation in Europe (OSCE) "between Vancouver and Vladivostok," which includes the two North American NATO states, Central Asia, and the Russian Federation. In the center of this Greater Europe lies geographical Europe. Here, regional and global interests of the United States and Russia overlap. Greater Europe includes four out of five permanent members of the UN Security Council and recognized nuclear powers and four out of six globally leading economic powers. Thus, the European security order is inextricably linked to the global security order and to other regional orders, in particular in the Middle East and North Africa, as well as to global functional orders such as the nuclear non-proliferation and disarmament regime.

As a result, the repercussions of cooperative or confrontational developments in Europe are inevitably felt globally. They either shape chances for cooperation on global security challenges such as internationally acting terrorism, failing and failed states, and proliferation of weapons of mass destruction, or produce obstacles to international responses and common action. Whether the international community can make progress on the way towards global nuclear arms control and, eventually, disarmament or whether it will witness a revival of the political role of nuclear weapons will depend to a large extent on the development of NATO–Russia relations in Europe. Similarly, US–Russian–European cooperation in ending civil wars, destroying terrorism, and stabilizing failed states in the Middle East will be influenced by the European security crisis. On the other hand, common action to regain some stability in the European periphery could encourage broader efforts to return to security cooperation in Europe.

2. ACTORS AND INTERESTS

(1) The first half of the twentieth century with its two world wars proved that *Germany* could develop the economic and military capabilities to dominate the continent but lacked the potential to be a world power. The United Kingdom and France lost their world power positions after 1945. Since then, preventing Germany from regaining power was not only an objective of the Soviet Union but also of the United Kingdom, France, and other European states; for instance, the Treaty of Brussels (1948) still reflected this rationale.[1] The foundation of NATO in 1949, however, already focused primarily on the other main problem of Europe, namely the threat of further expansion of a Soviet Union that had gained control of East and Central Europe after the Yalta decisions of February 1945. In that situation, Western Europeans drew the lesson that their security remained dependent on the political and military presence of the United States. Against this background, the transatlantic partnership became a core interest of the political class in West Germany, allowing it to overcome its postwar isolation and ensuring that (Western) Europe would not fall back into national rivalries. For the same reasons, Germany also pushed for European reconciliation and integration, with close Franco-German ties at the center.[2]

(2) At the same time, the *United States* had concluded that maintaining its global interest and containing the Soviet Union's expansionism required its direct and permanent political and military engagement in European

[1] See Günter Walpuski, *Verteidigung + Entspannung = Sicherheit, Texte und Materialien zur Außenund Sicherheitspolitik*, 2nd edn, Bonn-Bad: Godesberg, 1975, p. 44.

[2] Cf. Elysée-Vertrag, January 22, 1963, in Auswärtiges Amt (ed.), *Außenpolitik der Bundesrepublik Deutschland*, pp. 275–8.

affairs. However, in contrast to its European allies, the USA soon focused on a significant military contribution by West Germany to the common defense against and deterrence of the Soviet threat while embedding it firmly in the Western camp.[3] In consequence, West Germany built the second largest conventional military forces in Europe after the Soviet Union[4] and developed the third strongest economy globally. The Bundeswehr was fully integrated in NATO.

In the bipolar security order of Yalta, however, the lines of global confrontation still ran straight through Germany. During and even at the end of the Cold War, the "German question" remained the crucial issue in a divided Europe, as became obvious when *France* and the *United Kingdom* tried to resist the unification of the two German states in 1990.[5]

(3) In 1990, Europe succeeded in overcoming the Yalta order when compromises were found by key players on the German question, nuclear and conventional disarmament, and the creation of a cooperative security order for Europe and beyond. Such accord was interpreted as a "win-win" situation balancing strategic interests of major powers to end the Cold War rather than as "strategic defeat" of the Soviet Union. Its basic provisions are enshrined in the "Two-plus-Four-Treaty" on the unification of Germany, the Intermediate-Range Nuclear Forces Treaty,[6] the Treaty on Conventional Armed Forces in Europe (CFE), and the Charter of Paris.

- The *United States* did not deem it appropriate any more to contain an allied and democratic Germany and offered "partnership in leadership." It kept its political engagement with Europe, however, while it drastically reduced its military presence and shifted its strategic focus to the Middle East.
- The *Soviet Union*—financially exhausted from arms races and economic inefficiency—aimed at maintaining its security interests through a policy of cooperative balance of power and reciprocal geo-strategic restraint. It was based on arms control (CFE) and the OSCE as the institutional framework of a cooperative pan-European security community. This

[3] Wolfram Hanrieder has aptly characterized this US strategy as "dual containment": "integrating West Germany economically, politically and militarily in the European Community and NATO helped to contain both the Soviet Union and German revisionism simultaneously." See Wolfram Hanrieder, *Germany, America, Europe: Forty Years of German Foreign Policy*, New Haven, CT and London: Yale University Press, 1989.

[4] Presse und Informationsamt der Bundesregierung, *Weißbuch 1973/1974, Zur Sicherheit der Bundesrepublik Deutschland und zur Entwicklung der Bundeswehr*, Bonn: BMVg, 1974, p. 30.

[5] Helmut Kohl, *Vom Mauerfall zur Wiedervereinigung, Meine Erinnerungen*, Munich: Knaur Verlag, 2014, pp. 70–82, 317–24, 379–93.

[6] *Treaty between the United States of America and the Union of Soviet Socialist Republics on the Elimination of their Intermediate-Range and Shorter-Range Missiles*, December 1987, Selected Documents No. 25, Department of State Publications 9555, Washington, DC: Dept of State, December 1987 (reprint July 1990).

allowed a face-saving withdrawal of Soviet forces from its geo-strategic positions in Central Europe while keeping significant political influence in pan-European security affairs.

- *United Germany* stayed within the North Atlantic Alliance. It committed to limit its military forces, relinquish national possession of nuclear, chemical, and biological weapons,[7] promote security partnership with a changing Russia, and use its political weight and financial and economic power to strengthen the development of the European Union.[8]
- *France* and the *United Kingdom* retained symbols of their former global power status, namely nuclear weapons and permanent Security Council seats. Like Germany, they were eager to see a continued US presence in Europe, though with a new emphasis: after the dissolution of the Warsaw Pact, the collapse of the Soviet Union, the Russian military withdrawal from Central Europe, and the implementation of the CFE disarmament obligations, deterring Russia was no longer considered the rationale for the US military presence and NATO.

(4) The changes to this European security order of 1990 that sparked new geo-political rivalries after 2001 resulted from policy changes of the four leading Western powers and growing resistance by Russia against what Moscow saw as the unilateral abrogation by the United States and NATO of earlier agreements.

The *United States* changed its policy towards Russia several times: Presidents George Bush senior and Bill Clinton focused on strategic cooperation as agreed in the 1990s, but President George W. Bush pursued a geo-politically motivated "freedom agenda" in the Middle East and Eastern Europe. After the terrorist attacks on New York and Washington on September 11, 2001 and the subsequent military engagement in Afghanistan, this new policy culminated in the military intervention in Iraq (2003) and the pursuance of NATO's enlargement towards Russian borders—close to St. Petersburg in the north, near the Trans-Dnjestr conflict and the Russian Black Sea Fleet bases in Crimea in the center, and in the vicinity of the unstable Russian Caucasus flank in the south. In this, the US administration tried to rely on "new Europe" (Rumsfeld) rather than the "old" one, and thus risked the division of the Alliance.

In this context, in 2007 the USA stationed rotating conventional combat groups in Romania and Bulgaria and arranged the stationing of missile defense installations in Poland and the Czech Republic. It also supported Georgia's desire to regain control over the breakaway regions Abkhazia and South Ossetia and provided military advice, training, and equipment.

[7] Vertrag über die abschließende Regelung in Bezug auf Deutschland (September 12, 1990), Art. 3, in Bundesgesetzblatt 1990 II, p. 1318.

[8] Cf. German–French initiative of April 18, 1990, in Auswärtiges Amt (ed.), *Außenpolitik der Bundesrepublik Deutschland*, p. 669.

(Georgia, in turn, provided the temporarily third largest military contingent in support of US occupation forces in Iraq.) Already in 2001, President Bush had thinned out nuclear arms control, withdrawn from the Anti-Ballistic Missile (ABM) Treaty, initiated the build-up of a strategic missile defense system, and put conventional arms control on hold by blocking ratification of the CFE adaptation agreement. The USA also thwarted Russia's interest in a legally binding OSCE charter.[9]

President Obama acknowledged the growing problems in US-Russian relations and launched a "reset" policy in 2009. It showed first results with the New START Treaty, which was concluded, however, without solving the dispute on strategic missile defense. In contrast, the "reset" failed regarding European security affairs. As the backslide of democracy and human rights in Russia gained momentum, the Western confrontational tone of criticism persisted. Conventional arms control and the OSCE concept of a common and undivided European security space fell victim to new geo-political rivalry that initially manifested itself in territorial disputes in Moldova and Georgia. Its core issue, however, were attempts to reorder the post-Soviet space with the Ukraine in its center and tie it to the West.

A surprising change of US security policies was looming when President Trump during and after the election campaign in 2016 announced his intention to strike a deal with President Putin, concentrate political and military efforts on combating terrorism, and question US defense obligations towards NATO. In contrast, after a number of loyalty addresses to the Alliance of the US Secretaries of State and Defense, the continuation of the European Reassurance Program,[10] the prolongation of sanctions against Russia, the unilateral missile attack on April 7, 2017 against a Syrian air base, and the confirmation of nuclear guarantees for NATO's deterrence strategy, the classic US politics of interests seems to prevail in the military and diplomatic apparatus. Furthermore, the US Congress has curtailed the president's freedom of action. However, various and often contradicting signals have been sent from the White House and government quarters, multilateral US obligations are called into question(particularly in the field of trade and climate politics), and no long-term US political strategy has been outlined so far (December 2017). Therefore, there remains an element of uncertainty regarding US policies and a tendency to withdraw from multilateral commitments.

[9] Draft Charter of the Organization for Security and Cooperation in Europe submitted to the OSCE Permanent Council by the Russian Federation, PC.DEL/444/07, May 18, 2007; see also The Embassy of the Russian Federation to the United Kingdom of Great Britain and Northern Ireland, Russian Views of the OSCE Activities, http://www.rusemb.org.uk/osce/ [accessed September 8, 2016].

[10] See http://comptroller.defense.gov/Portals/45/Documents/defbudget/fy2018_ERI_J-Book.pdf [accessed November 30, 2017].

From a *Russian* viewpoint, NATO's enlargement contradicted the idea of a common, undivided security area and constituted a breach of earlier agreements. Russia was critical that NATO changed the European security order unilaterally instead of acting "in common" (i.e., with Russia) as agreed. Other contested issues included Western military interventions in violation of international law, the role of the OSCE within the European security architecture, and conventional arms control, which ensured overall and sub-regional military balances and geographic distance between NATO and Russia. Russia also suspects that the development of US strategic missile defense was undermining its second strike capability behind the pretext of an unrealistic threat assessment of Iranian nuclear and missile capabilities.

In particular, to Russia NATO's offer to Ukraine and Georgia to join the Alliance represents a direct threat to its own security interest. US military support to Georgia and the Georgian attack in summer 2008 against South Ossetia and Russian peacekeepers fueled such a perception,[11] as did Western support for the Maidan revolution in Kiev. Moscow drew a direct line to NATO in former President Yushchenko's warning during the Georgian war that Russian harbor rights in Crimea would be curtailed,[12] Yanukovich's fall in February 2014, and in an expected accession of a revolutionary government in Kiev. When it perceived the strategic position of its Black Sea Fleet to be at risk, the Kremlin reacted with the annexation of the Crimean Peninsula and support for the rebels in a barely concealed breach of international law. In this, Moscow overestimated the implications of the Maidan revolution and underestimated Western resolve.

Franco-German cooperation has been crucial for the development of the European Union and its cohesion in times of crisis. Cooperation and functional integration within the EU have given rise to common norms and positions, promoted consensus building and lent legitimacy to coordinated actions of its leading powers. Though occasionally old resentments reappear in political rhetoric, reservations against German dominance have generally been replaced by broad acceptance of German leadership where it is seen to represent European interests. In face of global security challenges and the Eastern neighbors' threat perception of a revisionist Russia, today most EU partners are less afraid of German dominance than of a lack of German leadership.

Although Germany is not a permanent member of the UN Security Council (UNSC), it cooperates with the five Permanent Members of the Council in

[11] See Independent International Fact-Finding Mission on the Conflict in Georgia (IIFFMCG/EUSR), Report Volume I, September 30, 2009, http://news.bbc.co.uk/2/shared/bsp/hi/pdfs/30_09_09_iiffmgc_report.pdf [accessed September 8, 2016].

[12] Interview with President Victor Yushchenko, *Die Welt*, September 11, 2008, http://www.welt.de/politik/article2429300/Ukraine-will-Russland-in-die-Grenzen-weisen.html.

addressing global and regional security problems such as the Iranian nuclear program or the war in Syria. Within the "Normandy format," Germany and France mediated between Ukraine and Russia to settle the Ukraine conflict. However, in contrast to the United Kingdom and France, Germany continues to hesitate with the use of military power beyond alliance defense obligations although it participates in a number of multinational operations abroad authorized by a UNSC mandate.

3. INSTITUTION, NORMS, AND PRINCIPLES

As opposed to the imposed Yalta order of 1945, the organizations, institutions, and agreed norms and principles of the European security order of Paris agreed in 1990 have largely been shaped by compromises between various national interests of its main actors and their allies.

3.1. NATO

During the Cold War, the North Atlantic Treaty Organization (NATO) focused on deterring the military threat against Western Europe posed by the conventional superiority of the forces of the Soviet Union and its Warsaw Pact allies. This purpose became obsolete with the end of the Cold War. NATO's other main purpose, however, persisted: the United States remained involved in Europe as a balancing and stabilizing factor. Even France, which traditionally has emphasized its strategic autonomy and thus remained somewhat aloof from NATO, returned to NATO's integrated (conventional) military structure, if only in 2008.

Although NATO as an alliance of sovereign nations decides by consensus, continued US involvement in Europe implies its political and military weight shape alliance strategies and actions in accordance with its own national interests. This harbors a potential for conflict within the Alliance, in particular when some members try to define a new purpose for the Alliance by refocusing it on "out of area"-deployments rather than on the defense of allied territories. The Alliance remained united in its enforcement role in Bosnia-Herzegovina after the conclusion of the Dayton Accord, the war over Kosovo in 1999, in invoking the defense clause (Article 5) of the Washington Treaty after 9/11, and in its military engagement in Afghanistan. However, the Alliance was thrown into turmoil when the USA requested solidarity in its war against Iraq in 2003, which collided with key principles of international law. As President Bush and his Defense Secretary replaced alliance consensus by ad hoc coalitions

("coalitions of the willing") banking on "new Europe" as opposed to the "old" one, NATO faced a political split and serious doubts about its future.

Such divergences also appeared during the debate in 2008 about possible membership of Ukraine and Georgia in the Alliance. NATO's first enlargement into Central Europe in 1999 had been embedded in a NATO–Russia accord geared to deepening cooperation, strengthening the OSCE, adapting the CFE Treaty, and mutual restraint in permanently stationing additional substantial combat forces.[13] NATO's enlargement in 2004 incorporated seven more Eastern European countries (with the 1999 accord not implemented), among them the Baltic Republics that were not party to the CFE Treaty. However, when the Bush administration launched its project to extend NATO farther, close to the Don River and the Caucasus region, "red lines" were crossed and any understanding with Russia was damaged. While several Central and Eastern European allies supported this, the USA met with opposition from Germany, France, and other Western European states. The compromise achieved in NATO's Bucharest Summit in April 2008, namely to offer a general accession perspective without a concrete "Membership Action Plan," satisfied nobody but kept the illusion of alliance unity.[14]

Despite such differences, NATO always tried to justify enlargement policies with normative political rhetoric, particularly with the right of states to choose their alliances. However, the Ukrainian case is not the only one that has demonstrated various, sometimes incompatible, national motives guiding the enlargement process: While the goal to stabilize the neighborhood without any anti-Russian sentiment dominated Franco-German considerations, the fear of a resurgent Russia and geo-political objectives prevailed in Eastern Europe and the United States. Both those policies and the rhetoric caused new tensions with Russia, which insisted on strengthening inclusive pan-European instruments, as agreed in the 1990s. The Georgian attack against South Ossetian militias and Russian peacekeepers in August 2008 significantly contributed to growing Russian doubts as to the real purposes of NATO's enlargement. In turn, Russia's military intervention and subsequent recognition of the independence of Abkhazia and South Ossetia in 2008 fueled existing threat perceptions of allies in Central and Eastern Europe.

President Obama's "reset" policies introduced in 2009 did nothing to change that geo-political context. NATO's Lisbon Strategic Concept of 2010 still describes NATO's further enlargement as an appropriate basis to ensure stability and security in Europe without any mention of the OSCE's project to

[13] NATO/Russian Federation, *Founding Act on Mutual Relations, Cooperation and Security between NATO and the Russian Federation, Paris*, May 27, 1997, https://www.nato.int/cps/en/natolive/official_texts_25468.htm.

[14] NATO, *Bucharest Summit Declaration*, Issued by the Heads of State and Government participating in the meeting of the North Atlantic Council in Bucharest on April 3, 2008 (= NATO PR(2008)049).

create a common security community.[15] Such efforts to change Europe's security order without Russia's participation and potentially against its interest contributed further to Russian frustration and threat perceptions. The NATO–Russia Council could not alleviate Russian concerns. In particular, it did not live up to the provisions agreed upon in the Rome Declaration (2002) that delegations would discuss important security issues in their national capacities rather than pursuing bloc positions.[16] Moreover, during the crises in Georgia and the Ukraine, NATO suspended the dialog exactly when it was most urgently needed.

The Ukraine crisis rekindled security concerns of NATO's Eastern European member states. They saw their suspicions about Russia's policies as revisionist and a direct threat to their own security confirmed, given that Moscow had annexed territory of the Ukraine and justified military intervention by invoking its "responsibility to protect" Russian minorities. During the Wales and Warsaw Summits in September 2014 and July 2016, NATO therefore decided to reassure allies by improving its crisis response capabilities, enhancing command, logistic, and air defense capabilities, and stationing on a rotational basis four battalion-size combat groups in Poland and the three Baltic States.[17] Germany, France, and Western European states held the view that such limited reassurance measures were meant to send a strategic message that no allied state could be isolated, without however suspending the NATO–Russia Founding Act. Such a position met with criticism in Eastern European and Anglo-Saxon countries where political and military pressure groups had proposed to build up a massive forward defense posture by stationing seven to eight heavy brigades. In this context, the USA on a national basis deployed an additional armored brigade to NATO's "eastern flank" and material stockpiles including 250 armored combat vehicles for another brigade in Germany, Belgium, and the Netherlands.

On a bilateral basis, the United States, the United Kingdom, and Poland also provided "non-lethal" logistical assistance and dispatched military trainers to Ukraine. In 2014/15, NATO conducted more than 160 military exercises to

[15] NATO, *Active Engagement, Modern Defence, Strategic Concept for the Defence and Security of the Members of the North Atlantic Treaty Organization*, Adopted by the Heads of State and Government in Lisbon, November 20, 2010, No. 27, https://www.nato.int/cps/en/natolive/official_texts_68580.htm.

[16] NATO–Russia Council, *Rome Declaration*, May 28, 2002, p. 4, https://www.nato.int/nrc-website/media/59487/2002.05.28_nrc_rome_declaration.pdf.

[17] NATO, *Wales Summit Declaration*, Issued by the Heads of State and Government participating in the meeting of the North Atlantic Council in Wales, Press Release (2014) 120, September 5, 2014, in particular Nos. 1, 16–23, http://www.nato.int/cps/en/natohq/official_texts_112964.htm?selectedLocale=en; NATO, *Warsaw Summit Declaration*, Issued by the Heads of State and Government participating in the Meeting of the North Atlantic Council in Warsaw, July 8–9, 2016, Press Release (2016) 100, July 9, 2016, in particular Nos. 37–41, https://www.nato.int/cps/en/natohq/official_texts_133169.htm [accessed November 30, 2017].

demonstrate political will and military capability to defend allies while Russia has increased significantly the number and size of snap exercises and the presence of forces along the Russian–Ukrainian border. The numbers of close-border flights of both sides have also reached a level unprecedented since the end of the Cold War and produced a sense of new military confrontation.[18]

This increase in unusual military activities indicates new mutual threat perceptions and underlines the level of tensions between the West and Russia. Despite the irritations created by President Trump's tweets, US policies within NATO have remained unchanged, and America remains committed to the defense of NATO, if necessary with nuclear weapons, as the Trump administration Nuclear Posture Review published in early 2018 made clear.[19] Yet at the same time both sides remain aware of the need to act in common against global security challenges, such as terrorist attacks by the Islamic State which threaten NATO states and Russia alike. Overall, NATO clearly has acquired new importance against this background of rising tensions within Europe, and the organization has also shifted back towards its traditional twin objectives of deterrence and détente in the management of European security.

3.2. The OSCE

The Organization for Security and Cooperation in Europe (OSCE) developed from the Conference for Security and Cooperation in Europe (CSCE) that was first convened in 1973. The CSCE sought to de-escalate tensions between East and West by accepting the territorial realities, banning the use of force to change the situation and establish human contacts in a divided Europe. In the Helsinki CSCE Final Act of 1975, thirty-three European states, the United States, and Canada agreed on a framework of ten principles to ensure peaceful coexistence between antagonistic political systems and military alliances in a time of confrontation and arms race.[20] The Act thus established provisions for strengthening peace and stability in Europe without changing the status quo of the "Yalta order."

[18] See Russia–West Dangerous Brinkmanship Continues, in European Leadership Network, March 2015, https://www.europeanleadershipnetwork.org/commentary/russia-west-dangerous-brinkmanship-continues/; Task Force on Cooperation in Greater Europe: Position Paper III: Avoiding War in Europe: how to reduce the risk of a military encounter between Russia and NATO, August 2015, pp. 1–2.

[19] United States of America. Department of Defense, Office of the Secretary of Defense: Nuclear Posture Review 2018, issued February 2018, https://media.defense.gov/2018/Feb/02/2001872886-1/-1/1/2018-NUCLEAR-POSTURE-REVIEW-FINAL-REPORT.PDF [accessed June 15, 2018].

[20] Schlussakte von Helsinki 1.8.1975, in Auswärtiges Amt (ed.), *20 Jahre KSZE,1973–1993*, 2nd edn, Bonn: Ausw. Amt, 1993, pp. 18–81.

However, it took another fifteen years of crises and arms racing before President Gorbachev initiated the new policies of *perestroika* and *glasnost.* Only then could the CSCE member states overcome the divisive "Yalta order" and establish a new European peace and security order. The Charter of Paris (1990) and its related arms control agreements marked the end of confrontation and postulated future cooperation of former adversaries under the umbrella of the CSCE (renamed OSCE in 1994). As the only inclusive and consensus-building regional organization, the OSCE is committed to a cooperative security order for Greater Europe based on a comprehensive three-dimensional security concept. This concept builds on the principles of international law and further develops the three traditional CSCE "baskets" on common political standards, human rights and the rule of law; strategic restraint and military transparency through arms control and Confidence- and Security-Building Measures (CSBMs); and economic and environmental cooperation.

The CFE Treaty—labeled the "cornerstone of European security"[21]—was signed in 1990 by former Warsaw Pact and NATO member states and ensured numerical equality at significantly lower force levels and geographical distance between the two blocs to curtail military potentials that could be used for massive cross-border operations. Its provisions were harmonized with the "Two-plus-Four Treaty" in which Germany agreed to reduce its own forces and reject the stationing of foreign troops or nuclear weapons on the territories of the former GDR or Berlin.

The Vienna Document aimed at improving transparency of military deployments and activities in Europe and Central Asia, promoting military contacts and supporting crisis management and risk reduction measures. Arms control and CSBMs were further enhanced by the Treaty on Open Skies, which provides for cooperative observation flights in the whole area between Vancouver and Vladivostok.

When NATO in 1996 started pursuing its first enlargement project in Central Europe, Russia voiced concerns about the motives of that project and held that it was contradicting the agreed OSCE objectives to create a common and undivided security area. Between 1997 and 1999 a compromise was found and agreed upon during the 1999 OSCE summit in Istanbul. While reaffirming the norms of the Paris order, it modified its security-related provisions and instruments as follows:

With the Charter for European Security (1999), OSCE participating states have agreed to strengthen the role of the OSCE and to create a common space of equal security from Vancouver to Vladivostok. While reaffirming the right of states to choose their security arrangements freely, all member states also

[21] OSCE, Charter for European Security, Istanbul, November 1999, in OSCE (ed.), *OSCE Istanbul Summit 1999*, Istanbul Document 1999, Istanbul, 2000, p. 7 (no. 29) (= PCOEW389).

committed not to strengthen their security at the expense of others. Accordingly, no state or alliance should have any pre-eminent responsibility for maintaining peace and stability or consider any part of the OSCE area as its sphere of influence.[22]

All CFE state parties signed an Adaptation Agreement to the CFE Treaty (ACFE) to adapt conventional arms control arrangements to NATO's first enlargement by Central European states that previously had belonged to the CFE Eastern Group of member states.[23] The ACFE intended to replace obsolete CFE bloc-to-bloc limitations with national and territorial ceilings to prevent destabilizing sub-regional force accumulations. With the opening of the Treaty for accession by all states within the area of application, the Agreement was to promote the creation of an inclusive and undivided OSCE security space in Europe.

Those provisions were expressly linked to the NATO–Russia Founding Act (1997). There, in context with NATO's enlargement, both sides had committed themselves to cooperate closely on security, inter alia through strengthening the OSCE, adapting the CFE Treaty and not to station additional substantial combat forces permanently. The foundation of the NATO–Russia Council (2002) also aimed at deepening security cooperation in a number of fields such as arms control and missile defense. Consultations in the Council were to be conducted without reference to bloc positions.

While the CFE disarmament provisions of 1990 had been fully implemented with Russia and Germany bearing the brunt of reduction obligations, the political stipulations of the Istanbul accord came under pressure shortly after it was adopted. Western states blocked ACFE ratification and demanded the withdrawal of Russian forces from disputed territories in Georgia and Moldova as a precondition for the ACFE to enter into force. Russia's position on territorial conflicts in the post-Soviet space stiffened the more NATO extended to the East and the USA increased its presence near the Black Sea and in the Caucasus region. Russian attempts to strengthen the political pre-eminence of the OSCE and its security-building role failed; instead, the USA and a number of allies concentrated their efforts on confronting Russia with democracy and human rights deficiencies.

Despite such regressive developments, the OSCE's field presence continued to be an asset, which was demonstrated by its stabilizing roles in Bosnia-Herzegovina, Kosovo, Moldova, and Kirghizstan and—up to 2009—in Georgia. The quiet implementation of arms control and CSBMs also contributed

[22] Ibid., p. 3 (no. 8).

[23] OSCE, Agreement on the Adaptation of the Treaty on Conventional Armed Forces in Europe, in OSCE (ed.), *OSCE Istanbul Summit 1999*, pp. 118–234; CFE Final Act of the Conference of the State Parties to the Treaty on Conventional Armed Forces in Europe, November 19, 1999, in OSCE (ed.), *OSCE Istanbul Summit 1999*, pp. 235–51.

significantly to military transparency until Russia suspended the CFE Treaty at the end of 2007 in response to allies' refusal to ratify the ACFE.

Moreover, the autonomous OSCE institutions—the Office for Democratic Institutions and Human Rights, the High Commissioner for National Minorities, and the Representative for the Freedom of the Media—still attracted political and public interest, e.g., in election monitoring. However, against the backdrop of growing geo-political rivalry the role of the OSCE as an inclusive security community lost political attention and the vision of a common and undivided security space fell into oblivion.

It was, therefore, after a decade of neglect that the role of the OSCE in crisis management was recognized again after the outbreak of the Ukraine crisis in February 2014. The OSCE proved to be the only regional organization capable of sustaining a widely accepted presence on the ground, monitoring the Minsk ceasefire agreements and facilitating stabilizing measures through the Trilateral Contact Group.[24] However, recent experience has also revealed the shortcomings of the OSCE crisis management tools. The OSCE Chair in Office lacks competencies to react rapidly during emerging crises, e.g., by dispatching fact-finding missions, and the CSBMs agreed are often not sufficiently intrusive, broad, and sustainable, and conventional arms control lacked attention in the security dialog in OSCE bodies in Vienna until Germany in 2016 launched a new initiative to revitalize this "corner stone" of European security.

While in Eastern Ukraine military offensive operations have been kept at bay since summer 2015 the political provisions of the Minsk Agreement have not yet been implemented, a fact which harbors a potential for new escalation. While the OSCE has demonstrated that common and inclusive crisis management is (still) possible, it will be able to continue this role and to attract Russian support only if its original vision of a common and undivided security space is pursued more vigorously. To that end, the role and status of the OSCE within the European security architecture have to be recalibrated. This is why the German OSCE chairmanship in 2016 aimed at reversing the unfavorable trends by "renewing dialogue, rebuilding trust and restoring security."[25] In this context, the then Foreign Minister Frank-Walter Steinmeier proposed to revitalize conventional arms control and established a "Group of Likeminded Countries" to promote such ideas. The "Structured Dialogue" the German OSCE chairmanship secured at the Ministerial Council meeting in December

[24] OSCE Permanent Council, Decision No. 1162 Extension of the Mandate of the OSCE Special Monitoring Mission to Ukraine, PC.DEC/1162 of March 12, 2015 (= PCOEW5968).

[25] Außenminister und amtierender OSZE-Vorsitzender Frank-Walter Steinmeier über die Beweggründe des deutschen OSZE-Vorsitzes, in *Ständige Vertretung der Bundesrepublik Deutschland bei der OSZE Wien*, Deutscher OSZE-Vorsitz, 2016, http//www.wien-osze.diplo.de/Vertretung/wienosce/de/011Vorsitz/Vorsitz_202016.html [accessed November 20, 2017].

2016[26] was taken up by the Austrian OSCE Chairmanship in 2017. The Dialogue aims to address principles and norms, threat perceptions, military doctrines, postures and activities, as well as crisis management. Its outcome will depend on the political will to de-escalate the tense situation.

3.3. The European Union

The European Union has significantly promoted integration, stability, and security in Europe. The sufferings in two world wars are still deeply ingrained in the collective memories of European nations. Preventing Europe from falling back into nationalism, fragmentation, and war has been the driving motive behind efforts to unite Europe, develop free and democratic societies, guarantee basic civil freedoms, human rights, and the rule of law, and promote good governance. To that end, the EU has created a unique set of political institutions, norms, and legal standards. Though proper implementation in all EU member states still leaves room for improvement, the EU is a success story. Wars between member states have become inconceivable.

The European Union is thus a political unity project rather than one of pure economic logic. Inherent frictions between those two driving factors at times require painful compromises. At least from a German perspective, harmonizing economy and trade-related standards and communalizing respective state functions are tools rather than an end in themselves.[27] However, no unified vision exists among member states as to what such an end state of the European Union should look like. Actually, the harmonizing of national security and defense policies is still in its infancy. It is obvious, therefore, that the EU has not replaced the role of nation-states and it seems unlikely that this will change in the near future. The EU Commission can only act on issues that member states have agreed to communalize. They are still the source of sovereignty; the European Parliament does not represent a "European nation" but the peoples of member states. In foreign and security policies, in particular, member states often act in their national capacities, as is demonstrated by largely autonomous action of European UNSC permanent member states, by different positions on military interventions outside Europe, or by divergent voting behavior on nuclear issues in the UN General Assembly.

[26] OSCE, Organization for Security and Cooperation in Europe, Ministerial Council Hamburg 2016, *From Lisbon to Hamburg: Declaration on the Twentieth Anniversary of the OSCE Framework for Arms Control*. MC.DOC/4/16 of December 9, 2016.

[27] See "Rede des Bundesministers des Auswärtigen, Dr. Kinkel, vor dem Deutschen Bundestag am 2.12.1992 anlässlich der Verabschiedung des Ratifikationsgesetzes zum Vertrag von Maastricht," in Auswärtiges Amt (ed.), *Deutsche Außenpolitik nach der Einheit 1990–1993. Eine Dokumentation*, Bonn, 1994, pp. 204–6; Helmut Kohl, "Ansprache des Bundeskanzlers, Dr. Kohl, aus Anlass des dreißigjährigen Bestehens des Elysée-Vertrags," Ibid., pp. 235–8.

Though EU member states have created a Common Foreign and Security Policy and a Common Security and Defense Policy, and in that context have tried to harmonize defense industries and beef-up defense cooperation, it is telling that they leave core defense functions in Europe to NATO while six EU member states stay nonaligned. In NATO, however, members act in their national capacities. The EU is not involved in European conventional arms control matters such as the CFE Treaty or its possible replacement; all this is handled exclusively by NATO.

Also the Permanent Structured Cooperation (PESCO) which twenty-five of twenty-eight EU member states agreed to on December 8, 2017 will not fundamentally change this picture. It is neither the founding act of a "European army" nor does it provide "strategic autonomy" from NATO's core defense functions. It aims, however, at strengthening the Alliance's European pillar, enabling the EU to carry out light stabilizing missions on its own and enhancing cooperation of armament industries in order to utilize defense budgets more efficiently and reduce the number of national armament projects. To that end, EU member states participating in PESCO have committed to steadily increasing and surveying defense budgets, improving command and control, mobility, logistics, medical support, maritime capabilities, training, readiness of the EU battalion-size battle groups, and collaborating on selected armament projects such as armored fighting vehicles. However, not all member states participate in every one of the seventeen concrete projects which have been agreed so far and all capacities developed within the PESCO framework will stay in the hands of individual nation-states.[28]

In contrast to these attempts of strengthening cooperation, the discussions between member states during past and current internal and external crises have revealed strong centrifugal tendencies within the EU. Together with the expected financial burden, this will temper the desire for further enlargement. Moreover, a linear progression of integration towards a European Federation cannot be taken for granted: the idea meets with reservations, particularly in Central and Eastern European member states, and has certainly contributed to Brexit. Further regression cannot be excluded, as the rise of anti-EU parties in several member states shows. On the other hand, new French initiatives under President Macron show that Brexit and new transatlantic uncertainties might also offer new chances to strengthen cooperation among remaining member states after the United Kingdom will have left the Union. At present, despite all attempts of harmonizing foreign and security policy, the EU cannot be regarded as a homogeneous actor in external affairs and security policies. At least, however, the classical leading European powers try to avoid, as far as

[28] See Council of the European Union, Council Decision 14866/17 establishing Permanent Structured Cooperation (PESCO) and determining the list of Participating Member States, Brussels, December 8, 2017.

possible, acting single-handedly, and they seek to enhance the legitimacy of their actions through coordinating with all EU member states.

Whether and to which extent the EU Eastern Partnership Policy and, in particular, the EU's offer to Ukraine of an Association Agreement including a "Deep and Comprehensive Free Trade Area" had a geo-political connotation and contributed to the Ukraine crisis has been the subject of controversial discussion.[29] Obviously, Russia was concerned that this offer could thwart its own Customs Union and Eurasian Union projects. It held that, given open borders and de facto free trade conditions between Russia and Ukraine, cheap EU products could flood the Ukrainian and even the Russian market to the detriment of national production and bilateral trade. However, such problems could have been dealt with in trilateral negotiations as the Presidents of France, Russia, Ukraine and the Chancellor of Germany suggested in their common statement of February 12, 2015.[30] In consequence, it was the polarizing interpretation of the Association Agreement by a few EU member states and certainly by the Maidan leaders that suggested a fundamental choice "...either for Russia or for Europe."[31] Such interpretations did not represent the views of the majority of EU member states and of the EU Commission. Brussels may have underestimated, however, the geo-political relevance of the Agreement against the background of deteriorating relations between Russia, the United States, and Eastern Europe after the war in Georgia.

Another question is to what extent preferential trade and exclusive economic arrangements of a number of OSCE member states can be made compatible with the OSCE vision of an inclusive and undivided security cooperation that includes the economic dimension. In this context, the idea of a Free Trade Zone between Lisbon and Vladivostok was mentioned in the statement of the Normandy format of February 12, 2015. Realities point in a different direction, however: in response to Russia's annexation of Crimea the EU implemented sanctions, and in a heated debate on energy security a number of EU member states expressed the view that dependence of their domestic energy markets on Russian natural gas imports could be used by Russia as a tool for blackmailing them as part of a strategy of "hybrid warfare."

[29] Cf. Stefan Meister and Marie-Lena May, *Die Östliche Partnerschaft der EU—ein Kooperationsangebot mit Missverständnissen*, Berlin, September 2009 (DGAP-Standpunkt 7).

[30] See Auswärtiges Amt, Pressemitteilung, February 12, 2015.

[31] See Michael Ludwig, Ein hoher Preis, Weshalb Armenien Russland der EU vorzieht, *FAZ*, October 8, 2014, p. 8; Georgi Gotev, EU loses Armenia to Russia's Customs Union, September 4, 2013, http://www.euractiv.com/europes-east/eu-loses-armenia-russia-customs-news-530224; Radio Free Europe/Radio Liberty: EU Officials Warn Yerevan Over "U-Turn," September 4, 2013, http://www.rferl.org/content/armenia-eu-customs-union/25095145.html.

4. A CRISIS OF THE EUROPEAN PEACE AND SECURITY ORDER

The European Peace and Security Order of Paris replaced confrontation with cooperation, reunited a divided continent, and solved the German question at its center. It was based on the cornerstones of adherence to principles of international law, common values, and a balance of security interests ensuring strategic restraint, in particular through arms control. Its central objective was to establish a common space of cooperative security based on equality and reciprocity.

Today, this order is in danger; NATO "frontline countries" deem it obsolete. Western states have reacted in a united way and strongly to Russia's intervention in Ukraine, which they see as a violation of international law and the very foundations of the order of Paris. However, tensions between the United States, a number of its allies, and Russia have been growing already since 2001, pointing to deeper roots of the conflict. The Paris order of 1990 was based on the assumption that a united Germany would stay within NATO and Soviet (Russian) forces would withdraw from Central Europe on the condition that NATO's military structures would not move forward and allied forces would not occupy positions that Russian forces had left. Close security cooperation and renunciation of geo-political zero-sum games were promised instead. At that time, all participants felt in such a "win-win situation" that everybody could keep face and guard basic strategic interests.

After the dissolution of the Warsaw Pact and the collapse of the Soviet Union, Russia and the West agreed that this order should be maintained. While the West wanted to assure stability in a fragmented post-Soviet space, Russia saw value in preserving the principles of mutual strategic restraint laid down in the "Two-plus-Four-Treaty" and the CFE Treaty with their concrete limitations and the geographical distance they put between Russia and NATO.

NATO's first enlargement changed this new status quo and required significant efforts to calm Russia's concerns. It held that the extension of military alliances contradicted the OSCE objective of creating a common space of cooperative security without dividing lines and geo-political competition. Nevertheless, through closer NATO–Russia ties (NATO–Russia Founding Act), adaptation of the CFE Treaty and strengthening the OSCE (European Security Charter) it was possible to alleviate Russian concerns.

After 2001, however, the Bush administration linked ratification of the ACFE to an end of Russian military and political influence in disputed territories in the post-Soviet space and promoted the accession of Georgia and Ukraine to NATO. The US withdrawal from the ABM Treaty and the build-up of strategic missile defense in NATO countries close to Russian borders triggered suspicions that this was to undermine Russia's second-strike capabilities. While the entry into force of the ACFE was blocked, NATO's second enlargement created potential deployment areas close to St. Petersburg without arms control restrictions. The USA in 2007 also stationed rotating combat groups near the Black Sea, labeled them "not substantial" and rejected Russian requests to negotiate.

At the same time, Russian proposals to provide the OSCE with a legally binding Charter, or to conclude a new security treaty, were blocked.[32] The OSCE Permanent Council was mainly used to confront Russia with its intransigent role in remaining territorial disputes as well as its democracy and human rights deficiencies, while Russian interests in sustaining basic security arrangements and adapting their instruments to a changing security landscape were ignored. Angry Russian accusations of Western "double standards" added to an increasingly poisoned atmosphere, indicating that the earlier understanding on strategic cooperation had dissolved and shifted back towards confrontation.

With the recognition of Kosovo by Western states and the Georgian crisis in 2008, relations between Russia and the United States, NATO, and the EU reached their first nadir after the Cold War. It is not clear yet why—in the presence of hundreds of US advisors and shortly after NATO's decision to offer Georgia a future accession option—the Georgian President resorted to a full-fledged attack against South Ossetia militias and Russian peacekeepers. This has fueled Russia's perceptions that a pro-Western course of neighboring countries in the "near abroad" will be followed by US military presence, the enlargement of the Western alliance closer to Russian borders and, eventually, military aggression. Russia's intransigence on territorial disputes grew with the US presence and reform movements in its immediate neighborhood: those territorial conflicts now became pawns in a larger geo-strategic game.

The new geo-political conflict shows that Russia has not yet found its place in the European security architecture. West and Central Europe have become more united under the umbrella of NATO and the EU, while the OSCE vision of a common space of equal security without geo-political rifts has faded. Decisions with far-reaching implications for the European security order were taken in Brussels while Vienna lost political attention. Dialog in established forums such as the G8 or the NATO–Russia Council was suspended during the crisis, while the OSCE bodies were becoming arenas for confrontational rhetoric rather than solution-oriented dialog. Moreover, after Russia's suspension of the CFE Treaty military-to-military contacts were reduced significantly, instigating growing mutual suspicion.

Russia saw the lack of respect for agreed assurances—such as a stronger role for the OSCE, adaptation of arms control, and closer NATO–Russia security

[32] European Security Treaty, Draft of November 29, 2009, in President of Russia, Official Web Portal, http://en.kremlin.ru/events/president/news/6152 [accessed December 3, 2009].

cooperation—not only as breaches of the security acquis but also as a humiliation.[33] In Moscow's view, Russia's interests were ignored, and a new narrative according to which Russia had "lost the Cold War" and was a "regional power" only replaced the interpretation of the Paris acquis as a "win-win situation." It feels that the West has not rewarded its fundamentally important historical concessions, such as replacing confrontation by cooperation, complete withdrawal of forces from its Central and Eastern European glacis, implementation of huge disarmament obligations, cooperation on the Dayton Peace Accord to pacify post-Yugoslavia, and agreeing to NATO's first enlargement on the basis of new adapted conditions, to name but a few. Instead, Moscow holds, the West has pushed its alliances closer to Russian borders, endangered crucial Russian strategic positions, and tried to split the Russian nation.

Moscow thus believed it had to win back Russia's national dignity and protect its strategic interest. Thus, its action in Ukraine in defiance of international law subjectively seems based on a strategic defense motive rather than on a master plan to restore Greater Russia in its historical borders. If this is true, Russia's political course could still be open to influence by measures accommodating Russian interests in exchange for its return to rules-based behavior.

5. CONCLUSIONS

Ending the Ukraine crisis through the full implementation of the Minsk Ceasefire Agreement will be an indispensable prerequisite for any attempt to reverse the current negative trend. A return to a cooperative and rule-based security order in Europe will be possible, however, if major stakeholders understand each other's threat perceptions, exercise military restraint, and seek a broad dialog on all open questions. Such an endeavor should focus on the pillars of the order of Paris—adherence to the principles of international law, common norms, and standards and security cooperation on the basis of arms control, reciprocity, and equality. Dialog should aim at reaffirming commitments of all states to international law but also address justifications of breaches such as inherited autonomy rights or stability oriented reasoning for supporting secession processes. The newly established "Structured Dialogue" within the OSCE could provide a valuable platform and narrow down the gaps between diverging threat assessments by establishing a common factual basis.

[33] Wladimir Putin, "Rede auf der 43. Münchener Sicherheitskonferenz," AG Friedensforschung (online), February 14, 2007, http://www.ag-friedensforschung.de/themen/Sicherheitskonferenz/2007-putin-dt.html [accessed November 10, 2017].

Strengthening the OSCE as the only inclusive regional organization in Europe with its objective to establish a common security space without geopolitical competition will be as important as a new NATO–Russia accord on cooperation and mutual restraint. Revitalizing conventional arms control to prevent destabilizing accumulation of forces that might be used for offensive operations or long-range precise strikes could provide mutual assurances.

A cooperative US–NATO–Russia threat analysis could focus on missile defense capabilities, in particular, to develop common perceptions and compatible countermeasures. Data exchange and mutual observation of exercises could assist in enhancing transparency to prevent misperceptions.

When addressing countries in the framework of the Eastern Partnership Policy the EU should consider its economic and security ties to Russia and Russian interest in promoting the Eurasian Union. An inclusive approach allowing for equal relations to both sides could help to bridge new lines of division in Europe and promote the OSCE's concept of inclusion.

In view of global security challenges, there is much potential for cooperation on maintaining the nuclear non-proliferation acquis with its link to and dependence on further nuclear disarmament, on combating terrorism and other transnational crime, and on stabilizing failed or failing states in the Middle East faced with the threat from the "Islamic State" and other jihadist and radical Islamist groups. While Russia will continue to play a major role in managing global security risks, common interests at that level of international order could be underpinned if cooperative solutions were to be found for open questions in Europe, and also vice versa.

7

The Middle Eastern Regional Order

Volker Perthes and Hanns W. Maull

To understand the Middle East as a "regional order" may seem somewhat confusing, given the violent disintegration not only of key states such as Syria but also the fact that the "old" Middle East—the Middle East as we knew it until 2011[1]—has disappeared, probably irreversibly. Yet if we consider patterns of interactions between the states in the Arab world there continues to be a regional security complex in the sense of Barry Buzan:[2] the countries are linked through interactions within a clearly demarcated system that are primarily about security, such as threats and military activities. The predominance of conflict interactions in both regional discourses and actions by states and non-state actors alike has in fact been characteristic of this regional security system for the last several decades, although there have also been many efforts to foster regional or sub-regional cooperation. However, none of them was able to shift the overall character of interactions in this region towards lasting cooperation.

1. THE MIDDLE EAST AS A REGIONAL ORDER

1.1. Geography of the Regional Order

Geographically, the Middle Eastern region includes all member countries of the Arab League but stretches beyond it. Within the Arab states, national

[1] Volker Perthes, *Das Ende des Nahen Ostens, wie wir ihn kennen—Ein Essay*, Berlin: Suhrkamp Verlag, 2015.

[2] Barry Buzan, *People, States and Fear: The National Security Problem in International Relations*, Brighton: Wheatsheaf Books, 1983, pp. 105f.; see also Barry Buzan and Ole Wæver, *Regions and Powers: The Structure of International Security*, Cambridge: Cambridge University Press, 2003.

political orders have often been contested violently, and also inter-state relations have been much more conflictual than might be expected against the background of historically powerful pan-Arab aspirations. Thus, secular nationalist states and conservative Islamic monarchies conducted an "Arab Cold War" that at times became quite hot (as, for example, in Yemen already during the 1960s, where Egypt and Saudi Arabia fought a proxy war, similar to the war today between Saudi Arabia and Iran).[3] Even between the Arab League member states, there has been a predominance of conflictual patterns of interaction. However, the region also includes several non-Arab states, notably Israel, Iran, and Turkey. Those states have been deeply involved with the Arab world for decades, mostly again through conflict. The Israeli–Arab conflict was long perhaps the most important conflict formation in the region, with the wars in 1948, 1967, 1973, 1982, and 2006 (and against the Palestinian Gaza Strip in 2008, 2012, and 2014) involving Egypt, Iraq (if only marginally), Jordan, Lebanon, and Syria in the major outbursts of open hostility. Moreover, the non-state actors Palestine Liberation Organization (PLO), Hezbollah, and Hamas also took part in the hostilities. The Iran–Iraq War from 1980 to 1988 was the longest inter-state war in the regional system. As other regional actors sided with either Baghdad or Tehran, this First Gulf War, as it was to be called later, may be seen as shaping the contours of a second major regional conflict formation which eventually would overshadow the Israeli–Arab conflict in its importance for the regional order: the conflict between the revolutionary Islamic Shi'ite regime in Iran and the conservative Sunni Arab states. The emergence of al-Qaida and, later, ISIS, two extremist Sunni Islamist non-state actors who celebrate terrorist violence as *jihad* (religious effort), have further exacerbated the tendency towards religious ideologization and sectarian polarization within the Middle Eastern regional order. Of course, this order also comprises non-conflictual economic, social, cultural, and political interactions, some of them involving substantial parts of the region's societies, but never, so far, becoming determining features of the region and its internal dynamics.

1.2. Subgroupings within the Arab Middle Eastern Regional Order

Since the 1990s, there have been efforts to form subgroups in attempts to organize economic cooperation and security on a sub-regional level. Although the outcome of those efforts has been mixed overall, the Maghreb more and more looks like a sub-regional order, though one without much formally institutionalized cooperation. The states of the Persian Gulf

[3] Malcolm H. Kerr, *The Arab Cold War, 1958–1964: A Study of Ideology in Politics*, Chatham House Essays, London: Oxford University Press, 1965.

form another sub-regional order. Again, this order is heavily conflictual as far as relations between Iran and its Arab neighbors are concerned. The conservative Arab monarchies on the Arabian Peninsula made significant progress in building their own regional organization, the Gulf Cooperation Council (GCC), mainly to enhance their common security. By 2017, however, the future of this structure has been cast into doubt as a simmering conflict between Qatar and some of its neighbors escalated beyond previously known levels.

One important conflictual aspect in this sub-regional order has centered on the distribution of power. Iran has traditionally aspired to obtain a hegemonic role in the Gulf, and Saddam Hussein's misguided attempt to integrate Kuwait into Iraq could be seen as a response to a failed attempt to form a strong Arab state coalition, with Iraq and the Gulf monarchies as its financiers. The growing weight of the sub-regional orders in the Persian Gulf and in the Maghreb reflects the realization of policymakers that the traditional core conflict of the Middle Eastern regional order, the conflict between Israel, its Arab neighbors, and the Palestinians, ultimately did not concern the rest of the Arab world all that much. Arab engagement in the Israeli–Arab conflict for those more distant Arab states was a matter of pan-Arab nationalist ideology and solidarity that did not actually involve the core interests of the nation-states in the Maghreb or in the Persian Gulf.

The Middle East regional order therefore has lost some of its previous cohesion while sub-regional orders have become relatively more independent from the central patterns of interactions in the system. Iran, however, maintains an ideologically fervent anti-Israel stance that integrates it into the Middle Eastern regional order much more than into the South Asian regional order: even though Iran borders on Afghanistan and Pakistan, there is much less interaction with these countries than with those in the Middle East.

2. THE DEMISE OF THE OLD ORDER IN 2011

2.1. The Old Order

This phase, which lasted until the British and the French withdrawal in the 1940s and 1950s, was marked by European dominance: all through the Maghreb and from there to Iraq, Arab societies lived under British or French mandate or colonial regimes. World War II dramatically weakened the European colonial powers and doubled nationalist fervor; with American support, this released the Arab world into independence. The last Franco-British effort to halt the process of Arab political emancipation from European colonial rule—their joint intervention in Egypt with Israel in 1956 after the nationalization of the Suez Canal—remained an episode that ended in failure, not least because it was undercut by the US administration of President Eisenhower.

After the European withdrawal during the 1940s and 1950s, the second phase of the Sykes–Picot order grew out of competition between the two superpowers in the context of the bipolar world order of the Cold War. That competition faded away after 1989. After the end of the Cold War and Saddam Hussein's invasion of Kuwait, US President George H. W. Bush made an attempt to comprehensively reorder the Middle East on the basis of a sustainable balance of power and international legitimacy: In contrast to the 2003 invasion, the United States-led intervention to liberate Kuwait from occupation and annexation by Iraq in 1991 kept strictly within the confines of the Westphalian order: the military alliance quickly defeated the Iraqi forces and pushed them out of Kuwait, but refrained from reordering the situation in Iraq itself through regime change. At that time, not only Republican hawks but also many Democratic internationalists in the United States argued that Bush should have ordered his troops to march on to Baghdad. He refused to do so, and thus clearly accepted the Westphalian principle for the regional order.

The successful liberation of Kuwait by an American-led, broad-based diplomatic and military coalition that included several Arab states also provided the opportunity for President Bush to declare the advent of a "new world order." By driving Iraq out of Kuwait, but accepting Saddam Hussein's hold on power in Baghdad, he had supported the existing states and their regional order; on that basis, he then tried to stabilize the situation by dealing with the core conflicts of the region through building a consensus with both regional powers and the then Soviet Union. At that time, the widely shared view was that the geo-political problems in the region would have to be dealt with first, starting with the Arab–Israeli and particularly the Israeli–Palestinian conflicts. That led to the Madrid Middle East Peace Conference and the following Israeli–Palestinian peace process. Revealingly, the United States and the Soviet Union *both* formally invited and chaired the Madrid conference.[4]

There was not enough political will to deal with the issues on an official interstate level, however, although Madrid was indirectly successful: it encouraged the secret track-two diplomacy that two years later led to the Oslo Agreement between Israel and the PLO, neither of whom wanted the whole region involved in the negotiations. For the degree of international support they required to go ahead, a small state like Norway was just fine; beyond that, both sides were much happier to deal with one another alone. Unfortunately, this preference did not stay that way. The Oslo Agreement, which was to be implemented within five years, remains unfulfilled to this day. By the time of

[4] The conference was co-chaired by the president of the United States, George H. W. Bush and Soviet leader Mikhail Gorbachev and attended by delegations from Israel, Syria, Egypt, and Lebanon, and a joint Jordanian–Palestinian delegation.

the agreement, the Soviet Union had fallen apart and President George H. W. Bush had failed to be re-elected. His successor Bill Clinton returned to a policy of keeping the Middle East at arm's length. When he finally took up the Israeli–Palestinian issue towards the end of his eight years in office, his push for a final settlement came too late.

The retreat of the great powers from the region would go on until 2003. Americans might see September 2001 as an important turning point, of course, and the invasion of Iraq in 2003 would be considered by them their reaction to 9/11. For the Arab world, however, which felt no responsibility for the terrorist attacks in the United States on that day in September 2001, the US invasion in Iraq 2003 was not so much an assault by the United States on one Arab country than on the Arab Middle Eastern order as such. For most of the Arab elites, even within countries that were considered pro-Western, the containment of Saddam Hussein's regime through a strong international sanctions regime was tolerable (despite real sympathy in other Arab countries for the Iraqi people and quite some profiteering from sanctions busting); regime change from outside, however, was seen as an unacceptable precedent.

2.2. The Transformation of 2011

The fundamental transformation of the Middle Eastern regional order took place in 2011 with what many then called the "Arab Spring" or the "Arab Uprisings." Not because they were successful (which they were largely not), but because people throughout the Arab world, including big, important Arab states like Egypt and Syria, started to look at domestic political issues, not least the autocratic and corrupt nature of the regimes, more than at the external conflicts that had long been used to mobilize societies and legitimize domestic political orders. In the course of events since 2011, with the revolts and revolutions more or less successful in Tunisia, failing in Egypt, and leading to civil wars in Libya, in Syria, and in Yemen, the Arab–Israeli conflict turned into a local conflict between Israelis and Palestinians. Not that it has come close to being resolved. On the contrary, new outbreaks of military violence and terrorism are likely as there does not seem to be an available political solution apparent that the political actors on both sides would be willing and able to implement. Israeli policymakers increasingly emphasize the virtues of conflict management rather than conflict resolution, and also see opportunities for Israel as the Israeli–Palestinian conflict no longer seems to stand in the way of improved relations, and even substantive security cooperation, between Israel and the monarchies in the Persian Gulf, governments in the Maghreb, and the new military regime in Egypt. This does not suggest that Arab leaders would openly or easily defend relations with Israel in their own countries.

Particularly if Israel was pushing for the establishment of official diplomatic relations, this would still be a hard sell to the public in most Arab countries. This does not preclude significant silent security cooperation between Israel and those countries, though. The year 2011 thus marks an important turning point in the Middle Eastern regional order, with the dominant pattern of conflict shifting away from an inter-state to an intra-state dimension within the Arab world. The old order has evaporated. Since the formation of the Arab Middle Eastern regional order in the post-Ottoman period and during World War I and its re-establishment under conditions of national independence in the post-World War II period, a few states, including Egypt, Syria, and at times Iraq, were the key actors that dominated Arab and Middle Eastern politics. Those states no longer dominate anything; in fact, some of them are not even able to control the dynamics of politics within their own countries. The American invasion in Iraq in 2003 somewhat paradoxically helped delay but also catalyze the demise of the old regional order. It brought about the destruction by external military intervention of one of those model authoritarian, bureaucratic Arab states: Iraq. By spreading fears about a repeat of such an external intervention, however, it also helped to stabilize authoritarian regimes in other Arab states, rather than promoting domestic restructuring and reforms. Ironically, such reforms had been demanded rather forcefully at around the same time by Arab intellectuals, development economists, and other professionals in the first Arab Human Development Report, which received considerable attention and triggered a broad debate.[5] The report identified serious shortcomings, such as insufficient participation of two large societal groups, women and youth, in economic activities and political decision-making, authoritarian governance, serious shortcomings in education, and other deficiencies as major causes for the bleak picture of human development in the Arab world. None of this was corrected, of course, by the American invasion of Iraq. Instead, anti-Americanism and anti-imperialist emotions were strengthened; the major beneficiaries were Islamist extremists.

The consequences of the demise of the old order are far-reaching. The regional order—which is often called the Sykes–Picot order because it was largely drawn by French and British diplomats during and after World War I—was a rather stable system; its member states and borders lasted for almost one hundred years, with only minor adjustments. Of course, there were wars and civil wars within that order, but if one compares that Arab Middle Eastern regional order to what happened in Europe during the same period, the relative stability of the Arab Middle Eastern regional order is striking. Even

[5] United Nations Development Programme, Arab Fund for Economic and Social Development, *Arab Human Development Report 2002*, available at http://hdr.undp.org/sites/default/files/rbas_ahdr2002_en.pdf.

the Islamic revolution in Iran 1979 did not undermine that order fundamentally, although it may have contributed to weakening some of the Arab regimes. The year 2011, however, overturned the old order because the political dynamics became local and took some of its most active states out of the equation. This destabilized the regional order from below, as it were, exposing the internal weaknesses of many of its states. These states had almost one hundred years to consolidate, or more than fifty years if one counts from their full independence from colonial powers after World War II. What emerged were bureaucratic authoritarian regimes like Egypt, Syria, and Iraq that were strongly centralized, highly securitized, and did indeed function as real states. These regimes were able to penetrate societies to a large extent, made significant progress (largely thanks to direct or indirect oil rents) in developing the economic and social infrastructure of their countries, and even displayed remarkable capabilities for interfering with their neighbors. Consider Syria's intervention in Lebanon, Egypt's in Yemen, or Iraq's even less successful attempt to annex Kuwait. What was lacking was a stable social contract between the regime elites and societies. Astonishingly, perhaps, most of the monarchies (Bahrain being the exception) did much better in weathering the storm of popular discontent that shook the region in 2011, than the increasingly "hereditary" republics.

3. CHARACTERISTICS OF THE MIDDLE EASTERN REGIONAL ORDER

3.1. Principles and Norms

One important norm for the old Middle Eastern regional order was the notion of one Arab nation that had common enemies, particularly Israel, but to some degree also non-Arab Iran. During the 1950s, 1960s, and into the 1970s, pan-Arab nationalism served as a source of legitimacy for a variety of Arab nationalist leaders, some of whom toyed with various unity projects between individual states, all under the ideological norm of "One [eternal] Arab nation." In practice, however, the Westphalian norm of national sovereignty for the individual Arab states prevailed, regardless of whether a regime's ideology was Arab nationalism, Islamism, or some form of hereditary monarchical secularism as, for example, in Jordan or Kuwait. Arab nationalism was repeatedly used to justify political and military interventions in other Arab states. At the same time, all states and rulers made clear that they would—where possible—ward off any such "brotherly" interference into their domestic affairs. Inter-Arab cooperation had to be voluntary, whatever the League of

Arab States had written into its Charter, and the only form of inter-Arab cooperation that really functioned reliably was the cooperation between the ministries of the Interior and their respective security agencies. All Arab states were security states—regime security was broadly considered the core national interest. The "authoritarian bureaucratic security state" became the de facto norm in the Middle East, with the exception of Israel and, for other reasons, Lebanon.

Ordinary people would realize that much of the official rhetoric on Arab unity was just that. If nothing else, significant restrictions on inter-Arab mobility made clear that Arabs had not become the citizens of a community of Arab states, but remained the subjects of individual states and regimes. In addition to other issues and grievances that were raised in the uprisings of 2011, activists often pointed at the gaps between the ideological claim that all Arabs belonged to one nation and the fact that it was much more difficult for young people from, e.g., Egypt, to get the necessary visa to travel to Morocco or to Tunisia than to travel to Europe. An ideological norm—pan-Arab unity—had simply moved out of touch with the social realities that the local people experienced in their daily lives. Yet national sovereignty and non-interference were hardly more credible as norms: some Arab governments practiced interference in other Arab countries extensively, such as Syria in Lebanon. Syrian political leaders used to speak of Lebanon as the soft underbelly of their country, where Israel could invade or conspiracies could be hatched against Syria's political order. In practice, the Syrian leadership left no doubt that it was Syria's national interest that defined their policies in the neighborhood, not some broader pan-Arab commitment. Regime survival and stability were the top priorities.

This was very much the case in other Arab states too. Commonly, regimes would use their extensive internal security forces to suppress dissent, but they would not hesitate to deploy the military, either. In 1982, Syria's president Hafiz al-Assad, father of the present ruler, quelled a Muslim Brotherhood-led uprising by overwhelming military force—the crackdown in the city of Hama alone may have cost up to 20,000 lives (some estimates go beyond that, but there are no reliable figures). Around the same time, comparable events on a smaller scale happened elsewhere, such as the Islamic extremist take-over of the Grand Mosque in Mecca (1979), in which the Saudi monarchy had no qualms in using the full panoply of military means, including the support of French special forces, to flush the rebels out. Iraqi strongman Saddam Hussein also repeatedly used military means to break down uprisings in the Shi'ite south and in the Kurdish north. All this was tacitly accepted by the other Arab states and by the international community against the background of continuing hostility and repeated wars between Arab states and their non-Arab neighbors, particularly Israel and Iran.

3.2. Interactions

The dominant interactions in this regional order were inter-state in nature, with a heavy emphasis on political and security issues, both cooperative and non-cooperative. Compared to the European regional order, for example, transnational social interactions were rather thin and largely confined to labor migration. In the Arab Middle Eastern regional order, even in the economic and social realms, state-led interactions dominate. For decades, much of the investment in industries and development projects in Syria, in Egypt, Tunisia, or Morocco came from the oil-producing countries, mainly from the development funds of Saudi Arabia, Kuwait, the Emirates and, to a lesser extent, Libya, but not from private business. Financially weaker Arab states would sometimes actively engage in a form of foreign-policy rent seeking. For a long time, Syria's self-proclaimed role as protector of Lebanon and defender of the Arab cause in its confrontation with Israel certainly paid out; so did Egypt's pretentions to act as the guardian of Gulf Arab security.

The most important economic flows within the regional order, however, came from intra-regional labor migration, mostly into the Gulf monarchies, Libya, and Iraq. The flow of remittances has given strong transnational underpinnings to linkages within the regional order. The people involved, however, were always skeptically eyed by the security apparatuses. Thus, the up to 500,000 Egyptian "work migrants" in Saudi Arabia engendered fears among Saudi authorities that this community (whose members spoke the same language and thus could easily build ties with local society) could become a risk to the stability of the political system in Saudi Arabia. At the same time, the authorities of the sending countries also critically eyed their own temporary out-migrants. The security bureaucracies worried about the ideas those people would bring back once they returned home. The system of transnational flows of remittances was therefore underpinned by strong economic and social interests, but also overshadowed by the paranoia of security agencies. Maltreatment of migrant workers also at times caused conflicts between states, as when Iraq, having imported several hundred thousand Egyptians as agricultural workers, mistreated them badly after the end of the Iran–Iraq War in 1988. When Iraqi soldiers were coming home from the front, the Egyptian workers were driven out to Egypt; some were even murdered. There were similar incidents between Libya and Egypt. Overall, labor migration in the Arab world therefore was a source of transnational contacts and linkages but also of inter-state frictions.

In sum, while the state order remained starkly Westphalian and authoritarian, economic asymmetries and interdependencies did create strong transnational links in the form of money flows and migrant workers. Labor migration also helped to spread a selective form of knowledge about one another between the people of different Arab states, not always positively connoted, however. Private business remained limited as long as most of the labor-exporting states maintained largely state-controlled economies. Since the beginning of this century, investments from wealthy private entrepreneurs in the Gulf in poorer Arab countries have significantly increased. Civil society exchanges have mainly been limited to a small intellectual elite. Popular culture—particularly Egyptian and Lebanese music, then movies and TV soaps from Egypt and Syria—traveled more easily. Of course, there is religious tourism, i.e., the pilgrimage to Mecca and Medina, which brings large numbers of Arabs, as well as Muslims from other parts of the world, to Saudi Arabia. Given its ideological, political, and security dimension, however, pilgrimage (not only to the holy shrines in Saudi Arabia but also, for example, to Shi'ite places of worship in Syria) has largely remained a state-organized affair.

4. AMERICA'S DISASTROUS INVASION OF IRAQ, "DEFENSIVE GEO-POLITICS," AND THE RETURN OF GREAT POWERS INTO THE MIDDLE EAST

Over the last twenty-five years, there has been a remarkable change in the way the Middle Eastern order has interacted with the outside world: states within the regional order have repeatedly tried to drag great powers into their local conflicts. During the Sykes–Picot phases of the regional order, outside powers had pushed into the region in response to the power vacuum created by the decay of the Ottoman Empire. Great power involvement in the region then continued, as we saw, until the end of the presidency of George H. W. Bush. For a decade or so following the end of the Cold War, the great powers largely tried to keep aloof from the Middle East. Power holders in the regional states, however, remained interested in keeping external players involved, trying to lever international political or military prowess to their own benefit in conflicts with neighbors.

4.1. America's Disastrous Intervention in Iraq and its Impact

From 2003 to 2008, we have seen a return of proactive great power involvement in the region under President George W. Bush, the son of G. H. W. Bush. The results were devastating not only for Iraq, but also for America's standing and influence in the region and the world. The glaring lack of success of American power play and the election of Barack Obama in 2008 initiated the most recent and last phase of the Sykes–Picot order before its dissolution. This phase was characterized by what we call defensive geo-politics—the reluctance of Western powers and Russia to get involved in the Middle East. Defensive geo-politics implies that great powers deal with the geo-political conflicts in the region, but rather from afar (or, literally, from the air), trying to contain what they see as risks emanating from the region rather than engineer political processes as the United States had done so disastrously in 2003. The logic of defensive geo-politics is about trying to prevent things from happening rather than shaping developments, and to work through proxies rather than through direct engagement.[6] All the different variants of defensive geo-politics that we can observe today share one leitmotif: Don't enter to determine political outcomes; work with the players that are there. Support them from outside to the extent you are prepared to, but otherwise try to hold the region at arm's length.

Except for the hastily conceived intervention in Libya, this reasoning still dominated Western (as well as Russian or Chinese) approaches during the so-called Arab Spring uprisings, sometimes justified with the somewhat cynical view that conflicts in the region needed to burn themselves out and that there were no good guys on any side. It was heavily shaped, of course, by the experiences of the United States in Iraq, of European countries in Afghanistan and, post 2011, of *both* European and American governments in Libya. Russia shared this attitude; they had learned their lessons in Afghanistan even earlier.

4.2. The Return of Interventionism

France first broke with that policy line by leading off the Libya intervention in 2011, taking other NATO partners and regional states along. In the following years, states from within and from outside the region began to intervene, directly or indirectly, in what became the most violent conflict in the region to this day, the war in Syria. In 2015, Saudi Arabia and the United Arab Emirates began their continued military intervention in Yemen. Although Syria is no longer an active player in regional politics, let alone a state that dominates others, it still lies at the core of the regional order, even—or particularly—of a dysfunctional order. One after the other, regional and international powers became directly involved in Syria: Iran has been present from 2012 with its own military "advisors," as well as through Lebanese, Iraqi, and Afghan militias. Russia sent in its air force and some ground troops in September 2015 when it feared that the Assad regime would otherwise lose Damascus and probably fall. The Obama administration had already started bombing the so-called Islamic State (IS) in the east of Syria, as well as in Iraq. Initially, this

[6] Chancellor Merkel has called her version of defensive geo-politics "Ertüchtigungspolitik"; it involves the upgrading, training, and arming of local allies such as the Kurdish Peshmerga forces.

could still be seen as an exercise in defensive geo-politics. After all, the United States was conducting its operation from far away and at high altitude. Since 2016 at the latest, Washington also has military advisors in Syria—an estimated 2,000 troops by the end of 2017—mainly to build and support the Kurdish-led Syrian Democratic Forces which became efficient partners in fighting the IS on the ground. Following the military defeat of the IS, at least as a self-declared "state" with control over large parts of Syria, the Trump administration began to justify its presence in Syria with the need both to stabilize areas liberated from the IS, and to deny Iran an extended influence in Syria.

Meanwhile, the wave of refugees that flooded from Syria to Europe had woken up the Europeans. They realized that the war in Syria could not simply be left to burn out by itself. Indeed, Syria did not implode; it exploded. The effects of this explosion affected Syria's neighbors and the countries of Europe not only in the form of human beings fleeing war and destruction. Europe also had to cope with the migration of hundreds of its own citizens who would join the Syrian war as foreign fighters and potentially come back from the region to commit terrorist acts on European soil.

5. CAN A SUSTAINABLE REGIONAL ORDER BE REBUILT?

5.1. Hesitant America, Inept Europe

Following George H. W. Bush's initiative in 1991, the United States did not undertake any real effort to create regional order in the Middle East. Rather, Washington supported sub-regional initiatives such as the Gulf Cooperation Council. The six participating monarchies share the same ideology, possess very similar political systems, and find themselves in the same geo-political environment; they thus face the same risks and should therefore find it easy to cooperate more closely among themselves—and with the USA to which they have been bound by a long history of common interests. Beyond that, Washington provided some support for sub-regional cooperation in the Maghreb. Then, after 2001, much of the US endeavor in the region was taken up by efforts to coordinate the fight against global terrorism.

Remarkably, Europe has not undertaken any serious efforts on its own to create regional order in the Middle East in the last decade and a half. The EU pursued economic cooperation with the region, of course, through the kind of arrangements that the EU has long pursued in its neighborhood: association agreements that will tie adjacent regions and their states to Europe through various preferential trade and aid arrangements. In the context of the Barcelona initiative of 1995, there had indeed been an attempt to create a regional dimension to this kind of neighborhood policy. This also included efforts to promote trade agreements within the Middle East: the so-called Agadir process was to deliver a free-trade agreement among the Arab states that could have included Israel at some point. This initiative failed because Europe underestimated the geo-political dimension of Middle Eastern conflicts and thought, somewhat naively, that if states could cooperate economically, their geo-political conflicts would fade eventually.

Efforts to build up a sustainable regional order from outside were thus rather feeble until 2003, and then distinctly counter-productive from 2003 to 2008. The authoritarian security states that dominated in the region, moreover, are probably particularly badly equipped to cooperate internationally. While democracies have a relatively high capacity for international cooperation,[7] the Middle Eastern security states are run by regimes that are unable to delegate power within their own countries and distrust their peoples. They will therefore find it hard if not impossible to delegate parts of their power upwards to cooperative regional or international governance mechanisms and very difficult to trust other regimes.

5.2. The Regional Order: Rotting from Below

Today, the Middle Eastern order is a defunct order that contains several more or less defunct states, including Libya and Yemen, but also core states like Syria and, to a lesser degree, Iraq. The system became defunct only recently, in 2011, but this is not to say that it was a functioning regional order before. The relative stability of the system has been noted; but it was a form of false stability in the way that authoritarian states seem stable up to the moment when they cease to be so. Genuine stability would allow for change and adaptation and thereby make systems sustainable. An order that is not sustainable is not an effective order. If we compare the Middle East with the European regional order, the latter seems remarkably stable and successful during the second half of the twentieth century, but it was indeed remarkably tumultuous and unstable during its first half, with dramatic changes of borders and large flows of migrants. The Arab Middle Eastern order certainly also had its crises and catastrophes, such as the waves of Palestinian refugees driven out of what was geographically Palestine after the establishment of the state of Israel, and of Jewish refugees driven out of Arab countries. Overall, however, we have had a comparatively stable system, despite the fact that it was built on

[7] Bruce Russet, *Grasping the Democratic Peace: Principles for a Post-Cold War World*, Princeton, NJ: Princeton University Press, 1993.

states with largely artificial borders that observers initially might have easily assumed to be unsustainable: After all, those states and boundaries were imposed by foreign powers and fiercely contested by nationalist movements. In the core Arab states in the Mashreq, the Arab East, in Syria, Iraq, Jordan, Lebanon, and also Saudi Arabia, three or four generations of political actors were socialized into perceiving the regional order in which they lived as illegitimate, and the nation-state they grew up in as having no right to exist because it really should be part of a bigger, pan-Arab state. Despite that, most of the individual states that make up this order have gained a high degree of legitimacy, internal struggles over power and political order notwithstanding. Today, in 2017, you could ask almost any Syrian (at least in the non-Kurdish parts of the country) what territorial form a future, peaceful Syria should have: the answer would very likely be the Syria as we see it on the map today. In other words, Syrians in the majority agree that they do not want their country to be divided into several mini states, nor do they want to attach it, or parts of it, to other countries.

The stability of the regional order was gradually undermined and eventually destroyed in the second half of the twentieth century by political stagnation in many of its constituent states. The challenge for the future will be how "better states" with better governance can be built within the given territorial borders. Regarding the stability of the system of states and borders, the Sykes–Picot order may have been a great success. Its ability to provide for the well-being of its people was quite low, however. While its legitimacy may have grown over time, the effectiveness of the Arab states and their regional order declined. Arguably, the nature of the political systems was the main factor in preventing societies from developing their potential.

It is instructive to compare economic performance and tertiary education indicators for the Arab world with East Asia in the 1950s and today. At that earlier time, the Arab world was far ahead in terms of education standards and of per capita GDP. Since then, both regions have experienced phases of foreign military intervention and war; states in both regions have been mostly governed by authoritarian dictatorial regimes. Yet in East Asia, regimes and elites recognized the importance of education, and societies were able to overcome the deficiencies of their national and regional orders and develop their countries economically, socially, and eventually politically.

5.3. The Arab League: Deficiencies of Institutionalized Regional Cooperation

Nothing comparable happened in the Middle East. One reason was the context: processes that comprehensively civilize societies can take place sustainably only if their regional environment permits a political take-off. Yet today, a society of states in a meaningful sense has hardly ever existed in the Middle East. States prefer to cultivate unpredictability to foster their national interests, rather than work together to create a more predictable regional environment. The Arab League has largely been an ideological project, driven by the popularity of Arab nationalism that peaked in the mid-1960s. At times, it was dominated by a few states driving the Arab League forward, even if that involved bending the rules, as in the case of support for the American intervention to drive Saddam Hussein out of Kuwait. In those instances, states with dissenting views were simply marginalized. Most of the time, however, the rule of unanimity in decision-making paralyzed the organization. It was therefore probably much more legitimate than it was effective. (There is an interesting contrast here with the European Union, which seems to be less legitimate than it is effective.) Increasingly, however, people in the region grew disillusioned with their governments' rhetoric about the grand common Arab cause: they wanted solutions to their own problems and demanded that their leaders focus on the development of their own nation-states.

Whatever legitimacy the Arab League enjoyed originally was damaged when people realized that it did not deliver. It never fulfilled its promises to the Palestinians about the liberation of Palestine or about international diplomacy to settle the conflict with Israel. It was unwilling or unable to resist foreign and regional intervention, as in the cases of Lebanon, Kuwait, Iraq, or, most recently, Libya, Syria, and Yemen. It failed in all the cases of Arab–Israeli wars. Arguably the only exception was the October war of 1973, when the Arab oil producers threw their weight behind Egypt's and Syria's struggle and the Arab states were able to gain at least some initial battlefield success.[8]

Nor was the League able to respond to the high hopes in inter-Arab cooperation. Many Arabs expected that the enormous oil revenues of some Arab countries would be used for the benefit of the entire Arab region, making life better for everybody. The notion that the oil resources in the region belonged to the Arab people as a whole, and that the Gulf States should therefore share their oil income, was very popular in Egypt, Syria, Jordan, and Lebanon. Unsurprisingly, it was not popular at all in Saudi Arabia and in other major oil-producing countries. Elites were willing to be generous to their poorer brethren, but decisions about the degree of such generosity were to remain their sovereign right. Here again, the norm of pan-Arab unity, the idea that all Arabs belonged to one nation whose resources should be shared collectively, fell on the very hard ground of nation-state interests. Yet the idea keeps coming back: In intellectual debates in the Arab world, there are always voices that try to resuscitate pan-Arab nationalism in one form or another—be it authoritarian or democratic. During the upheavals in the Arab

[8] Hanns W. Maull, *Oil and Influence: The Oil Weapon Examined*, Adelphi Paper No. 117, London: IISS, 1975.

world from 2011 onwards, it was fascinating to observe how easily slogans traveled from the Maghreb to the Mashreq and back. While civil society interaction had, as we observed above, not at all been strong before, suddenly the same slogans were heard all over the Arab world, one movement using quotes from the other. As the wave of revolts began in Tunisia, slogans that had been invented there were used by demonstrators in Libya and Egypt and fired at protesters in Yemen. The boys who triggered the first heavy-handed reaction of the Syrian state were using slogans that they had seen on television broadcasts from Tunisia and Egypt. In this way, the enthusiastic atmosphere of the first days and months of the Arab uprisings in 2011, for a short while gave the idea of Arab unity a new, democratic lease of life. People were defining their own collective identity once more as that of Arabs sharing the same grievances and ideas. In contrast to the official Arab nationalist discourse, which still focused on external enemies, public anger was vented at corrupt domestic elites. Some regimes reacted with brutal force to suppress such sentiments, others—notably Morocco, Jordan, and Oman—tried and managed to deflect the anger with more or less substantial political reforms. The uprisings did not bring about any fundamental change of the political systems, or the regional order. But the drama of 2011 demonstrated that the idea of a common purpose of the Arab peoples remained revivable, and may again be revived in the future, most likely in different forms and by new actors.

6. THE MIDDLE EAST IN WORLD ORDER

Today, the relevance of the Middle Eastern order for the rest of the world comes by default. It is defunct, and a defunct order creates problems and exacerbates disputes for other, adjacent orders. It invites outside interventions which of course are driven by the self-interests of the intervening powers rather than by the interests of the region itself. A defunct regional order creates fears that can lead to defensive geo-politics, to an attitude that would ideally have the outside world build a wall around the region and leave it to itself.

In fact, a defunct regional order resembles, in its inability to deal with problems peacefully and competently, a failed state. Yet as is often the case with failed states, the export of the Middle East's oil and gas resources continues to function surprisingly well. The geo-political relevance of those resources has been diminished, however, as the importance of the Middle East for world energy supplies has declined significantly. This is particularly true for oil exports, but also for transit routes. The Suez Canal, to mention but one example, no longer has the importance it used to have before big container ships could easily sail around the African continent. Yes, the Suez Canal is still there and yes, Gulf oil will continue to be relevant because its production is much cheaper than that of most other oil sources. As long as the world burns oil for energy, therefore, the Gulf States will export it. Yet its relevance for Western energy security that it used to have in the 1970s and 1980s has diminished significantly. This applies not only to the United States which has become largely self-sufficient in energy, but also for Europe. Disruptions in Middle East oil supplies nevertheless still can have a significant impact on international oil markets. Abundant Middle Eastern oil exports can also be a real pain for producers like Russia if Middle Eastern oil continues to remain as cheap as it is today, in late 2016. Moreover, oil is still used as a geo-economic weapon, for example in the conflict between Saudi Arabia and Iran. Middle Eastern oil and gas will continue to be attractive sources of energy for China and Asia-Pacific. Yet it probably has lost its utility as a weapon with which the Arab oil could be used to exert pressure on the rest of the world.[9]

Today, the relevance of the region for the international order mainly lies in the threats that we perceive as emanating from it, and from the region's geo-political location at the crossroads between continents and religiously defined transnational communities. If it were not so close to Europe, we would probably be much less interested in it. For example, we might not feel the need to try and help improve the situation in a country like Egypt, that is not very responsive to initiatives from Europe; or to continue working on a settlement for the Israeli–Palestinian conflict where the responsiveness of the protagonists themselves is also very limited, to put it mildly. Yet as the Middle East is so close to Europe, we ignore developments there at our peril.

As for the Middle East's impact on functional partial orders, the nuclear non-proliferation regime stands out: it has certainly been affected heavily by negative spillovers from the Middle East. This includes the nuclear programs of Israel, Pakistan (though related to the South Asian rather than the Middle Eastern conflict system), and Iran. Iranian nuclear ambitions may have been contained with the help of the Iran nuclear agreement (Joint Comprehensive Plan of Action or JCPOA), which can strengthen the nuclear Non-Proliferation Treaty if it is honored by all signatories. More broadly speaking, a badly governed Arab Middle Eastern region can create enormous problems throughout the world. We have already mentioned terrorism, migration, and geo-economic threats as challenges that will require broad international cooperation to be dealt with successfully.

The Middle East also connects the Mediterranean basin with countries around the Indian and the Atlantic Oceans. If Africa finally were to take off, a badly governed Middle East would almost certainly hamper and slow down

[9] Ibid.; see also, Edward L. Morse and Amy Myers Jaffe, OPEC—Can the Cartel Survive another Fifty Years?, in Jan H. Kalicki and David L. Goldwyn (eds.), *Energy and Security: Foreign Policy Strategies for a World in Transition*, 2nd edn, Washington and Baltimore: Wilson Center Press/Johns Hopkins University Press, 2013, ch. 5.

that development. Thus by location, by sheer size, and by means of its population growth, the Middle East will retain a large conflict potential and remain a region of considerable significance for world order. Will it also remain a region without any functioning regional order? At present, unfortunately, that seems quite likely. Any change would probably have to start at the very bottom of regional order by rebuilding communities and states, then subregions. Only after viable national orders and the will to cooperate between them have re-emerged, could a new, more effective regional order for the Middle East as a whole become possible once more.[10]

[10] This chapter is based on an interview with Volker Perthes by Hanns W. Maull.

8

East Asia's Evolving Regional Order and its Global Implications

Charles E. Morrison

1. INTRODUCTION

For those who fear that the "liberal international order" is decaying or fragmenting, East Asia raises two kinds of issues. One concerns Asia "regional order." Is there one? If so, what is the nature of this order and how enduring might it be? If not, will the various conflicts within East Asia result in destabilizing cold or hot conflict? Because of the region's demographic and growing economic and political weight in the world, a second set of issues concerns the impact rising East Asia may have in shaping the global order. Does the rise of Asia drive the nails into the coffin of the liberal economic order? Or can East Asia even come to its rescue?

It is, of course, impossible to answer such questions with any certainty. This chapter makes only guesses about the future of the regional and global order based on the current outlook, trends, and aspirations. With respect to the regional order, it argues that underlying trends are causing East Asia to become more rather than less stable. But there are significant international relations downside risks, notably over shifting power relationships and Chinese and American policies. As for the second set of issues, East Asia undoubtedly will continue to exercise growing weight in global society. On the whole, East Asia participation in international regimes reinforces their global character, but reduces like-mindedness, shifting the emphasis perhaps more toward order rather than liberalism. But East Asia, even China, so far projects no alternative ordering principles.

It is useful to bear in mind that the values associated with the "liberal international order" and developed over centuries in the Western world were not deeply embedded elsewhere.[1] With Asia's rise, a truly global international order might well be emerging from it, but it will be a little different.

2. REGIONAL TRENDS

Reviewing the broader Asian security order at the beginning of the last decade, Muthiah Alagappa concluded that "Asia has become a more secure and predictable region"[2] and that the regional security order "is not fragile."[3] He did not discount the region's security challenges, but pointed out that Asia had then avoided war for more than two decades, that few states faced existential threats, and that although instrumental, the regional order was increasingly based on an accepted normative base.

These observations mostly remain valid. There has still been no military conflict and there are today even fewer serious internal conflicts.[4] Nevertheless, increased questions about Sino-American relations and the future of both countries' policies and the status quo in the Korean peninsula have augmented feelings of insecurity. Let us examine, first, some of the key longer-term trends affecting the region and their impacts. These trends include the changing intra-regional distribution of power, demographic change, consolidation of the nation-state at the domestic level, economic and human integration, and regional institution-building.

2.1. Distribution of Power

Historically, the East Asia system consisted of one heavy-weight—China—placed geographically and economically in the center of the region, with smaller kingdoms and local lords mostly to the east and south interacting with it.[5] It was only after the display of the superiority of Western military technology in the first Opium War of 1839–42 that China went into steep decline and the Sino-centric world and the "tribute system" associated with it

[1] Adda B. Bozeman, *Politics and Culture in International History*, 2nd edn, Piscataway, NJ: Transaction Publishers, 2002, pp. 513–22ff.

[2] Muthiah Alagappa (ed.), *Asian Security Order: Instrumental and Normative Features*, Stanford, CA: Stanford University Press, 2002, pp. xi and 3. In contrast to this essay, Alagappa's Asia included South Asia.

[3] Ibid., p. 572.

[4] The US Pacific Command is the only US regional command that has not been involved in military fighting within its area of responsibility since the end of the Vietnam War.

[5] Even its foreign rulers, the Mongols and the Manchus, were Sinicized and acted internationally as if they were Chinese emperors.

came to an end. China's recovery in recent decades to be the dominant regional power is thus not an aberration, but a restoration of a historical norm, at least for the resident powers. By 2010, China's GDP surpassed that of Japan, a country with a tenth its population, and now substantially exceeds it. The disparity between East Asia's largest economy and its second largest will only grow, while the gap between Chinese and American power has greatly narrowed.

With China's recovery and what Xi Jinping calls "national rejuvenation," there is a natural tendency for China to reassert its central role in an East Asia system, with consequences for its neighbors.[6] The difference today from the historical norm, however, is that East Asia is part of a global system and that the smaller nations of Asia have had an alternative in their relationships with the United States. Increasingly China resents this, testing US alliances, discouraging close US relations with the smaller states, and suggesting that the United States is an outsider playing a disruptive regional role and promoting containment of China. The other states are torn between trying to reinforce their American ties to counterbalance China or to accommodate it.[7] Uncertainty regarding US policy, especially after the election of Donald Trump as president with a Republican majority in both houses of Congress, makes this even more acute. The adjustment to this changing distribution of power is probably the most difficult challenge facing East Asia's new regional order since neither the Sino-centric model nor a US-centric alliance system is likely to be an acceptable basis for the future order. The other trends in the region, however, generally favor order over conflict.

2.2. Demographic Change

Demographically, East and Southeast Asia account for 30 percent of world population, but the sharp decline in fertility and the aging of populations has drastically changed the demographic complexion of most Asian societies. So has rapid advance of urbanization. In Northeast Asia, demographic changes that took a century or more to unfold in Europe have been telescoped into three to four decades. Japan, South Korea, Taiwan, Singapore, and urban parts of other countries are experiencing fertility rates significantly below replacement level. This is beginning to shrink labor forces and greatly increase the ratio of elderly dependents. Japan, whose population is declining in absolute

[6] See, in particular, *Secure a Decisive Victory in Building a Moderately Prosperous Society in All Respects and Strive for the Great Success of Socialism with Chinese Characteristics for a New Era*, Report of October 18, 2017 to the 19th Congress of the Chinese Community Party. English text available at http://news.xinhuanet.com/english/special/2017-11/03/c_136725942.htm.

[7] For example, the Philippines shifted from the former strategy under President Benigno Aquino to the latter strategy under his successor, Rodrigo Duterte, who took office in June 2016.

terms, is at the forefront: by mid-century, more than a fifth of its population will be above age seventy-five. Japan will then have become humanity's first super-elderly society, while South Korea, Singapore, and Taiwan will be about a decade or so behind. China, too, has begun to experience an absolute decline in the size of its labor force, and in response has shifted from a "one-child" to a "two-child" policy, a move unlikely to affect population growth significantly.[8]

These changes clearly have enormous social implications for tax systems, social security systems, and healthcare, but their implications for international relations have not been carefully studied. One might expect that older, highly urbanized societies would be more risk averse and protective of their scarcer youth, their property, and the infrastructure accumulated in cities. On the other side, there are also fears that the heavier burden of supporting the elderly, combined with other factors such as growing income inequalities and gender imbalances, could create high rates of stress and domestic anomie that could spark greater nationalism and worsen regional relations.[9]

2.3. Consolidation of the Nation-State

As Asia has modernized, introducing national educational systems, military service, parliaments, national media, and other institutions, the Asian nation-state system has been consolidating. "Nation-state" is a European, not an Asian conception, but like the European conception of national sovereignty, it has been widely embraced in Asia. Some countries, notably Japan and Korea, have long established national identities, based on common ethnicity, language, and culture. For them, political unity is the norm.[10] Others, including China, Vietnam, and Thailand, have large majority populations for whom again political unity is a norm, but not without challenge from territorially

[8] Cai Fang and Lu Yang suggest relaxation of the one-child policy will boost fertility by about 0.2 percent. Cai Fang and Lu Yang, Take-Off, Persistence, and Sustainability: The Demographic Factor in Chinese Growth, East Asia Bureau of Economic Research, Working Paper 96, 2015, available at http://papers.ssrn.com/sol3/papers.cfm?abstract_id=2808296.

[9] Neil Howe and Richard Jackson make this point but argue that it may be bad for international order as the more developed countries will have less resource and will to protect themselves against a more disorderly developing world. On China, they suggest a "massive age wave" could slow growth and precipitate a political crisis. Neil Howe and Richard Jackson, Global Aging and the Crisis of the 2020s, *Current History* 110:732 (January 2011), pp. 20–5, available at https://csis-prod.s3.amazonaws.com/s3fs-public/legacy_files/files/publication/110104_gai_jackson.pdf. Others have been concerned about the domestic social impact of a rising male to female ratio in China, arguing it could spill over into foreign relations. See Andrea den Boer and Valerie Hudson, The Security Risks of China's Abnormal Demographics, *Washington Post*, April 30, 2014. A similar bulge in the male–female ratio in South Korea has already mostly closed.

[10] Now divided, Korea has been a single kingdom during most of the past millennium. This legacy makes its current division less likely to endure.

based minorities. In these cases, as well as for the almost entirely colonially constructed countries of the Philippines, Malaysia, and Indonesia, building national identity entirely on an ethnic, cultural, or religious base is highly problematic. Elites therefore seek alternatives in more modern cultural elements (such as the spread of a national language as in Indonesia) or the characteristics of civic society (for example, Singapore, which fosters pride in civic institutions such as the education system, healthcare, and quality of governance).

While the region contains both old and new nations, state structures and their guiding principles are all generally quite new: most constitutions and modern political institutions date from the mid-1940s or later and are not fully accepted. In many instances, fundamental political issues are still contested. These may include independence of the courts, the role of the military and of religion, the scope of individual rights, mechanisms of accountability, and the distribution of authority between local, regional, and central governments. Some of these issues have the potential to fracture the body politic, and unstable states would make for unstable regional order.

So far, however, nation- and state-building has been relatively successful, especially over the longer-term. Most states are internally stable. The region-wide respect for the norms of sovereignty and non-interference to guide state behavior has supported this consolidation. Thus, no state overtly supports dissident or separatist groups that challenge the established territorial status quo or the internal political order of another state.[11] Internally, most states have demonstrated some ability to incorporate rising social forces and minorities in national political life. There has also been a continuing slow extension and improvement of government services, including in minority areas.

Sub-national identities based on ethnicity, history, language/dialect, or simply geography and circumstances (such as in Okinawa), may remain strong, but gradually become local elements within the national framework, rather than the basis for secessionism. Political parties in South Korea, Taiwan, and Thailand, for example, have regional bases but aim for national control. Taiwan's ambiguous status is a potential challenge to the regional order, but China has little incentive to force this issue as long as the Taiwanese do not, and there is a consensus in Taiwan not to. The only successful secession in recent East Asian history has been East Timor, which took place when Indonesia was in transition. Virtually everywhere else secessionism is at low ebb, confined to specific localities or subgroups that are often seeking better treatment or autonomy rather than full independence.

[11] This was not always the case: China frequently was engaged in domestic politics of neighboring countries in ancient history as well as the 1950s and 1960s when it supported communist insurgencies in Southeast Asia, and Vietnam, until an even later period, was active in the politics of Cambodia and Laos.

2.4. Economic Interdependence and Human Interactions

Rapid economic development in East Asia has also been associated with economic integration and vastly increased cross-national interaction. Modern economies have become highly interdependent both with each other and with the rest of the world, as countries and corporations have taken advantage of the relatively open international economic order. Despite considerable differences in development patterns, certain common features appear. These include emphasis on manufacturing in the early stages of development, high savings, and integration into the international economy. China was a latecomer, but followed a similar trajectory, with trade still accounting for about 40 percent of its GDP, a high share for an economy of its size.[12]

The share of intra-regional to total East Asian trade rose remarkably from about 37 percent in 1980 to 55 percent a quarter of a century later, with almost all of that growth resulting from components trade in manufactured goods that reflected the growth of regional production networks.[13] This puts the percentage of intra-regional trade above that within North America, although still below that within the EU. Unlike the other two regions, however, a very high share, almost half, of East Asian final manufactured products serve markets outside the region. Interdependence should have a positive impact on the regional order in that it raises the costs of conflict (but does not necessarily prevent them), builds international networks based on common interests, and helps drive the development of institutions, norms, and rules to advance these interests.

With economic growth, interdependence, urbanization, and electronic forms of social interactions, non-governmental, people-to-people international interactions in business, education, the arts, and tourism have also increased astronomically over the past quarter century, developing a pattern that looks more like the human connectivity within Europe and North America. With the exception of North Korea, people easily traverse routes that were once complicated, dangerous, or completely blocked by political barriers. This has contributed to a much denser network of air routes connecting not only capitals, but also second-tier cities with each other. Other physical infrastructure has yet to catch up, but there is enormous investment in connectivity—roads, railways, pipelines, fiber optic cables, and port facilities. One can envisage in twenty or thirty years a connectivity pattern more similar to that in North America.

[12] The World Bank has this figure above 60 percent in the 2005–7 period. See World Bank, Trade (% of GDP), http://data.worldbank.org/indicator/NE.TRD.GNFS.ZS?end=2015&start=2013.

[13] Razeen Sally, *Regional Economic Integration in Asia: The Track Record and Prospects*, ECIPE Occasional Paper, 2 (2010), p. 3, available at http://ecipe.org/app/uploads/2014/12/regional-economic-integration-in-asia-the-track-record-and-prospects.pdf.

2.5. Building Regional Institutions

While in years past, East Asia has been described as "under-institutionalized," there is now what Henry Kissinger calls "a dazzling array of multilateral groups and bilateral mechanisms."[14] These are not necessarily the same as those in Europe. The notion of formal intergovernmental institutions entailing national obligations is entirely new to the region; there are no prototypes in East Asian history. Most of the new institutions are voluntary; they do not strive to develop formal regional regimes or curtail the exercise of sovereignty. But they contribute to regional order through strengthening mutual understanding, building personal ties, and socializing leaders into widely understood behavioral norms. Regional forums also frequently have been venues where problems were symbolically laid to rest or put on hold. Even when there are no binding outcomes resulting from deliberations in such regional institutions, there usually will be statements or communiques incorporating some general principles and promising actions. Because of their less formal nature, intra-Asian institutions and those connecting East Asia with other regions have been remarkably resilient, continuing to do business even when member states were not getting along. The growth of regional cooperation is an element for regional order-building, with the Association of Southeast Asian Nations (ASEAN) being especially important as a force for orderly relations among its ten members, and as a bargaining tool for their relations with larger powers.

3. CHALLENGES TO REGIONAL ORDER

Many of the observable trends are contributing to strengthening the regional order. But there is also much that could go wrong. The most obvious potential forms of disruption are great power geo-strategic rivalry or an American withdrawal from the region, conflict in Korea, intensified economic conflict, and internal disorder. The first four of these to varying extents involve conflicts between regional behavior and liberal norms.

3.1. China and Geo-Strategic Rivalry

From the perspective of both international relations theorists and the publics, there is deep concern about the potential for conflict between a rising China's

[14] Henry Kissinger, *World Order: Reflections on the Character of Nations and the Course of History*, New York: Penguin Books, 2014, p. 210.

regional pretensions and the long-standing US interest in opposing a potential hegemon in Asia. John Mearsheimer sees conflict as inevitable,[15] while Hugh White argues that in order to avoid a clash, the United States should share power with China in a regional concert of powers including Japan and India.[16] The territorial conflicts in the East and the South China Sea often are interpreted as symbolic touchpoints of this rivalry. Security specialists and politicians in both China and the United States frequently portray the other country as a rival and easily leap to worst-case conclusions about its behavior. Many Chinese fear that US policy aims to "contain" China, and many Americans believe that China would like to expel it from the region.

Like other major powers, and President Trump makes this crystal clear for the United States, China's fundamental commitment is not to "the international order" as such, but to its conception of its national interests. This leads to contradictions. On one hand, China values order, and sees many aspects of the current East Asian regional order and the global order as congruent with its national interests. But on the other hand, perceived security interests, historical claims, nationalism, and traditional notions of international order in China's neighborhood and toward certain issues has resulted in claims and conduct at odds with widely accepted international law and liberal norms. As China acquires more capabilities, it is in a stronger position to assert its own authority and reinterpret the "rules" to its own liking, especially in its neighborhood. As Richard Fontaine and Mira Rapp-Hooper have noted, China "can contest regional rules while buttressing global ones and will do so as its interests dictate."[17]

China's expansive claims and artificial island-building in the South China Sea and its territorial dispute with Japan provide obvious examples. They are dangerous because they are driven by nationalism and thus inspire nationalism elsewhere, and because they involve the use of military or paramilitary forces. At the same time, the Chinese have kept their tactics below a level that would provoke a military reaction. The United States' support for its allies and friends, its insistence on "rules-based" solutions based on the UN Convention on the Law of the Sea, its "freedom of navigation" exercises as well as its capabilities make it the principal protagonist opposing China. Both China and the United States have claimed that the other is driving up tensions, while both perceive themselves responding to provocations.

Chinese tactics have had some success. Chinese provocations around the Senkakus (Daioyutai), its curtailing of normal political relations with Japan,

[15] John J. Mearsheimer, *The Tragedy of Great Power Politics*, New York: W. W. Norton, updated edition 2014, chapter 7.

[16] Hugh White, *The China Choice: Why We Should Share Power*, Oxford: Oxford University Press, 2012.

[17] Richard Fontaine and Mira Rapp-Hooper, The China Syndrome, *The National Interest* 143 (May/June 2016), pp. 10–18.

and its limited use of economic penalties resulted in a Japanese acknowledgment that China had claims. In the South China Sea too, China has gradually intimated ASEAN rival claimants.

Territorial issues are just one aspect of a complex China–US relationship marked by interdependence and competition. The most positive result would be a routinized, depoliticized interaction in which each side defends its own interests in symbolically important ways that would not, however, challenge the status quo to the point of provoking conflict. For example, for years the United States has regularly conducted "freedom of navigation" exercises, and the majority are routine. Almost unnoticed, they have involved Indonesia, Malaysia, the Philippines, South Korea, Taiwan, and Vietnam, with multiple challenges to all except Taiwan and Vietnam.[18] The de-politicization of the Chinese-declared Air Defense Identification Zone in the East China Sea following its promulgation in November 2013 also provides some hope of routinization.

The past and current leaderships of both countries recognize the dangers of politico-military conflict. Chinese President Xi Jinping has spoken of avoiding "the Thucydides trap," "win-win" diplomacy, and a "new kind of great power relations." The United States welcomes China as a global player and a "responsible stakeholder" in the international system, while China claims to accept US legitimate interests in the Asia-Pacific region and welcomes US participation in Chinese-led initiatives such as the Asian Infrastructure Investment Bank (AIIB) and Belt and Road Initiative (BRI).[19] During the G. W. Bush administration, the two established regular annual high-level dialogs, and these continue under new guise with each US administration. It appears that politicized elements in the relationship are often managed in ways that defer and deflect; as a result, China–US relations so far rarely have displayed the highly destructive, emotional quality of the worst periods of Japanese–American economic tensions in the 1970s and 1980s. This was certainly the case in the first year of the Trump administration when the USA prioritized Chinese support on North Korean sanctions and both leaders emphasized establishing personal rapport.

Nonetheless, if China wants in the end to re-establish a traditional regional order in which it is clearly acknowledged as the dominant power, this will eventually come into conflict with America's long historic imperative of preventing a rival hegemon in either Europe or Asia. The traditional order, which did not accept other Asian countries as equal, is also not acceptable to China's

[18] US Department of Defense, *Freedom of Navigation Report for Fiscal Year 2014*, available at http://policy.defense.gov/Portals/11/Documents/gsa/cwmd/20150323%202015%20DoD%20Annual%20FON%20Report.pdf. Most of the rationales for these challenges involve excessive baselines (South Korea, Vietnam, Taiwan, and the Philippines).

[19] Xi Jinping speech in Seattle, September 22, 2015, available at https://www.ncuscr.org/content/full-text-president-xi-jinpings-speech [accessed September 24, 2016].

neighbors, most of whom find an active US presence reassuring, although not to the point of open confrontation. At the present time, however, the region is unsure about the steadfastness of US policy.

3.2. The American Wild Card

The election of Donald Trump as President of the United States after a campaign in which he had promised to terminate multilateral trade arrangements and questioned the US alliance system introduced a new element of uncertainty to the East Asian and global systems. US policies are addressed elsewhere in this volume, but it is important to note here that the alliance system and US trade policies were long pillars of the East Asian regional order and were consistently pursued even at times of other significant policy changes such as the withdrawal from Vietnam and the shift in recognition from the Republic of China on Taiwan to the People's Republic of China.

There has been considerable reluctance in the region to believe that the new US president would seriously jeopardize long-standing commitments and the economic arrangements. It was hoped that once in office and surrounded by foreign policy expertise, Trump would conduct American policy along more traditional lines as had previous politicians once elected. To some extent this happened. Although Trump immediately abandoned the Transpacific Partnership (TPP), he, Vice President Michael Pence, and his Cabinet secretaries have repeatedly reassured Japan and South Korea regarding defense commitments, most recently reinforced in November 2017 when Trump visited the three Northeast Asian countries on an extended trip to attend the Asia Pacific Economic Cooperation (APEC) Leaders Meeting in Vietnam. Seeming to rely heavily on personal relations at the top, he had met all three leaders earlier in the United States, and by all appearances established good relationships with them.

The abandonment of the TPP, the passage of which would have been uncertain in the Congress under any circumstances, eliminated the economic centerpiece of the previous administration's "rebalance toward Asia" approach. Trump has put the region on notice that he intends to renegotiate trading arrangements, including the bilateral Korea–US Free Trade Agreement, and insist on "balanced" trade, but his first focus was on the North American Free Trade Agreement. Many of the notions associated with the new administration—that bilateral imbalances denote unfair trade, that manufacturing jobs can be "brought back" to the United States, and that concessions can wrung from bilateral as opposed to multilateral negotiations—are out of touch with economic and diplomatic realities. For these reasons, there will be business pressures on Trump to make compromises or find other means of showing that he has won concessions. Once again, so far, he has deferred the more extreme campaign statements to hike tariffs or declare countries currency manipulators in favor of more legalistic approaches. These, of course, will trigger complaints to the World Trade Organization (WTO), but it is uncertain whether the Trump administration will accept WTO adjudication despite a high US success rate at the WTO.[20]

On the security side, dire predictions that Trump would pull American forces from forward positions and encourage Asia allies to acquire nuclear arms have not materialized.[21] But the president's style, which is to set out bargaining positions often without consultation with his Cabinet, is very different from what the region or indeed the world is used to in an international leader. While this has resulted in efforts in Japan and China, especially, to accommodate Trump by flattery and concessions, it is not a strategy that is conducive to longer-term order-building, which requires a step-by-step approach based on principles and enduring commitments. Perhaps most disturbing has been the new administration's approach to North Korea, where there is concern that its interpretation of American national interests could create a disaster for allies and thus jeopardize the future of the US alliance system in Asia.

3.3. The Korean Peninsula

The division of the Korean Peninsula is a legacy of events in the 1940s and 1950s. The northern half has been ruled the entire period by a family regime, originally propped up with substantial Soviet and later Chinese assistance. From an international order perspective, North Korea's behavior is as perverse as that of any established government. At different points, it has kidnapped foreign citizens, blown up a South Korean airliner, unsuccessfully attempted to assassinate the South Korean president in Myanmar killing many senior political and bureaucratic leaders in the process, sold illicit drugs through embassies, shipped illicit arms, shelled a South Korean island, torpedoed a South Korean corvette, and murdered the current ruler's half-brother in Malaysia.[22] For years it has pursued a nuclear weapons program in defiance of international reprobation and sanctions.

[20] See Chapter 1 by Bernard Hoekman in this volume.

[21] See, for example, Van Jackson, Donald Trump's Asia Policy Would Be a Disaster, *The Diplomat*, September 2015.

[22] North Korea has admitted to some of this, including the kidnappings of Japanese citizens. It has denied other charges, including responsibility for the sinking of the *Cheonan*, a South Korean naval corvette, in 2010. A South Korea-sponsored international investigation concluded the ship was sunk by a torpedo from a North Korean midget submarine, and it is hard to imagine any other explanation.

Because it withdrew from the Non-Proliferation Treaty (NPT), North Korea believes it can legitimately pursue a nuclear weapons program. It also argues that it must do so for its defense, citing US–South Korean exercises, even though it has never been punished militarily for any of the misbehaviors cited above nor has there been any overt threat since 1953. North Korea's ability to launch a massive artillery attack on the city of Seoul has obvious deterrent power.[23] The nuclear issue is discussed in another chapter in this volume, but here we just note that the program seems driven by the regime's prestige and survival needs. Lacking a secure basis of legitimacy, the Kim regime thrives on having powerful enemies and appears unable to engage in significant economic changes without suggesting that the policies of previous revered leaders were wrong. It also wants security guarantees, but since Pyongyang's main security threats are either self-generated or internal, the outside world cannot guarantee its long-term survival.

Having come quite far toward its goal of being able to deliver a nuclear warhead on an intercontinental ballistic missile capable of reaching the North American mainland, North Korea is very unlikely to abandon its weapons program, although it might at some point no longer require testing. The question here is the potential impact on the regional order. There are several ways North Korea's behavior could be devastating:

- If it causes other regional countries to develop nuclear weapons capabilities. It has encouraged some discussion of this in South Korea, but neither Seoul nor Tokyo has much incentive to do so as long as they are anchored in the US alliance.
- If it encourages a China–US confrontation. But both these countries have taken pains to magnify areas of cooperation and minimize differences over North Korea, especially in the current administration.
- If the United States undertakes a preventive strike against North Korea without consultation with its allies. This could result in devastating losses, mainly in Asia, and, if it appeared the USA had sacrificed Asian lives to hypothetically save Americans ones, it is unlikely the US alliance system would survive.

In 2018, however, there was new hope that North Korea could be incorporated within the system as a more "normal" country.

[23] In an unusually candid statement, Steve Bannon, then a White House advisor, told an interviewer that because of this, Washington could "forget" a military option in dealing with Pyongyang. The United States, however, would never rule out the option in the event of North Korean aggression, similar to China's refusal to rule out a military option should Taiwan declare independence. The Trump administration, however, has brandished this option more openly, in hopes that it would impress North Korea and help persuade Beijing to strengthen sanctions. See Jeff Rogin, Bannon Is Right About North Korea, *Washington Post*, August 17, 2017.

3.4. Economic Architecture

Trade issues could also potentially be divisive, but at the present time, they seem more likely to divide the United States from the region than the regional countries with each other. In recent years, there has been a proliferation of bilateral and multilateral trade arrangements within the region as well as by its countries with non-regional partners. Many of these have been criticized as "trade light,"[24] more symbolic and political, than geared towards genuine trade liberalization.

Prior to Trump's election, the main concern was that of competing architectures: the TPP, in which the United States was the largest economy versus the Regional Comprehensive Economic Partnership (RCEP) in which China was the largest. The withdrawal of the USA from the TPP ended this, and while the remaining TPP countries, with Japan's leadership, still hope to conclude the TPP, the majority of them are also in the RCEP negotiation.

In this integrating and innovative region, trade issues will undoubtedly continue to be contentious, although less so within the region than with its trading partners, especially the United States. The key issue is whether issues will be resolved through orderly processes. In their trade relations with each other, Asian countries have a tendency to prefer informal modes of settlement, although the issues may also be brought to the WTO.

3.5. Domestic Disorder

An orderly inter-state system depends on stable, functioning states as its building blocks. Regions with national units riven with unresolved social fault lines, as in the Middle East and Africa, present the biggest challenges to regional order-building.[25] A full assessment of the Asia-Pacific order from this perspective would require a more thorough analysis of domestic political stability than can be attempted here, but the importance of the domestic foundations of regional order in East Asia should be acknowledged.

As discussed in section 2.3, the state system in East Asia has been consolidating, but several countries face significant challenges. Where these countries are systemically important, political instability could have broader regional implications.

Instability in China would be destabilizing not only for the region but for the world. From time to time, it is argued that China needs more fundamental

[24] Sally, *Regional Economic Integration in Asia*, p. 6.

[25] For an analysis including studies from other regions, see Jeffrey Herbst, Terence McNamee, and Greg Mills, *On the Fault Line: Managing Tensions and Divisions within Societies*, London: Profile Books, 2012.

political reform to avoid serious dislocations associated with slowing economic growth, rising rates of income disparities, and increased expectations for political participation, and that increased repression makes a crisis more rather than less likely.[26] The political leadership in China may face difficult challenges as growth inevitably slows to "a new normal," and regime insecurity could also lead to the increased use of nationalism as a source of legitimacy or distraction. So far, however, there is little evidence of domestic unrest and most demonstrative expressions of nationalism have been short-term reactions to perceived slights, condoned by government, but not to point of disrupting policy.[27]

With the 19th Party Congress in October 2017, Xi Jinping assumed an even more dominant leadership position. This may reduce some incentives for posturing in the shorter-term. But the longer-term question of how effectively China is governed and whether in a manner conducive to good relationships with the outside world is a key question for regional and global order.

4. EAST ASIA AND GLOBAL LEADERSHIP

East Asia has been gradually building a stronger regional order, although with clear geo-strategic risks. Now let's turn to the related question of its impact on the global order. Will the region as a whole, or China as the region's biggest actor, play a significant global regional leadership role in the near or longer-term future? These questions are neither idle nor insignificant in light of the accelerated withdrawal of the United States from some elements of global leadership under the Trump administration and the strong aspiration of President Xi Jinping of China to be recognized as a global leader.

4.1. East Asia and Global Regimes

Many of the world's present partial functional political and economic orders that together make up the present liberal international order (LIO 2.0) were

[26] For a concise version of this argument, see David Shambaugh, The Coming Chinese Crack-Up, *Wall Street Journal*, March 6, 2015. Shambaugh argues that the "political system has become the primary impediment to China's needed social and economic reforms."

[27] This is especially true of the social media, dominated by young people. At the end of 2012, the average Chinese Internet user was young (54.4 percent between 10 and 29), urban (72.1 percent), male (55.8 percent), and on a low income (53.2 percent earning under 2000 yuan a month). A quarter are students: Geremie R. Barmé and Jeremy Goldkorn (eds.), *Civilising China*, Canberra: Australia National University, 2013, p. 324. This would appear to be fertile demographic ground for virulent and emotional nationalistic statements following an incident, but may not be that relevant to longer-term policy direction.

constructed when Asia was weak. The speed at which East Asia has been recovering its position in the world economy is little short of breathtaking. When China took over Japan's place as the leader of the Asian economic "miracle," in the early 1990s, Asia's rise accelerated, driven by the rapid rise in GDP in a country of over 1 billion people. Today, East Asia counts for almost 30 percent of world product, about the same as Western Europe or North America, and it has much greater potential growth. China is the world's second largest economy on an exchange rate basis. It ranks first in number of billionaires, first in value of exports, first in foreign exchange reserves, first in Internet users, first by far in length of high-speed railways, first in the number and capacity of its supercomputers, first in outbound tourists, and first in the production of many minerals and manufactured goods including cars, ships, and solar panels. Japan ranks second in car production, third in economic size and the length of its high-speed railways, and fourth in exports. South Korea ranks first in proportion of college-age population in higher education, first in per capita patents, first on R&D spending as a proportion of GDP, and first in the production of some electronic products such as mobile cell phones, flat screen televisions, LCD displays, and memory chips. It is the world's fifth largest exporter.

Some institutional reforms have been made over the years in global organizations to accommodate a more diverse set of actors, but there is an obvious disjunction between Asia's current economic size and its weight in international organizations. Asian complaints include lack of sufficient representation, retention of "vetoes" by earlier members, and the notion that transatlantic norms and values embedded in these institutions are "global" ones. For example, "the responsibility to protect" is frequently perceived in Asia as interventionist and is unpopular where many countries secured their national sovereignty only several decades ago.

Nonetheless, so far East Asian countries have not sought to replace the existing order. Quite to the contrary, the importance of the liberal international order, or at least its economic dimensions, in the region's rise in recent decades is generally recognized and appreciated. Being highly integrated with major markets and financial institutions in Europe and North America and dependent on external sources of energy and other resources, East Asia countries have sought to engage, join, and participate in global institutions, and only later to reform incrementally.[28] The dependence on global markets and global supplies has spurred trade- and transportation-related infrastructure investments, favored unilateral economic reforms to facilitate integration into the world economy, and encouraged membership in international trade regimes.

[28] One notable exception was North Korea's leaving the Non-Proliferation Treaty (NPT).

It made sense to adopt global norms and standards, in part because there aren't distinctive East Asian norms, and it would be very difficult to develop them. Most assertions of separate norms have been reactive. For example, stung by American criticism of its governance and form of democracy, Singapore in the early 1990s strongly pushed an "Asian values" campaign designed to underscore commonalities in Asian cultural norms that allegedly privileged authority over democracy and social good over individual good. Although it gained support in Malaysia, China, and elsewhere, this campaign disappeared as American criticism subsided and the Asian financial crisis exposed some of the institutional weaknesses of the region.[29]

East Asian countries are not united, either domestically or regionally, around an alternative set of values. Japan, for example, is much more conflicted about its East–West international identity than China.[30] In general, Japan and South Korea were eager to join the ranks of the advanced nations. But China prefers to style itself as "an advanced developing country" with its own special characteristics. Could China then become a pole of global leadership, playing a comparable role to the United States?

4.2. China as a Global Leader

Global leadership requires a capacity to acquire and use the major elements of power (economic, diplomatic–military, cultural) as well as to identify national interests to some considerable degree with broader systemic interests thus helping to give international leadership legitimacy. China has many elements of power and clearly has potential to become the world's most powerful nation.[31] It also has aspirations to provide leadership in the realm of economic globalization.[32] But it is unclear whether China's current behavior in the

[29] As Amartya Sen (among others) noted, East Asian cultures are "remarkably diverse," with "no homogeneous worship of order over freedom in any of these cultures": Democracy as a Universal Value, *Journal of Democracy* 10:3 (1999), pp. 3–17.

[30] Kent Calder and Min Ye, *The Making of Northeast Asia*, Stanford, CA: Stanford University Press, 2010, pp. 119–20. The authors argue that Japan should "seek a formula for Asian regionalism that allow[s] Tokyo both to play a leading role and to marginally enhance its autonomy [from] the West without alienating its important American ally."

[31] The US National Intelligence Council suggests that China may well become the world's leading power in terms of a comprehensive measure of power before the middle of the century: National Intelligence Council, *Global Trends 2030: Alternative Worlds*, Washington, DC: NIC, December 2012, p. 16.

[32] Xi says that "China champions the development of a community with a shared future for mankind, and has encouraged the evolution of the global governance system. With this we have seen a further rise in China's international influence, ability to inspire, and power to shape; and China has made great new contributions to global peace and development": Xi Jinping speech in Seattle, September 22, 2015. Hugh White, for example, magnifies China's strengths, while David Shambaugh emphasizes China's insecurities. See White, *The China Choice*, and David Shambaugh,

economic, diplomatic, or security realms match that of a global leader or confer legitimacy.

Like other East Asian countries, China joined and participated in regional and global institutions.[33] It has also shown flexibility, allowing Hong Kong and Taiwan (styled as Chinese Taipei) to join economic institutions such as the Asian Development Bank and APEC forum. But China makes firm distinction between economic institutions and political institutions that only sovereign nations, not Hong Kong or Taiwan, may be members of, and between economic globalization, which China supports, and political globalization. Regarding itself as an advanced developing country, China has mainly defined its global role as that of a model and leader for developing countries, not for the world as a whole.

Over the past two decades, China has appeared to become increasingly internationally self-confident. It long called for a "new international order," but originally mostly defensively, with emphasis on protection of national sovereignty and multipolarity in the face of "single superpower" rhetoric. From the late 1990s onward, it has begun taking leadership roles within an expanding comfort zone. This most notably included establishing the Shanghai Cooperation Organization from 2001 and in 2006, institutionalizing the annual meetings of the BRICS (Brazil, Russia, India, China, and, after 2010, South Africa). After the 2008 global financial crisis, China began financing developing country infrastructure in earnest. This was "branded" by President Xi as the Belt and Road Initiative (BRI), a program of long-term, massive investments in Eurasian and African infrastructure.[34] Financial development initiatives included the New Development (BRICS) Bank, the Silk Road Fund, and the AIIB.

The BRI recycles savings, provides work for China's construction and materials industries, and creates economic opportunities for western as well as coastal China. Externally, it provides a large, if somewhat vague, Chinese vision of connectivity around and across the world's great land hemisphere. Since it reaches into Europe, it somewhat expands from China's initial emphasis on developing countries.

China has also sought to develop non-governmental institutions or meetings to rival Western-led ones, including the Boao Forum (read: World Economic Forum) and Xiangshan Forum (read: Shangri-La Dialogue). These do not

China goes Global: The Partial Power, Oxford: Oxford University Press, 2013. Joseph Nye is also skeptical that China will overtake the United States: Emanuel Pastreich, Interview: Joseph Nye, *The Diplomat*, October 30, 2015, available at http://thediplomat.com/2015/10/interview-joseph-nye-2/ [accessed September 24, 2016].

[33] See Chapter 12 by Zhongying Pang in this volume.

[34] David Dollar, *Is China's Development Finance a Challenge to the International Order?* Brookings Institution Report, November 2017. The BRI was originally called "One Belt, One Road" in English.

attempt to supplant the institutions they have been modeled on, but are a form of emulation, benchmarking existing models but providing Chinese decision-makers with more comfortable, China-centric dialogs around the same issues on their home ground. They involve many non-Asian participants.

Following the election of Donald Trump, Xi increasingly has projected himself as the protector of the aspects of the global system in which China was already invested. In January 2017 in Davos, he strongly backed the Paris Climate Agreement and "economic globalization," arguing that inward-looking trade policies are a counterproductive response to inequities associated with globalization. In his report to the 19th Party Congress, he reaffirmed these views and called for China to increasingly expand its activities in the world at large.

Do these Chinese efforts amount to a gambit for China global leadership in the short- or long-term? Clearly Xi is desirous of recognition of China's rejuvenation and achievements, and seems to be enjoying the space afforded by Trump's lack of interest in the Paris Agreement, the TPP, or in multilateralism generally. Xi's posture is also rooted in Chinese domestic political and economic interests, since improving China's environment, stimulating innovation, and maintaining orderly markets are clearly high domestic priorities. But China also faces many obstacles.

In David Shambaugh's terms, China still remains a "partial" power on many of the indices of power, particularly weak in global military projection capabilities. And as noted in section 2.1, it is also burdened by the history of the tribute system, which relegated neighbors to subordinate positions. As China's power has grown, these neighbors have become more nervous, and it is difficult to be a global power when engaged in petty quarrels with neighbors.

Moreover, China so far appears to have failed to develop any credible model of alternative multinational leadership. In the political sphere, it supports a new kind of large power relations, peaceful resolution of disputes, and win-win solutions, but such statements are typically not connected with practical modes to achieve these goals and are disconnected from behavior that many neighbors regard as bullying.

This leaves China embracing the areas of globalization it supports, but without an embedded value system that supports it. Except with respect to infrastructure, China appears to be largely responding to initiatives from elsewhere rather than developing distinctive visions of its own. Even with respect to neighboring North Korea where China has power to both reward and punish, it has been mostly reactive, with little diplomatic initiative of its own. China is therefore likely to continue to benchmark the existing system, focusing on the BRI and the AIIB as its signature initiatives within its present comfort zone. However, it should also be capable of adapting its policies to fit the realities of a new era of world history.

5. CONCLUSION

When order-building is examined in a longer-term perspective, the world appears to be on the cusp of developing the first truly global world system. Regional and functional orders are part of this complex system. The East Asia component, although facing challenges particularly as a result of the geopolitical change and the Korea questions, has the potential to be a significant and stable element of the global system, comparable to Western Europe and North America.

The ascendancy of the West in the past century and a half was accompanied by a significant spurt of European, transatlantic, and global order-building punctuated by the enormous economic and political catastrophes of the first half of the twentieth century. This order-building, however, drew almost exclusively on the political culture, philosophy, and history of Europe. Since Europe had a long tradition of multipolarity, accommodation of diversity, and the development of diplomacy and international law, it provided the best and perhaps only feasible model for global order. It was still during the ascendancy of the West that this model was embedded in the United Nations and other institutions that are today global rather than transatlantic in character.

East Asia's recovery is both a great achievement of the liberal international order and a challenge to it. It was a heroic assumption that East Asian cultures with their own long and different traditions, histories, and domestic politics could easily accept the values and assume the responsibilities associated with the transatlantic-based order, becoming "responsible stakeholders" in the system. Nonetheless, with varying degrees of success, East Asian countries are contributing to global order-building. This engagement is enlarging and deepening a global system that will probably still have at its core the values based on European traditions. But in the process what has been called the global system has lost some of its like-mindedness, somctimes stymying action or encouraging coalitions of those willing to take actions on their own.[35] This is probably a transition until a deeper consensus is developed around the global norms of the future. Developing this consensus and the policies and enforcement mechanisms to address the world's enormous global economic, political, and humanitarian issues is the foremost order-building challenge of the present day.

[35] This is not just a matter of new international actors but also newly empowered domestic ones in the West, seizing power from traditional foreign policy elites.

9

The State and regional Order in East Asia

Chaesung Chun

1. INTRODUCTION

In modern history, the regional order in East Asia has evolved dynamically through several major stages. Traditionally, there was no "inter-national," as empires that claimed universality and refused to recognize the concept of sovereignty for other states and empires had vied for domination in the region. From the nineteenth century onward, however, Western imperialism implanted "internationality," and the modern state system began to take root in East Asia. Given the presence of several global powers in East Asia, the region has long been exposed to the interference of world politics (indeed, the region in that sense could be called "porous"). Great power competition and cooperation between the United States, the United Kingdom, Russia, China, and Japan have defined the security, economic, and cultural landscape of East Asia throughout the modern era. In the late nineteenth and the first half of the twentieth century, imperial or hegemonial ambitions among these states led to two world wars. Since then, we have had bipolar confrontation between the United States and the Soviet Union, a period of unipolar American dominance after the end of the Cold War, and now, since about 2008, increasing rivalry between the United States and China, accompanied by efforts of Russia and Japan to secure the status of great powers for themselves, too.

Yet power politics of the realist kind has not been the only factor shaping the East Asia regional order. The rapid development of liberal market economies in East Asian countries has given rise to domestically influential economic actors that needed a stable and peaceful international environment. This, in turn, has instigated cooperation and coordination between governments, as well as between governments and business, both in the context of the international and the regional order. The liberal notion of commercial peace therefore has taken root and shaped East Asia as well.

Despite setbacks, the march toward democracy has turned out to be a megatrend in national politics throughout the region. The growth of civil society in most East Asian countries helped to foster transnational interactions, and these have had an impact on government policies. Public diplomacy has been one response to this transnational dimension of regional order by governments: US soft-power diplomacy and Chinese "charm offensives" have become important elements of their great power rivalry. The existence of democracies, and the potential for further advances in democratization in presently authoritarian states, underpin the vision of a "democratic peace" in East Asia.

From the past development of regional order, East Asians retain multi-layered political identities. At one level, the modern sovereign state has developed firm roots, reinforcing nationalism and national identities. At another level, enabled by the information and communications revolution citizens have cultivated regionalism and cosmopolitanism. Cultural elements such as Confucianism, Buddhism, and the strong influence of traditional Chinese culture have shaped collective identities as well. At the same time, there remain important unresolved tasks to complete the modern nation-state transition: some territorial boundaries still need to be settled, and diverging knowledge, perceptions, and interpretations of modern history continue to divide East Asians. Politicians sometimes manipulate these perceptions for their own purposes, playing games with the politics of memory. The politics of identity will therefore remain another factor shaping the future regional order in East Asia.

This chapter traces the trajectory of the East Asian regional order in its security and economic aspects and examines the nexus between the two. Lacking strong regional security institutions, East Asia suffers from uncertainties and great power competition. At the same time, intra-regional economic transactions have grown persistently and in a highly dynamic fashion. Deepening economic interdependence within the region has created interesting patterns of interference with the regional security order. Sometimes, economic interactions had the effect of assuaging strategic mistrust and competition, reminding states of their common interests and the need for cooperation. At other times, governments glibly securitized economic interactions and the regional economic architecture to promote domestic or geo-political objectives; this has helped create a mercantilist atmosphere in regional inter-state relations and fostered the logic of institutional balancing. Hence, the so-called "Asian paradox"—the surprising combination of high levels of intra-regional economic interdependence and intensifying security competition between states.

2. THE EAST ASIAN SECURITY ORDER SINCE THE END OF THE COLD WAR

2.1. Pathways to East Asian Order-Building

Asia has enjoyed relative peace for more than two decades. Since the beginning of the Cold War, there have been two great wars in Asia—the Korean

War and the Vietnam War; they catalyzed the rise of two sub-regional orders in Northeast and Southeast Asia. Since the Vietnamese invasion of Cambodia in 1978 and the Chinese punitive attack on Vietnam in 1979, however, there have been no further major conflicts. International institutions or informal regimes, such as the Association of Southeast Asian Nations (ASEAN) Regional Forum, certainly have contributed to this stability, especially in the post-Cold War period. Yet East Asia basically has remained a realist world. Crises around several flash points, such as the Korean Peninsula, cross-straits relations between mainland China and Taiwan, and maritime territorial disputes in the East and South China Seas, have been defused through great powers' negotiations or accommodations during the remainder of the Cold War and since then, even with the rising rivalry between the United States and China.[1]

The question is what has caused this relative stability, including the absence of major wars. In this volume, we distinguish three kinds of international order: order through competition and power, order through cooperation, and order through transformation. Undoubtedly, East Asian regional order has largely been shaped by competition and power. Looking back on the evolution of the Westphalian system in Europe, European states eventually succeeded in developing a regional security arrangement, the Concert of Europe, based on multilateral norms and commitment to diffuse reciprocity that maintained peace for an extended period before breaking down. After two painful world wars, Europe succeeded in transforming the sovereign states system by forging an integrative regional order out of several major components, from economics though culture to politics and defense. It remains to be seen whether European countries will achieve the final stage of consolidating pooled sovereignty; "Brexit" certainly represents a critical setback. However, other regions struggling to achieve sustainable peace based on cooperation and transformation still take the European experience as the standard to follow.

Non-Europeans envy the European experience of transcending the sovereign nation-state system at least to the extent that they could create a regional union in which worries about physical security were generally mitigated. East Asians have longed for the critical moment of transition from order-building through competition and power to order-building through cooperation—but has this moment arrived? Lacking strong regional security arrangements and firm cultural common ground, such as a "usable" shared past from which East Asia could forge a common collective identity,[2] regional cooperation still appears to rest on rather weak foundations. By contrast, Europe referred back to the past of Christendom for the present community as the communal

[1] Muthiah Alagappa (ed.), *Asian Security Order: Instrumental and Normative Features*, Stanford, CA: Stanford University Press, 2003, p. 3.

[2] Aaron L. Friedberg, Ripe for Rivalry: Prospects for Peace in a Multipolar Asia, *International Security* 18:3 (Winter 1993–4), pp. 5–33 (24).

and cultural basis of regional union. Already in early modern times, there had been intellectual efforts to design a European republic, among which is Kant's idea of perpetual peace.

For now, the distribution of power among great powers and their strategies will continue to dominate the evolution of the East Asian regional order. Since the end of the Cold War, this power distribution broadly speaking was unipolar until 2008, and then shifted toward bipolarity as a result of the rapid rise of China. As this volume assumes, however, the same order can contain distinctive sub-orders for different issue areas. Closer inspection therefore yields a more complicated picture: while post-Cold War East Asia today still seems defined by American unipolarity in its security architecture, in economic relations China has established itself as undeniable second pole that competes with the United States. In cultural relations, things are more complicated still, because all nations in the region try to pursue their own nationalist agendas and identities and strive to deny the great powering prevalent influence. In politics, we witness tensions between a trend to develop multilateralist pathways to regional order and strong forces upholding nationalism, populism, and conservatism.

2.2. 1990 to 2008: East Asian Security Order and American Unipolarity

Some regions are highly sensitive to shifts in the distribution of global power, whereas other regions are not. The relative porousness of a regional order to global changes thus obviously differs between regions, but almost all Third World regions appear to be rather heavily affected by changes in the global distribution of power. Given the presence of global powers in the region, the East Asian order, however, seems particularly sensitive to global changes. Four great powers, the United States, China, Russia, and Japan are both regional powers and great powers shaping the regional order.

During the Cold War period, the East Asian regional order tended to mirror changing shapes of Cold War rivalry. For example, the era of détente between the United States and the Soviet Union and between the United States and China affected almost all East Asian countries. The two Koreas, fiercely adversarial and repeatedly engrossed in military clashes, launched their own "mini-détente" when Washington and Beijing strengthened the East Asian security architecture through conciliatory arrangements. North Korea's leader Kim Il Sung, encouraged by the implosion of South Vietnam and its unification with the North, wanted to continue his aggressive military and diplomatic efforts to subvert South Korea, but Chinese pressure to put détente in place on the Korean Peninsula narrowed North Korea's strategic leeway.

The post-Cold War era in East Asia can be roughly divided into two phases. Phase one, American unipolarity, lasted from 1991 to 2008. Phase two is about the transition to bipolarity; it began in 2009 and continues to the present. During the Clinton and Bush administrations, the United States enjoyed dominant military prowess and economic prosperity. Washington tried to sustain the network of alliances that had been forged during the Cold War. With the Cold War enemies gone (with North Korea as the exception), both America's Northeast Asian allies, South Korea and Japan, and its Southeast Asian allies, especially the Philippines, began to reconsider their need for a security alliance with the United States. The continuing threat from North Korea, heightened further when the country was caught developing a nuclear weapons program and walked out of the Non-Proliferation Treaty in March 1993, justified the continuation of the US alliance with South Korea and Japan. The need to maintain regional security provided a further powerful *raison d'être* for the US-centered bilateral alliances network. After 9/11, South Korea and Japan embraced US requests to send troops or provide financial assistance to the global war on terrorism, despite debates about the geographical reach of their respective bilateral security arrangements with Washington at home.

Under unipolarity, the regional security order had to face several important questions. Was unipolarity sustainable? Was American unipolarity special and thus particularly well placed to ensure sustainability? Was the unipolar regional order more peaceful than others were?[3] Liberal theoretical arguments supporting the sustainability of US unipolarity focused on the lack of balancing intentions of other nations because American leadership rested on multilateral institutions, democratic inclusion, and open liberal market economies. Further, it was argued that the peculiar domestic foundations of American power would be able to resist the temptation of imposing imperial rule. This would prevent balancing acts by others to defy the sole hegemon and thus uphold American leadership well into the twenty-first century.

In East Asia, these arguments seemed to be supported by much evidence: American liberal hegemony was generally recognized as beneficial to regional stability and peace, and as compatible with multilateralism and democratic ideals. With no enemies (apart from North Korea) left, most East Asia's American allies decided to preserve their alliance relationships with Washington. The emerging powers, such as China and India, needed regional peace,

[3] Charles Krauthammer, The Unipolar Moment, *Foreign Affairs* 70:1 (Winter 1990–1), pp. 23–33; Christopher Layne, The Unipolar Illusion Revisited: The Coming End of the United States' Unipolar Moment, *International Security* 31:2 (Fall 2006), pp. 7–41; Christopher Layne and Bradley Thayer, *American Empire: A Debate*, New York: Routledge, 2006; Paul K. MacDonald and Joseph M. Parent, Graceful Decline? The Surprising Success of Great Power Retrenchment, *International Security* 35:4 (Spring 2011), pp. 7–44; Kenneth Waltz, The Stability of a Bipolar World, *Daedalus* 93:3 (Summer 1964), pp. 881–909; William Wohlforth, The Stability of a Unipolar World, *International Security* 24:1 (Summer 1999), pp. 5–41.

stability, and open international markets. The public goods provided by Washington, such as functioning international trade and financial arrangements, in fact supported the rise of these powers.

While American leadership may therefore appear quite sustainable in this phase of the East Asian order, its peacefulness was a different matter.[4] To maintain global unipolarity, the United States waged wars. Since the end of the Cold War, the USA has deployed major forces in four inter-state wars: against Iraq in 1991, in Kosovo in 1999, in Afghanistan from 2001 to the present, and again in Iraq between 2003 and 2010. America thus has been at war for thirteen out of the twenty-seven years from 1989 to 2016.[5] Monteiro argues that unipolarity creates conflict-producing mechanisms that are likely to involve the unipolar power itself. War among great powers is surely unlikely under such conditions, but the strategic choices of the unipolar power can trigger conflicts with other powers, or among the latter.[6] For example, recalcitrant minor powers are likely to test the limits of the status quo and try to enhance their position by challenging the power and authority of a hegemon by trying to make revisions such as small territorial conquests, altered international alignments, or increases in their relative power.[7]

The case of non-proliferation illustrates this argument. Although the United States so far has provided the global public good of non-proliferation of weapons of mass destruction largely successfully, dissident states challenge US leadership, in part because they feel threatened by some aspects of American counter-proliferation policies.[8] A recent study by the Center for Strategic and International Studies concludes that

> ... a major stimulus for a faster rate of nuclear proliferation is U.S. conventional military superiority. This causes nonnuclear nation-states (such as North Korea, Iran, Iraq, Syria, and Libya) to pursue nuclear weapons as a counter or offset to U.S. military prowess. It also leads nuclear-armed states with interests in opposition to the United States (Russia, for sure, but perhaps China [*sic*!]) to increase their reliance on nuclear weapons, much in the way that the United States did during the Cold War.

This will, in turn, affect security strategies of friendly states:

> More nuclear-armed regional adversaries (to the United States and its allies) and increased reliance on nuclear weapons by major powers in competition with the United States will lead U.S. nonnuclear allies to rely more on U.S. extended nuclear deterrence. However, the credibility of U.S. extended deterrence will have been weakened by the failure of U.S.-led efforts to prevent the nuclear proliferation that led to the increased demand from its allies for help in deterring

[4] See Chapter 10 by Daniel Deudney in this volume.

[5] Nuno P. Monteiro, Unrest Assured: Why Unipolarity is Not Peaceful, *International Security* 36:3 (Winter 2011/12), pp. 9–40 (11).

[6] Ibid., p. 20.

[7] Ibid., p. 27.

[8] See Chapter 4 by William Walker in this volume.

> nuclear-armed adversaries. This vicious cycle is likely to continue unless the United States moves forcefully to counter it.[9]

The case of North Korea's nuclear development highlights the non-peacefulness of a unipolar world. Former socialist states have had to make painful adjustments to the structural imperative of global and regional unipolarity. China chose to open its economy to and to maintain cooperative relations with Washington. Other socialist regimes in East Asia, such as Vietnam, similarly attempted to find new trajectories of reform and opening. These frequently entailed domestic political, economic, and ideological transformations. North Korea, on the other hand, endeavored to preserve its totalitarian regime without substantial reform and opening. Fear of being absorbed by more powerful and prosperous South Korea has driven the North to the alternative of developing nuclear weapons, which has inevitably antagonized the United States. Since March 1993, when North Korea withdrew from the Non-Proliferation Treaty, Pyongyang has repeatedly made it clear that it wants to conclude a peace treaty with Washington. However, its military provocations against the South and its development of nuclear weapons have become formidable obstacles to genuine peace and stability in East Asia.[10]

2.3. 2009 to Today: The Rise of China and the Transformation of the East Asian Security Order

Many different causes have contributed to the relative decline of United States global dominance since 2008, but the enormous expense on the global war on terror certainly was one of them. After September 11, 2001, the first administration of President George W. Bush decided to conduct this fight with its wars in Iraq and Afghanistan. This exhausted America's public financial resources. The wars also gravely damaged the legitimacy of US leadership, as international public opinion turned increasingly skeptical of America's way of fighting terrorism through military unilateralism. Moreover, increasing budget deficits and growing skepticism about American global interventionism significantly weakened the domestic consensus behind America's hegemonic grand strategy.[11] The multiple crises in American and international financial markets and the world economy, as much as overstretched military

[9] Clark Murdock, Samuel J. Brannen, Thomas Karako, and Angela Weaver, *Project Atom: A Competitive Strategies Approach to Defining U.S. Nuclear Strategy and Posture for 2025–2050*, Washington, DC: Center for Strategic & International Studies, 2015, p. vi.

[10] Yong Chool Ha and Chaesung Chun, North Korea's Brinkmanship and the Task to Solve the "Nuclear Dilemma," *Asian Perspective* 34:1 (2010), pp. 87–109.

[11] See Chapter 11 by Marco Overhaus in this volume.

assets and declining legitimacy at home and abroad, called for a new global security strategy for the United States, and the two administrations of President Barack Obama responded to this need by adopting a grand strategy of retrenchment and the so-called pivot to Asia. This strategy conceded that US resources had to be concentrated on core interests of the United States in the East Asian region. Accordingly, the Obama administrations decided to focus on Asia and rebalance US strategic resources by retrenching in Europe and the Middle East.[12] This strategy of retrenchment turned out to be insufficient to attenuate American public anti-interventionist sentiment, however, which led to the surprising victory of presidential candidate Donald Trump in the November 2016 elections in the United States. President Trump's "America first strategy," which he tried to implement from his very first days in office, gravely affected East Asian perceptions of the US presence in the region. As indicated by President Trump's Asia tour in November 2017, he emphasized the importance of US economic interests based on fair trade and fair sharing of alliance burdens. Trump justified this with the East Asian trading partners' alleged unfair trade and investment practices, and he seemed willing to make full use of American military power and commitment in the region to solve the United States' own domestic economic problems.

American hegemony may be in decline, but decline is a relative phenomenon. It is true that the American strategy of primacy brought about symptoms of overstretch that put pressure on US budgets. New threats, notably global terrorism, also rapidly exhausted American power without solving the root causes of terrorism in the Middle East and elsewhere. China, meanwhile, has displayed steady and rapid economic development for the last two decades, with GDP growing by more than 10 percent per year on average, and this economic growth has translated into a rapid expansion of military power. The Chinese government increased annual defense spending by almost 12 percent every year and thus fueled the People's Liberation Army's continuous drive for modernization.

The power shift between the United States and China will be the most essential element in the coming years in East Asia's regional order. Some argue that war between them will be inevitable. Violent hegemonic succession in modern times (between Spain and France, then between France and the United Kingdom) reinforces the prediction that the rivalry between the United States and China will end with an all-out military clash. If those arguments are correct, bipolar competition, confrontation, and power politics will define the pathway of international order in East Asia. In this argument, the two great

[12] Mark E. Manyin, Stephen Daggett, Ben Dolven, Susan V. Lawrence, Michael F. Martin, Ronald O'Rourke, and Bruce Vaughn, *Pivot to the Pacific? The Obama Administration's "Rebalancing" Toward Asia*, Congressional Research Service, March 28, 2012, available at https://china.usc.edu/sites/default/files/legacy/AppImages/crs-2012-pivot-pacific.pdf.

powers will divide the region and tighten their alliances and their strategic partnerships. Power transition theory also holds that high levels of dissatisfaction of the rising power precipitate hegemonic war.[13] Others also see the danger that the old hegemon might attack a rising power preemptively in order to foreclose any conceivable challenge to its hegemony.[14]

One should not over-theorize the future of the US–China relationship, however. Moreover, the rapidly globalizing environment of international order now seems to be changing so rapidly that past experience may not provide adequate guidance for the future. Moreover, there are good reasons to doubt some of the claims of power transition theories. First, the American-led international liberal order has enabled China to rise, and China therefore seems unlikely to challenge or replace that order any time soon. This assumption is corroborated by the positive feedback from international economic transactions on the regional security order in East Asia, making the liberal argument of commercially induced peace more plausible. The socio-economic interdependence between the two countries has grown deep roots not just through trade, but also in the realms of financial and direct investment. There are a great number of stakeholders and vested interests in China that cherish cooperative relations with the United States, and Chinese leaders are well aware of that: "[F]or the political leadership of the PRC, economic security is arguably at least as important as conventional sovereignty," and "without continuing rapid development the legitimacy of the extant regime will be increasingly called into question with potentially fatal consequences."[15] Chinese leaders are also well aware that China needs to stick to international norms that liberal states such as the United States have formulated in the past. Thus, while President Trump weakens the American position by unilaterally revoking the Transpacific Partnership (TPP) agreement, President Xi tries to project the image of a China that preserves and develops the global economic order. In his report to the 19th Party Congress, President Xi emphasized the so-called "major country diplomacy with Chinese characteristics" to "encourage the evolution of global governance." Power competition guided by norms and principles will not develop easily into a manifest power clash, and institutional balancing will loom large in the coming power shift between the two countries.

[13] For the interpretation of China's assertiveness, see Alastair Iain Johnston, How New and Assertive Is China's New Assertiveness? *International Security* 37:4 (Spring 2013), pp. 7–48; see also Michael Swaine, Perceptions of an Assertive China, *China Leadership Monitor* No. 32 (May 2010). It is quite uncertain that this applies to the case of China. China has risen under the framework of international order provided by the United States, and the issue of dissatisfaction involves many problems of definition and measurement.

[14] Steve Chan, *China, the U.S., and the Power-Transition Theory: A Critique*, New York: Routledge, 2008.

[15] Mark Beeson, Hegemonic Transition in East Asia? The Dynamics of Chinese and American Power, *Review of International Studies* 35:1 (2009), pp. 95–112 (102).

Second, there is the effect of nuclear deterrence between the two. As the United States and China each retain broadly based second-strike capabilities, neither country would likely start a war that could be susceptible to nuclear escalation. Although strategic mistrust looms large between Washington and Beijing, both parties are keenly aware of the importance of the nuclear balance and mutual deterrence. There may, however, be a stability–instability paradox here: both powers might be tempted to use force below the nuclear threshold to achieve their objectives, but any military option is likely to be expensive and risky.

Third, changes in the East Asian regional order toward higher levels of institutionalization are increasingly gathering support from the smaller East Asian countries that all face a similar dilemma in how to maintain favorable relations with both Washington and Beijing. The best option for small states under conditions of great power rivalry is multilateralism, through which great powers can resolve their problems through negotiations based on shared norms and principles. As such mechanisms are insufficiently developed in East Asia, they have responded with diverse forms of hedging strategies, as well as by undertaking their own efforts to contribute to lessening the strategic distrust between the United States and China.

Yet Beeson's view that "... China has of late demonstrated a greater enthusiasm for multilateral engagement than has the US, which was the architect of the very system in which China has become an increasingly effective part"[16] is only partly right. In fact, the United States has continued to put more emphasis on the so-called "hub and spokes" approach than on East Asian multilateral mechanisms, although in the twenty-first century, Washington has put increasing emphasis on the latter as a supplement to its bilateral alliances. Having East Asian neighbors on one's own side would increase one's perceived power position in hegemonic competition; both great powers have therefore conducted charm offensives.[17] China also "... has engaged with international institutions to burnish its own credentials as a 'responsible' international actor, a tactic that not only highlights possible American failings by contrast, but which makes it more difficult for the U.S. to 'contain' China as a result."[18] These efforts contribute to forming a more participatory and inclusive regional order, alleviating the rivalry between the two great powers and enhancing the legitimacy of regional order.

Judging from how the relationship between the United States and China has evolved since 2008 to today, the pessimistic predictions appear somewhat presumptuous. The leaders of both countries are well aware of the danger of

[16] Ibid., p. 104.

[17] Joshua Kurlantzick, *Charm Offensive*, New Haven, CT: Yale University Press, 2007.

[18] Beeson, Hegemonic Transition in East Asia?, p. 104.

falling into the "Thucydides trap,"[19] and they try to invent new pathways towards more cooperative regional and international orders. When US–China relations worsened in the years 2009–10 due to, among other issues, the failure of the Copenhagen climate conference, US arms sales to Taiwan, and tensions over Korea, both the United States and China took steps to mend the relationship. Thus, in 2013 President Obama and President Xi Jinping agreed to work towards a "new type of major powers' relationship." Since then, the US–China relationship has tried to move away from competition over specific issues and instead focused on implementing solutions for outstanding controversial issues on the basis of shared norms and standards. Examples quoted by the two presidents in their summit meeting in June 2013 included the North Korean nuclear problem and cyber-security. The principle of nuclear non-proliferation and mutually agreeable principles in the cyber area supported this new mechanism of enhancing common interests. By adopting principles that are mutually advantageous, both countries tried to position themselves favorably with a view to possible future conflicts that lie beyond the horizon and cannot be predicted. This suggests a deeply rooted belief on both sides that US–China competition will continue for an indefinite period. Furthermore, there is a shared view that they can better exert their diplomatic influence by securing the support of other countries in the region.

As President Obama's term came to an end, the concept of a "new type of major powers' relationship" was criticized on both sides. The realistic perception now seemed to be that there clearly existed incompatibilities between core interests of both sides.[20] During the presidential campaign, President Trump ferociously attacked President Obama for sacrificing US interests to Chinese unfair trade practices. Most Republicans, including President Trump, seem to believe firmly that the rise of China will be a threat not just to the United States but also to its allies in the region. Realizing the power gap between the United States and China, Chinese leaders, on the other hand, for the time being seek to maintain a stable international environment to pursue their own national development, but they also keep in mind their long-term plan to replace American hegemony.

In sum, the East Asian regional order has gone through two major phases, one of American unipolarity and one marked by the power shift between the United States and China. East Asia's regional security architecture has been particularly affected by the shifting power distribution and rivalry between the

[19] Graham Allison, The Thucydides Trap: Are the U.S. and China Headed for War? *The Atlantic*, September 24, 2015, available at https://www.theatlantic.com/international/archive/2015/09/united-states-china-war-thucydides-trap/406756/.

[20] US–China Economic and Security Review Commission, China Seeks a "New Type of Major-Country Relationship" with the United States, June 25, 2013, p. 2, available at https://www.uscc.gov/sites/default/files/Research/China%20Seeks%20New%20Type%20of%20Major-Country%20Relationship%20with%20United%20States_Staff%20Research%20Backgrounder.pdf.

USA and China. Lacking strong multilateral security arrangements, relations between the great powers, including their military power, have largely determined the regional order's trajectory. However, China and the USA are trying to develop new norms and to regulate their relationship, and both also compete with each other for the support of the smaller countries in the region as the influence of lesser powers in the region is becoming stronger. Moreover, even the big two powers find that they are heavily dependent upon each other in many ways. Cooperation and its institutionalization may therefore come to define the East Asian order increasingly in the future, perhaps even making it more harmonious and peaceful in the process.

3. EAST ASIAN INTERNATIONAL ORDER IN ECONOMIC AREAS

3.1. The Theoretical Nexus between International Security and Economic Interdependence

The world economy has to be understood as embedded in a global political and strategic context. Systemic factors such as polarity, power shift, and hegemonic dominance therefore will affect the formation and maintenance of international economic governance.[21] In the aftermath of great powers' wars in the past, great powers have tended to design an international economic order reflecting the underlying distribution of power amongst each other. Today's international economic governance originated in the post-World War II settlement of 1944/5, the so-called Bretton Woods system. The United States created, defended, and expanded this liberal economic order that promoted American strategic interests, but also the interests of its allies. By providing international economic public goods, the United States functioned as a system maker and elicited cooperation from other major powers. Informal agreements between the United States and its partners supported the US leadership, providing Washington with certain privileges that came with its leadership in global economic governance.[22]

Those arrangements, however, proved to be unsustainable after the end of the Cold War. First, with the arrival of the US unipolarity, its economic partners no longer required US security patronage, which deprived the United States of its past privilege. The preponderance of US power no longer

[21] Avery Goldstein and Edward D. Mansfield, *The Nexus of Economics, Security, and International Relations in East Asia*, Stanford, CA: Stanford University Press, 2012.

[22] Michael Mastanduno, System Maker and Privilege Taker: U.S. Power and the International Political Economy, *World Politics* 61:1 (2009), pp. 121–54.

translated into direct influence in situations where its partners were unwilling to make economic concessions to the United States. Both Japan and certainly China do not rely on the US military power to sustain their security. But both countries recognize that the liberal economic order supported by the US market and the US-led international economic institutions benefitted their export-led growth strategy. Japan and even China also supported US efforts to uphold the present international economic governance as long as they considered it beneficial to their own growth.

However, the United States is no longer in a position to request economic collaboration and adjustment from other major economic powers, because they no longer depend on US protection, at least not in the same way and to the same degree. China, in particular, which certainly does not feel it depends on the US security framework for its own security, will not easily make concessions in matters of global economic governance. This may have important implications for the East Asian regional order. While the United States therefore may manage to maintain its position as the strongest economy and its leadership in the maintenance of the international economic order, it is unlikely to retain its old privileges as unrivaled hegemon.

Moreover, the domestic foundations of US hegemony have recently been crumbling. As the inequalities of wealth and income among American citizens have grown and the economic hardship of the middle classes has been aggravated, President Trump and the Republican Party won the US elections in November 2017. Although there are many reasons for America's economic problems, starting with the neoliberal reform from the 1980s that widened the income gap, the development of automation which deprived workers of their jobs, and the budget deficit, President Trump prefers to attribute the current situation to unfair practices by America's partners in the country's external economic relations. Yet his attacks on free trade agreements and on free-riding on American military commitments to induce economic concessions from allies and partners will ultimately undermine US leadership in the economic order architecture in East Asia.

3.2. US–China Rivalry and the Evolution of International Economic Order in East Asia

Since the end of the Cold War, countries in East Asia—hoping to benefit from the pacifying potential of a changing regional security order—established a series of regional economic institutions such as Asia Pacific Economic Cooperation, ASEAN+3, the East Asia Summit, the Chiang Mai Initiative and its Multilateralization, and the Trilateral Summit meetings of the leaders of South Korea, Japan, and China. The mushrooming of institutions, however, apparently did not consolidate the economic norms and principles leading to a convergent economic architecture for the region. Rather, middle powers such as the ASEAN countries tried to hold their ground with their own initiatives in the midst of great power politics, where the United States and China pursued institution-building in ways tailored to their own interests.

National or sub-regional interests thus meshed with universal norms and principles that also flourished in the region, producing a combination of liberal market mechanisms within a profoundly realist logic. This encouraged the phenomenon of institutional balancing. As Kai He indicates, states want to "counter pressures or threats through initiating, utilizing, and dominating multilateral institutions, as an overlooked realist strategy for states to pursue security under anarchy." When economic interdependence is high, as in East Asia, institutional balancing will replace power balancing: "The traditional definition of balancing mainly refers to power balancing or 'hard balancing' in a military sense. Institutional balancing, however, is a new form of balancing—'soft balancing' behavior."[23]

In East Asia, competition and rivalry will continue despite all the new rhetoric of cooperation. Although practical considerations and norms embedded in regional institutions may moderate it, competition between China and the United States actually seems likely to become stronger and in the process acquire new dimensions. That strategic competition may indeed lead to competitive institution-building is already apparent in today's regional economic architecture. Present arrangements reflect the growing rivalry between the United States and China, with Washington trying to maintain its status as a system leader while Beijing, with support from Asian partners, seems intent on replacing US economic leadership. For example, the United States under President Obama promoted the TPP as a means to shape the principles, norms, and rules of future Asia-Pacific trade. The logic of institutional balancing clearly came through in President Obama's following statement: "TPP allows America and not countries like China—to write the rules of the road in the 21st century, which is especially important in a region as dynamic as the Asia-Pacific."[24]

China challenged this American approach to institution-building. Foreign Ministry Spokesperson Lu Kang, responding to questions about President Obama's statement, described Beijing's position as follows:

> We never believe that world trade rules can be made by any specific country alone. We have never thought that China or any other specific country could

[23] He Kai, Institutional Balancing and International Relations Theory: Economic Interdependence and Balance of Power Strategies in Southeast Asia, *European Journal of International Relations* 14:3 (2008), pp. 489–518 (492–6).

[24] Barack Obama, Statement by President Obama on the Signing of the Trans-Pacific Partnership, February 3, 2016, available at https://obamawhitehouse.archives.gov/the-press-office/2016/02/03/statement-president-signing-trans-pacific-partnership.

> decide by itself how to write the rules or agenda of global trade in the 21st century. We always maintain that the World Trade Organization (WTO) play a leading role in making global trade rules [. . .] There is no need to politicize the economic issue. Don't make people feel that the US is pursuing some political ends throughout the process of promoting the TPP.[25]

In response, China has been very active in devising its own economic institutions, such as the RCEP (Regional Comprehensive Economic Partnership) to compete with TPP, and the Asian Infrastructure Investment Bank (AIIB). As Terada notes, "the launch of AIIB, as a key financial institution to bolster China's 'One-Belt, One Road' strategy, may contribute to China's development model being more popular and gaining more supporters, challenging the US preference for democracy and a market economy." Conscious of the TPP's growing momentum after Japan joined in July 2013, China redoubled its efforts to establish its regional counter-FTAs (Free Trade Agreements) such as RCEP or the Free Trade Agreement of Asia and Pacific framework, in which it could set its own standards for regional integration according to its own schedule.[26]

Reflecting these Chinese efforts, a high-level Chinese government official remarked:

> China believes that the RCEP negotiation should give consideration to the development level and bearing capacity of different countries involved in the negotiation, and be inclusive. Under the background of slower increase in the world economy at present, entering into the agreement on RCEP as soon as possible is of great significance for all participants to expand opportunities of market access, strengthen industrial cooperation and shore up the confidence in economic development. China will continue to strengthen the communication and cooperation with all other parties to promote the completion of the negotiation as soon as possible in 2016.[27]

It is still to be seen whether the RCEP will draw consensus among its members for the launch, but most people are pessimistic. Chinese inclinations towards institutional balancing are also apparent in this quote:

> The AIIB is both inclusive and open, and a global financial institution that believes in equality. [. . .] It is important to note that the Philippines joined the AIIB despite having a maritime dispute with China. The bank's openness is also

[25] Ministry of Foreign Affairs of the People's Republic of China, Foreign Ministry Spokesperson Lu Kang's Regular Press Conference (Ministry of Foreign Affairs), February 5, 2016, available at http://www.fmprc.gov.cn/ce/cech/ger/fyrth/t1338870.htm.

[26] Terada Takashi, Japan and Geo-Economic Regionalism in Asia: The Rise of TPP and AIIB, East Asia Institute Issue Briefing, February 3, 2016, available at http://www.eai.or.kr/data/bbs/eng_report/20160203166284.pdf.

[27] Ministry of Commerce of the People's Republic of China, Regular News Conference Held by the Ministry of Commerce, January 6, 2016.

> reflected in the flexibility for the countries that have not yet ratified Trans-Pacific Partnership Agreement—and will not exclude members from the trading bloc even if they fail to ratify the agreement before the deadline expires.[28]

As President Trump withdrew from the TPP on the first day of his inauguration and tries to dismantle President Obama's legacies, China will have even more room for maneuver to shape the region's economic architecture, and Beijing can also be expected to make full use of its economic power to wield more political and security-related influence over other regional powers.[29] In his report to the 19th Party Congress, President Xi mentioned "a community with a shared future for mankind, to build an open, inclusive, clean, and beautiful world that enjoys lasting peace, universal security, and common prosperity" which can be interpreted as an ambitious design for global leadership. The pathway towards this community does not deviate, however, from existing norms, at least not in principle, when President Xi promises to "promote trade and investment liberalization and facilitation, and make economic globalization more open, inclusive, and balanced."[30]

To conclude from all this that economic norms and principles in the East Asia region reflect the logic of competition and power politics would thus be misleading, as this is only part of the truth. The nexus between security and economic order may well work both ways: there is no a priori reason to believe that strategic interests will dominate the logic of economic cooperation. With increasing levels of economic interdependence driven by continuing globalization, the habits and practices of cooperation with the help of other Asian countries could well alleviate strategic tensions between the United States and China. Economic integration in East Asia will continue to be fostered in the midst of competition between the two countries and thus prevent dividing the region into two opposing camps. The different versions of economic integration pursued at present on different trajectories even may merge eventually into a common region-wide international economic cooperation framework.

4. CONCLUSION

Not only one, but three pathways—competition/power politics, cooperation, and transformation—will contribute to order-making in the region and shape the norms, principles, and rules of regional order in East Asia. Within that

[28] *China Daily*, Inclusive AIIB to boost sustainable growth, January 15, 2016.

[29] See Chapter 12 by Zhongying Pang in this volume.

[30] Xi Jinping keynote speech at World Economic Forum, Davos, January 17, 2017, Jointly Shoulder Responsibility of Our Times, Promote Global Growth, available at https://america.cgtn.com/2017/01/17/full-text-of-xi-jinping-keynote-at-the-world-economic-forum.

order, moreover, different issue areas are interwoven horizontally in complex ways: sometimes, they reinforce each other, whereas at other times, they pull in different directions. The relationship between the regional security and the regional economic sub-orders is particularly complex, which makes the future of regional order uncertain and open. Economic transactions are often securitized to conform to the logic of power politics, whereas the grim picture of power politics sometimes is lightened up by the touch of commercial peace.

We cannot know whether the world presently is undergoing a postmodern transformation towards an entirely new organizing principle. From a realist point of view, the changing balance of power among major countries may produce a shift to a new order with entirely different organizing principles, such as a monopoly of power from a single center or a condominium of several actors. Liberals may argue that globalization creates the space for universal norms and principles based on global markets and the advent of a cosmopolitan civil society. Constructivists will point to the salience of universal norms and principles that easily find their ways into the minds of global villagers thanks to information technology and the communications revolution. State sovereignty, which has wielded unparalleled power by monopolizing military force, directing a nation's economic activities, and reinforcing nationalism, now gradually may have to give way to non-state actors, such as the Islamic State with its ruthless use of violence, economic actors with unparalleled amounts of financial capital at their disposal, and supranational or transnational actors such as international organizations and transnational civic groups.

What is certain, however, is that the technological dynamics that made possible these changes will continue to revolutionize politics, the economy, knowledge, and communications. Non-state actors such as terrorists will therefore have even easier access to terrible violence at relatively low cost, and economic interactions will spread even farther into every corner of the world. The development of information and communications technology may lift human minds imbued with nationalism to a new global domain. Technological advances may well defy both the optimism of hyper-globalists and the conservatism of stubborn statists.

To ensure a more cooperative and multilaterally grounded future, the great powers in East Asia must dissolve strategic distrust to overcome the security dilemma and avoid offensive actions that would instigate predictable responses. Middle powers can help to warn against the tragic potential of great power politics, suggest better ways of realizing mutual interests, and ultimately transform the regional order. Technological advances and an ever more vibrant transnational civil society are also likely to favor processes of transformation in the international order. The result might be a more civilized states system in East Asia, with stronger institutional mechanisms of cooperation, or even an international order transformed and reliant on a new organizing principle beyond anarchy.

Part III

"Ordering Powers"

10

Hegemonic Disarray—American Internationalisms and World Disorder

Daniel Deudney

A quarter century ago, with the peaceful resolution of the Cold War, the collapse of the Soviet Union, and the end of the systemic challenge of the international communist movement, the United States stood in a position of unparalleled power, influence, and confidence. The American world order, initially put into place in the wake of World War II, appeared to ensure a degree of international order unprecedented in world history.[1] Over the last fifteen years, however, beginning with the terrorist attacks of 9/11 and the American-led "global war on terrorism" that produced the disastrous American invasion of Iraq in 2003, darker trends have begun to dominate international politics, with a seemingly endless series of civil wars and jihadist terrorist campaigns in the Middle East, Russia's return to authoritarian government and great power revisionism,[2] the Crash of 2008 and the ensuing "Great Recession," the weakening of the European Union, the failure of "democratic transitions" in many countries, the resurgence of Maoist traditionalists and regional hegemonic aspirations in China, and the harnessing of the Internet to strengthen authoritarian regimes.[3]

Changes have also affected the domestic foundations of the liberal international order. Within the established liberal democracies, growing nativist, nationalist, xenophobic, far-right, and anti-globalist movements have challenged the old order. In the United States, the elections of November 2016 resulted in a sharp shift to the Right in Congress and brought President

[1] For the definitive account of this role, see G. John Ikenberry, *Liberal Leviathan: The Origins, Crisis, and Transformation of the American World Order*, Princeton, NJ: Princeton University Press, 2011.

[2] Daniel Deudney and G. John Ikenberry, The Unraveling of the Cold War Settlement, *Survival* 51:6 (December/January 2009/10), pp. 39–62.

[3] Ronald J. Deibert, Cyberspace Under Siege, *Journal of Democracy* 26:3 (July 2015), pp. 64–78.

Donald Trump to power. In Europe, nationalist forces that openly call for withdrawal from the European Union, the abnegation of global trade agreements, and the dissolution of the NATO alliance continue to threaten the domestic political foundations of the liberal international order, despite the victory of Emmanuel Macron and his new political movement "En marche" in the presidential and parliamentary elections in France.[4] The victory of the "Brexit" vote in the UK introduced what seems likely to be a long period of uncertainty in Great Britain and the European Union. Rapidly growing populations in the poorest parts of the world, combined with stagnant or declining populations in Europe, Russia, and Japan are creating growing incentives for migration, further exacerbating nativist backlashes in the developed world.

1. HEGEMONIC TROUBLES

Until 2016, the United States seemed to sit within this swirling set of problems as if in the deceptively calm eye of a hurricane. Yet even within the country that has played such an outsized role in shaping world order for the better part of a century, winds of disorder were making themselves felt. Domestic political support in the USA for international involvements has been steadily waning.[5] Despite the net benefits of lowered trade barriers for the US economy, in the 2016 presidential race not only candidate Donald Trump, but also his Democratic opponent Hilary Clinton voiced strong criticisms of new international trade agreements, even though robust public support exists for economic "globalization" generally.[6] The voices of anti-globalist sentiment are growing in America, too, and populist anger on both the Left and the Right increasingly focuses its ire on unaccountable "global elites" devoting themselves to cosmopolitan, rather than American national, interests.

1.1. Will America Turn Inward Again?

Within American elite foreign policy discourse, increasingly influential neo-sovereigntists, libertarians, and "realists" advocate a retrenchment to "off-shore" balancing and even the acquisition of nuclear weapons by Japan

[4] Nick Corasaniti, Alexander Burns, and Binyamin Appelbaum, Trump Takes Aim at Trade Deals and "Globalism," *New York Times*, June 28, 2016, p. A1.

[5] Charles A. Kupchan and Peter L. Trubowitz, Dead Center: The Demise of Liberal Internationalism, *International Security* 32:2 (Fall 2007), pp. 7–44.

[6] Adam Taylor, Despite Campaigns' Rhetoric, Majority of Americans Polled Favor Globalization, *Washington Post*, September 7, 2016, p. A7.

and South Korea.[7] This raises the prospect of an "Amexit," an American retrenchment somewhat analogous to that after World War I, but with potentially even greater consequences for world order. Such an "Amexit" would represent the implosion of the American-led international order driven by changes in the core of the system, rather than by pressures from its periphery or the rise of rival great powers.[8] The election of Donald Trump in November 2016 demonstrated that such concerns could hardly be dismissed.

Even before the result of that election came in, however, Washington's political capacity to conduct a coherent foreign policy had been declining, calling into question the ability of the United States to play its traditional role as hegemonic leader and problem-solver. However, the political order of the United States has always been ill-suited to the conduct of great power diplomacy, largely by design. Our historical baseline for thinking about the political capacity of the American system to conduct the kind of coherent and rational foreign policy required for hegemonic ordering derives from World War II and the Cold War. In both these periods, there was a "clear and present danger" from powerful foreign great powers that made it possible for the United States to forge and implement something approaching a coherent "grand strategy."

These two periods, however, were in important ways anomalous within the overall pattern of the American conduct of foreign policy. The historical norm has been extreme partisanship and the routine exploitation of the many veto-points in the American constitutional order to thwart international initiatives. Over the last decade or so, partisanship has again grown greatly. The extreme partisan reception of the nuclear agreement with Iran in July 2015, in which not a single Congressional member of the opposition party offered support, was a clear symptom of the new partisan domestic context for American foreign policy. If the rancor evidenced in this episode became the "new normal" in American foreign policy, the United States would increasingly lack the political capacity to play the role of hegemon, whatever its "hard" economic and military capabilities.

1.2. Hegemonic Disorder

Thinking about hegemony by international relations theorists has emphasized that hegemons provide a degree of order to international systems. In this view,

[7] John Fonte, *Sovereignty or Submission: Will Americans Rule Themselves or be Ruled by Others?* New York and London: Encounter Books, 2011; Christopher Preble, *The Power Problem: How American Military Dominance Makes Us Less Safe, Less Prosperous, and Less Free*, Ithaca, NY: Cornell University Press, 2009; John J. Mearsheimer and Stephen M. Walt, The Case for Offshore Balancing: A Superior U.S. Grand Strategy, *Foreign Affairs* 95:4 (July/August 2016), pp. 70–83.

[8] Amitav Acharya, *The End of American World Order*, Oxford: Polity Press, 2014.

a hegemonic system sits in-between a simple anarchic system and one marked by the hierarchy characteristic of empires. The United States has indeed provided order in a variety of important ways since the end of World War II, but it also has been, and continues to be, a major source of disorder in international politics. In the early years of the twenty-first century, the contribution of the United States to international disorder has grown, particularly in the Greater Middle East, in the wake of American military interventions and the now chronic drone campaign. Several hundred thousand people (and about five thousand Americans) have been killed, millions of refugees have been created, and violent religious extremism, the most ostensible object of American violence, has, if anything, become more pervasive. Political scientists have created a small cottage industry of studying "failed states," but have given little attention to the phenomenon of "smashed states," such as Iraq and Libya, which were demolished by American military power, creating political and military vacuums which the United States lacked the ability (Iraq) or the will (Libya) to fill with viable alternatives.

A key notion of hegemony theory has been the idea that the hegemonic state facilitates international cooperation. In the decade and a half of the twenty-first century, the United States has indeed been an important catalyst for international cooperation in anti-terrorism activity, but this cooperation has been decidedly anti-liberal in its consequences. The objective of combating "terrorism" is widely shared by the other members of the international "community" and in the wake of 9/11, a wide array of new international cooperative policing and surveillance measures have been put in place, with American "leadership" and the support, often enthusiastic, of non-liberal states such as Russia and China. The effect of anti-terrorism measures worldwide has been to strengthen state policing and surveillance capabilities to squeeze individual rights. These measures have ample historical precedents in the era of the European Concert of Powers in the first part of the nineteenth century, when anti-revolutionary agendas united many of the leading European powers, and then again in the late nineteenth century when anarchist terrorism drove states into a variety of cooperative measures on intelligence sharing.

2. RE-THINKING AMERICA IN WORLD ORDER

How did the United States come to be a source of disorder in world politics? Many Americans are in a state of denial about the ways in which the foreign policy of the United States has become a disordering influence. Many Americans tend to view the problems afflicting world politics as something that exists *despite* the strenuous efforts of Americans to solve them, but after seventy years in which the United States has played such a major role in so many parts of the world, it is hard to sustain the illusion that the United States has only contributed to order, not disorder. There is simply too much evidence for the claim that many problems exist because of American actions and policies. For some critics of American foreign policy, such as Noam Chomsky and members of the global old Left, the expansion of American influence is straightforwardly the source of oppression and war. But such views are too one-sided, in failing to recognize the many positive impacts of American foreign policy. They are also too simple, in failing to acknowledge the diverse ways in which the United States has dealt with diverse problems.

This essay offers a more complex picture of the sources of America's disordering influences. The main argument is that the disorders produced by American influence stem from the *unintended consequences* of earlier choices and successes—consequences that often are ironic and tragic. In playing its role as hegemon, the United States has used its preponderance and exercised its leadership in a wide variety of ways. Hegemony provides the indispensable basis for influence. Yet the ways in which this influence is exercised, and the aims it seeks to realize, cannot be derived or deduced from the fact of hegemony. To understand these ways and aims it is necessary to understand the diverse internationalist visions of world order that have been employed by American leaders at different times to frame how the United States defines and solves problems, and views its interests.

The following argument proceeds in two main steps. There will be, first, a brief examination of some of the overlapping and conflicting strands of American internationalism. This will be followed by a consideration of three important problematic features of the impact of American foreign policies on contemporary world politics—the American National Security State (NSS), the turmoil in the Greater Middle East, and climate change.

2.1. Variants of American Internationalisms

The United States is often characterized as a "liberal hegemon," and the foreign policies the United States has pursued over the last seven decades to build international order are commonly referred to as "liberal internationalism." Yet the concepts of hegemony and liberal internationalism obscure as much as they reveal about the logics and patterns of American foreign policy. The internationalism that America has pursued is in fact an uneasy amalgam of several distinct world order strategies, which are sometimes reinforcing each other, but sometimes contradictory. Despite the importance of this topic, and all that has been written about it, there is nothing approaching a commonly accepted set of categories and terms for the different international policies and aims which the United States has pursued. Despite the absence of settled nomenclatures and typologies, for the purposes of this brief exposition, four major strands can be identified: *Westphalian internationalism*, *republican-constitutional internationalism*, *Rooseveltian internationalism*, and *techno-material globalism*.

It is commonly thought that any "internationalism" aims for something that is incompatible with the Westphalian international order, and aims to go beyond it. Yet this assumption overlooks the existence of *Westphalian internationalism*, an orientation that places great emphasis upon the universalization and moderation of an international system in which nation-states, not empires, are the primary units of world politics.[9] With empire as its adversary, the Westphalian internationalist is strongly committed to the maintenance of an international balance of power. For Westphalian internationalism states with significantly more capacities than others, the great powers, have a particular responsibility to maintain international order.[10] A key feature of this approach to world order, which is embodied in the core elements of the United Nations Charter, is a strong aversion to inter-state aggression. Westphalian internationalism is, in the language of the theorists of the "English School," committed to "pluralism" rather than "solidarity" and as such is comfortable with a great diversity of domestic regime types, as long as those regimes behave in ways consistent with minimal standards of international behavior. Because of its commitment to the preservation of internationally recognized borders, Westphalian internationalism has a pronounced status quo bias, and it is hostile to the ambitions of revisionist states. Although the United States is often cast, both by its admirers and its detractors, as an essentially revolutionary state due to its strong commitment to democracy and human rights, the actual conduct of American foreign policy has largely followed patterns consistent with the dictates of Westphalian internationalism.

In contrast, *republican-constitutional internationalism* is a particularly American approach. This internationalism places primary emphasis upon the preservation of the limited government constitution of the United States itself, and views a large national security state as a fundamental threat to this domestic order. In this view, threats to security arise from unchecked power, whether in anarchy or hierarchy. From the founding until the beginning of the twentieth century, this American internationalism sought to realize its goals through a policy of geo-strategic isolationism, combined with strong support

[9] Hedley Bull, *The Anarchical Society: A Study of Order in World Politics*, New York: Columbia University Press, 1977.

[10] Mlada Bukovansky, Ian Clark, Robyn Eckersley, Richard Price, Christian Reus-Smit, and Nicholas J. Wheeler, *Special Responsibilities: Global Problems and American Power*, Cambridge: Cambridge University Press, 2012.

for the "law of nations." In the context of the international system that emerged in the early twentieth century, this internationalism saw its vocation as the protection of limited government at home by moderating other states and the inter-state system in which they operated. This was to be achieved through the spread of liberal democracy within other states and through the creation of international institutions to pacify inter-state relations. The republican-constitutional motivation behind American internationalism is often overlooked.

Another internationalism that has played a prominent role in American foreign policy is what G. John Ikenberry and this author have referred to as *Rooseveltian internationalism*,[11] an American version of what Hanns Maull has called "social democratic internationalism." Although concern for commercial interests and the contribution of wealth to the achievement of power and security have been a feature of the (mercantilist) Hamiltonian tradition in American foreign policy since the eighteenth century, Rooseveltian internationalism is a distinctly twentieth-century variant. It recognized that industrial capitalism could only be made compatible with political and social democracy through the creation of strong government institutions to regulate markets, redistribute wealth, and sustain high levels of economic growth.

The last form of internationalism considered here is what might be called *technomaterial globalism*. The basic assumption of this approach is that the industrial revolution has transformed the material foundations of human life in a multitude of ways, creating high levels of interdependence and complexity that sit awkwardly on the territorial framework of nation-states; they therefore require international regulation and governance. This approach inspired many of the functional partial orders or international regimes, such as those for the regulation of nuclear weapons,[12] the governance of various extraterritorial spheres such as the oceans, the atmosphere, the electromagnetic spectrum, and outer space, and the protection of the planetary biospheric life-support systems. Far from being distinctively "liberal," technomaterial globalism is not linked to any particular domestic political regime type, as long as it is modern and competent; it is notable that the Soviet Union was a key contributor to those forms of order. With the planetary problem of climate change, the attraction of this approach to building international order is rapidly growing.[13]

[11] Daniel Deudney and G. John Ikenberry, Unraveling America the Great, *The American Interest* 11:5 (May/June 2016), pp. 7–17.
[12] See Chapter 4 by William Walker in this volume.
[13] See Chapter 2 by Joyeeta Gupta in this volume.

2.2. The National Security State (NSS) in American Global Diplomacy

The various internationalisms the United States has pursued in the twentieth century are commonly seen as a great break from the isolationism that allegedly characterized US foreign policy from its beginnings to the turn of the twentieth century. Many accounts of American "liberal internationalism," particularly those offered by self-described "realists," present the primary impulse behind this approach to world order as essentially humanitarian, as the pursuit of "ideals" and "values" rather than interests and security.[14] This view seriously misinterprets the nature of republican-constitutional internationalism that sits at the center of the cluster of internationalisms known as liberal. The key insight of the American founders was that insecurity resulted from both the extremes of anarchy and hierarchy, and that governments that were too powerful were potentially as great a security threat to the people as extremes of both internal and external anarchy.[15]

Recognizing that the perpetual threat of war contributed to the growth of powerful central governments, the founders wanted to interact with the international system in ways that minimized central state power and avoided large standing military establishments. During the first century of the American republic, this led to a foreign policy of "isolationism" with regard to security alliances and involvement in foreign wars, but support for the "laws of nations" and trade as a means to moderate the relations among states in an anarchic international system. In avoiding what Washington referred to as "foreign entanglements," the great behemoth of domestic despotism could be kept at bay. It was widely recognized that those foreign policies were feasible only because of the relative geographic isolation of the United States.

Around the turn of the twentieth century, this posture toward the world became increasingly untenable. The technologies of the industrial revolution undermined the Atlantic Ocean's value as a protective "moat," and the United States found itself drawn into wars to preserve the balance of power in Europe. The program of modern American liberal internationalism was formulated in response to this dilemma. Its essential goal was to change the world in order that the world would not change the United States. This meant promoting the transformation of other states into constitutional liberal democracies, and moderating inter-state anarchy through the development of international law,

[14] Thus, the influential commentator Walter Russell Mead sees the "Wilsonian tradition" and "liberal internationalism" as animated by the ethical impulse to eliminate war. See Walter Russell Mead, *Special Providence: American Foreign Policy and How It Changed the World*, New York: Routledge, 2002. See also Robert E. Osgood, *Ideals and Self-interest in America's Foreign Affairs: Great Transformation of the Twentieth Century*, Chicago, IL: University of Chicago Press, 1953.

[15] Daniel H. Deudney, *Bounding Power: Republican Security Theory from the Polis to the Global Village*, Princeton, NJ: Princeton University Press, 2007.

organizations, and regimes. As Woodrow Wilson put it, the goal was to "make the world safe for democracy." Although the implications of this policy for other states and the international system were profoundly revolutionary, its essential goal was markedly conservative with regard to the American domestic constitutional order.

2.3. The Rise of the National Security State

Since the middle years of the twentieth century, however, the United States has been forced to make great exertions to sustain the international balance of power in the face of powerful revisionist states, most notably Nazi Germany, Imperial Japan, and the Soviet Union. To preserve the plural state-system, the United States has been mobilized for global total war since the early 1940s.[16] Americans have generally recognized that these steps were necessary for the survival of the country, but were perilous for the domestic order; many feared that the United States would become a "garrison state."[17] As late as 1961, when President Dwight Eisenhower in his Farewell Address warned of the unwarranted influence of a "military industrial complex," this concern was widely voiced in American foreign policy discourses.

Over the long decades of the Cold War, as well as in its wake over the last quarter century, a giant National Security State has become a significant feature of the American political landscape. At the same time, the international system, which the United States in important ways had pacified and sustained through the American alliance system and international institutions, nevertheless essentially remains unsettled and illiberal. The decades of American pre-eminence, far from benefitting the United States (as many critics of American foreign policy would have it), have changed the United States in ways that are profoundly at odds with the animating vision of republican-constitutional internationalism: America's enlarged role in the world has created exactly what its Founding Fathers had hoped most to avoid, namely a large national security state. This is what I have elsewhere referred to as "the tragedy of American global diplomacy."[18]

[16] James Ledbetter, *Unwarranted Influence: Dwight D. Eisenhower and the Military–Industrial Complex*, New Haven, CT: Yale University Press, 2011.

[17] Bartholomew Sparrow, From the Outside, in Sparrow, *World War II and the American State*, Princeton, NJ: Princeton University Press, 1996; Michael J. Hogan, *A Cross of Iron: Harry S. Truman and the Origins of the National Security State, 1945–1954*, Cambridge: Cambridge University Press, 1998.

[18] Deudney, *Bounding Power*, p. 189.

2.4. Implications for International Order

This national security state, created as a means to secure some vital foreign policy objectives, influenced American world policy in two major ways that undercut not only the original vision of America's domestic order, but international order as well. First, its influence has increasingly been at odds with the pursuit of international order. Along with the growth of the NSS, new doctrines of exaggerated national "sovereignty" have gained ground in American foreign policy conversations, among them the "new sovereigntist" view that any foreign treaty or authoritative organization is intrinsically a threat to "American sovereignty" and "constitutional integrity." This doctrine essentially reverses the original American approach to sovereignty. Where the Founders viewed sovereignty as an ultimate source of authority vested in the people as a whole and feared usurpation by enlarged and ambitious governments, the new sovereigntists have essentially imported the theory of sovereignty of European authoritarian and autocratic regimes, which places complete authority and autonomy in the head of state and views any external obligation as intrinsically incompatible with its prerogatives. Perhaps the most salient case in this regard is the International Criminal Court (ICC), long a dream of internationalists. While Americans played a major role in the negotiations leading to the Treaty of Rome of 1998 establishing the ICC, the United States government bowed to the preferences of the US military and kept the ICC at arm's length.

Second, the enlarged American NSS has resulted in the atrophy of the other instruments of American influence, with the result of an excessive militarization of American foreign policy. The American national security elite and many parts of the American public under its influence view the world in highly militarized terms, routinely inflate threats, involve the United States in conflicts all over the world, and see military power as a universal solution to problems.[19]

3. THE UNITED STATES AND THE GREATER MIDDLE EAST

The region of the world most marked by disorder today is the Greater Middle East.[20] Over the last quarter century, there has been a steady deterioration of order in this region, and today violent civil wars, insurgencies, and terrorism

[19] This view was expressed by former president Barack Obama himself. See Jeffrey Goldberg, The Obama Doctrine: The U.S. President talks through his hardest decisions about America's role in the world, *The Atlantic*, April 2016, available at https://www.theatlantic.com/magazine/archive/2016/04/the-obama-doctrine/471525/ [accessed January 4, 2018].

[20] See Chapter 7 by Volker Perthes and Hanns W. Maull in this volume.

are endemic, notably in Afghanistan, Iraq, Syria, Libya, and Yemen. Hopeful events, such as the Camp David accords, the democratizing "Arab Spring," and the arms control agreement between Iran and the international community appear as exceptions to the general trend. "Spillovers" from conflicts in this unsettled region, most notably terrorism and refugee flows, have contributed to political instability in neighboring regions of Europe and northern Africa.

The involvement of the United States in the disorders of the Middle East has been extensive and growing steadily for several decades, with no clear end in sight. In many ways American involvement has been a prime contributor to *disorder*, rather than *order* in the region. With the commitment of the United States to defend the Persian Gulf monarchies in the "Carter Doctrine" of 1980, and then the massive American-led military campaign to expel Iraq from Kuwait in 1991, the American posture in the region evolved from something resembling an "off-shore balancer" into that of a "regional hegemon."[21] With the 9/11 terrorist attacks on the United States in 2001 and the subsequent military intervention in Afghanistan in 2002 to overthrow the Taliban regime, and then the 2003 invasion of Iraq and overthrow of the regime of Saddam Hussein, American activities in the Greater Middle East have come to dominate US foreign policy and heavily influence American domestic politics.[22]

More than any other set of actions, what the United States has done in the Middle East in the last fifteen years has diminished its stature as a source of world order. The direct costs to the United States so far have been some four trillion dollars, about five thousand battle deaths, and several tens of thousands of serious injuries. Relations with long-standing allies in Europe have been frayed.[23] United States practices in the "war on terrorism," ranging from torture and extrajudicial kidnapping to increasingly intrusive surveillance through the Internet, have greatly tarnished American legitimacy and international standing. These costs loom large in the arguments of those in the United States who want America to withdraw from the global leadership role it has played over the last seven decades. This party of American retrenchment views "liberal internationalist" policies such as the Iraq War and American ambitions to recast the region in its own image as disastrous examples of the conduct of American foreign policy.

[21] Andrew Bacevich, *America's War for the Greater Middle East: A Military History*, New York: Random House, 2016; Robert Jervis, *American Foreign Policy in a New Era*, New York: Routledge, 2005; Jeffrey Record, *Wanting Iraq: Why the Bush Administration Invaded Iraq*, Washington, DC: Potomac Books, 2010.

[22] John Kenneth White, Terrorism and the Remaking of American Politics, in William Crotty (ed.), *The Politics of Terror: The U.S. Response to 9/11*, Boston: Northeastern University Press, 2004, pp. 37–63.

[23] David Andrews (ed.), *The Atlantic Alliance Under Stress: US–European Relations after Iraq*, Cambridge: Cambridge University Press, 2005.

3.1. Threats from Allies

How the United States came to be involved in the conflicts of this region so deeply is a complex and controversial story. A particularly troublesome feature of the current disorders in the region is that the threats of radical jihadist violence to the United States and its allies originate not from regimes that are *adversaries* of the United States, but rather from its traditional *allies* and clients in the region, particularly Saudi Arabia. Osama bin Laden, the leader of the al-Qaida terrorist network, was the scion of a prominent Saudi family, and almost all the 9/11 hijackers were Saudi citizens.[24]

It is important to underscore just how deeply implicated Saudi Arabia and its lavishly subsidized Wahhabi clerical establishment have been in the rise of anti-modern and violently jihadist Islam. The Saudi monarchy, which dates to the late 1920s, came into existence through, and continues to be based on, an alliance between the House of Saud, now counting several thousand family members, and the Wahhabi sect of Islam, which is extremely puritanical and anti-Western. Wahhabism emerged among the Bedouin tribes in the harsh deserts of Arabia during the eighteenth century. The legal system of the kingdom, based on Sharia law, enshrines oppression of women and minorities, capital punishment for apostasy, and the complete prohibition of all other religions within the kingdom. From the standpoint of the "human rights" standards that the United States and its European allies have sought to institutionalize worldwide, the Saudi regime is among the worst. Even more troubling, Saudi Arabia has been aggressively exporting its brand of Islam, especially since the seizure and bloody battle for the Grand Mosque of Mecca in 1979. All over the world, clerics trained, educated, and generously subsidized by the Saudi religious establishment have pulled Islamic communities sharply in radically conservative directions.

While the Saudi regime, itself a target of radical terrorism, officially condemns and opposes violent jihadi activity, the Islamic communities shaped by its influence have offered fertile recruiting grounds for jihadi activism all across the globe. It is notable that the regime that was established during this decade in the Sunni parts of Syria and Iraq, known as "Islamic State in Iraq and Syria" (ISIS) or "Islamic State in Iraq and the Levant" (ISIL), was in many ways a rough-hewn version of Saudi Arabia. After taking power in several cities, the ISIS militants, confronting the tasks of running a government, simply imported Saudi textbooks for its schools. Its numerous beheadings, which horrified the civilized world, emulate a routine Saudi practice.

[24] Lawrence Wright, *The Looming Tower: Al-Qaeda and the Road to 9/11*, New York: Knopf, 2006.

Some indication of the global influence of the Saudi religious network can be seen in the evolution of Islamic communities in Kosovo, the part of the former Yugoslavia that a NATO intervention led by the United States liberated from Serbian genocide and ethnic cleansing in 1999.[25] Historically, Kosovar Muslims had been tolerant and comfortable with secular freedoms, but with extensive training and subsidies from Saudi Arabia, Kosovar clerics drew many congregations toward the Saudi version of Islam, and Kosovo became a recruiting ground for violent jihad, with many of its young men joining ISIS.

3.2. The Road Not Taken

Viewing the forces in conflict in the region, many American commentators ask "where are the Arab moderates?" The short answer to this question is that the United States and its allies crushed them. In the fateful struggle for the direction of the Arab world during the era of decolonization, the United States lined up on the wrong side and is now reaping the consequences. Like other peoples under European imperial rule elsewhere, the Arab world witnessed the rise of nationalist movements that aspired to make the Arab world independent of European rule and to build modern societies. In those, religion and tradition would have greatly diminished roles, and national Arab identity would dominate over traditional ethnic, religious, and gender identities. During the middle years of the twentieth century, this movement was very successful, coming into power in Egypt, by far the most populous Arab country, as well as in Syria and Iraq, through military coups (at that time, the officer corps was the spearhead of secular Arab nationalism).

Because the Arab nation, like the German and Italian peoples before their political unifications in the nineteenth century, was divided into multiple states, many of them weak and dominated by outside powers, a central objective of the Arab nationalist program was the political unification of the Arab world. From the secular nationalist perspective, the oil-rich regimes of the Persian Gulf region were illegitimate bastions of reactionary religious ideology, as well as clients of outside great powers and squanderers of the hydrocarbon patrimony of the Arab nation.

By the first decade of this century, the secular Arab national modernization project had largely disappeared. The failure of the Arab modernization and political unification project in the Middle East contrasts with the success of numerous other nationalist postcolonial projects, in Latin America during the nineteenth century and elsewhere in Asia in the middle years of the twentieth century. As the Middle East expert Ian Lustick has pointed out, efforts by

[25] Carlota Gall, How Kosovo Was Turned Into Fertile Ground for ISIS, *New York Times*, May 22, 2016, p. A1.

outside powers to thwart Arab unification and modernization started as early as the mid-nineteenth century. With the waning of European colonial powers in the wake of World War II, the Suez Canal Crisis of 1956, and the retreat of Britain from "East of Suez" in 1971, the United States stepped in to play this role.[26]

In many ways, American opposition to the Arab national modernization and unification project was an anomaly in the US response to the aspirations of colonial peoples to independence. As the "first new nation" born from a successful revolt against European colonial rule, the United States generally supported anti-colonial struggles, and Americans held up their "republican" project as antithetical to imperialism.[27] In the wake of World War II, the United States prodded the Europeans to accede to the independence of peoples in Indonesia, India, and Africa. They deviated from this posture, however, where communists coalesced with nationalist movements, most notably in Vietnam—and in the Arab world.[28]

American access to the oil wealth of Saudi Arabia plays some role in explaining this posture. Although a united Arab nation would certainly have been eager to sell oil to the United States and its Cold War allies, the commercial interests of American oil companies would have suffered, yet on numerous occasions, the US government over-rode commercial interests when larger strategic objectives were at stake.[29] Another factor was the Cold War competition with the Soviet Union. However, a strong and unified Arab nation would have been a much stronger bulwark against Russian advances than the patchwork quilt of weak states that came to make up the region. The alliance with conservative Islam against atheistic communism, not just in the Middle East but in the southern parts of the Soviet Union as well, appealed to American governments committed to the anti-Soviet project. This unholy alliance played a key role in the success of the resistance to the Soviet occupation of Afghanistan during the 1980s. The survival of the state of Israel also would have been in doubt if Arab nationalism had achieved its aspiration to unite the Arab-speaking world.

[26] Ian S. Lustick, The Absence of Middle Eastern Great Powers: Political "Backwardness" in Historical Perspective, *International Organization* 51:4 (Autumn 1997), pp. 653–83.

[27] Ian Tyrrell and Jay Sexton (eds.), *Empire's Twin: U.S. Anti-Imperialism from the Founding Era to the Age of Terrorism*, Ithaca, NY: Cornell University Press, 2015; Seymour Martin Lipset, *The First New Nation: The United States in Historical and Comparative Perspective*, New York: Basic Books, 1963; David Armitage, *The Declaration of Independence: A Global History*, Cambridge, MA: Harvard University Press, 2007.

[28] William Roger Louis, *Imperialism at Bay: The United States and the Decolonization of the British Empire, 1941–1945*, Oxford: Oxford University Press, 1978.

[29] Stephen D. Krasner, *Defending the National Interest: Raw Materials Investments and U.S. Foreign Policy*, Princeton, NJ: Princeton University Press, 1978.

4. FROM ECONOMIC PROSPERITY TO CLIMATE CATASTROPHE

Another major instance of yesterday's solution becoming today's problem is visible in the relationship between economic prosperity and climate change. The Earth's climate is starting to change in ways that threaten to cause widespread disruption in the decades ahead, and slowing climate change is now one of the major problems confronting the international system. The primary cause of climate change is the emission of "greenhouse gases," most notably carbon dioxide from the burning of fossil fuels by electricity generating plants and automobiles. Critics from the Left proclaim that "green is the new red" and argue that climate change is a planetary emergency caused largely by capitalism that can only be remedied by the replacement of capitalism with another, more environmentally sustainable system of economic production.[30]

In many ways, however, the emerging planetary climate problem is rooted in the success of liberal democratic capitalism's response to mass impoverishment. The years since the end of World War II have witnessed unprecedented growth in both the American and the world economy. Among the great powers and ideological movements that vied for global supremacy in the upheavals of the twentieth century, both the United States with its system of liberal democratic capitalism and the Soviet Union with its system of democratic centralism and state socialism, were distinctive from other rivals (such as Japan or Nazi Germany) in that they aimed for universal prosperity. The question of which system could best deliver on this goal was one of the decisive fronts in the long struggle between Soviet communism and Western capitalism. Freedom from "Want" was one of Franklin Roosevelt's "Four Freedoms" that defined the American vision of war aims and postwar order.[31] The Great Depression of the 1930s called the future of capitalism into question and contributed to the rise of radical anti-democratic movements on both the Left and the Right. In response, Roosevelt's New Deal and then the European Christian Democratic and Social Democratic versions of the welfare state revived capitalism's widespread ideological appeal as a model for development and prosperity. The appeal of the "American way of life" with its high-consumption lifestyle has been felt in every corner of the world, as the period of American ascendancy coincided with unparalleled economic growth in many regions of the world.

As it turns out, however, the solution to yesterday's problem of mass poverty has become the source of today's problem of planetary ecological

[30] See, for example, McKenzie Wark, *Molecular Red: Theory for the Anthropocene*, London: Verso, 2015.

[31] Jeffrey A. Engel (ed.), *Four Freedoms: FDR and the Evolution of an American Idea*, Oxford: Oxford University Press, 2016.

destruction. The impact of capitalist economic activity is about to create a fundamentally new world, in which the twentieth-century American model is no longer viable.[32] Even the characterization of the dominant economic system as "capitalism" is increasingly called into doubt, as it privileges consumption at the expense of depleting the "capital" of the Earth's capacity to support humans. In that sense, we do not have capitalism, but anti-capitalism. With a human population that numbered only two billion in 1930 now swollen to well over seven billion and barreling toward nine to ten billion at mid-century (with much of the growth in the poorest parts of the world), both population and economic "corrections" of ghastly proportions seem increasingly likely.

Climate change, in particular, seems destined soon to swamp all other global problems; if all goes well, the next hegemonic leader will emerge as the global problem-solver in this context.[33] The ability of the United States to lead the world in grappling with the demands of the "Anthropocene" will be determined by a political struggle within the United States. On the one hand, there is a powerful coalition of fossil fuel industries with the countryside and religiously inspired skeptics of climate science. On the other hand, there is the broad-based environmental movement, which has already made significant inroads toward a low carbon future through energy conservation and the promotion of renewable energy sources, most notably wind and solar, and dominates politically in many cities and some states, most notably California.

5. CONCLUSION: THE TRAGIC IRONY OF AMERICAN GLOBAL DIPLOMACY

This survey of America's disordering impact on the present international order as the result of unintended consequences of its different internationalist projects has revealed that yesterday's solutions became a source of today's problems. The agenda of Westphalian internationalism to preserve the global balance of power required the creation of a vast national security state. It also led the United States to oppose Arab national modernization and support conservative regimes in the region that are now a significant source of terrorist

[32] One indicator of the magnitude of this problem is the recent claim that, if the cost of "un-externalized externalities" is taken into account, there has been no net economic growth over the last several decades. See Robert Costanza, Ralph d'Arge, Rudolf de Groot, Stephen Farber, Monica Grasso, Bruce Hannon, and Karin Limburg, The Value of the World's Ecosystem Services and Natural Capital, *Ecological Economics* 25:1 (April 1998), pp. 3–15; Paul Hawken, Amory B. Lovins, and L. Hunter Lovins, *Natural Capitalism*, Boston: Little, Brown, 1999.

[33] See Chapter 13 by Daniel Krahl in this volume.

threats. The NSS solution to the problem of inter-state aggression has militarized American foreign policy and impeded the creation of international regimes and organizations to solve global problems and moderate inter-state anarchy. Similarly, the agenda of republican-constitutional internationalism to "make the world safe for democracy" has expanded the zone of democratic governance in the world at the cost of eroding its foundations at home. And the great success of Rooseveltian internationalism in providing for decades of prosperity both domestically and internationally now inadvertently threatens the life-support systems of our planet. The United States' internationalism and its role in the world are therefore both ironic and tragic.

6. POST-SCRIPTUM: REFLECTIONS ON THE FIRST YEAR OF PRESIDENT DONALD TRUMP

This essay was largely written in the summer of 2016, when the election campaign in America was in full swing. The outcome of those elections and the experiences with the first year of US foreign policy under President Trump validate its core argument about the tragic and ironic consequences of US hegemony. Donald Trump's victory reflects both the enormous material and human burden that America's misguided policies in the Middle East imposed on US society and the failure of its democratic order to distribute this burden fairly. His foreign policies have taken up some of the demands of his nativist, nationalist, and xenophobic base, as with his decisions to take the USA out of the Transpacific Partnership (TPP) on his third day in office, to terminate US government participation in the Paris Agreement to combat climate change, and to recognize Jerusalem as the capital of Israel in defiance of the policies of all previous US administrations since 1990. Although on balance the foreign policy record of this administration in 2017 was erratic and inchoate, rather than outright destructive, the specter of "Amexit" still looms large: in a perceptive essay, Evan Osnos characterized Trump's foreign policy as "retreating from the front," as opposed to President Barack Obama's alleged doctrine of "leading from behind."[34] Its National Security Strategy paints a Darwinian image of an "extraordinarily dangerous world" of zero-sum competition, in which China and Russia, as "rival powers" were "aggressively undermining American interests around the globe"[35] and—while it does not outright discard its alliances and the

[34] Evan Osnos, Making China Great Again: How Beijing learned to use Trump to its advantage, *The New Yorker*, January 8, 2018, available at https://www.newyorker.com/magazine/2018/01/08/making-china-great-again [accessed January 4, 2018].

[35] President of the United States, *National Security Strategy of the United States of America*, Washington, DC, December 2017, available at https://www.whitehouse.gov/wp-content/uploads/2017/12/NSS-Final-12-18-2017-0905.pdf [accessed January 4, 2018], p. 1.

multilateral institutions of the liberal international order—offers little to its allies whose support for its policies it persistently evokes and requests.[36] With its one-sided reliance on Saudi Arabia's present leadership, its recognition of Jerusalem as Israel's capital, and Trump's determination to undermine the nuclear agreement with Iran concluded by his predecessor with all the other permanent members of the UN Security Council, Germany, and the European Union, this administration seems bound to continue America's dysfunctional role in the Middle Eastern regional order.[37] The same also seems true for the partial functional order on climate change, where President Trump not only has announced America's withdrawal from the Paris Agreement but initiated a number of policy changes that favor the fossil fuel industries to the detriment of renewable energy. There, too, this administration's contributions to international order are likely to be dysfunctional.

Will that help or hinder the future evolution of the international order? Will the Trump administration further undermine it, or in the end perhaps—in another ironic twist—encourage the rise of an alternative, post-Western order, that would most likely be guided by China? At present, disorder seems more plausible than a revival of international order, under whatever auspices. However that may be, the future evolution of international order will reverberate strongly not only around the globe, but also within the national political order of the United States itself, as the Founding Fathers understood very well.

[36] *National Security Strategy of the United States of America.*
[37] See Chapter 11 by Marco Overhaus in this volume.

11

The United States and Regional Security Orders in the Middle East, East Asia, and Europe

Marco Overhaus

1. INTRODUCTION

The United States of America is still the only power with the capability to have a major impact—for better or for worse—on the security orders in all major geographical regions of the world, most notably the Near/Middle East, East Asia, and Europe. For seven decades after World War II, the USA has defined its international role in *liberal* terms, that is to say as a power that pursues a broader set of objectives, including security, free trade, and the rule of law, and that builds its leadership role not only on military might but also on international organizations, diffuse—as opposed to transactional—reciprocity, and self-restraint.

This liberal concept of American leadership and hegemony had already been challenged in all of the major world regions well before Donald Trump entered the scene. The new president's words and deeds have created additional uncertainty about the future course of US foreign policy. While Trump's National Security Strategy, published in December 2017, is full of references to international cooperation and liberal values, *in essence* it depicts the world and its geographic regions as arenas in which states compete for power.[1] At the same time the USA seems to have diminished in power to shape regional dynamics.

The simultaneous erosion of regional security orders and US liberal hegemonic power raises the question of how these phenomena relate to each other.

[1] President of the United States, *National Security Strategy of the United States of America*, Washington, DC, December 2017, p. 25, available at https://www.whitehouse.gov/wp-content/uploads/2017/12/NSS-Final-12-18-2017-0905.pdf.

This chapter addresses this question by looking at the principal dynamics inside each of those three regions. While there is an abundance of literature on US foreign and security policy, the specific ambition here is to assess the interaction of US security policies and regional dynamics across geographically defined security sub-orders in the Middle East, East Asia, and Europe from a comparative perspective. This view makes it possible to identify interference between America's approaches to different regional orders and the responses to those policies in the respective regions.

2. SIGNS OF EROSION

As is argued in the Introduction to this volume, one important measure of whether political orders can be considered *effective* is whether they successfully contain the use of threat and violence among the major participants in the system, "prevent unchecked aggression or abuse" of force and help "to prevent or rapidly contain civil war, at least in strategically significant states."[2] Measured by this benchmark, the erosion of regional security is most obvious in North Africa and the Middle East where not only civil strife is spreading but where major powers are also engaged in proxy wars. Wider Europe, too, is experiencing a civil war with external intervention in Ukraine that is to a significant degree spurred by a power struggle between the "West" and Russia. The regional security order in East Asia is still working in the sense that the use of force between states has been contained so far. Yet, signs of erosion are visible here as well. Tensions between China and its neighbors over territorial claims in the East and South China Seas have intensified since 2010, raising the risk of armed conflict in this region as well. In 2017 North Korea successfully tested an intercontinental ballistic missile while tensions between Washington and Pyongyang reached previously unknown levels. A war with North Korea would have devastating consequences far beyond Northeast Asia.

The erosion of regional security orders has coincided with indications of a declining willingness and ability of the United States to shape these orders. This includes Obama's "red line" being crossed by Syria's Assad regime when it used chemical weapons against the civilian population with impunity, and political allegations that American weakness has enabled Russia to step into the void in Syria.[3] Yet, it is not only the perception of American weakness but

[2] Bruce Jones and Thomas Wright, The State of the International Order, Washington, DC: Brookings, February 2014, pp. 4f. (= Policy Paper 33). See also the Introduction to this volume by Hanns W. Maull.

[3] For a discussion of Russian policy in Syria and how it relates to US policy, see Julia Ioffe, Russia's Game Plan in Syria Is Simple, in *Foreign Policy*, September 25, 2015, available at

also of American disinterest that is raising doubts in the region about the US security role. The shale revolution in the USA, with its unprecedented levels of exploitation of unconventional gas and oil[4] and Obama's eagerness to strike a deal with Iran over its nuclear program have led to allegations, especially among the Arab Gulf monarchies, that Washington's Middle East policy is unreliable and that the USA is disengaging from the region.[5]

Such suspicions have made the relationships between the USA and the Arab countries much more complex. At the same time, America's relations with other traditional allies in the region have deteriorated as well. Israel's government felt alienated by the Obama administration's vocal criticism of its settlement policies. In Egypt, Washington pursued a rather ambivalent policy after the military, led by General Abdel Fattah al-Sisi, ousted then president Mohammed Morsi in July 2013.

America's troubles in the Middle East have resulted both from its own policy shortcomings and more difficult regional dynamics. In any case, these troubles certainly cannot be solely attributed to the Obama presidency. The United States had lost legitimacy and influence in the Middle East long before and, according to Joel Migdal, its position by 2010 had become tenuous: popular support for the USA had declined in most countries of the region and "there were no full-blown strategic allies to which Washington could outsource regional responsibilities."[6]

President Trump's policy in the Persian Gulf and in the wider Middle East departs from his predecessor's in some crucial ways. He relies, first and foremost, on the alliance with Saudi Arabia which is backed up by a massive armaments cooperation package.[7] At the same time he wants to abandon the nuclear agreement with Iran as it stands and to contain and roll back Tehran's influence in the region.[8] While this policy shift is much to the liking of the rulers in Riyadh or Abu Dhabi it is questionable if Washington has the

http://foreignpolicy.com/2015/09/25/russias-game-plan-in-syria-is-simple-putin-assad/ [accessed February 13, 2017].

[4] Kirsten Westphal, Marco Overhaus, and Guido Steinberg, *The U.S. Shale Revolution and the Arab Gulf States: The Economic and Political Impact of Changing Energy Markets*, Berlin: SWP (German Institute for International and Security Affairs), November 2014 (= Research Paper RP 11).

[5] Emile Hokayem and Becca Wasser, *The Gulf States in an Era of American Retrenchment*, London: Routledge for IISS, 2014, pp. 135–64 (152) (= Adelphi Series No. 447–8).

[6] Joel S. Migdal, *Shifting Sands: The United States in the Middle East*, New York: Columbia University Press, 2014, p. 329.

[7] Aaron Mehta, Revealed: Trump's $110 Billion Weapons List for the Saudis, *Defense News*, June 8, 2017, available at https://www.defensenews.com/breaking-news/2017/06/08/revealed-trump-s-110-billion-weapons-list-for-the-saudis/ [accessed December 15, 2017].

[8] In October 2017 President Trump published his "New Strategy on Iran." See Office of the Press Secretary, The White House: President Donald J. Trump's New Strategy on Iran, Washington, DC, October 13, 2017, available at https://www.whitehouse.gov/briefings-statements/president-donald-j-trumps-new-strategy-iran/ [accessed December 15, 2017].

resources and instruments to keep Iran in a box and if the policy shift will afford the USA more leverage in the Gulf.

The United States' ability to shape regional security has also declined in the other two regions. While America is still the "hub" in East Asia's regional security order, it is no longer able to shape the security developments in this region to the same extent as in the past. In both political and economic security terms, the East Asian order is undergoing, in the words of James B. Steinberg and Michael O'Hanlon, "massive, tectonic change, driven primarily by China's remarkable economic rise in recent decades."[9] China's military modernization is beginning to challenge the US military posture in Asia-Pacific and has made it much more difficult for Washington to manage its numerous bilateral security alliances and arrangements with regional actors while simultaneously engaging with, but also hedging against, a rising China. Obama's policy of the "rebalance" towards Asia was also meant as an attempt to deal with these complexities. One of Trump's first policy decisions was to withdraw the United States from the economic leg of the rebalance, the Transpacific Partnership (TPP) trade agreement. At the same time he is likely to sustain, and potentially expand, the US military presence in the region.[10]

In Europe, US leadership had been tested during the Balkan wars in the 1990s. Until 2014, however, wider Europe (the European Union and its eastern neighborhood) was mostly seen in Washington and European capitals as a source of security and stability rather than insecurity (the 2008 Georgian war notwithstanding). The Russian annexation of Crimea and the civil war in Ukraine have strongly challenged these assumptions. While a direct military confrontation between NATO and Russia still looks like a remote possibility, Moscow's assertiveness has highlighted security vulnerabilities of the Atlantic Alliance's eastern region, especially in the three Baltic Republics.

These recent developments have re-emphasized the significance of the US security and military presence in Europe for both traditional military and more "hybrid" scenarios. European NATO members remain critically dependent on the United States' strategic enablers, such as air protection, intelligence, and airlift. However, threat perceptions widely diverge among European NATO allies today. Trump's ambivalent statements on NATO's relevance[11] have also raised questions about the future US role as an

[9] James B. Steinberg and Michael O'Hanlon, Keep Hope Alive: How to Prevent U.S.–Chinese Relations from Blowing Up, *Foreign Affairs*, June 16, 2014, available at https://www.foreignaffairs.com/articles/asia/2014-06-16/keep-hope-alive [accessed April 21, 2017].

[10] Patrick Cullen, The Rebalance to Asia under Trump: What Comes Next? *The RUSI Journal* 162:2 (April/May 2017), pp. 8–15 (8).

[11] During the election campaign Trump suggested that the United States' willingness to defend its allies in Europe and Asia will depend on the USA being "reasonably reimbursed for the tremendous cost of protecting these massive nations with tremendous wealth": David E. Sanger and Maggie Haberman, Transcript: Donald Trump on NATO, Turkey's Coup Attempt

indispensable security guarantor in Europe. Within the USA it is debated—often through the lenses of party politics—to what extent US retrenchment or, on the contrary, US overreach has damaged the country's standing and influence in regional contexts. Thus, Brat Stephens claims that "global disorders [were] spurred by American retreat."[12] An alternative view is that imperial overreach and hubris first led to the disintegration of Iraq, a process that eventually spread into Syria and the Middle East as a whole.[13] Chester Crocker adopts a third, more structuralist view according to which the erosion of international order is not primarily caused either by deeds or omissions of the United States but rather by "unregulated diffusion of authority, agency, and responsibility."[14] According to this view, states in general, not just the United States, have lost some of their authority and their capacity for action while problems such as migration and cyber-security have proliferated, thus causing a "system overload" and eventually "a world adrift."[15]

3. THE FUTURE OF LIBERAL HEGEMONY

Liberal hegemony is a suitable *ideal-type* to assess the role of the United States in regional security orders for both empirical and normative reasons. The perception of the United States—both inside and outside the country—as a crucial and *legitimate* provider or even guarantor of regional security orders has predominantly been based on the notion of liberal internationalism and hegemony. After World War II, in Germany and most West European countries as well as in Japan and South Korea (though much less so in the Soviet space and the Middle East), the view of America's role was shaped by liberal internationalism. In the geographical spaces outside the West, America's public appeal often rested also on its engagement with liberal principles. Post-World War II international institutions, such as the United Nations and the World Bank, were founded on these principles.

Liberal internationalism has also been the dominant approach inside the USA.[16] The preference for an active foreign and security policy, including a

and the World, *New York Times*, July 21, 2016, available at https://www.nytimes.com/2016/07/22/us/politics/donald-trump-foreign-policy-interview.html [accessed December 15, 2017].

[12] Brat Stephens, What Obama Gets Wrong: No Retreat, No Surrender, *Foreign Affairs* 94:5 (September/October 2015), pp. 13–16 (16).

[13] See Chapter 10 by Daniel Deudney in this volume.

[14] Chester A. Crocker, The Strategic Dilemma of a World Adrift, *Survival* 57:1 (February/March 2015), pp. 7–30 (13).

[15] Ibid., p. 23.

[16] Raphael S. Cohen and Gabriel M. Scheinmann, Can Europe Fill the Void in U.S. Military Leadership? *Orbis* 58:1 (Winter 2014), pp. 39–54 (39).

strong military posture abroad, complemented by foreign assistance, free trade, and multilateralism within international institutions, has stretched to the mainstream of both Republicans and Democrats as long as these parties were both relatively broad-based in ideological terms.[17] Barry Posen posits (with a critical undertone) that after the end of the Cold War, US policy was still characterized by a "consensus grand strategy of liberal hegemony,"[18] a strategy that includes a preference for an assertive foreign and security policy as well as the promotion of democratic governance, rule of law, free market capitalism, and international trade.

According to G. John Ikenberry, liberal hegemony is hierarchical while at the same time it rests on "political bargains, diffuse reciprocity, provision of public goods, and mutually agreeable institutions and working relationships" while the hegemonic state "operates to a greater or lesser extent within those rules and institutions."[19] Liberal international order is "sustained through consent rather than balance or command"[20] which is what distinguishes it from other systems such as geo-political blocs, exclusive regional spheres, or closed imperial systems.

Against this background, the ability to forge *winning coalitions* is crucial for the hegemon's ability to shape regional security orders. A "winning coalition" is a coalition of states and non-state actors that is both willing and able to maintain effectiveness of the order. Liberal hegemony is thus based on the assumption that effectiveness of the regional or global order can best be achieved if one or a few great powers provide for the public international good.[21] In the area of security, the United States is still the only power that is potentially able to fulfill such a role across all regional security orders.

To be sure, liberal hegemony has both a cooperative and a coercive dimension. On the one hand, the United States aims to reassure the members of its coalition that their security will be safeguarded as part of the security of the system as a whole.[22] What matters most to keep the coalition together is legitimacy among a sufficiently large number of other countries of the system

[17] Steven Hurst, Parties, Polarization, and U.S. Foreign Policy, in Inderjeet Parmar, Linda B. Miller, and Mark Ledwidge (eds.), *Obama and the World: New Directions in U.S. Foreign Policy*, 2nd edn, London and New York: Routledge, 2014, pp. 95–106 (96).

[18] Barry Posen, *Restraint: A New Foundation for U.S. Grand Strategy*, Ithaca, NY and London: Cornell University Press, 2014, p. 5.

[19] G. John Ikenberry, *Liberal Leviathan: The Origins, Crisis, and Transformation of the American World Order*, Princeton, NJ: Princeton University Press, 2011, p. 26.

[20] Ibid., p. 18.

[21] Ulrich Menzel, *Die Ordnung der Welt: Imperium oder Hegemonie in der Hierarchie der Staatenwelt*, Berlin: Suhrkamp, 2015, p. 37.

[22] For a more abstract explanation, not just limited to the realm of security, see Andrew Kydd, In America We (Used to) Trust: U.S. Hegemony and Global Cooperation, *Political Science Quarterly* 120:4 (2005–6), pp. 619–36 (620f.).

rather than coercion or domination.[23] On the other hand, the hegemon must be able to credibly deter or punish those states or actors that threaten the security and rules of the system, using the political, financial, and military instruments at its disposal.

The great power(s) provide the international public good called "security," help create rules and institutions which to some extent also restrain their own behavior, and offer lesser states some opportunities to influence their policies and the system as a whole.

Clearly, the United States has played such a role—albeit in different forms and to different degrees—in the regional security orders of Europe, Asia, and the Middle East. Within the NATO framework it reassured West European states over fears of a rearmed West Germany and the Soviet threat while offering all states a say in Washington's security and defense political choices (e.g., with regard to "nuclear sharing"). In East Asia, the United States has performed a similar role vis-à-vis Japan and China by embedding the former into a military alliance and thus reassuring other states in the region against both nations. In the words of Lee Kuan Yew, the USA has been the "least distrusted power" in the region.[24] Even China accepted the USA's hegemonic role because it benefitted economically from it.

In the Middle East, America inherited Britain's hegemonic status. It gradually enhanced its role in the region and by the end of the Iran–Iraq War in the 1980s, the USA had become the dominant political and military power in the Persian Gulf. The stabilization of international oil markets and efforts to mediate the Israeli–Palestinian conflict were the "liberal" aspects of US hegemony in this region. Free trade, multilateralism, or the promotion of democratic governance have not been central pillars of Washington's policy in the Middle East.

In view of the current turmoil in the Middle East, one shortcoming of liberal internationalism (as well as of alternative approaches to US foreign policy) already is obvious: It is focused almost exclusively on states and thus still rests on the assumptions of the Westphalian model of international order. From this point of view, the demise of order within states—often termed "failing states"—is primarily seen as a security challenge to be managed rather than as a crucial feature of the demise of regional security orders themselves.

It is not only dynamics abroad that affect Washington's ability to play its hegemonic role in regional security orders. Sufficient support at home, within the United States, for international liberalism is also an important factor. The latter mainly concerns the political will of major domestic actors, as well as

[23] Nick Kitchen, Hegemonic Transition and U.S. Foreign Policy, in Parmar et al. (eds.), *Obama and the World*, pp. 80–92 (84).

[24] Quoted in Nick Bisley, Neither Empire nor Republic: American Power and the Regional Order in the Asia-Pacific, *International Politics* 43 (2006), pp. 197–218 (199).

their willingness to help mobilize the financial resources to underpin America's hegemonic role.

Economic woes—the rising levels of public debt, eroding infrastructure, underperforming education systems, and the fallout from the financial crisis of 2008—as well as the costly, unsuccessful, and open-ended foreign policy entanglements in Afghanistan and Iraq—have combined to incite a mood of "inwardness" and a critical view on the global responsibilities of the United States.

These factors have surely facilitated the election of Donald Trump. However, they should not be equated with an isolationist turn in the United States. Barack Obama had widely been criticized, and not only by Republicans, for his administration's alleged lack of engagement and decisiveness in foreign and security policy. Trump wants to preserve American military superiority based on forward military presence, globally mobile forces, and extended nuclear deterrence.[25] What distinguishes him from his predecessor is that he does not seem to be interested in "order building"—and certainly not if it involves extending US commitment to multilateral institutions.

4. REGIONAL DYNAMICS AND US APPROACHES

4.1. Near and Middle East

In the Near and Middle East—spanning North Africa, the Levant, the Arabian Peninsula, and the Persian Gulf—the erosion of the regional security order is most obvious: state order has collapsed in Libya, Syria, Iraq, and Yemen. This vacuum has enabled terror organizations such as the "Islamic State" to spread and it also fanned proxy wars and interventions by the two major regional powers, Saudi Arabia and Iran.[26]

The so-called "Arab Spring" was the climax of a long process of social mobilization driven by declining development standards[27] and increasing frustration with authoritarian rulers. The uprisings had two faces: they gave rise to "...vibrant civil organizations bridging sectarian, ethnic and other differences," but they also catalyzed "...social violence between various religious, kinship, and ethnic groups—communities that had often [...] coexisted peacefully [...] under the thumb of autocrats."[28] Although the US intervention in Iraq in 2003, driven by the neoconservative agenda of the first George W. Bush administration to bring democracy to the Middle East,

[25] *National Security Strategy* 2017, p. 3.
[26] See Chapter 7 by Volker Perthes and Hanns W. Maull in this volume.
[27] Migdal, *Shifting Sands*, p. 317. [28] Ibid., p. 333.

helped to accelerate the demise of regional security, the national and regional dynamics that made it so fragile had developed over the previous decades.

While Washington's role and influence in the Middle East had increased at the beginning of the 1970s, it tried to secure its hegemony with a light security and military footprint, effectively playing the role of an "external balancer." For this approach to work, the USA had to rely on alliances with Israel, Arab states (first and foremost Saudi Arabia), and Iran (still under the Shah). These alliances were much more fluid (and far less institutionalized) than in Western Europe, yet the system worked at times rather well. As a consequence, Washington enjoyed an influential position in the region that could build on a broad coalition.

The Yom-Kippur War of 1973 surely diminished the USA's hegemonic role. However, after Egypt and Israel concluded a peace treaty in 1979—and after Egypt left the Soviet orbit—Cairo became a member of the American-led coalition.[29] Improved relations with the Arab Gulf states also helped, especially after the creation of the Gulf Cooperation Council in 1981.[30]

The Islamic revolution in Iran, which long had been an important regional power, resulted in an important shift away from the dominance of pro-Western forces in the region.[31] The fall of the Taliban regime in Afghanistan in 2001 and of Saddam Hussein in Iraq in 2003 further strengthened Iran's influence in the Middle East as it eliminated two of the country's "greatest strategic threats in its immediate neighbourhood."[32] The increasingly fierce struggle between Iran and Saudi Arabia exacerbated tensions between Shi'ite and Sunni Islam, further destabilizing both the domestic and regional orders in the Middle East. As a consequence, the influence of the United States in the region has been eroding as can be witnessed in Bahrain, Iraq, and Yemen.

While Iran had already started its involvement in Lebanon and Iraq soon after the revolution in 1979, the fall of Saddam Hussein in 2003 emboldened Tehran to pursue an even more assertive regional agenda.[33] In the future, the balance likely will shift further in Iran's favor: the wealth (and hence the power) of the Arab Gulf states depends on finite oil and gas reserves whose world market prices have been hugely volatile. This is to a lesser extent also true for Iran which, however, also has a relatively young and well-educated population with "tremendous potential once its isolation ends."[34]

In the past, successive US governments had great difficulties in adapting their regional strategies to the changes and power shifts occurring in the region. Since taking office at the beginning of 2009, President Obama's

[29] Ibid., p. 311. [30] Ibid., p. 311. [31] Ibid., p. 323.

[32] Lawrence J. Korb and Daniel de Wit, Beyond Iraq: Lasting Issues for the U.S. in the Middle East, in Robert E. Looney (ed.), *Handbook of U.S.-Middle East Relations: Formative Factors and Regional Perspectives*, London and New York: Routledge, 2009, pp. 25–37 (25).

[33] Ibid., p. 28. [34] Jones and Wright, The State of the International Order, p. 31.

approach to the region aimed at restoring US legitimacy while reducing the US military footprint in Iraq and Afghanistan. In order to gradually disentangle America, Obama sought to delegate more responsibility to local allies while cautiously engaging Iran (limited at first to the nuclear dossier). For this strategy to work, the USA would have to remold its alliances and relationships with key regional actors on a broader and more balanced basis.

During his first year in office President Trump has taken the opposite direction. He builds his Middle East policy almost exclusively on the US alliances with Saudi Arabia and Israel while shutting the door on any positive engagement with Iran. This policy calls into question the nuclear agreement with Iran even though it has decreased the risk of nuclear proliferation in the region. The unconditional siding with Saudi Arabia has also fueled tensions inside the Gulf Cooperation Council (especially between Riyadh and Doha). Trump's unilateral recognition of Jerusalem as Israel's capital in December 2017 has further discredited Washington as a broker between Israelis and Palestinians.

The dilemma for any future US administration, whether Democratic or Republican, is that the intensification of regional competition and the simultaneous collapse of state orders has made it much more difficult—if not impossible—to build a *winning coalition* in order to sustain the regional security order in the Near and Middle East. Ideally, the liberal hegemon would try to promote negotiated solutions to regional conflicts, most notably in Syria, Yemen, and Israel/Palestine. The track record of past administrations, including under Obama, had already been rather mixed in this regard. Under Trump, prospects for the United States to play the role of a peace broker seem to be even more remote.

4.2. East Asia

North Korea has developed into the gravest risk to regional security in East Asia. The regime in Pyongyang has made unexpected progress in the development of nuclear weapons and ballistic missiles. In 2017 it was on the verge of reaching the ability to threaten the mainland of the United States with a nuclear strike.[35] While tensions over conflicting territorial claims in the South and East China Seas have also risen, open military confrontations involving China, the other maritime claimant states from the region, and the United States were still largely avoided. The state orders *within* the nations in East Asia were mostly stable. Even where domestic unrest did occur, as in Thailand

[35] William J. Broad et al., This Missile Could Reach California. But Can North Korea Use It With a Nuclear Weapon? *New York Times*, September 3, 2017, available at https://www.nytimes.com/interactive/2017/08/22/world/asia/north-korea-nuclear-weapons.html [accessed December 15, 2017].

or Myanmar/Burma, the confrontations remained short of civil war. Non-traditional security problems such as terrorism or piracy are serious, but they do not fundamentally threaten the regional security order as such.[36]

It is commonplace that China's military, political, and economic rise is the most significant driver of regional dynamics.[37] Just like the power shifts in the Middle East, it has to be understood as a longer-term process involving a changing balance among the key powers of the region. Whereas during the Cold War, the regional security order was mostly shaped by the interactions among four powers—the United States, China, the Soviet Union, and Japan—today the "G-2," consisting of the USA and China, "is the most consequential bilateral relationship of our time."[38] The foreign and security policies of Southeast Asian countries are to a significant degree defined by how they "balance," "bandwagon," or "hedge" against China, using different forms of cooperation with Washington. While China's rise has been in progress for decades, regional security tensions in the South and East China Seas have erupted since 2010.[39] There are different explanations for what has caused these tensions. Some observers focus on the consequences of the 2008 financial crisis for Asia and China. According to this reading, economic uncertainties have further inflamed nationalism to which the region had been prone anyway due to its unresolved colonial heritage.[40] In China, nationalism has played a crucial role as a substitute ideology after the demise of communism.[41] This might be one, if not the only, factor explaining changes in Chinese foreign policy towards a more assertive stance. An alternative view sees the announcement of the Obama administration to rebalance US policy towards Asia as a potential source of instability rather than stability as it puts additional pressure on China to adopt a more assertive stance in regional security.[42] In the course of the rebalance policy, the USA only modestly increased its military presence in the region. More importantly, not least from China's perspective, has been

[36] See Chapter 8 by Charles E. Morrison and Chapter 9 by Chaesung Chun in this volume.

[37] Oliver Turner, The U.S. "Pivot" to Asia Pacific, in Parmar et al. (eds.), *Obama and the World*, pp. 219–30 (219).

[38] James Steinberg and Michael O'Hanlon, *Strategic Reassurance and Resolve: U.S.–China Relations in the Twenty-First Century*, Princeton, NJ: Princeton University Press, 2014, p. 1

[39] Gudrun Wacker, *Security Cooperation in East Asia: Structures, Trends, and Limitations*, Berlin: SWP (German Institute for International and Security Affairs), 2015, pp. 13–15 (= SWP RP 4, May 2015).

[40] Thomas J. Christensen, Obama and Asia: Confronting the China Challenge, *Foreign Affairs* 94:5 (September/October 2015), pp. 28–36 (28).

[41] On the role of nationalism in China see Robert Sutter, East Asian Security, Policy Debates, and American Leadership, in Elena Atanassova-Cornelis and Frans-Paul van der Putten (eds.), *Changing Security Dynamics in East Asia*, Basingstoke and New York: Palgrave Macmillan, 2014, pp. 27–46 (44).

[42] Turner, The U.S. "Pivot" to Asia Pacific, p. 222.

the fact that Washington upgraded its defense relations with select countries in the region.

Whatever the causes, rising tensions in the region have accelerated a worrying armament race between China and the United States as well as within the region. China's military budget has undergone an annual estimated increase of 10 percent while "between 2007 and 2011 arms imports across the South East Asian region increased by 185 per cent."[43]

A more positive development in the Asian security order has been the revaluation of regional institutions that also cover security issues. While obviously Asia does not have the same degree of institutionalized cooperation evident in Europe under EU or NATO auspices, there is no lack of institutions per se. For the post-Cold War period, Press-Barnathan observes a growing interest in multilateral cooperation as indicated by the growing number and scope of regional cooperation institutions (creation of the Association of Southeast Asian Nations (ASEAN) Regional Forum in 1993, of Asia Pacific Economic Cooperation in 1989, or of the East Asia Summit in 2005).[44]

Traditionally, the security policy of the United States has been based on selective bilateralisms with key actors in the region which still form the backbone of Asia's regional security order.[45] Washington has formalized bilateral security alliances with Thailand, the Philippines, South Korea, Australia, and Japan, while the US relationship with Taiwan is a quasi or de facto alliance.

The United States has been gradually changing its security and political posture in Asia. The most significant programmatic change under the Obama administration has been the *rebalance* to Asia. It has been constructed as a multi-dimensional policy that includes a political, a military, and an economic dimension (the TPP).

As part of the political dimension of the *rebalance*, the Obama administration started to engage more deeply in regional security structures. In July 2009 the United States acceded to a key document of ASEAN, the "Treaty of Amity and Cooperation in Southeast Asia" and in 2010 Washington established a permanent US Mission to ASEAN.[46] Washington has also become more proactive promoting common policies of ASEAN member states vis-à-vis the territorial disputes in the South China Sea.[47] The political dimension of America's pivot to Asia can be seen as a renewed effort to build coalitions and thus legitimacy in Asia. The security concerns among Southeast Asian

[43] Ibid., p. 226. The author cites the Stockholm International Peace Research Institute "Military Expenditure Database" of 2012 as his source.

[44] Galia Press-Barnathan, The Impact of Regional Dynamics on U.S. Policy toward Regional Security Arrangements in East Asia, *International Relations of the Asia Pacific* 14:3 (2014), pp. 357–91 (368).

[45] Wacker, *Security Cooperation in East Asia*, p. 7.

[46] Press-Barnathan, The Impact of Regional Dynamics, pp. 380f.

[47] Wacker, *Security Cooperation in East Asia*, p. 30.

countries with a view to China's rise are balanced by increasing interdependence in the economic realm.

The Trump administration has not followed the *rebalance* policy of its predecessor but neither has it, at least until the end of 2017, replaced it with a different strategy towards Asia.[48] Individual statements by Trump and some of his advisors indicate that the new administration will emphasize the military aspects of the US presence in Asia-Pacific (or the Indo-Pacific as the Trump administration now calls it). Two of Trump's advisors, Peter Navarro and Alexander Gray, have called it a "peace through strength" vision for regional security,[49] which also became one of the four major themes of the National Security Strategy of 2017. "Peace through strength" is also in line with the president's plans to enhance significantly the size of the US Navy over the next one-and-a-half decades.

At the same time, Trump does not show much interest in the liberal aspects of US engagement in Asia-Pacific. One of his first decisions was to abandon the TPP which had set high standards for economic governance (including amongst state-owned companies, financial services, and intellectual property). Yun Schüler-Zhou and Margot Schüller summarize a widespread perception when they state that the "Trump administration's retreat [from the TPP] work[s] against the strategic U.S. interest of shaping the region based on liberal values and open markets."[50]

4.3. Europe

Before Russia's annexation of Crimea, it was widely assumed that Europe had become a producer rather than a consumer of security. With the return of open conflict between the USA/the EU and Russia and the ongoing civil war in Eastern Ukraine, it is plain to see that the European security order, too, has been eroding.[51]

Since the end of World War II, the western half of the European security order (European Communities and NATO) rested on two major pillars: First, on security reassurance that was mostly provided by the United States and

[48] Tim Huxley and Benjamin Schreer, Trump's Missing Asia Strategy, *Survival* 59:3 (June/July 2017), pp. 81–9.

[49] Alexander Gray and Peter Navarro, Donald Trump's Peace Through Strength Vision for the Asia-Pacific, *Foreign Policy*, November 7, 2016, available at http://foreignpolicy.com/2016/11/07/donald-trumps-peace-through-strength-vision-for-the-asia-pacific/ [accessed December 15, 2017].

[50] Yun Schüler-Zhou and Margot Schüller, *Trump's Shadow over U.S.–China Economic Relations*, Hamburg: German Institute for Global and Area Studies, July 2017, p. 8, available at https://www.giga-hamburg.de/en/system/files/publications/gf_asien_1704_en.pdf [accessed December 15, 2017].

[51] See Chapter 6 by Wolfgang Richter in this volume.

second, on institutional enlargement, initially within Western Europe, and after the fall of the Iron Curtain towards Eastern Europe as well.

With the end of the Cold War, the United States' interest in European security diminished considerably. The US military presence was reduced from more than 350,000 troops in 1986 to about 67,000 permanently stationed troops in 2014.[52] Military bases and infrastructure have been substantially dismantled as well. Decisions since 2011 in Washington to cut the defense budget have reinforced these trends and increased pressure from Congress to close even more American military installations in Europe (even though the actual costs of European bases to the defense budget are almost negligible).[53]

Post-1991, the rationale for the remaining military presence in Europe shifted from collective NATO defense towards crisis management and global power projection. US military commanders justified bases in Europe before Congress on the basis that Europe is an "unsinkable aircraft carrier,"[54] i.e., a platform for US power projection into the Mediterranean, the Middle East, and Africa. In his testimony before Congress in April 2014, Commander General Philip Breedlove of the US European Command (EUCOM) stressed that 70 percent of NATO operations and 60 percent of EU operations took place outside of Europe.[55]

During his first term in office, President Obama had not given significant priority to European security either.[56] The *Strategic Defense Guidance* of 2012 and the *Quadrennial Defense Review 2014*, which were written under Obama's watch, contained a clear regional prioritization: Asia-Pacific comes first, the Middle East second, and only then does Europe find a place in the security and defense strategy of the United States.[57]

The deterioration of the European security order since 2014 has surely had an impact on Washington's policies towards Europe. Due to the Ukraine

[52] Defense Manpower Data Center (DMDC), US Department of Defense Personnel, Workforce Reports and Publications, Active Duty Military Strength by Service (Updated Monthly), available at https://www.dmdc.osd.mil/appj/dwp/dwp_reports.jsp.

[53] Adam Grissom from the RAND Corporation assesses that "... [e]ven if sequestration is implemented the American presence in Europe will still account for less than 1 percent of the residual defense budget": Adam Grissom, The United States, in Clara Marina O'Donnell (ed.), *The Implications of Military Spending Cuts for NATO's Largest Members*, Washington, DC: Brookings, July 2012, p. 26 (= Analysis Paper).

[54] James Stavridis, *Testimony of Admiral James Stavridis, United States Navy Commander, United States European Command, Before the 113th Congress*, Stuttgart: European Forces Command (EUCOM), 2013, p. 4.

[55] Philip Breedlove, *Statement of General Philip Breedlove, Commander U.S. Forces Europe, Congressional Posture Statement*, Stuttgart: European Forces Command (EUCOM), April 1, 2014, pp. 4f.

[56] Anne Applebaum, Obama and Europe: Missed Signals, Renewed Commitments, *Foreign Affairs* 94:5 (September/October 2015), pp. 37–44.

[57] Department of Defense, *Sustaining U.S. Global Leadership: Priorities for 21st Century Defense*, Washington, DC: Department of Defense, January 2012, p. 3; Department of Defense, *Quadrennial Defense Review 2014*, Washington, DC: Department of Defense, March 2014.

crisis, the US administration has stopped, for the time being at least, the longer-term trend to decrease the number of permanently stationed troops in Europe and at the same time has increased temporary deployments—initially battalion-sized and since 2015 brigade-sized—in the European theater.[58] Probably the most visible step was US Defense Secretary Ash Carter's announcement of June 2015 to deploy 250 armored vehicles to Europe. It was only in 2013 that the United States had withdrawn its last battle tank from the continent, a step that was now reversed. Washington also reinforced the Air Force and naval presence over and on the Baltic and Black Seas. In parallel to these reinforcements, America has stepped up its bilateral and multilateral training exercises with European partners that are focused on collective defense rather than crisis management scenarios.

In February 2016, the Obama administration presented its budget request to Congress for the fiscal year 2017 that included financial allocations to the European Reassurance Initiative (ERI)—which is the major fund for the rotations, reinforcements, and enhanced exercises in Europe—of US$3.4 billion. This represented a fourfold increase over the 2016 enacted defense budget.

Despite his "America First" rhetoric, the Trump administration has continued to honor the US pledges to bolster security and defense reassurances to European states made by the previous administration. This includes, among other things, the European deployment of an additional Army Brigade Combat Team, consisting of roughly 3,500 troops and 87 tanks.[59] Moreover, the USA is the lead nation for one of four NATO multinational battle groups that form the "Enhanced Forward Presence" of the alliance in Eastern Europe.[60] Politically even more relevant is the fact that Trump asked Congress to allocate US$4.8 billion for the ERI, a significant increase. While Washington's decisions since 2014 do not add up to a complete reversal of the longer-term trend of a shrinking US military footprint in Europe, there is no indication that Trump is planning to reverse American military contributions to European security and NATO reassurance.

Comparable to the situation in other regional settings, the crucial question is what role the United States will play in European security beyond military deployments. Since 2014 the Atlantic Alliance has regained some relevance as

[58] Andrew Tilghman, EUCOM Base Closure Will Not Affect Force Levels, *The Military Times*, January 9, 2015, available at http://www.militarytimes.com/story/military/pentagon/2015/01/08/eucom-base-closures-will-not-affect-force-levels/21453321/ [accessed April 17, 2107]; John Vandiver and Michael Darnell, Army Looking to Store Tanks, Equipment in Eastern Europe, *Stars and Stripes*, January 25, 2015, available at https://www.stripes.com/army-looking-to-store-tanks-equipment-in-eastern-europe-1.325693 [accessed April 17, 2017].

[59] US Army Europe Public Affairs Office, *Atlantic Resolve Fact Sheet*, updated April 1, 2017, available at http://www.eur.army.mil/AtlanticResolve/.

[60] North Atlantic Treaty Organization, *NATO's Enhanced Forward Presence Factsheet*, updated May 2017, available at https://www.nato.int/nato_static_fl2014/assets/pdf/pdf_2017_05/1705-factsheet-efp.pdf.

a multilateral forum to discuss fundamental topics such as relations with Russia and the future of arms control in Europe. The risk is that Trump will reduce alliance relationships to the defense spending and burden-sharing debates. His initially ambivalent remarks on NATO's relevance did not help either. During the first year of his term, relations with Russia remained a heavy domestic burden on Trump—due to accusations of Russia's meddling in the presidential elections of 2016 and of his campaign's collusion with Russian officials. Hostility in Congress towards Russia remains high, both among Democrats and Republicans.[61] These domestic factors mean that the Trump administration's leeway for political initiatives vis-à-vis Moscow will remain very small.

5. CONCLUSION

During the last decade, the regional security orders in the Near/Middle East, East Asia, and Europe have eroded to different degrees, as has the leadership role of the United States as a liberal hegemon within these orders. The interaction between US security policies and the regional dynamics varies significantly across the regions, however.

The liberal characteristics of hegemony encompass a willingness to pursue a broader set of goals and instruments to promote regional security, including foreign aid, democracy promotion, and economic openness. Procedurally it involves support for multilateral institutions, reciprocity, and self-restraint as a basis to build "winning coalitions" under changing circumstances. As defined at the outset of this chapter, a "winning coalition" is a coalition—including states and non-state actors—that is both willing and able to maintain effectiveness of the regional security order at hand.

In the *Near and Middle East*, the liberal elements both of US hegemony and of international order—multilateral institutions based on principles of consent, democratic governance, and economic openness—have been the least developed among the three regional orders discussed in this chapter. The erosion of the Middle East security order has been driven, first, by societal mobilization that had the net effect of weakening statehood in the region. Second, the longer-term power shift from Arab countries to non-Arab countries, most notably Iran, has contributed to increasingly fierce competition over influence that eventually turned internal conflicts into proxy wars. By

[61] In July 2017, the US House of Representatives and the Senate passed the "Countering America's Adversaries Through Sanctions Act" by wide bipartisan majorities. The act also includes additional sanctions against Russia. More information is available at https://www.congress.gov/bill/115th-congress/house-bill/3364 [accessed December 15, 2017].

intervening militarily in Iraq in 2003, the United States has itself massively advanced these longer-term processes. Most importantly, Washington was slow to build a broader-based coalition and instead has continued to rely first and foremost on autocratic Arab countries.

Under Obama, official policy in Washington was that the 2015 deal over Iran's nuclear program was exclusively aimed at strengthening the regional and global non-proliferation of nuclear weapons. However, it could also be read as a cautious effort—or maybe a trial—to rebuild a broader basis for Middle East security that included America's and the Arab states' most relevant competitor. President Trump has ended this trial and instead seeks to contain and roll back Iranian influence in the region by coercive means. At the end of 2017 it is still too early to tell what the effects of his policy shift in the region will be. Developments so far—the escalation between Qatar and other Gulf Cooperation Council states in June 2017, the political crisis in Lebanon in the autumn, and renewed violence between Israel and Hamas in the wake of Trump's unilateral recognition of Jerusalem as Israel's capital in November—indicate that this policy shift is leading to less rather than more security.

In *East Asia*, China's economic and military rise is a long-term process but since 2010 it has coincided with heightened tensions in the South China and East China Seas. North Korea's rapid progress in developing nuclear weapons and ballistic missiles has raised tensions in the region further and even raised the prospect of a devastating war. These developments, too, have made it more challenging for the United States to build and sustain coalitions with its Asian partners. The Obama administration sought to meet these challenges with its multi-dimensional *rebalance* approach which included a multilateral trade agreement, more visible support to regional organizations, and a modest shift of military capabilities into the region. President Trump is sticking to the military dimension of the rebalance but seems to have abandoned the other two.

Finally, in *Europe*, the United States has been disengaging over the past twenty-five years while the major friction in the European security order—the antagonism between EU/NATO-Europe and Russia—had only been concealed (at best) rather than resolved. Today, America and its European partners are in the midst of a realignment process: Washington is adopting a partial and hesitant re-engagement with Europe, and Western/Central Europe is trying to find political strategies vis-à-vis Moscow. What is clear, though, is that institutional enlargement—a central pillar of the post-Cold War European security order—has reached its limits.

In all three geographical regions, the erosion of security orders has been driven by regional dynamics which in turn have been reinforced by the demise of the United States as a liberal hegemon. Some major developments—such as the "Arab Spring" in North Africa and the Middle East, or China's rise in Asia—cannot be attributed to policy decisions in Washington. Other developments—the disintegration of Iraq since 2003, the escalating conflict with North Korea, or Russia's hostility towards NATO—are more closely linked to the role of the United States in regional security. A positive contribution by America to regional security orders depends not only on its military presence but also on the liberal features of its leadership role, not least its ability to support mutual agreements and exercise self-restraint.

A review of the major dynamics in regional orders shows that American hegemony has always been short of liberal ideal-type expectations. Even before Trump, liberal US hegemony has been eroding alongside the effectiveness of regional orders in the Middle East, East Asia, and Europe. One year into his presidency, the contours of Donald Trump's foreign and security policy are still nebulous in many ways.

Trump's election shows that a skeptical view on America's global responsibilities has become stronger inside the United States. Domestic political support for building and sustaining a liberal international order has waned. It is important to note, though, that Trump has not given up the idea that the United States is involved in the business of *order building* as such. Trump's new "Strategy on Iran," published in October 2017 and the idea of "peace through strength" in Asia-Pacific assume a leading role for America in these regional contexts. At the same time, the Trump administration sees the international and regional security orders primarily as arenas for regional power competition in which economic and military might are the most relevant currencies. Multilateral institutions, a non-transactional sense of reciprocity, and self-restraint seem to be either a second thought or completely absent from his thinking and policy decisions.

It would be simplistic and misleading to say that the erosion of regional security orders is the result of the deeds and omissions in Washington. The missing liberal hegemon will make it much harder, though, to reverse the trend and to rebuild these orders from within and from the outside.

12

China and the Struggle over the Future of International Order

Zhongying Pang

1. INTRODUCTION

In the past, China (that is, the ruling Chinese Communist Party and its state, the People's Republic of China)[1] usually addressed the issues of the international order in its five-yearly key policy statements. In the era of "(economic) reform and development and opening up" from the late 1970s to 2010s as China joined the existing international institutions, particularly financial and trade organizations, those statements became increasingly symbolic rather than substantively meaningful: during that period, China was largely intent on joining, rather than modifying the existing international order. However, following the 2008 global financial crisis, from 2009, and particularly since late 2012, when the current Chinese political leadership around Xi Jinping was installed, China has been pushing for reforms to existing international institutions (especially international financial organizations), as well as building new ones of its own as a top priority in China's foreign policy.

Scholars in International Relations have been confronted with a series of critical questions on China's role within the struggle over the future shape of international order: What role does China play today in the existing international order? Why is China no longer satisfied with its position in that order and increasingly seeking to reform existing global institutions? Do China's new international enterprises, such as the Belt and Road Initiative (BRI) represent an attempt to build an alternative international order? How will China, as a "rising power," deal with US responses to China's policies? What

[1] Internationally, China is usually regarded as a "party-state." This is not exact. The People's Republic of China is not simply a "party-state." It should be regarded as a "party and its state" (*Dang He Guo Jia*) because constitutionally and institutionally, the party and its state coexist: while the party leads the state, they are actually two governing bodies.

does China's embrace of "global governance" mean at a time when forces of "de-globalization" appear to be on the rise worldwide? This chapter discusses these questions and proposes some tentative conclusions concerning China's current foreign policy transformation, bearing in mind that this transformation is still in its early stages and has to grapple with its inherent contradictions, difficulties, and uncertainties.

2. THE EVOLUTION OF CHINESE POLICIES ON INTERNATIONAL ORDER

2.1. The Background

With the foundation of the People's Republic of China (PRC) in 1949, Chinese foreign policy underwent a revolution. At the core of the PRC's revolutionary diplomacy was the complete overhaul of the old foreign policy tenets and their replacement with a comprehensive set of new guidelines. These included leaving the "liberal" and joining the "other" international order (*Ling Qi Lu Zao*). Thus, China became a member of the Soviet-led order of Communist states and movements and was drawn into the Cold War in Asia-Pacific.

Since that early time, the *Ling Qi Lu Zao* approach has waxed and waned, but it never disappeared. Although China has recently denied repeatedly that it still follows the approach of *Ling Qi Lu Zao*, under the current Chinese leadership and with its new policies, *Ling Qi Lu Zao* actually may make a comeback as the PRC's approach to international order.

From the late 1950s to the early 1970s, as the People's Republic and the Soviet Union began to split and their relationship progressively deteriorated, China became increasingly isolated internationally. It tried to break out of this isolation using different stratagems. Thus, it started "exporting the Chinese revolution" to Asia and Africa, and engaged in secret strategic negotiations with both the USA and Japan. China's support for African independence and decolonization movements was reciprocated by the new-founded states in Africa: their support enabled the PRC in 1971 to replace the Republic of China (Taiwan) at the United Nations in New York as the representative of China. This included the Security Council, where China, as a founding member, has one of five permanent seats with veto power. Together with China's rapprochement with the USA, entry to the United Nations (UN) helped to pave the way, after the death of Mao Zedong and the end of the Cultural Revolution, for China's "opening up": it launched its economic reforms at home and began to engage with the US-led liberal international order, in particular with its economic institutions.

In the context of the strategic cooperation with the USA against an expansionist Soviet Union, China also opened up to other parts of the "capitalist world." In 1972, China and Japan normalized their diplomatic relations, and in 1975, China established diplomatic relations with the then European Community. In late 1978, China finally normalized its diplomatic relations with the USA by exchanging ambassadors. Deng Xiaoping visited America at the time of the Chinese New Year in 1979 to celebrate this "honeymoon" between China and America.

All these diplomatic breakthroughs significantly contributed to China's economic reforms and improved its geo-political position. China's attitudes and policies towards the Western-dominated international institutions during this period, particularly international economic and financial institutions, became thoroughly positive. As an important step in its opening-up, in the early 1980s, China (re-)joined the International Monetary Fund (IMF) and the World Bank. In 2001, after fifteen years of tough negotiations with the USA, the European Union (EU), and other developed states, China became a member of the World Trade Organization (WTO).

Today, China holds membership in almost all existing universal intergovernmental institutions. From the early 1980s to the late 2000s, China, in its keen quest for (re-)entry, accepted the principles, rules, and norms of those institutions almost without reservations. Thus, China became de facto a "status quo power" in the international order.[2]

Deng Xiaoping died in 1997 but his foreign policy doctrines continued to shape the policies of the two subsequent Chinese leaderships around Party chairmen and presidents Jiang Zemin and Hu Jintao through the 1990s to the late 2000s. With regard to the international order, Deng Xiaoping's attitude can be summarized as follows: China's "peaceful development"—the growth and development of China's economy—depends on a friendly and cooperative international environment (read: on a functioning international order). A central task of Chinese foreign policy, therefore, had to be to secure such an environment to its own benefit.

That China has indeed benefitted in many ways from its long engagement with the existing international order is still generally acknowledged to this day. China was able to use its membership in those institutions to speed up its domestic market-oriented reforms (*Dao Bi*). Its entry into the WTO was a particularly important step on this path to deepen economic reforms.

Deng Xiaoping asked China never to take the lead (*Bu Dai Tou*). Gradually, however, China has begun to change this traditional role and explore the idea of Chinese leadership in international affairs. Thus, China played an

[2] Alastair Iain Johnston, Is China a Status Quo Power? *International Security* 27:4 (Spring 2003), pp. 5–56.

important role in making possible the Paris Agreement on climate change in 2015.[3] Like the WTO entry, China's international leadership on climate change policy has obvious domestic aspects: China needs the UN climate change governance to solve its serious domestic climate change challenges.

2.2. A New Approach to International Order?

Since 2008–9, however, when the international financial and economic crisis struck the USA, the EU, and other Western economies, China has begun to revisit its relations with the existing international order. As the implications of China's ascendancy for the international order became a prominent feature in international discourses about China as a "rising power,"[4] China now sees its relationship with the existing international order at a crossroads.

A major judgment made by China's National Foreign Policy Conference in 2014 was that the future of international order was increasingly contested internationally and that this struggle might last some time.[5] In China's view, decisions about international order should not just be taken by the USA and its allies in Europe and Asia, but by all member states of the UN. China sees this as a contribution to the "democratization of international relations" (*Guo Ji Guan Xi Min Zhu Hua*), which as part of the new doctrine of Chinese foreign policy seeks not only the reform of existing international institutions but also the building of new ones.

To promote this doctrine, China's foreign policy is unilaterally sponsoring a number of new initiatives, such as the Belt and Road Initiative (BRI), and is multilaterally building new international financial institutions such as the Brazil, Russia, India, China, and South Africa (BRICS) Contingent Reserve Arrangement, the New Development Bank (NDB), and the Asian Infrastructure Investment Bank (AIIB). The NDB is widely perceived as a (miniature) "alternative" to the IMF and World Bank. The BRICS argue, however, that the NDB is not a rival to existing international financial institutions (IFIs) but a partner.[6] The NDB tries new business practices that differ from the "traditional"

[3] See Chapter 2 by Joyeeta Gupta and Chapter 13 by Daniel Krahl in this volume.

[4] Partly, those discourses may be seen as reactions to a debate in the USA about the challenge China might pose to the existing (American) order. In 2015, US discourses seemed to turn towards a possible fall of the rising power. The chorus was led by David Shambaugh. See David Shambaugh, The Coming Chinese Crackup: The Endgame of Communist Rule in China Has Begun, *Wall Street Journal*, March 6, 2015. Other prominent US voices have sounded similar views on the future of China.

[5] According to news releases, the conference took place on November 28 and 29, 2014 in Beijing.

[6] See: Not here to compete with IMF, World Bank: NDB chief KV Kamath, July 9, 2015, available at http://economictimes.indiatimes.com/news/economy/finance/not-here-to-compete-with-

approaches and methods used by the IFIs.[7] The AIIB has not positioned itself openly against the World Bank, but defines itself ambitiously as "a first class multilateral development institution with 21st century governance."[8] The Obama administration criticized the creation of the AIIB and ruled out US membership of the organization. There is no sign that the Trump administration will want to join the AIIB, either. Even if America were to become an AIIB member, however, Washington would have no power of veto on decision-making. As China does not pursue a dominating role in AIIB, the organization can be seen as a new international institution without hegemony, hence as an example of what China's "New International Relations" might mean. AIIB and the other new institutions that China has created in international development finance and international monetary cooperation show obvious parallels in their functions with existing IFIs; they could therefore be regarded as a challenge to them.

In a time of de-globalization, as the new US administration embraces "America first" policies and revives economic nationalism, China is trying to become the new driving force for saving globalization, with the People's Republic's new paramount leader Xi Jinping becoming its leading defender.[9] At home, China intends to continue economic reforms and further promote the opening of its economy. A measure of this commitment to "deepened economic reforms" and a "furthered opening" is China's historic move to open its financial sector to more foreign ownership, which was announced during Donald Trump's swing through Asia (including China) in early November 2017, on which the new American president explained why his administration would withdraw from existing multilateral arrangements.

In his address to the United Nations General Assembly in September 2015 to celebrate its seventieth anniversary, Xi launched a series of Chinese initiatives to strengthen existing global governance, including a ten-year, US$1 billion China–UN Peace and Development Fund, a Chinese peacekeeping stand-by force of 8,000 troops, and a significant contribution to the UN sustainable development goals, such as the creation of South–South Cooperation College at Peking University and China Center for International Knowledge Development. This

imf-world-bank-ndb-chief-kv-kamath/articleshow/48002259.cms?utm_source=contentofinterest&utm_medium=text&utm_campaign=cppst [accessed August 29, 2016].

7 See: New BRICS bank in Shanghai to challenge major institutions, *Financial Times*, July 21, 2015, available at http://www.ft.com/cms/s/0/d8e26216-2f8d-11e5-8873-775ba7c2ea3d.html#axzz4JGzZw7Bk [accessed August 29, 2016].

8 Jin Liqun, *Building Asia's New Bank*, Brookings Institution, Washington, DC, October 21, 2015, p. 5, available at http://www.brookings.edu/~/media/events/2015/10/21-aiib-jin-liqun/20151021_asia_infrastructure_bank_transcript.pdf [accessed August 29, 2016].

9 Xi Jinping's remarks on globalization at the Davos World Economic Forum on January 17, 2017 were well received by European and other observers. The first Belt and Road Initiative Summit in Beijing on May 14–15, 2017, organized and chaired by Xi, served to explore the possibilities of a "new globalization."

speech presaged an important shift in China's recent policy towards international order: the significance China now attaches to global governance. Before 2009, China's official documents had intentionally neglected, cast serious doubt on, or even openly criticized the concept of global governance as it was coined and practiced in the West; the Communist Party and the People's Republic never used the term "global governance" in their political statements.[10] On October 12, 2015, however, at a regular study session of the Political Bureau of the Communist Party of China Central Committee, Xi Jinping stressed that the existing global institutions urgently needed reforms to achieve "new rules for the international order" and to "decide in which direction the world will head." According to Xi, the rise of developing nations including China (the global South) has brought about "revolutionary changes to world order."[11]

2.3. A Reconfirmed Reformist Approach to International Order

The reinterpretation of China's foreign policy guidelines and the recent initiatives described above demonstrate that China since 2008–9 has become a reformist state actor within the existing international order, with a particular focus on the international financial, monetary, trade, and development functional orders. For instance, in 2009 the President of China's central bank, Zhou Xiaochuan, appealed for the reform of the international monetary system. In his statement, he called for the replacement of the US dollar as the dominant world currency with "... an international reserve currency that is disconnected from individual nations and is able to remain stable in the long run."[12]

With other major developing nations, then Chinese president Hu Jintao joined the G8 summit in L'Aquila (Italy) in 2009 ("8+5") to explain China's official stance on global economic governance (this was the first time a Chinese leader used the term "global governance" internationally). The year 2009 also marked the beginning of the BRICS, a global grouping China sponsored together with Brazil, India, Russia, and (as a later addition) South Africa. Together with the G20 summit process, the birth of BRICS ended the old G8 temporary outreach format of the 8+5 that had existed since 2003.

[10] Zhongying Pang and Hongying Wang, Debating International Institutions and Global Governance: The Missing Chinese IPE Contribution, *Review of International Political Economy* 20 (2013), pp. 1189–214.

[11] Qin Yaqin, an internationally recognized constructivist theorist in international relations and president of China Foreign Affairs University, was invited to lecture on why global governance does matter to China.

[12] Zhou Xiaochuan's Statement on Reforming the International Monetary System, available at https://www.bis.org/review/r090402c.pdf.

BRICS is not just cooperation among five major developing nations but a collective platform to coordinate their policy stances on global issues. Thus, BRICS' joint declaration at its Sanya Summit in 2011 under Chinese presidency called for the reform of existing international financial institutions. Within the G20, BRICS has become a caucus, parallel to the G7 of the Western industrialized countries and the "middle power" group MIKTA (Mexico, Indonesia, Republic of Korea, Turkey, and Australia);[13] China also has used its membership in the G20 to push for reforms in international financial institutions. Thus, the G20 agreed to the reform of IMF quotas and IMF governance in 2010.[14] Since then, China has joined other G20 members in implementing the agreement and repeatedly called on the USA to honor its commitment and do so as well. The US Congress finally approved the changes to the IMF statutes in late 2015.

China's reformist role in the international order does not relate to all global issues, however. For example, China does not call for a major reform of the United Nations Security Council (UNSC); on this issue, China is remarkably cautious, even conservative. Thus, China's Position Paper for the seventieth anniversary celebrations of the United Nations in 2015 argued that "... controversial topics should be avoided during the 70th anniversary year to uphold unity of UN membership and prevent distraction to discussions on key items on the UN agenda."[15] BRICS members Brazil and India, on the other hand, have long tried to secure permanent seats for themselves in a reformed UNSC, working with Germany and Japan in the so-called G4. China's stance on the reform of the UNSC therefore fundamentally differs from that of Brazil and India, creating a split in policies towards international order within BRICS.

3. THE BELT AND ROAD INITIATIVE: A "COMMUNITY OF SHARED FUTURE FOR MANKIND"?

China's Belt and Road Initiative (BRI) represents an unprecedented Chinese intervention in the struggle for a new international order. Although it now clearly is at the core of China's foreign policy, the policy messages from Beijing on BRI are still complicated and contradictory. One school argues that BRI is a "strategy" to guide China's new role in the twenty-first century world. This implies that the initiative aims at changing the current international order. According to another school of thought, however, the BRI is an international

[13] This grouping was formed in 2013, but remains confined to meetings of foreign ministers only.

[14] See http://www.imf.org/external/np/exr/faq/quotasgov.htm.

[15] Available at http://www.fmprc.gov.cn/mfa_eng/zxxx_662805/t1298420.shtml.

economic "initiative" for helping improve the infrastructure in the developing world from Asia to Africa and even Latin America. This also tends to be how China's diplomacy presents the BRI.

We need to consider China's future economic growth perspectives to understand why China uses BRI to work for a new international order. Thus, the economist Zhang Jun asks: "Can China sustain rapid GDP growth within the confines of the current global order, including its trade rules, or must the current U.S.-dominated order change drastically to accommodate China's continued economic rise?"[16] Zhang seems to have doubts whether China would be able to realize its development ambitions fully within the context of the present international order. The present leadership's blueprint for China's future development is summarized under the two labels of "the two 100-year strategies" and "China dreams."[17] The former goes back to Deng Xiaoping and focuses on the early 2020s when the Chinese Communist Party (CCP) will commemorate its centenary. By that time, according to present plans, China's economy will be relatively developed by international standards, and it even might have become the world's largest economy not just in terms of purchasing power parity, but also according to conventional exchange rate calculations. By 2049, when the People's Republic of China celebrates its one hundredth birthday, the world's largest economy should also have joined the ranks of developed economies. Yet would this development trajectory envisaged by the CCP be possible at all under the existing international order? Is the existing order flexible enough to accommodate China's future economic development? If not, how does China go about designing, promoting, and ultimately realizing an alternative international order that would serve its development ambitions better? Can China avoid conflict with other major state actors in the pursuit of a new order? If not, what would be the consequences of possible clashes between China and others over their differences on how to shape the future international order?

There are no clear answers to these questions at this time. Yet the linkages between China's future economic development and the future of the international order must be taken seriously. In practice, many in China may want the Chinese economy to continue to operate under the existing principles, norms, and rules of an America-dominated liberal order, but they feel the order should be reformed. Many also worry that the reforms may need to be delayed or even fail to materialize. The experience so far with reforms has certainly been disappointing: in the existing international order as of today,

[16] Zhang Jun, China's Pursuit of a New World Order, available at http://www.project-syndicate.org/commentary/china-new-world-order-by-jun-zhang-2015-06?barrier=true [accessed January 11, 2017].

[17] The "strategies" and "dreams" can be found in every political statement delivered by Xi Jinping since the 18th CCP National Congress in 2012. Most recently, he repeated these at his speech for the 95th anniversary of the CCP on July 1, 2016 in Beijing.

China is still not adequately represented. (For example, in the reformed IMF, Japan's voting power as the third largest economy is still higher than that of China, the second largest economy.) More fundamentally, China worries about being excluded in a changing international order. Although some old institutions such as the Arctic Council (where China has had observer status since 2014), the International Energy Agency (observer status since 2015), and the European Bank for Reconstruction and Development (membership since 2016) have opened up to include China, some new groupings organized by the USA with the intention of shaping the international order for the next generation do not include China. The most important example of this is the Transpacific Partnership (TPP) in trade and investment, from which China feels painfully excluded. Such worries contributed to China's drive to initiate new international institutions such as the AIIB: seen from this perspective, they represent safeguards for providing the Chinese economy with the kind of new international order it needs to prosper in the future. Of course, President Trump took the USA out of TPP almost immediately after he took office, but even after America's exit from the TPP, the eleven other members, led by Japan, have pledged to continue TPP. There is still no Chinese seat, although some TPP nations have suggested the inclusion of China.

As pointed out in section 2.1, the BRI is an interesting case of China's new *Ling Qi Lu Zao* in a time of uncertainty over the future of international order. Although China emphasizes that the BRI is based on existing international rules including the United Nations Charter, it originally was a unilateral initiative. Beijing's designation of the BRI as a way to promote a "community of common destiny" or "community of shared future for mankind" (or *Ren Lei Ming Yun Gong Tong Ti*) shows that China does explore an alternative international order.

There can be no doubt that the BRI creates frictions between China and the United States—not least because it seems destined to trigger a struggle over who gets to define and design the future international order. Yet China sees the BRI as an inclusive project that is open to the USA, as well as to others, just as China also repeatedly invited the USA to join the AIIB and other China-sponsored international institutions.[18]

The BRI has been given much prominence politically as a way to realize a "community of human destiny." Xi Jinping used the term repeatedly in Africa, Asia, in the G20 context and elsewhere,[19] and senior diplomats have tried to explain the implications of the BRI for the community of shared future for mankind. Thus, a former Chinese ambassador links the BRI with the "community of human destiny" as "one coin, two sides." In other words, the BRI is

[18] Jin Liqun, *Building Asia's New Bank.*

[19] Jin Kai, Can China Build a Community of Common Destiny?, available at http://thediplomat.com/2013/11/can-china-build-a-community-of-common-destiny/.

an instrument to realize the "community of human destiny."[20] Fu Ying presents the BRI as a way to improve the supply of international public goods for an "inclusive and open international order"[21]—that is, a "community of human destiny."[22] Behind these diplomat-turned-scholar words, the doctrine of "community of human destiny"[23] may in fact signal a foreign policy shift towards a new Chinese role in the shaping of the future of international order. Under Deng Xiaoping's foreign policy doctrines, from the late 1970s to the early 2000s China avoided touching issues of political values, and there were no efforts to export political ideology. This was a move away from Mao Zedong's line that emphasized the export of political revolution. The BRI aims at connecting not only the Chinese economy but also China's society and politics with others. The "community of human destiny" is China's political and ideological offer to the world. China therefore seems ready again to export immaterial goods, including what might be labeled "illiberal" political values such as the "China model" in domestic governance.

4. A CLASH OF CONCEPTS OF INTERNATIONAL ORDER BETWEEN CHINA AND THE USA?

Henry Kissinger argues that ancient China saw itself at the center of its own hierarchical universal order and thus believed in a concept that strove to "...order the world primarily by awing other societies with its cultural magnificence and economic bounty, drawing them into relationships that could be managed to produce the aim of 'harmony under heaven.'"[24] Today, together with the USA, China is one of two "indispensable pillars of world order,"[25] but Kissinger warns that between the two countries there are many tensions resulting from different views and actions on world order. To reconcile the differences between the two "pillars" for a truly global order, the two nations "must" achieve a "partnership."[26]

The differences between China and the USA on issues of international order begin with the vocabulary. The United States favors the term "world order,"

[20] In an interview with the author on January 11, 2016.

[21] Fu Ying, Speech at the 52nd Munich Security Conference, February 13, 2016, available at https://www.securityconference.de/en/activities/munich-security-conference/msc-2016/speeches/speech-by-fu-ying/.

[22] Author's interview with senior official on April 26, 2016 in Beijing, China.

[23] The official English formula came to be "a community of human destinies." This was later changed to "a community of shared future for mankind."

[24] Henry Kissinger, *World Order: Reflections on the Character of Nations and the Course of History*, New York: Penguin Books, 2014, pp. 4–5.

[25] Ibid., p. 226. [26] Ibid., pp. 231–3.

while China prefers to talk about "international order"—a subtle but interesting divergence! From a substantive perspective, the tensions between the two diverging concepts are not necessarily bad for the future of international order: they even may facilitate, rather than hinder, the emergence of a new international order. Although China began to explore so-called "constructive interventions" (*Jian She Xing Jie Ru*) in the context of the international discussion about a "responsibility to protect" (R2P), China still emphasizes the international principles of "sovereignty" and "non-interference," not least to rebut America's interventions in China-defined domestic and Asian regional affairs. There, China sees America as a non-Asian country that heavily intervenes in Asian affairs as, for example, in the South China Sea disputes where China criticizes the USA as a "non-South China Sea" claimant that nevertheless meddles.

China stresses that it is not an outsider but already an insider in the existing international order. "China has been asked frequently: are you challenging the U.S. as leader of the world order? Or are you making a parallel order? The answer is: of course not, we are part of the international order."[27] However, after three decades of connecting with the US-dominated international order, China in reality still feels deeply alienated politically by the USA; in particular, "the U.S.-led military alliance puts their interests above others' and pays little attention to China's security concerns."[28] In fact, China is seen as an "illiberal" state in a "liberal" world order.[29] Conceivably, China could experience political changes in the future that would allow it to join the world of democracies. At present, however, China's political change towards democratic governance is uncertain. As long as this is the case, an "illiberal" China would find itself in conflict with the leader of the existing liberal international order.

The conflict between the USA and China is not only about different political concepts of international order, however. China opposes the way in which America tries to use existing international rules to achieve its narrow geopolitical and strategic goals in its competition with China over regional and global influence. The USA sees itself as a defender of "freedom of navigation" and "freedom of flights." Yet China claims it also needs "freedom of navigation" and "freedom of flights." This struggle between China and the USA ultimately seems futile: in the last analysis, "freedom of navigation" and "freedom of flights" are principles of universal common interests.

[27] Fu Ying, Speech at the 52nd Munich Security Conference.

[28] Fu Ying, China and the Future of International Order, lecture at Chatham House, London, July 6, 2016, available at https://www.chathamhouse.org/sites/files/chathamhouse/events/special/2016-07-08-China-International-Order_0.pdf, p. 3.

[29] Wim Muller, China: An Illiberal, Non-Western State in a Western-Centric, Liberal Order? *Baltic Yearbook of International Law* 15:1 (2015), pp. 216–37, available at http://papers.ssrn.com/sol3/papers.cfm?abstract_id=2575643 [accessed September 6, 2016].

A key controversy concerns the attitude and the actions of the United States towards China in the South China Sea (SCS). In 2002, China agreed to a Declaration on the Conduct of Parties in the SCS with the Association of Southeast Asian Nations (ASEAN) to manage the SCS maritime territorial disputes peacefully,[30] and has agreed to negotiate a Code of Conduct in the SCS with ASEAN. The dominant sea power in the SCS, however, is not China but America. The USA criticizes China's actions as challenges to the existing maritime order represented by the United Nations Convention on the Law of the Sea (UNCLOS), but as a member of the UNCLOS China actually does not challenge the existing maritime order but relies on it. Moreover, the USA is not a party of the UNCLOS. Although the American government claims to adhere to UNCLOS, it also uses the principles of "freedom of navigation" and "freedom of flights" to intervene in the South China Sea. Clearly, the USA sees itself as the global policeman in the SCS.

To manage the struggle for international order in China–US relations, since 2013 China has been trying to transform this bilateral relationship into "a new model of great power relations" (read: a new kind of relationship between a rising power, like China, and an established power, like the USA).[31] This chapter argues that China's "new relations" doctrine is a response to the need to avoid a Cold War-like conflict, or even the "Thucydides trap" of a real war, between the USA and China in East Asia and the Pacific. In other words, the two discourses are linked: China realizes that it has to try to avoid the Thucydides trap; Beijing's answer is the "new relations."

Since 2009, the Obama administration made it quite clear that it did not want to let China write trade and investment rules in the TPP negotiations. President Obama repeatedly argued that the "United States, not China must write trade rules for Asia."[32] Thus, just as Russia's membership in the G8 was suspended in 2014, China has been excluded from the TPP.[33]

As for the regional security order in Asia, China proposes that it should be organized not by any "external powers" (*Yu Wai Shi Li*), but by the Asian countries themselves. At a Conference on Interaction and Confidence-Building Measures in Asia in 2014, President Xi Jinping said that "Asian issues should be solved by Asians" and "Asian security should be maintained

[30] ASEAN claims it includes all Southeast Asian nations. Yet China is also a Southeast Asian nation. This is an exclusion problem that China is facing in Asia.

[31] China's official translation is "a new model of major-country relationship" with the USA: "no-conflict, no-confrontation, mutual respect and win-win cooperation." Note: China does not use the term "power" but "country."

[32] Fu Ying, Under the same roof: China's view of world order, *Huffington Post*, November 11, 2016, available at: http://www.huffingtonpost.com/fu-ying/china-global-order_b_8537918.html [accessed January 14, 2017].

[33] "Amazingly enough, this remark has prompted some in China to find out what the rules are, how they are affecting us and what we should do": ibid.

by Asians."[34] This notion forms the core of the "new security concept" that China has been advocating since 2014. In the USA, it is widely criticized as "China's Monroe Doctrine."[35]

In responding to the "rise of China," the Obama administration implemented its "pivot to Asia" (later called the rebalancing) strategy to balance a rising China between 2011 and 2016. The BRI represents China's response to America's "pivot to Asia"—it also could be seen as China's pivot to the world.[36]

5. IS CHINA "BOUND TO LEAD" IN GLOBAL GOVERNANCE?

Joseph Nye coined the phrase "Bound to Lead" in the late 1980s to describe America's continuing leadership in the international order.[37] In his *Tao Guang Yang Hui* doctrine (section 2.1), Deng Xiaoping to the contrary postulated that China should "not take the lead" (*Bu Dai Tou*) in international affairs. Now, however, the PRC has begun to act as an international leader: since 2013, China has shown a much stronger commitment to take a proactive role (*Feng Fa You Wei*) in constructing, improving, and strengthening global governance. However, there are no good precedents for China's role as an international leader in a globalized world either in terms of the role expectations of others from the People's Republic or of its own role concept. Yet an international discourse on China's leadership has emerged and is growing.[38]

The way to take the lead that the PRC proposes itself is global (economic) governance. Thus, Li Daokui writes: "China's organization of the AIIB is widely regarded as an experiment or a pilot for the emergence of China's (global) leadership in global governance... (that)... will be a great opportunity for China to demonstrate what it wants for a new model for global

[34] See Xinhua, China Focus: China's Xi proposes security concept for Asia, May 21, 2014, available at http://news.xinhuanet.com/english/china/2014-05/21/c_133351210.htm [accessed August 20, 2016].

[35] Roger Cohen, China's Monroe Doctrine, *New York Times*, May 8, 2014, available at http://www.nytimes.com/2014/05/09/opinion/cohen-chinas-monroe-doctrine.html [accessed August 20, 2016].

[36] See Wang Jisi, China's Search for a Grand Strategy: A Rising Great Power Finds Its Way, *Foreign Affairs* 90:2 (March/April 2011), pp. 68–79.

[37] Joseph S. Nye, *Bound to Lead: The Changing Nature of American Power*, New York: Basic Books, 1990.

[38] For example, Gregory Chin and Hugo Dobson, China as G20 Host in 2016: Dawn of Asian Global Leadership? *Global Policy Journal*, March 3, 2015, available at http://www.globalpolicyjournal.com/blog/03/03/2015/china-g20-host-2016-dawn-asian-global-leadership [accessed August 20, 2016]; William C. Kirby and F. Warren McFarlan, China still isn't ready to be a true global leader, *Harvard Business Review*, January 5, 2015, available at https://hbr.org/2015/01/china-still-isnt-ready-to-be-a-true-global-leader [accessed September 9, 2016].

governance."[39] The quest for a leadership role in international order can be defined as China's attempt to mobilize normative power[40] to influence international rule-making.[41] In doing so, however, China will have to overcome some very serious challenges. Today, the PRC's "hard power" certainly is much "harder" than it was two decades ago, but it is perhaps not hard enough, at least not in terms of economic hard power: unlike the United States or the European Union, analysts hold that China, the second largest economy in the world, still lacks the capacity to regulate the global economy independently.[42] Another major challenge is that it has no formal or informal political alliances or "coalitions of the willing" to achieve an international agenda that bears China's imprint. China's official policy is still one of non-alliance (*Bu Jie Meng*). Realizing the shortcomings of this principle, however, China has begun to revise the non-alliance policy: as President Xi Jinping has stated, China now wants to "forge international partnerships" (*Jie Ban*).[43]

In early 2014, President Xi said in a meeting with the German Körber Foundation: "We will contribute the Chinese vision to the management of contemporary international relations, offer the Chinese solution for improving global governance, and make our own contribution to the efforts of mankind in meeting various challenges of the 21st century."[44] However, the lack of progress and success at the national governance level—such as the delayed political reforms towards democracy—may constitute a serious constraint on China's ambition and commitment for global governance. The economic "rise" of the Chinese economy is slowing, but there is no alternative to its continuation. World history tells us that after the "rise" to world power status, the "fall" of great powers often begins rather quickly.[45] Will the PRC

[39] Li (David) Daokui, The AIIB as China's Pilot Attempt to Reform the Global Economic Governance, *Foreign Affairs Journal* (Beijing) (Summer 2015), pp. 27–36.

[40] An equivalent in Chinese to the concept of "normative power" and its usages in international affairs may be seen in Confucius' notion of Wang Dao (王道).

[41] Actually, there are several cases where China began to seek a multilateral leadership role even before it launched the BRI. For example, together with Russia, China tested such a role in the organizing and structuring of the Shanghai Cooperation Organization, which was founded in 2001. See Jia Qingguo, The Shanghai Cooperation Organization: China's Experiment in Multilateral Leadership, Japan Slavic Research Center (SRC), 2007, available at http://src-h.slav.hokudai.ac.jp/coe21/publish/no16_2_ses/05_jia.pdf [accessed September 9, 2016].

[42] Zheng Yongnian, What the reform of "supply-side" answers [in Chinese], available at http://www.zaobao.com/forum/expert/zheng-yong-nian/story20160216-582045/page/0/1 [accessed September 9, 2016].

[43] Xi Jinping, Forging a Strong Partnership to Enhance Prosperity of Asia, Institute for Southeast Asian Studies (ISEAS), Singapore, November 7, 2015, available at http://www.fmprc.gov.cn/mfa_eng/wjdt_665385/zyjh_665391/t1313923.shtml [accessed January 13, 2017].

[44] Available at http://www.fmprc.gov.cn/mfa_eng/wjdt_665385/zyjh_665391/t1148640.shtml [accessed January 13, 2017].

[45] Zheng Bijian, China's "Peaceful Rise" to Great Power Status, *Foreign Affairs* 84:5 (September/October 2005), available at https://www.foreignaffairs.com/articles/asia/2005-09-01/chinas-peaceful-rise-great-power-status [accessed September 9, 2016].

conform to this law? The Chinese government's current "supply-side structural reform" confirms the end of the "rise" and signals the arrival of the "new economic normal" (*Xin Chang Tai*), but it refuses to acknowledge the possible beginning of the "fall." The structural reforms are intended to find new driving forces for future economic growth and thus for a continuing "rise"—but will they succeed in doing so?

The Chinese leadership is willing to embrace multilateralism fully. The initial success of the AIIB may encourage China to go further and help it to expand the knowledge and practical experience that are the essence of multilateralism. Whether China can succeed in multilateralizing its initiatives, especially the BRI, nevertheless is uncertain. If it failed to do so, it would not be able to sustain the People's Republic's international leadership role.

A wiser option for China might be to cultivate its "middle-ness" in global affairs. For now, China is neither a US-like hegemonic power nor an EU-like normative power, but it could be a "middle" power. Its middle-ness could be developed into a powerful combination of China's economic weight (even if its economy were to slow down, most countries in the world would have to rely on China as their largest overseas market) and its influence on countries that are interested in China's model of effective governance (Chinese politics can be considered as a "third way" between the traditional democratic and non-democratic national political orders).

Today, the Middle Kingdom, for the first time in recent history, is deeply obsessed with "great country diplomacy" (*Da Guo Wai Jiao*: China's officials intentionally do not use the term "great power" but "great country"). Chinese leaders argue that "China is unprecedentedly close to the center of the global stage for the first time in the modern era" (*Zhong Guo Qian Suo Wei You di Zou Jin Shi Jie Wu Tai de Zhong Xin*). Politically, a position at the center of global governance is an advantage, and with the development of AIIB and the 2016 presidency of the G20, China has been moving there.[46]

6. CONCLUDING REMARKS

China continues to deepen its relations with the existing international order, and it demands to be treated not only as an important member, but also as its defender, as China's economic rise since the late 1970s has been a crucial factor in globalization. Notice that hardline populists, such as Donald Trump's

[46] The Chinese government conceived the logo for the 2016 G20 Summit as "...a stylized bridge consisting of 20 layered lines. The bridge signifies that the G20 is a bridge for global economic growth, international cooperation and a win-win future." Available at http://www.g20chn.org/English/China2016/Logo/index.html.

former strategist Stephen K. Bannon,[47] have been blaming China as a major external source of the perceived woes of globalization in both Europe and the USA.

Within this international order, it is both reasonable and necessary that China acts as a reformist state actor. As long as the reforms improve the openness and inclusiveness of the international order and allow members like China to have a greater say in global governance, this helps strengthen the existing rules-based international order, even if those reforms may not necessarily be in the United States' narrowly defined national interests. Other states, however, may choose to support China's reform efforts. For example, China's initiative at the G20 to reform the IMF in 2010 was supported by most other G20 members including all the forum's European member states. Such Chinese actions would avoid the dangers of a pluralization of global governance while increasing China's contributions to global public goods at a time when the US administration withdraws from several key international organizations.

On the other hand, the consequences of a slow-down, let alone a failure, of such reforms on the existing order could be serious indeed. Thus, this might encourage—indeed even create—incentives for some within the existing international order to search for alternatives. This does not just concern China, but also the declining hegemonic power America itself, which might be tempted to consider alternative arrangements that from its own point of view might seem more attractive. In recent years, the great powers have not done enough to strengthen existing global institutions but have preferred instead to focus on building exclusive new institutions. (Thus, China built the BRICS Research Data Alliance, AIIB, and BRI, and the United States the TPP.) Both the BRI and TPP not only violate the principles of the existing liberal international order but also risk making global governance more fragmented, hence more difficult and perhaps finally impossible.

China-built new institutions such as the AIIB, however, do not go beyond the existing order. Jin Liqun, the first AIIB president, stated: "Both the World Bank Group and Asian Development Bank have contributed substantially to Asia's poverty reduction over the decades, but poverty reduction is hard to achieve, not just because of lack of funding, but more importantly because of the approach. I have a deep conviction that the poverty reduction program in and of itself will not go very far in making a difference in the livelihood of the poor and the needy. In most of the cases, the approach needs to be refined, needs to be improved."[48] Yet although China, through AIIB and in other ways, contributes to global governance within the framework of the existing

[47] Stephen K. Bannon made an important long speech in Tokyo, Japan on China, the USA, and globalization: see http://www.asahi.com/ajw/articles/AJ201711160052.html.

[48] Jin Liqun, *Building Asia's New Bank*.

international order by providing public goods, the emergence of Chinese leadership will inevitably create conflict with the USA as the present leading power in this order. This is a conflict of power, influence, and interests, and as such a geo-political disturbance to effective global governance within a rules-based and open international order.

The opposition of the United States and Japan to China's rise, however, also provides a huge warning sign that it is not only in China's, but also in the world's interest that the PRC refrain from seeking a less open, less cooperative, and less rules-based order. Fortunately, so far, the parallel institutions China has designed and built seem perfectly compatible and therefore can coexist and cooperate with others that reflect US hegemony. China reassures others that it does not seek hegemony in the new institutions. China accepts that others in the China-sponsored institutions contribute to managing and governing China multilaterally through them. Of course, they challenge the existing institutions, but those challenges are not a bad thing. They could even be quite useful, as new institutions might help promote the reform of the old ones.

13

The Paris Agreement—China's Kind of (International) Order?

Daniel Krahl

Since its accession to the United Nations in 1971, China has broadly engaged with post-World War II liberal international order and its institutions. It perceives these institutions as forums in which China would participate to utilize, and eventually change, this international order in line with its own preferences. Since 2001 China has also participated in founding new institutions and even initiated its own, sometimes excluding other world powers. This should not come as a surprise, considering that China has several issues with the existing international order. The most important of those are what Beijing perceives as Western attempts to use existing arrangements to change China's behavior or to even halt its global rise. China resents this not least because of what it calls the West's double standards: the USA, it argues, has repeatedly failed to comply with existing international norms itself and abused international institutions as tools of American hegemony. At the same time, membership has taught China the value of institutions both for its own development and as a means to sustain the kind of favorable international environment that has made possible China's rise over the last decades.

China's desire to shape international institutions to reflect the new geo-political and geo-economic realities once it had gained the possibility to do so is hardly surprising. Yet the direction in which Beijing would like to nudge the international order so far seems rather opaque. One way to clarify China's intentions behind its efforts to reform the present international order is to look at Beijing's ideas about order. In the last few years, Western attention has shifted from the question of how China could best be integrated into the existing international order to how China is changing the global order by establishing its own institutions, starting from the Shanghai Cooperation Organization (SCO) in 2001 to the announcements of the One Belt One Road initiative (OBOR, now usually referred to as the Belt and Road Initiative, BRI) and the Asian Infrastructure Investment Bank

(AIIB) in 2013.[1] These initiatives have grabbed the headlines, not only because they are interesting, which they are, or important, which they might be, but mostly because they fit into fears that China might build up parallel institutions to the established Western arrangements.[2]

Ironically, China's potentially most vital contribution to future international order, its support for the Paris Agreement (PA) on climate change in December 2015, so far has met with comparatively little attention in debates on international order. Yet the potential impact of the PA on the future of international order could well be deeper and longer lasting than that of any of China's own new institutions.[3] The agreement provides for reorienting a world economy that has been based on carbon fuels for the last 250 years onto a largely carbon-neutral track by 2050 and thus envisions the biggest reorientation in human economic activity since the industrial revolution.

Seen from the perspective of global order, the PA is very different from the early post-Cold War partial order on climate change that the UN Framework Convention on Climate Change (UNFCCC) and the Kyoto Protocol represented.[4] It was structured specifically in ways that would make it possible for China, by then the biggest emitter of greenhouse gases, to participate, and thus might offer a new paradigm for the future international order at a time when great power conflict has returned to the international arena with a vengeance. China knows that new global challenges such as climate change can only be addressed through global institutions and that, as a latecomer, it cannot completely renegotiate the liberal international order. Learning how to engage China in such efforts, instead of simply expecting it to behave according to Western rules, might be a better way to keep a developing China within the bounds of an international order acceptable to all sides. This, however, might mean accepting some of China's ideas about the future international order.

1. CHINESE CONCEPTS OF INTERNATIONAL ORDER

Chinese concepts of international order have to be understood as an evolving process, not as a fixed set of ideas. China has had a difficult relationship with

[1] See, for example, David Dollar, China's Rise as a Regional and Global Power: The AIIB and the "One Belt, One Road," *Horizons* 4 (Summer 2015), pp. 162–72.

[2] See, for example, Sebastian Heilmann, Moritz Rudolf, Mikko Huotari, and Johannes Buckow, China's Shadow Foreign Policy: Parallel Structures Challenge the Established International Order, *China Monitor* No. 18 (2014), available at http://merics.org/fileadmin/templates/download/china-monitor/China_Monitor_No_18.pdf [accessed September 28, 2016].

[3] The attention has been mostly by the climate change community itself, less so from the international relations community.

[4] See Chapter 2 by Joyeeta Gupta in this volume.

international society ever since its first encounters with European colonialism in the sixteenth century.[5] Until the nineteenth century, China was embedded in its own world, often referred to as the *tianxia* ("all under one Heaven"). From the imperial Chinese perspective, this world was not made up of equal Westphalian states, but was ordered hierarchically, with one benevolent state in the center, the Middle Kingdom (*zhongguo*). That order was stable, or so it was claimed, as every state received its proper status and role through this hierarchy.[6]

This world ended when Western powers forced China to become a member state of a Westphalian system of nominally equal nation-states through a series of wars and unequal treaties between 1839 and 1901.[7] Step by step, the Middle Kingdom turned into "China." As part of this process, catching up with the "modernized" West has dominated Chinese political thinking to this day, despite recurring conservative backlashes. The "birth of modern China" was fraught with colonial occupation and exploitation, as well as with an extended civil war and a desperate struggle against the invasion of imperial Japan, making this transformation, which includes redefining China's status and role in the international order, a painful and traumatic experience.[8] After the founding of the People's Republic, China found itself squarely in the socialist camp, but the ideas of "national rejuvenation" (*fuxing/zhenxing*) and becoming a "strong and rich great country" (*fuqiang daguo*) remained

[5] For the Western perspective of one-way socialization see Barry Buzan, China in International Society: Is "Peaceful Rise" Possible? *The Chinese Journal of International Politics* 3:1 (2010), pp. 5–36.

[6] Shih Chiyu, Assigning Role Characteristics to China: The Role versus the Ego State, *Foreign Policy Analysis* 8:1 (2012), pp. 71–91 (77). On the tributary system, see David Kang, *China Rising: Peace, Power, and Order in East Asia*, New York: Columbia University Press, 2007; for a critical assessment of the *tianxia* concept, see David Callahan, Chinese Visions of World Order: Post-Hegemonic or a New Hegemony? *International Studies Review* 10:4 (2008), pp. 749–61. The influence of the tributary system on role conceptions in Korea and Vietnam, and the continuing navigation in the role location exercise on the regional level between the USA and China is described in Joon-Woo Park, Gi-Wok Shin, and Donald Keyser (eds.), *Asia's Middle Powers? The Identity and Regional Policy of South Korea and Vietnam*, Stanford, CA: Walter H. Shorenstein Asia-Pacific Research Center Books, 2013.

[7] Shih Chiyu, Assigning Role Characteristics to China, p. 82.

[8] For China's encounter with the West, see Jonathan D. Spence, *The Search for Modern China*, New York: W. W. Norton, 1990 and Jürgen Osterhammel, *China und die Weltgesellschaft*, Munich: Beck, 1989. An important part of this narrative is that only the determined leadership of the Communist Party was able to save China from the "Century of National Humiliation" (*yi bai nian guochi*). The "Century of National Humiliation" is a historical frame used by the Chinese government to describe the years between the first Opium War (1839–42) and the "Liberation of China" by the Communist Party of China: see Wang Zheng, *Never Forget National Humiliation*, New York: Columbia University Press, 2012. It is an important part of the overall narrative of the rejuvenation of China through the leadership of the Communist Party and plays a huge role both in terms of the construction of China's own identity and of its relations with the West, for example in the context of the patriotic education campaign. On this, see also William Callahan, *China: Pessoptimist Nation*, Oxford: Oxford University Press, 2010.

the principal guidelines for Chinese foreign policy.[9] Deng Xiaoping retained the frames of the "anti-hegemonic struggle for the third world" and the "detached balancer between the superpowers"[10] but saw foreign policy above all as a tool to support China's own economic development through its integration into the world economy.[11] The post-Mao Party legitimizes its rule through its ability to safeguard China's sovereignty and advance its economic development, making sovereignty and trade the two overarching principles of Chinese foreign policy.[12] In pursuing those principles, however, Chinese foreign policy had to steer a difficult middle way between adapting itself to its international environment and challenging it, resulting in shifts between "keeping a low profile" and the urge to change the "unjust world order" created by the "ideological discrimination and military alliances stressed by the West."[13]

1.1. The Four Pillars of China's Order

China's approach to international order contains four pillars (*si da zhizhu*):[14]

(a) *China's great power status.* Acceptance of its status as a great power is probably the most important aspect of China's foreign policy. As this depends on status recognition by other countries and great powers, especially the USA, China has proposed the "Great Power Relationship

[9] For a discussion of China's tactical use of internationalist rhetoric for nationalist purposes, especially in its relationship with the USSR, see Anne-Marie Brady, *Making the Foreign Serve China: Managing Foreigners in the People's Republic*, Lanham, MD: Rowman & Littlefield, 2003, pp. 79–117. She questions the adequacy of realist internationalist thinking among the Chinese leadership. For a discussion of the importance of Chinese foreign policy rhetoric and its recent changes, see Dominik Mierzejewski, From Morality to Morality: The Rhetoric of Chinese Foreign Policy over Four Decades, in Bin Wu, Yao Shujie, and Chen Jian (eds.), *China's Development and Harmonization*, Abingdon: Routledge, 2013. The concept of "rejuvenation" to make China a "rich and powerful country" has been around since the beginning of the twentieth century, and has been the core aim of Chinese foreign policy for a long time. See Evan Medeiros, *China's International Behaviour*, Santa Monica, CA: RAND Corporation, 2009, p. 7. These concepts have been re-emphasized by the present leadership since 2012.

[10] Shih Chiyu, Assigning Role Characteristics to China, p. 81.

[11] However, Wang Yizhou argues that the idea of national interest was not new to the China of the 1980s, but was actually also prevalent during the times of Mao's socialist foreign policy, when it was simply taboo to talk about them due to Maoist internationalist rhetoric. Wang Yizhou, Rethinking State Interests, in Cai Tuo (ed.), *Chinese Perspectives on Globalization and Autonomy*, Leiden: Brill, 2012, pp. 157–80 (166).

[12] Ibid., p. 173.

[13] Yang Jiemian, The Self-Consciousness of Chinese-Characteristic Diplomatic Practice and Theory, in Zhao Jinjun and Chen Zhirui (eds.), *China and the International Society: Adaptation and Self-Consciousness*, Hackensack, NJ: World Century Publishing Cooperation, 2014, p. 3.

[14] Ibid., p. 12. See also Medeiros, *China's International Behavior*, p. 93 and Robert Sutter, *Foreign Relations of the PRC: The Legacies and Constraints of China's International Politics since 1949*, Lanham: Rowman & Littlefield, 2013, p. 19.

of a New Type"[15] with America, demanding reciprocity in accepting the status of the other and its interests. In this context, China would accept the global leadership of the USA if America accepted China as its equal on the global stage and stopped interfering in China's domestic political order and its regional sphere of influence in East Asia.

(b) *China's relations with its neighbors.* In the Chinese view, the East Asian region is its priority sphere of influence.[16] For Beijing, the territorial disputes over Taiwan and the East and South China Seas touch on its core interests. East Asia therefore is the only region where China sees itself as having a real strategic vision and an emphasis on governance through multilateral institutions including or even led by China.[17] China conceives of the proper order for that region with itself on top, reflecting the old *tianxia* system. For Beijing, this is the "natural" state of regional order in East Asia, which is prevented only by US interference.[18]

(c) *China and other developing countries.* Perhaps the most important historical legacy of Mao's foreign policy outlook is China's self-conception as a developing country and the emphasis it puts on the relationship with other developing countries. Deng Xiaoping promised in 1984 that China would always be a "Third World country even if it

[15] Paul Mancinelli argues that the New Type of Great Power relationship is actually a rather consistent outgrowth of the Russian–Chinese relationship. It was first proposed as a model for Sino-US relations by State Councillor Dai Binguo in 2008, but only used again in this context by then Vice-President Xi during his visit to the USA in 2012. See Paul Mancinelli, Conceptualizing "New Type Great Power Relations": The Sino-Russian Model, *Jamestown Foundation China Brief* 14:9 (May 7, 2014), pp. 12–16. The concept remained an enigma for many observers due to China's understanding of this frame as a process rather than a fact, so Chinese Foreign Minister Wang Yi felt obliged to explain it in 2013: "China had to become a great power and pursue great-power relations but that it should not do so in the mould of previous great powers. This means that China will not tolerate interference from foreign forces in its diplomatic decisions and will not seek alliances or hegemony. Instead, Beijing will pursue a path of peaceful development": see Zhao Kejin, Guiding Principles of China's New Foreign Policy, Carnegie-Tsinghua Center for Global Policy, September 9, 2013, p. 2, available at http://carnegietsinghua.org/2013/09/09/guiding-principles-of-china-s-new-foreign-policy-pub-52902 [accessed November 26, 2016].

[16] Yong Deng, Better than Power: "International Status" in Chinese Foreign Policy, in Yong Deng and Wang Feiling (eds.), *Power and Motivation in Chinese Foreign Policy*, Lanham, MD: Rowman & Littlefield, 2005, pp. 51–72 (64).

[17] Jörn Dosch, Relations between China and Southeast Asia: A New Regional Order in the Making?, in Lowell Dittmer and George T. Yu (eds.), *China, the Developing World, and the New Global Dynamic*, Boulder, CO: Lynne Rienner, 2010, pp. 61–82 (61); interview with Chinese foreign policy expert at China Foreign Affairs University, Beijing, April 2013.

[18] While most of China's neighbors seem to be worried about its rise and have welcomed the Obama administration's "pivot to Asia," Beijing does not understand their concerns, ascribing them purely to hostile inference by the USA. See Zhao Kejin, Guiding Principles of China's New Foreign Policy, p. 4. For a debate on the impact of China's rise on Asian security and perceptions of its own periphery, see Li Mingjiang and Kalyan Kemburi (eds.), *China's Power and Asian Security*, Abingdon: Routledge, 2015; for a more discourse and role-oriented approach, see Niv Horesh, Kim Hyun Jin, and Peter Mauch, *Superpower China: Historicizing Beijing's New Narratives of Leadership and East Asia's Response Thereto*, Singapore: World Scientific, 2015.

had developed."[19] This approach has two advantages for China. First, China is aware that many developing countries are unhappy with the existing world order, which they perceive as favoring the developed countries. Second, it enhances its own self-understanding as a civilizational state beneficent to others. China therefore still defines itself as the leader of the Third World, a Mao-inspired role that today can be understood as a supplement to the traditional hierarchy of the *tianxia* system.[20] This does not imply Soviet-style support for resistance against the Western-dominated international order, however, but instead promotes China's own model of making use of the international order and then changing it from the inside.[21]

(d) *Multilateralism*. This is the most recent addition to complete the four pillars that, according to Evan Medeiros, only emerged in 2005.[22] China for some time hesitated to get involved in regional multilateral activities because of its distrust of alliances and its emphasis on sovereignty, but later came to appreciate that multilateralism allowed it to deflect interventionist tendencies in East Asian regionalism and launch security dialogs with its neighbors while concentrating on its peaceful rise.[23] Thus, China has increasingly turned towards (regional) multilateral institutions as both a way for achieving the other three pillars and a tool.

These concepts of order have been evolving over the last thirty years, dynamically interacting with China's gradual integration into the existing international order. China's inclination to accept a new international order

[19] Mel Gurtov, Changing Perspectives and Policies, in Dittmer and Yu (eds.), *China, the Developing World*, pp. 13–36 (18).

[20] Lowell Dittmer, China and the Developing World, in Dittmer and Yu (eds.), *China, the Developing World*, pp. 1–12 (1).

[21] "Beijing avoids involving itself in direct confrontation with the global power and instead coaches the local power on how to make a concession to restore harmony in the structure": Shih Chiyu and Yin Jinwu, Between Core National Interest and a Harmonious World: Reconciling Self-Role Conceptions in Chinese Foreign Policy, *The Chinese Journal of International Politics* 6:1 (2013), pp. 59–84 (74). For China's policy towards Africa in the new millennium, see Larry Hanauer and Morris Lyle, *Chinese Engagement in Africa: Drivers, Reactions and Implications for U.S. Policy*, Santa Monica, CA: RAND Corporation, 2014.

[22] Medeiros, *China's International Behavior*, p. 94.

[23] Bates Gill, *Rising Star: China's New Security Diplomacy*, Washington, DC: Brookings Institution Press, 2007, pp. 21, 69–70. See also Wang Jianwei, China's Multilateral Diplomacy in the new Millennium, in Yong Deng and Wang Fei Ling (eds.), *China Rising: Power and Motivation in Chinese Foreign Policy*, Lanham, MD: Rowman & Littlefield, 2004, pp. 159–200 (163). According to Wang Jianwei, for China, multilateralism "...does not merely indicate China's vision of what the world should be but also contains instrumental elements that are more closely related to what the perceived world is and to China's own foreign policy objectives. On the one hand, multilateralism is increasingly perceived as a more effective tool to counterbalance U.S. unilateralism at global and regional levels. On the other hand, multilateralism has been applied as a more-charming and less-threatening form of exercising China's influence in the world and in the region."

will depend on whether those four pillars are accommodated, or at the very least not challenged, by it.

2. FROM THE UN TO THE WTO—CHINA INTEGRATES

Membership in the United Nations (UN) in 1971 was the beginning of the People's Republic's real engagement with the international system. After the internationalist rhetoric of the Cultural Revolution, this implied the definitive acceptance of a Westphalian-type international order. This formally guaranteed China's sovereignty and, through its membership in the UN Security Council (UNSC), awarded recognition of China's status as a great power. As Beijing's elevation to the UN took place mainly with the support of developing nations from Africa and the Middle East, multilateralism allowed China to achieve three of its foreign policy goals: status as a great power, champion of the developing world, and regional status as the sole Asian country in the UNSC.

China still sees the UN as the main forum of its international role and continues to widen and deepen its engagement within the vast web of UN institutions. This engagement can be understood as a key element in China's socialization into the international order, as it offers China the opportunity to engage voluntarily in global governance activities. China has been quite successful in defending the principle of sovereignty wherever it sees its own interests at stake, though it is still the UNSC member that has used its veto least.[24] In this process of socialization, China has adopted those aspects of global governance it considers compatible with its desire for global stability and development. Peacekeeping operations, once reviled as "imperialist," were first accepted and later actively engaged in as a way to participate in global governance and the search for stability.[25] Yet China's approach to international law is instrumental rather than principled, as demonstrated by Beijing's

[24] For China's voting record in the UNSC, see Joel Wuthenow, *Chinese Diplomacy and the UN Security Council: Beyond the Veto*, New York: Routledge, 2012.

[25] From the 1980s onwards, China started to participate more actively in these missions and is today one of the most important contributors of troops and especially finance to UN peacekeeping operations, shifting gradually to more combat-oriented troops since it first sent armed police officers to then East Timor (now Timor Leste) in 2000. In Lebanon, South Sudan, and Mali, China's deployments were rapid and sometimes decisive. See Stephen Olson and Clyde Prestowitz, *The Evolving Role of China in International Institutions*, prepared for the US–China Economic and Security Review Commission, January 2011, p. 57, available at http://origin.www.uscc.gov/sites/default/files/Research/TheEvolvingRoleofChinainInternationalInstitutions.pdf [accessed November 26, 2016].

refusal to cooperate with the Permanent Court of Arbitration in The Hague on China's South China Sea (SCS) claims and its blunt rejection of its Award.[26]

At the regional level, China's commitment to multilateralism has generally been less enthusiastic. When it joined the Asian Regional Forum and later the Asia Pacific Economic Cooperation (APEC), its main intention probably was to prevent both bodies from getting involved in any of its core interests, like Taiwan or the SCS.[27] Later, Beijing pushed the ASEAN+3 talks as a way to counter the US-dominated APEC[28] and used a Free Trade Agreement (FTA) with ASEAN to weaken its ability to build a united front against the big neighbor in the north.[29]

FTAs and even bilateral trade arrangements play an important role in China's foreign policy. Yet the second most important context of China's integration into international order after the UN was its membership in the World Trade Organization (WTO) in 2001.[30] This set off a period of rapid expansion in exports and drove domestic market reforms. In the brief golden age of neoliberal institutionalism and free trade when China "joined the club of rule-abiding countries," its entry into the WTO served as a coming of age ceremony of China as a trading nation and as an important status symbol of acceptance by international society.[31] Still, while China has undoubtedly benefitted from membership, the long and painful negotiations to secure it were seen as humiliating in China and undermined its trust in America's leadership in global governance.[32] Moreover, Chinese enthusiasm for the WTO waned quickly once the demanded reforms were considered complete in 2006; China's policy focus shifted towards bilateral trade negotiations and FTAs instead of WTO reform.[33] Western optimism about the socializing effects of WTO membership and hopes that China would become a liberal market economy have also waned; US and EU trade officials continue to complain about unfair barriers to market access in China.[34]

[26] China, however, can point to the fact that it is a ratified member of the United Nations Convention on the Law of the Sea (UNCLOS) and thus present itself as a better global citizen than the United States. See Ben Cardin, The South China Sea Is the Reason the United States Must Ratify UNCLOS, *Foreign Policy*, July 13, 2016, available at http://foreignpolicy.com/2016/07/13/the-south-china-sea-is-the-reason-the-united-states-must-ratify-unclos/ [accessed December 15, 2016].

[27] Gill, *Rising Star*, p. 32.

[28] Susan Shirk, *China: Fragile Superpower*, Oxford: Oxford University Press, 2007, p. 120.

[29] For China's strategic interaction with ASEAN see Dosch, Relations between China and Southeast Asia.

[30] China sees bilateral FTAs (including with those regions like ASEAN or the Gulf Cooperation Council (GCC)) as more promising than pushing forward WTO negotiations on a multilateralist track. Interview with Chinese Academy of International Trade and Economic Cooperation (CAITEC) researchers, Beijing, May 17, 2013.

[31] Shirk, *China: Fragile Superpower*, p. 132. [32] Ibid.

[33] Interview with CAITEC researchers, Beijing, May 17, 2013.

[34] See United States Trade Representative, *2015 Report to Congress on China's WTO Compliance*, available at https://ustr.gov/about-us/policy-offices/press-office/reports-and-publications/

China's membership in international financial institutions like the International Monetary Fund and the World Bank has been understood by Beijing less as a chance to drive global policy than as an opportunity to learn and gather experience for its own experts, whom it has vigorously involved in both organizations. China has been able, mostly through the success of its economic and international aid policies, to modify the prevailing perspectives in these organizations.[35] China's most successful use of institutions for capacity-building has been its participation in the Asian Development Bank, where China proved an ardent learner of institutional processes to increase its expertise and train qualified personnel at a time when its resources were limited. Later, China turned into a champion for other developing countries in the bank.[36] Participation helped China understand the often inefficient procedures and mechanisms of multilateral institutions, which tend to put off prospective beneficiaries, and improve upon them once it started to develop its own institutions. Yet Beijing seems to have concluded that to change institutions so fundamentally tied to neoliberal ideology would be more difficult than creating its own institutions, which would allow China to present itself as great power and champion of the developing world.[37]

Western reactions to China's integration into the existing (Western-designed) international order have been rather mixed. While overall China is credited with having integrated itself relatively successfully, there is also a certain disappointment in the West that some of the expected effects, notably China's conversion to those institutions' Western-inspired norms and values, did not materialize. China, in turn, came to understand better the limits of how much it can change these institutions from within. The benefits of the integration process, like knowledge-transfer, access to markets, and channels of diplomacy, that China received through its membership in the UN and the WTO probably remain unquestioned in China, but Beijing resented having to knock on doors for membership and what it sees as attempts to interfere with its sovereignty. It was therefore an obvious choice for China to make use of the lessons learned from integrating into international society to invent its own institutions in ways that made them better suited to represent and promote the changed international order that China would like to see.

2015/2015-report-congress-chinas-wto [accessed August 9, 2016], and interview with German industry representative, Berlin, July 2016.

[35] The most notable example came in 2010 when the IMF acknowledged the benefits of capital controls. See Olson and Prestowitz, *Evolving Role of China*, p. 21.

[36] Ibid., pp. 68–74. [37] Ibid., p. 35.

3. FROM THE SCO TO THE BRI—CHINA LAUNCHES ITS OWN INSTITUTIONS

The Shanghai Cooperation Organization (SCO) was the first institution that China helped launch. It was formally established in Shanghai in 2001 and was the outcome of a multilateral process initiated in 1996 to negotiate the borders between China and the successor states of the Soviet Union.[38] With its security-oriented framework, the SCO was seen by many as a reaction to increasingly assertive Western policies that had reached a climax with the Kosovo War in 1999. In particular for China, it was conceived as a response to trans-border terrorism in Central Asia. Since its foundation, a marked shift has taken place within the organization, with China becoming the driving force for further integration.[39] Yet the main importance of SCO may well have been the lessons it taught China in the art of institution-building.

Beijing put those newly acquired skills to good use when it launched its first own institutions in 2004 with the Forum of China Africa Cooperation (FOCAC) and the China Arab Friendship and Cooperation Forum. Both built on the long-standing tradition of "Third World solidarity" with the African Union and the Arab League.[40] Both institutions also pioneered a new format of "China + x," in which all the other members would sit opposite their "big brother" China. (The 16+1 mechanism with Eastern European countries, initiated in 2012, was the first time that China established such a mechanism with a group of industrialized countries).[41] This was a format that differed from other institutions, including the SCO, where China was just one member among many, and has given rise to debates, especially in the West, whether these summits are modern versions of tribute missions. China still understands world politics as a hierarchy,[42] and critics accuse China of using the old *tianxia* frame in a revised form to legitimize its exploitation of other

[38] Wang Jianwei sees this as a "northward drive" of Chinese regional cooperation following its earlier "southward drive" towards Southeast Asia. See Wang Jianwei, China's Multilateral Diplomacy, p. 177 and p. 166 respectively.

[39] Nadine Godehardt and Daniel Krahl, "Friedensmission 2010": China als zentralasiatischer Akteur? *GIGA focus*, October 2010, available at https://www.giga-hamburg.de/de/system/files/publications/gf_global_1010.pdf [accessed October 16, 2016].

[40] Yun Sun, *Xi and the 6th Forum on China–Africa Cooperation, Major Commitments, but with Questions*, Washington, DC: Brookings Institution, 2015, available at https://www.brookings.edu/blog/africa-in-focus/2015/12/07/xi-and-the-6th-forum-on-china-africa-cooperation-major-commitments-but-with-questions/ [accessed September 12, 2016].

[41] Jurica Simurina, *China's Approach to the CEE-16*, ECRAN Short-Term Policy Brief 85, January 2014, available at http://eeas.europa.eu/archives/docs/china/docs/division_ecran/ecran_is107_paper_85_chinas_approach_to_the_cee-16_jurica_simurina_en.pdf.

[42] For a more thorough discussion of China's multilateralist turn, especially with regard to the SCO and FOCAC, see Yong Deng and Wang Feiling (eds.), *Power and Motivation*, pp. 200–44.

countries and its own civilizing projects in its perceived periphery.[43] In this view, China's new international institutions, where African heads of state would convene around the Chinese president to receive investment from China, are merely modern versions of tributary rituals, where representatives of foreign lands came to the "center" of the civilized world. In this way, China's Third World policy re-enacts "the drama of giving without taking," similar to the presents the emperor gave foreign delegations. Beijing would insist, of course, that this foreign policy behavior does not include hierarchy: China does not dominate or exploit, as other states do.[44] Yet the channels of influence provided by FOCAC have certainly been useful to China in other, established international organizations. Thus, seven African nations paid homage to China during the 2006 FOCAC summit by recognizing China's market economy status in the WTO,[45] and African nations' votes were decisive in electing Margaret Chan as the Director-General of the World Health Organization just after the 2006 FOCAC summit.[46]

The BRICS (Brazil, Russia, India, China, and South Africa) summits do not follow that particular format. This multilateral institution helps underline China's role as a "rising power"[47] and shows the West that keeping rising powers out of the inner circle of established institutions like the G7, simply leads them into founding their own institutions. While representing both the great power and the developing country aspect, the BRICS also signals China's determination to cultivate its global reach and a new approach to tackling global challenges, symbolized by a united front with the other BRICS in WTO negotiations and climate talks.[48]

The establishment of the AIIB and the OBOR project in 2013 seems like a logical continuation of the policies described above, though their scale, both in aspiration and in material underpinning, makes them stand out. OBOR now draws together China's separate regional strategies, connecting Eastern Europe and Africa to China and its neighborhood, through a new version of the Silk Road.[49] From the beginning, Western observers differed in their

[43] For a critical assessment of the *tianxia* concept including its meaning for China's relationship with developing countries, see Callahan, Chinese Visions of World Order.

[44] Shih Chiyu, Assigning Role Characteristics to China, p. 80.

[45] Chi Zhang, *The Domestic Dynamic of China's Energy Diplomacy*, Singapore: World Scientific Press, 2015, p. 205.

[46] Ibid., p. 207. [47] Ibid.

[48] For a more thorough debate of China's role in the BRICS, see Daniel Krahl, China: Aus den BRICS herausgewachsen? *Aus Politik und Zeitgeschichte (APuZ)* 63:50–1 (2013), pp. 36–41, available at http://www.bpb.de/apuz/173803/china-aus-den-brics-herausgewachsen?p=all [accessed October 16, 2016]; similarly also Michael A. Glosny, China and the BRICS: A Real (but Limited) Partnership in a Unipolar World, *Polity* 42:1 (2010), pp. 27f.

[49] One Belt, One Road, *Caixin Online*, October 12, 2014, available at http://english.caixin.com/2014-12-10/100761304.html [accessed October 16, 2016].

interpretation of AIIB and OBOR: they were seen either as part of a Chinese hegemonic project, or simply as a way to facilitate Chinese investment.[50]

Overall, Western reactions to Chinese attempts to establish new institutions have tended to be nervous. They were often perceived as attempts to establish parallel structures to Western institutions and symbols of new Chinese hegemonic aspirations. Thus, the EU initially responded cautiously to China's appearance in Eastern Europe but over time came to appreciate the potential benefits of China's investment in its impoverished backyard.[51] China's most poignant success with its own multilateral institutions came when the USA tried to prevent other states from joining the AIIB: even close US allies like the United Kingdom and Germany joined within a short time, arguing that by doing so, they were able to influence the new institution.[52] There were also attempts by Western powers, however, to accommodate China's quest for status and to integrate it (with other emerging powers) into the established Western world order, especially through the elevation of the G20 after the 2008 financial crisis. Until 2016, however, China was reluctant to be drawn into such a role, let alone commit significant resources.[53]

With the election of Donald Trump as the forty-fifth president of the United States, however, this began to change. As the new US administration started to withdraw from the multilateral order that America itself had built with considerable expense of blood and treasure, Beijing's reluctance gave way to increasingly explicit efforts by the Chinese leadership to assume the mantle of defender of globalization and leader in the liberal international order (LIO 2.0). While, in the words of Evan Osnos, the Trump administration's doctrine seemed to consist of "retreating from the front,"[54] President Xi stepped into the breach.

4. THE PARIS AGREEMENT—CHINA'S KIND OF INTERNATIONAL ORDER?

The concept of order that is implicit in the Paris Agreement differs from those discussed above. At the seemingly disastrous Copenhagen climate change

[50] For a detailed discussion of OBOR and AIIB, see Chapter 12 by Zhongying Pang in this volume.

[51] Simurina, *China's Approach to the CEE-16*.

[52] Jane Perlez, China Creates a World Bank of Its Own, and the U.S. Balks, *New York Times*, December 4, 2015, available at http://www.nytimes.com/2015/12/05/business/international/china-creates-an-asian-bank-as-the-us-stands-aloof.html?_r=0 [accessed October 16, 2016].

[53] See Jörn-Carsten Gottwald and Niall Duggan, Hesitant Adaptation: China's New Role in Global Policies, in Sebastian Harnisch, Cornelia Frank, and Hanns W. Maull (eds.), *Role Theory in International Relations: Approaches and Analysis*, London: Routledge, 2011, pp. 234–51 (246–9).

[54] Evan Osnos, Making China Great Again, How Beijing Learned to Use Trump to its Advantage, *The New Yorker*, January 8, 2018, available at https://www.newyorker.com/magazine/2018/01/08/making-china-great-again [accessed January 3, 2018].

conference of 2009, where China for the first time had taken center stage in international climate negotiations, Beijing found itself accused of having blocked a successful outcome of the conference.[55] In fact, the Kyoto approach was unacceptable to several other states besides sovereignty-conscious China, including the United States. After Copenhagen, negotiators realized they needed to build a multilateral framework different from the Kyoto Protocol to accommodate the two largest emitters, the USA and China, as a precondition for achieving the ultimate objective of the UNFCCC. It took six more years until in Paris the balance was found that made a universal agreement possible.

UNFCCC, the legal and institutional context in which international climate negotiations take place, was modeled after the blueprint of its mother organization, the UN. It therefore displayed some of the characteristics of this organization that China had always been comfortable with, like sovereignty and equality of all members. In the 1990s and early 2000s, China was more than happy not to play a major role in the climate change negotiations beyond posing as "champion of the developing world" through the G77 + China format. As such, it insisted that only developed nations, or Annex-I states, which historically accounted for the bulk of previous emissions, had to undertake reductions of CO_2 emissions, from which non-annex members like China were to be exempt under the "common but differentiated responsibilities" (CBDR) principle and the Annex architecture of the Kyoto Protocol.[56]

As a result of China's economic rise, the debate shifted, however: China now was rapidly becoming a major emitter itself, overtaking the USA as the world's biggest source of CO_2 emissions in 2006. Fighting climate change without China's participation seemed increasingly unrealistic. The Bush administration (2001–9), not eager to comply with any climate change regime itself, refused to contribute as long as China was allowed a free ride on emissions.[57] An arrangement that had so far served China's interests well by imposing costly responsibilities on developed countries while shielding

[55] See, for example, Mark Lynas, How do I know China wrecked the Copenhagen deal? I was in the room, *The Guardian Online*, December 22, 2009, available at http://www.guardian.co.uk/environment/2009/dec/22/copenhagen-climate-change-mark [accessed September 13, 2016].

[56] He Lichao, China's Climate-Change Policy from Kyoto to Copenhagen: Domestic Needs and International Aspiration, *Asian Perspective* 34:3 (2010), pp. 5–33. See also United Nations, *United Nations Framework Convention for Climate Change*, 1992, available at https://unfccc.int/resource/docs/convkp/conveng.pdf [accessed October 17, 2016]; Lester Ross, Changing Climate: What the Paris Accord means for China, *Law360*, New York, March 18, 2016, available at http://www.law360.com/articles/767558/changing-climate-what-the-paris-accord-means-for-china [accessed October 17, 2016].

[57] Daniel Bodansky, *The Copenhagen Climate Change Conference: A Post-Mortem*, 2010, p. 3, available at http://www.fao.org/fileadmin/user_upload/rome2007/docs/Copenhagen_Climate_Change.pdf (accessed November 26, 2016). China became the biggest CO_2 emitter in 2006: see John Vidal and David Adam, China overtakes U.S. as world's biggest CO2 emitter, *The Guardian Online*, June 19, 2007, available at https://www.theguardian.com/environment/2007/jun/19/china.usnews [accessed September 13, 2016].

China from them, was now being used by the United States to put pressure on China. China reacted by accusing the USA of "climate imperialism," arguing that the West wanted to use the climate change issue as a means to halt China's rise. Remarkably, Beijing nevertheless does not even seem to have considered leaving the UNFCCC at that point. Instead, shortly before the Copenhagen conference, China responded by forming BASIC (the BRICS countries minus Russia) which was to block any attempt by the West to change the CBDR principle.[58]

Since Copenhagen, climate change has become a central pillar of China's foreign policy, in which it tried "balancing its domestic needs with its international aspirations."[59] For Beijing, negotiating climate agreements became synonymous with negotiating the future global order and China's role in it. "China's climate-change diplomacy has now become a key component of its foreign policy because of the issue's global strategic significance. [...] Internationally, China wants to participate more fully in shaping the international environmental regime and expects to exert more influence generally over the rules of international affairs."[60] For China, climate change negotiations therefore assumed a geo-political importance that it did not have in the perception of most Western decision-makers.

In the nervous atmosphere before Copenhagen, an agreement containing binding reductions for China seemed as abhorrent as a "new Plaza accord."[61] From a Chinese perspective, the West was trying again to impose its norms on China, but Beijing would not be seen as budging under Western pressure.[62] The notion that China simply was stalling to evade climate policy responsibility was always more Western framing than reality. For the Copenhagen Accord, the seemingly meager outcome of the conference in 2009, contained a provision that would show the way forward: a pledge to reduce global emissions by 80 percent by 2050. In accepting this clause China had in principle agreed to developing countries' emission reduction contributions for the first time, since this clearly would be impossible without major reductions by developing nations.[63]

This non-binding clause became the basis of the Paris Agreement. The negotiations were still mostly shaped by the EU and the USA; during the climate change negotiations in Cancun 2010 and Durban 2011, China tried to stay out of the limelight not least because of dwindling support from other developing countries, which now supported EU efforts to build on the voluntarist approach suggested by the Copenhagen Accord. At Durban, China

[58] Bodansky, *Copenhagen Climate Change Conference*.
[59] He Lichao, China's Climate-Change Policy, p. 6. [60] Ibid., p. 8.
[61] Interviews at China Foreign Affairs University Beijing, January to February 2010.
[62] Ibid.
[63] Daniel Bodansky, The Paris Climate Change Agreement: A New Hope? (May 17, 2016), *American Journal of International Law* 110 (2017), p. 7, available at https://papers.ssrn.com/sol3/papers.cfm?abstract_id=2773895 [accessed November 26, 2016].

remained silent during the last hours of negotiations, thereby isolating India, and thus quietly acquiesced to the roadmap that would lead to Paris.[64]

In 2014, China then announced a bilateral agreement with the USA at the margins of the APEC summit in Beijing. At the Lima climate change conference towards the end of the same year, Beijing now committed China to cap its CO_2 emissions "around 2030," possibly even at an earlier date, and to generating 20 percent of its primary energy from non-fossil fuels in exchange for reduction commitments by the United States.[65] With this agreement, China paved the road for Paris. Beijing had cleverly used the stage of APEC and great power diplomacy to present itself as a responsible power and a leader in global governance. By taking the initiative, it evaded the impression that it had caved in to Western demands, instead presenting itself in a new role as part of a "G2" with the USA.

Just before Paris, China again assumed an important role in climate change negotiations when it submitted its Intended Nationally Determined Commitments (INDCs) already in late June 2015,[66] putting pressure on other emerging economies like India to follow suit. To be sure, China's commitments in themselves were not overly ambitious.[67] The importance of China's INDC submission lay in its commitment to the Paris Agreement process and its acknowledgment of the need to provide for an early peak in its emissions. This turned the division of the world along the annex firewall of the Kyoto Protocol into a thing of the past. There is little doubt that the Paris Agreement could never have been reached without China; without China, moreover, any agreement would have had a very limited effect on global warming, given China's massive contributions to global emissions. At a time when China and the United States seemed to be on a collision course geo-politically, China thus proved its ability to work together with the USA and others to address global issues, as long as this cooperation acknowledged China's interests and accommodated its preferred policy approaches.

That China took a leading role in building the Paris Agreement climate change order can be explained by domestic changes and a modification of its foreign policy. While domestic factors such as air pollution and the desire to accelerate technology transfer have often been highlighted,[68] China's willingness to assume

[64] Interview with German climate negotiator, Berlin, July 20, 2016; see also Bodansky, The Paris Climate Change Agreement, p. 8.

[65] Ross, Changing Climate. See also Chapter 2 by Joyeeta Gupta in this volume.

[66] UNFCCC newsroom, China submits its climate action plan ahead of 2015 Paris summit, June 30, 2015, available at http://newsroom.unfccc.int/unfccc-newsroom/china-submits-its-climate-action-plan-ahead-of-2015-paris-agreement/ [accessed October 17, 2016].

[67] China was already trying to transform its economy towards being less resource intensive even without international pledges: see Ross, Changing Climate.

[68] See Barbara Finnamore, Sam Geall, Angel Hsu, Johanna Lewis, and Li Shuo, Beijing Is Finally Getting Serious About Climate Change, *Foreign Policy*, July 11, 2015, available at http://foreignpolicy.com/2015/07/11/china-climate-change-greenhouse-united-states-policy/ [accessed October 17, 2016].

a leadership role in global governance also reflects a modified foreign policy role concept. This change took place over a longer period but became apparent after Xi Jinping came to power in 2012. It reflected a new vision of China's future global role and its relationships with the international order.[69] From this perspective, it is easy to understand why China agreed to the precedent that the Paris Agreement established: it supports three pillars of China's foreign policy without affecting its core interests in its East Asian periphery. First, China managed to give substance to the "new type of great power relationship" with the United States in a way that underlined China's equal status as one the world's two great powers. Second, the Agreement allowed China to cast itself as the champion of developing countries, which after Copenhagen had grown increasingly critical of China. As a "responsible power," China therefore now forcefully supports developing countries on financial compensation demands by putting pressure on developed countries to make funds available for the Green Climate Fund. Moreover, China also launched its own, independent South–South Climate Cooperation Fund.[70] This approach has three advantages: China can ingratiate itself with the Third World, get more involved in green energy and climate investment in Africa, and garner support for its positions in the UNFCCC institutions. Lastly, Paris symbolizes the kind of flexible multilateralism that China appreciates. No supranational body will have authority to sanction China if it does not reach its INDCs; thus, China safeguards its sovereignty. With its voluntary commitments that it has to re-submit every five years, Beijing retains the freedom to adjust them in line with its greatest priority, economic development.

The international functional order that emanated from Paris fits China's vision of global governance by following, rather than driving, national policies, but it also sets international standards.[71] It ensures that all states are included and will have to deliver, preventing other developing nations from gaining competitive advantages over China. Finally, Beijing batted away the nightmare of a "new Plaza accord," under which the established powers would force a rising power to give up some of its advantages. With the Paris Agreement, China and the United States for a brief moment took over the leadership role in climate policy once claimed by the EU.

5. DONALD TRUMP AND THE PARIS AGREEMENT AS POST-AMERICAN ORDER

This joint leadership role ended on November 8, 2016, when Donald Trump was elected US president. His frequently indicated intention to leave the PA, finally

[69] He Lichao, China's Climate-Change Policy, p. 7. [70] Ross, Changing Climate.
[71] Bodanksy, The Paris Climate Change Agreement, p. 2.

announced on June 1, 2017, already overshadowed the Marrakesh climate talks in November 2016 and raised questions about the very survival of the PA. It was China that saved the agreement by reaffirming its commitment to it. Beijing has since been careful not to overstate its leadership role in the PA that many awarded to it, but by the end of 2017 it seemed as if the Agreement might even have been strengthened, rather than weakened, by the fall-out of Trump's decision. If so, this was obviously due to China rejecting a climate change policy race to the bottom with the USA, but trying to portray itself as a responsible power.[72] There seemed to be an understanding in Beijing that the rapid decline of American power and standing in the world, and its reluctance to use its influence in ways that would benefit others, not just itself, might speed up the transition in global power much more than expected and probably wished for in Beijing.

Since the election of Donald Trump, the US involvement in its self-created liberal multilateral system has weakened significantly. This has strengthened China's role, which now stands as a pioneer in free trade and multilateral agreements. The withdrawal of the United States from a proactive liberal trade policy, demonstrated most dramatically by the US departure from the Trans-pacific Partnership, has made the East Asian countries even more dependent on China. Even staunch Asian US allies like Japan under its China-critical right-wing Prime Minister Abe had to seek rapprochement with China.[73] As China itself has been repeatedly accused of protectionist economic policies, the EU or Canada continue to find it hard to come to free trade agreements with China, despite the fact that Beijing has become the only possible serious ally on free trade for lack of alternatives.

On climate change, however, things are much easier, as China seems to be a truly like-minded partner.[74] It is clear that the PA would not survive if China were to drop out, too. By simply restating its commitment China therefore has been cast in the role of savior of the global climate. As Chinese environment and energy policies at home have recently become much more credible in their efforts to reduce the growth of Chinese emissions (Beijing now calls for the creation of an "ecological civilization"), China's international image as a responsible global actor has been enhanced further.[75]

[72] Christine Loh, As the U.S. dithers, China cements its climate leadership role, *South China Morning Post*, November 22, 2017, available at http://www.scmp.com/comment/insight-opinion/article/2120923/us-ditherschina-cements-its's-climate-leadership-role-opening [accessed December 22, 2017].

[73] SCMP, Japan ready to cooperate with China on global trade plan, Shinzo Abe says, *South China Morning Post*, December 4, 2017, available at http://www.scmp.com/news/china/diplomacy-defence/article/2122846/japan-ready-cooperate-china-global-trade-plan-shinzo [accessed December 22, 2017].

[74] SCMP, China, EU step up ties to fight climate change, *South China Morning Post*, September 18, 2017, available at http://www.scmp.com/news/china/policies-politics/article/2111657/china-eustep-ties-fight-climate-change [accessed December 22, 2017].

[75] Loh, As the U.S. dithers.

The PA marks a further step away from the old international order centered on Western power, and it fits well into Chinese attempts to create a post-American order that rests on great power diplomacy within a framework of multilateralism and cooperation among developing countries, as exemplified by its Belt and Road Initiative. The PA allows China to leverage the internal fight against pollution and the restructuring and upgrading of its economy for the pursuit of international status. While China still refuses to assume a true leadership role within the PA for fear of committing itself too much, as a regulatory institution the PA has so far shown itself to be flexible enough to keep China involved. The downside of this light regulatory touch that characterizes the PA is, of course, its uncertain impact on global warming.

The PA also demonstrates that the integration of China into the international order now proceeds along a trajectory that differs markedly from the assumptions of traditional integrationist theories in the West. While the West originally thought that it was China that would change as it integrated into international institutions, China is now changing the global world order from within these institutions. Although the specific favorable circumstances that allowed for the new model of the Paris Agreement may not exist in all areas of international order, the PA nevertheless provides a promising example for the type of institutional arrangement that might integrate a more active and powerful China into an international order that accommodates its needs yet may still deserve to be called "liberal."

6. CONCLUSION

Looking back at forty-five years of Chinese attempts to come to terms with the established liberal international order (LIO 2.0), China has been very successful in becoming a respected member of this order and increasingly also in adapting it in ways that suit its own evolving concepts of global order. When it arrived on the international scene, China chose to adapt to the institutions as it found them because it understood that it was more effective to change them from within than to fight them from outside. In this way, China was also able to make full use of the resources that these institutions and the international order as a whole afforded it to advance its own economic and social development, and Beijing thus has come to appreciate the benefits that international institutions can provide. As its capacities grew, China has increasingly paid back into these institutions, thereby benefitting other members and the institutions themselves. This experience led China to define multilateralism as one of the pillars of its foreign policy and a major tool with which to advance the other three pillars of that policy, its relations with great powers, with its neighbors, and with developing countries.

Ultimately, China wants an international order that reflects its own growing importance. This involves modifying global institutions away from their Western characteristics, as the world around them is changing. To this end, China needed to build its own institutions along a learning curve—from learning how to participate in others' organizations to creating one's own and teaching others about the conduct of international cooperation. These new institutions may well turn out to be what China sees as beta-version building blocks in its vision of a new international order. They not only reflect China's greater capabilities, but also serve specific Chinese foreign policy interests, such as enhancing China's status in the present, transitional international order.

At the same time, China knows that it cannot solve global problems alone or deal with other great powers, notably the USA, only through its own new institutions. As it needs others to tackle global challenges, it also has to work together with them in common institutions like the UN.

The Paris Agreement, as an offshoot of the UNFCCC, could therefore provide a model for a future international order that would reconcile China's domestic needs, its global interests, and its own vision of international order. This functional order helped China to engage other great powers and established it as one of the two indispensable powers for tackling global climate change. At the same time, the PA allowed China to present itself as a champion of developing countries. It also safeguarded China's sovereignty while binding all participants into a framework of voluntary cooperation, and it served China's domestic purposes of economic and technological transition and environmental protection.

China's search for a new international order remains an ongoing process, and Paris is not a blueprint for solving all international problems. Yet the PA showed that a new order can be created when China is included from the beginning. The Paris negotiations became a unique exercise in global cooperation at a time of global uncertainty because the West understood that it needed China, the world's biggest source of greenhouse gas emissions, as part of any meaningful policy to contain climate change, but that at the same time it had little leverage to secure compliance through pressure. It therefore had to accommodate Chinese interests. The result was an arrangement that for the first time seriously included non-Western nations in designing a new functional order on climate change.

Of course, China's multilateralism differs from the European approach. For Europe, multilateralism has always been a way to augment its limited capabilities, hoping that it would be able to constrain the great powers through universal institutionalism. China's concept of multilateralism is compatible with great power politics and supports their policies. It moderates the impact of geo-political changes, such as its own rise, without preventing them, and it allows Beijing to partake in global governance at limited costs. This multilateralism reflects, rather than drives, national policies, but it also tries to set international standards. It is designed to be acceptable to countries like China, yet still intends to be effective.

Whether the Paris Agreement really can deliver the effective containment of climate change, especially without the United States, remains to be seen, of course. Still, the PA may offer a first glimpse of the new international order—an order that would still comprise many elements of the old liberal international order, such as a central role for the UN and for international principles, norms, and rules. Europe would still have an important role to play, and the USA would continue to be indispensable. Yet this order would have overcome the remnants of unipolarity and bipolarity, and more broadly the prevalence of Eurocentric approaches to global standards based on integrationist concepts of multilateralism, in favor of looser forms of global governance. This order would focus on tackling global challenges in less interventionist, more voluntarist ways. In short, the Paris Agreement could become a first step towards an international order with truly common responsibilities.

Conclusions

The Rise and Decline of the Liberal International Order

Hanns W. Maull

This volume began with the Atlantic Charter of 1941, the original blueprint for what we call the (post-Cold War) "liberal international order 2.0" (LIO). Future historians may well come to regard 2016 as the year when this order expired. It was a year in which brutal military force was applied by Russia and its allies to help win a civil war in Syria and reshape the politics of the Middle East, and in which China (and Taiwan) brusquely rejected the Permanent Court of Arbitration Award to the Philippines in its territorial dispute and thus demonstrated that it was not to be constrained by international law in the pursuit of its territorial objectives in the South China Sea. Within Western democracies, the rise of populist nationalist and anti-globalization sentiment also animated Brexit, the UK's decision to leave the European Union, and set Donald Trump on his way into the White House as president of the United States.

The decline of the LIO 2.0 to a considerable degree resulted from the remarkable achievements of the liberal international order. Its original version had succeeded in containing Soviet expansionism—albeit at the price of the establishment of a national security state in the United States. The LIO made possible the socio-economic miracle of the *trente glorieuses*, the decades of remarkable growth, full employment, and the rise of the welfare state in Western democracies from 1950 to 1973—though that golden age encouraged a revolution of rising expectations and promoted the proliferation of vested interests.[1]

The LIO was also able to integrate "rising powers" into its arrangements. This started with the former adversaries (West) Germany and Japan, and then

[1] See Mancur Olson, *The Rise and Decline of Nations: Economic Growth, Stagflation, and Social Rigidities*, New Haven, CT: Yale University Press, 1984.

continued with several waves of newly industrializing countries, starting with the "four tigers" Singapore, Hong Kong, the Republic of Korea, and Taiwan and ending, for now, with the People's Republic of China and Vietnam. Since 1990, the LIO came to be consolidated and expanded into the universal political framework that enabled and embedded globalization as the LIO 2.0. Yet globalization turned out to be highly corrosive for the Western democratic welfare state model and the cohesion of Western societies.

Although the LIO was conceived and partially implemented already in the aftermath of World War II, it really came into its own only with the end of the Cold War in Europe and Asia. The dissolution of the Soviet bloc with its institutions, the Warsaw Pact and Comecon (roughly comparable to the North Atlantic Treaty Organization (NATO) and the General Agreement on Tariffs and Trade), and the entry of many of the formerly socialist countries into Western institutions such as NATO, the European Union, and the World Trade Organization (WTO), meant that the liberal international order now had become truly global in reach, as its original architects had hoped. Its earlier promise in the immediate aftermath of World War II, which gave birth to the United Nations and daring internationalist projects such as the Baruch Plan for the international control of nuclear weapons and, as late as mid-1947, produced an American invitation to the Soviet Union and its Eastern European satellites to join the Marshall Plan, floundered under the deepening distrust and growing tensions between Washington and Moscow and thus remained a brief episode. From 1947 onward, the liberal international order was superseded by a divided world with two different partial international orders, one dominated by the United States, the other by the Soviet Union.

This final chapter will try to draw some conclusions from our journey through the universe of the LIO 2.0 to answer the questions posed in the Introduction: How has the international order changed since 1990? What trends can be identified, and how are they to be evaluated? What have been the strategies and policies of major ordering powers? To do so, the following sections will attempt to summarize what happened in the partial orders surveyed with regard to (a) their effectiveness and legitimacy, (b) the incidence of violence and the use and threat of force, (c) the enforcement of order through collective action, (d) the evolution of principles, norms, rules, and institutions, (e) dominant interaction patterns and actors, and (f) the evolution of partial orders over time (section 1). We will then devote particular attention to the two ordering powers, the United States and China, that are likely to be most influential players in the twenty-first century, with a view to evaluating their roles in the international order (section 2) and how they have changed (section 3). Section 4 will offer some explanations for what has been happening to the LIO. We conclude with some reflections on implications of our findings (section 5).

In brief, the LIO since 1990 experienced, after a period of consolidation under fire (1990 to 1995) remarkable advances towards both more inclusive and more highly developed arrangements of global governance (1995 to 2000). The first years of this century (2001 to 2005) constituted a major turning point, however, and with the fallout from the world financial and economic crises in 2008/9, the unraveling of the LIO accelerated. By 2016, this disintegration had assumed major, possibly systemic dimensions, transforming the LIO into something else, a new, weaker international order with as yet undefined characteristics. Those changes were driven by the remarkable acceleration of technological change, which created new opportunities for social advancement, but also brought new problems, risks, and threats. In response, political processes were challenged across the board by societal demands for more, and better, governance of a globalizing, turbulent world; often, their response fell behind expectations and needs, pointing towards an opening gap between what is demanded of political order and what it can supply.

1. STATES, PARTIAL ORDERS, AND THE INTERNATIONAL ORDER: A SUMMARY

As explained in the Introduction to this volume, we approached the evaluation of the state of the international order through an assessment of its regional and functional components. (Figure C.1 gives a schematic presentation of how we conceive the international order.) How effective, how legitimate have they been? How much recourse to violence occurred? What were the rules? Were they enforced? Who were the dominant actors, and what were the principal patterns of interaction? How did the partial order, and the policies of the ordering powers, evolve over time?

1.1. Effectiveness and Legitimacy

We consider political order as *effective* if it achieves its—stated or implicit—objectives at least to some significant extent. This implies that the principles, norms, rules, and institutions established to secure these objectives are broadly respected, and that the order is able to adapt over time to changing circumstances. An order is *legitimate* if those concerned generally support its aims, norms, and institutions. Such support is expressed not only by compliance but also through efforts by those who live in it to sustain the order and achieve its objectives.[2]

[2] Both effectiveness and legitimacy will vary, of course, between issue areas and over time. We grade them on a scale from 0 (zero effectiveness/legitimacy) to 3 (high effectiveness/legitimacy) and also assess the evolution of those grades over time (rising/declining effectiveness/legitimacy).

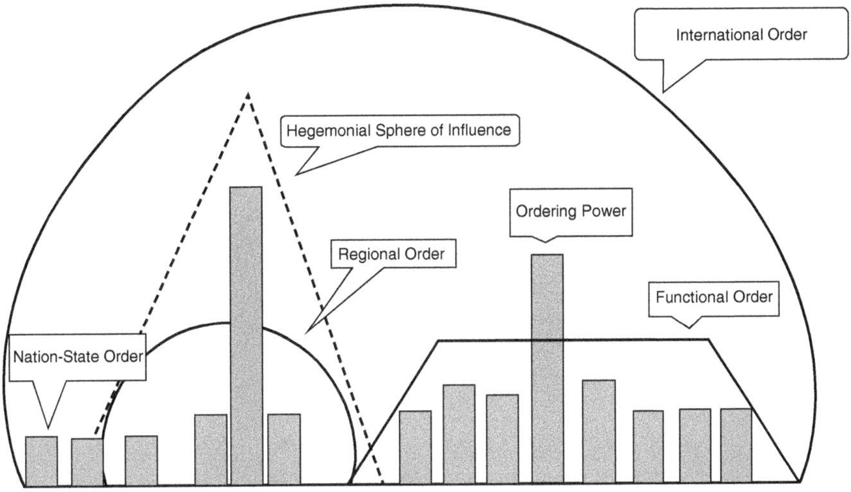

Figure C.1 The international order
Source: own design

Legitimacy and effectiveness are the two (interrelated) pillars of political order that support its *authority* (i.e., the capacity to govern). Our survey of partial orders shows wide differences, from partial orders with very low levels of authority to some that function impressively well. Among the three regional orders we considered, only one (the East Asian regional order) has been reasonably stable until now; its resilience in the face of the major new challenge of power transition is increasingly tested, however.[3] The Middle Eastern order, which had remained remarkably unchanged in its essential features for close to a century despite frequent wars, was overthrown by the Arab uprisings in 2011 and their aftermath, while the post-Cold War pan-European order has been thrown into disarray by Russia's intervention in Eastern Ukraine and the annexation of the Crimea. Among the six[4] different functional partial orders surveyed here, only one (the order for *international public health emergencies*) today (early 2018) clearly appears effective, legitimate, and authoritative. One functional order (*climate change I*) has been transformed into a qualitatively different but as yet untested order (*climate change II*); two others (the arguably two most important and consequential orders governing *international trade* and *nuclear*

[3] See, for example, Michael D. Swaine, with Wenyang Deng and Aube Rey Lescure, *Creating a Stable Asia: An Agenda for a U.S.–China Balance of Power*, Washington, DC: Carnegie Endowment for International Peace, 2017.

[4] We see the Paris Agreement as a fundamentally new attempt to address the problem of climate change and therefore have two different functional orders on this one issue.

weapons), have been limping along for some time, while the last functional realm we considered (*cyberspace*) so far remains largely ungoverned. Moreover, with the exception of the *international public health emergency regime*, the trends regarding both effectiveness and legitimacy in all partial orders are either uncertain or (in most cases) negative; our authors observed erosion, if not serious deterioration, almost everywhere. This is true even in the case of international trade, one of the most impressive and important partial orders of all: the legitimacy of the WTO order is increasingly contested within member states societies and, since Donald Trump was elected president of the United States, even by the government of its chief architect. Before that, the shift towards Free Trade Agreements (FTAs) with geo-political connotations by all major trading powers threatened the effectiveness and authority of the WTO order.

Effectiveness and legitimacy appear closely linked in most of the partial orders surveyed. There are also examples of disjunction, however. In the case of *international trade* (see Chapter 1 by Hoekman), in what we call the *climate change order I* (1992–2015, see Chapter 2 by Gupta), in the *Arab Middle East* (see Chapter 7 by Perthes and Maull) and, following the analysis of Morrison (Chapter 8), in *East Asia*, trends concerning legitimacy and effectiveness do not run in lockstep. Thus, the WTO order governing world trade presently seems more effective than legitimate, suggesting the urgent need to adapt this order to ensure its survivability. The gap in the perceptions of the legitimacy of the *climate change policy order I* ("Kyoto Protocol order") between the United States and most other countries contributed to the Copenhagen COP 15 disaster in 2009 and the eventual transformation of the old order into the *climate change policy order II* ("Paris Agreement order"). The *Middle Eastern regional order* enjoys legitimacy only insofar as its peoples broadly support their respective nation-states; this does not necessarily extend to their respective regimes. Nor has popular identification with the nation-states always prevented their disintegration, or facilitated their reconstitution where they have fallen apart. In the case of the *East Asian regional order*, the lack of legitimacy (which contrasts strikingly with its effectiveness so far) is affected by fundamental differences between the United States and China over what the regional order should look like in the future (Table C.1).

1.2. Violence and Unilateral Use of Force

As explained in the Introduction to this volume, we take the incidence of violent conflict to reflect failures in political order: the coercive threat and use of military force usually engender risks of escalation that not only can cause appalling human suffering but also risk leaving all parties worse off. From this

Table C.1. Effectiveness and legitimacy of partial orders compared

	IPHE (health)	Trade	Nuclear weapons	Cyber	Climate change I	Climate change II	Pan-Europ. order	East Asian order[1]	Middle Eastern order
Effectiveness									
Status:	3	3	2	0	2	uncertain	1	2/2	1
Trend:	steady	down	down	uncertain	down	uncertain	uncertain	down/uncertain	down
Legitimacy									
Status:	3	2	2	1	3 (but lower in US)	3	1	2/1	1 (nationalism) 0 (pan-Arabism)
Trend:	up	down	down	uncertain	uncertain	uncertain	uncertain	Down/down	Dissolution, transformation
Contentiousness									
Status:	1	3	3	3	3	2	3	2/2	3
Trend:	steady	up	up	uncertain	uncertain	uncertain	uncertain	down/down	Dissolution, transformation

Scale: 0 – 3 (0 = nil; 1 = low, 2 = significant, 3 = high); [1] = Chun and Morrison assessments diverge

perspective, major failures appear in two of the three regional orders we surveyed: in Europe and the Arab Middle East, wars have been fought, mostly during the first half of the 1990s and again over the last decade.[5] The epicenters of violence seem to have shifted towards warfare within states, often with the involvement of outside powers or transnational violence (e.g., Ukraine, Syria, Libya, Yemen; in the Middle East, international terrorist organizations such as al-Qaida or the so-called Islamic State (IS) have been a significant factor in such transnational violence). In the third regional order, East Asia, the threat and use of force plays a major role in underpinning, but also in challenging the regional order: the region in recent years has experienced a significant increase of military expenditure and an extensive arms build-up; some experts see aspects of arms racing.[6] In our survey of functional partial orders, however, the threat and use of force played a role in only one case, that of the nuclear weapons order. The most important, but not the only incidence of military intervention in that context was the US-led military intervention in Iraq.[7]

Trends regarding military preparations and use of force are thus worrying in all three regional orders, underlining the return of power politics to international relations. All established nuclear powers, as well as India, Pakistan, and, most disturbingly, North Korea are pushing ahead with plans to modernize their arsenals of nuclear weapons and their delivery systems, while nuclear arms control and disarmament are withering. The recently negotiated Nuclear Weapon Ban Treaty seems unlikely to change the behavior of nuclear armed states and alliances. The only major positive development in recent years was the Joint Comprehensive Plan of Action between Iran and the international community—an achievement that was undermined, however, by the result of the US presidential election in November 2016. Conventional military modernization and expansion is also taking place in all three regions, pushing up not only military expenditure in current dollar terms, but also military expenditure *per capita* and as a percentage of GDP.

[5] Erik Melander, *Organized Violence in the World 2015: An Assesment* [*sic*] *by the Uppsala Conflict Data Program*, available at http://www.pcr.uu.se/digitalAssets/61/c_61335-l_1-k_brochure2.pdf [accessed January 10, 2017].

[6] Sheryn Lee, *Crowded Waters: Naval Competition in the Asia-Pacific*, Australian Strategic Policy Institute: ASPI Special Report, July 2015. The increase in defense spending has been quite large in absolute figures, but in relation to the size of local economies they have declined rather than gone up. See International Institute for Strategic Studies (ed.), *The Military Balance 2016*, London: International Institute for Strategic Studies, 2016, pp. 212–306 (214).

[7] Apart from Iraq 2003, only Israel has used military force to prevent nuclear proliferation (bombing reactors in Iraq and later in Syria). Arguably, the alleged existence of weapons of mass destruction was more a pretext for the US invasion of Iraq than its cause; this view would significantly reduce, but not altogether eliminate, the incidence of violence in the nuclear weapons order.

1.3. Principles, Norms, Rules, and Institutions

The Atlantic Charter, the founding document of the liberal international order, defined eight principles for the LIO: (1) no territorial or other aggrandizement for the victorious powers, (2) inviolability of territorial borders (territorial changes were permissible only with the consent of the people concerned), (3) free elections, self-determination, and self-rule, (4) free trade and free access to raw materials, (5) improved labor standards, economic advances and social security for all, (6) international peace and freedom from fear and want for all, (7) freedom of navigation, and (8) international abandonment of the use of force. A recent effort to identify the basic principles, norms, and rules of the liberal international order today[8] arrives at a slightly larger catalog of ten such "rules"; beyond those to be found already in the Atlantic Charter, the list includes the obligation to combat terrorism and to safeguard global commons, such as the world's climate. Interestingly, it also shifts the emphasis on the principles relating to domestic political order towards democracy and human rights, but tacitly drops the principles of full employment/social stability and distributional justice. This shift reflects the impact of neoliberal thinking on Western liberalism during the 1980s and 1990s: the principle of social fairness now was relegated to a back seat, if not discarded altogether.[9] What was lost in the LIO 2.0 was the emphasis that its original version had placed on the need to ensure domestic support for the LIO in its key Western member states.

Our synopsis shows the major adjustments undertaken in the LIO's principles and norms since 1990 to ensure its sustainability (e.g., through the precautionary principle), promote international fairness (e.g., through the principle of "common but differentiated responsibilities"), and strengthen the international rule of law (e.g., through adjudication of trade disputes). The *freedom to exploit technological advances and commercial opportunities* to ensure growth and prosperity continues to be a central but also an increasingly contested norm, particularly in the functional orders addressing nuclear proliferation and cyberspace. The same is true about the Westphalian principle of *sovereignty*, which came under attack in the context of gross human rights violations by governments. The principles of *trust* and the norm of

[8] Stewart Patrick, World Order: What, Exactly, are the Rules? *The Washington Quarterly* 39:1 (2016), pp. 7–27.

[9] The relevant passage in the Atlantic Charter suggests that the governments of the United States and the United Kingdom "... desire to bring about the fullest collaboration between all nations in the economic field, with the object of securing *for all* [emphasis added, HWM] improved labor standards, economic advancement, and social security." The Atlantic Charter, *Declarations of Principles issued by the President of the United States and the Prime Minister of the United Kingdom*, August 14, 1941, available at http://www.nato.int/cps/en/natohq/official_texts_16912.htm [accessed January12, 2017].

confidence-building as ways to overcome mutual suspicion and cultivate opportunities for international cooperation also figure importantly in the aspirations of the pan-European and East Asian regional orders, as well as in the nuclear non-proliferation and cyberspace functional orders. Distrust nevertheless remains one of the most important obstacles to a sustainable international order.

International organizations play a central role only in three partial orders, namely in the order dealing with *international public health emergencies* (the World Health Organization (WHO)), the *world trading order* (with the WTO, in particular its Dispute Settlement Body), and the *nuclear order* (through involvement of the International Atomic Energy Agency (IAEA) and the UN Security Council). In the *Middle East*, regional, but also global institutions such as the UN have largely been irrelevant. *Europe*, on the other hand, has long enjoyed a dense network of regional organizations (e.g., NATO, the European Union, the Council of Europe, and the CSCE/OSCE), and *East Asia* has been catching up rapidly since 1990: it now counts a large number of regional organizations (e.g., Association of Southeast Asian Nations (ASEAN); the ASEAN Regional Forum; the East Asia Summit).[10] The impact of those regional security organizations on security and stability has at best been mixed, however.

1.4. Rules Enforcement through Collective Sanctions

Political order largely functions on the basis of voluntary compliance, but it will sometimes also have to rely on the threat and the use of collective force and/or economic and diplomatic sanctions to enforce its norms and rules. Only a few partial orders have seen the collective use of legitimate force, namely the nuclear weapons order (Iraq 1991–8, see Chapter 4 by Walker), the Middle Eastern regional order (again, Iraq 1991, see Chapter 7 by Perthes and Maull), the pan-European regional order (Balkans 1995–9,[11] see Chapter 6 by Richter), and, arguably within the East Asian region, the case of East Timor (1999–2000). Economic and diplomatic sanctions as coercive means to secure compliance were also much more relevant in regional than in functional partial orders: they have played important roles in all three of them (e.g., in the Balkans against Serbia and in the Ukraine conflict against Russia; in the Middle Eastern order, against Israel and Iraq; in East Asia against Myanmar and the Democratic

[10] See Nick Bisley, *Building Asia's Security*, London: Routledge for IISS, 2009.

[11] NATO's Kosovo intervention in 1999 was a borderline case—it did not have a UNSC mandate as Russia and China cast vetoes, but was widely considered legitimate as a means to halt another episode of ethnic cleansing by Serbia in Kosovo.

People's Republic of Korea (DPRK)). In the international trade order, the WTO has successfully developed quasi-judicial means of enforcement through rulings of its Dispute Settlement Body (see Chapter 1 by Hoekman), but the *international public health emergencies* order, perhaps the most effective and legitimate of all partial orders we surveyed, has no coercive means to ensure compliance (see Chapter 3 by Hunger). This argues against any clear relationship between enforcement capacity and effectiveness (Table C.2).

1.5. Dominant Interaction Patterns and Actors

Dominant interaction patterns within the nine partial orders surveyed in this volume differ hugely. At one end of the spectrum, we have the functional order to manage *international public health emergencies*, in which international cooperation dominates. Here, as Hunger explains in Chapter 3, the WHO stands at the center, interacting with member governments but also with civil society actors; cooperative interactions between states and independent activities by civil society actors are also significant but clearly secondary. At the other end, we find the (now defunct) *Middle Eastern order* surveyed by Perthes and Maull (Chapter 7). In this regional order, political and religious strife is pervasive, and violent conflict and military activities dominate. Those are conducted primarily by states but recently increasingly also by non-state actors (al-Qaida, Hezbollah, the so-called Islamic State). Even in economic interactions, states weigh heavily; the search for commercial opportunities by private citizens and corporations and interactions between civil society actors are closely regulated and supervised by governments. The dominant actors in this region are Egypt, Saudi Arabia, Iraq (to 2003), Syria (to 2010), Iran, Turkey, and Israel, as well as the outside powers America and, recently again, Russia.

In several other partial orders, we find somewhat contradictory patterns of interaction, in which cooperation *and* competition, the pursuit of commercial opportunity by non-state actors *and* of national (regime) security by governments enjoy roughly equal weight. This particularly characterizes the *East Asian order* analyzed in Chapters 8 and 9 by Morrison and Chun, respectively, the *pan-European regional order* surveyed in Chapter 6 by Richter (with a marked shift towards adversarial competition since about 2010 in both regional orders), and the domains of *world trade* and *cyberspace* (surveyed in Chapter 1 by Hoekman and Chapter 5 by Dunn Cavelty, respectively). Although the WTO plays an important independent role in adjudicating trade disputes, it has no autonomous power to act. Thus, the most important players in the world trade order continue to be governments, notably the USA, China, and the EU, but also coalitions of like-minded countries. Each of those has the ability to block any further progress in developing and adapting the

Table C.2. Incidence of violence/trends in violence and collective sanctions in partial orders

	IPHE (health)	Trade	Nuclear weapons	Cyber	Climate change I	Climate change II	Pan-European order	East Asian order	Arab-ME order
Violence	0	0	2	0	0	0	2	1	3
Trend V	–	–	uncertain	–	–	–	uncertain	uncertain	rising
Trend M	–	–	rising (modernization and expansion of nuclear arsenals)	rising	–	–	rising	rising	rising
Collective sanctions	–	Economic (DSB rulings)	Economic and military	–	–	–	Economic and military	Economic	Economic

Scale: 0–3 (0 = zero; 1 = low: important role of threat of military force; casualties of actual use of force < 100; 2 = significant: important role of threat of military force; casualties of actual use of force > 100; 3 = high)
Trend V = levels of actual violence (casualties); *Trend M* = levels of military preparations
DSB = Dispute Settlement Body

Source: compiled by the author

WTO further, though none of them can impose its management blueprint on others. Through their compliance with the present WTO order, however, they also enable that order to function.

As in world trade, multilateral negotiations dominated the pre-Paris *climate change policy order I* (analyzed in Chapter 2 by Gupta), in this case within the UN Framework Convention on Climate Change (UNFCCC) and the Conferences of the Parties of that agreement (COPs). The most significant result of those negotiations was the Kyoto Protocol, signed on December 11, 1997, that entered into force on February 16, 2005 despite Washington's refusal to ratify. In the Paris Agreement (*climate change policy order II*), national targets and strategies are coordinated and monitored multilaterally, but the responsibility for formulating and implementing them squarely has returned to the exclusive sovereignty of the member states. Both functional orders illustrate well the dual nature of present international relations, in which dense webs of interdependence create both great benefits and great risks, unevenly distributed. Reaping the benefits and avoiding the pitfalls will require broad-based international cooperation. In *cyberspace*, according to Dunn Cavelty in Chapter 5, we have a similarly ambiguous pattern of interactions, with huge potential collective gains but also large risks. There, the political framework to embed and manage those interactions, however, is as yet largely inexistent. As regards the *nuclear order*, Walker shows in Chapter 4 that patterns of interaction are marked by both competition and cooperation, with states vying for commercial and goe-political advantage whilst being driven to cooperate, at times, in the regulation of nuclear activity for the individual and common good. Despite significant achievements, the partial order is today fragile and riddled with contention. The present US administration of President Donald Trump further weakened it through its—mutually contradictory—policies towards Iran (unilateral withdrawal from the JCPOA) and the DPRK (the Singapore summit Kim-Trump).

In none of our case studies have international organizations played important autonomous roles as actors. Non-state civil society and business actors have been significant in a number of partial functional orders, as well as in the Middle Eastern regional order (terrorist organizations, such as the so-called Islamic State) and in East Asia (transnational corporate webs of interdependence). The European Union appears as an autonomous actor only in the context of the WTO order, while the United Nations Secretary General does not appear at all in such a role. The closest example of independent and semi-autonomous action by the head of an international organization concerns the WHO Director-Generals during the late 1990s and the early 2000s, Gro Harlem Brundtland and Jong-wook Lee. The latter boldly took up crisis management in the SARS emergency, considerably broadening the WHO mandate in the process. He did so, however, in anticipation of a mandate by the World Health Assembly that was already moving in this direction (see Hunger, Chapter 3). Overall, states clearly remain by far the most important actors in the international order (Table C.3).

Table C.3. Dominant interaction patterns and actors compared

Partial order	*Dominant interaction patterns*	*Dominant actors*
IPHE (health)	WHO with civil society actors and member governments	WHO; member states, civil society
Trade	Quasi-judicial, cooperative: DSB as courts; WTO as arena for negotiations	Member states, corporations, DSB
Nuclear technology	Power (balance, hegemony, alliances, enforcement of compliance); cooperation (esp. arms control and the non-proliferation regime); civil nuclear trade	Nuclear weapon states (esp. USA and Soviet Union/Russia, increasingly China and India) and their agencies; groups of non-nuclear weapon states; nuclear industry; NGOs
Cyberspace	States: cyber-attack/defense; transnational individual/organized crime activities Transnational commercial activities	States (including "irregulars"); business; "hackers"
Climate change I	Cooperation: multilateral negotiations, binding agreements (Kyoto Protocol)	Annex One states, Annex Two states; USA, China, India
Climate change II	Cooperation: multilateral negotiations, non-binding; autonomously defined national targets; multilateral coordination and supervision	USA, China; France, EU
Pan-European regional order	Cooperation (economic, political); power competition (spheres of influence)	EU member states; USA and Russia
Middle Eastern regional order	(Military) power, violence; alignments and alliances	USA, Russia; Iran, Saudi Arabia; Israel, Turkey; non-state actors (IS)
East Asian regional order	Cooperation (economic); Power (security)	USA, China; Japan, the two Koreas, ASEAN

Source: compiled by the author

1.6. Partial Orders: Evolution Over Time

Our analysis shows widespread and frequently significant advances in international order during the 1990s, particularly during the second half of that decade: several of the partial orders surveyed experienced notable, some even far-reaching progress both in strengthening existing partial orders and in bringing in new members.

Perhaps the most important advances were made in *international trade*. The successful conclusion of the Uruguay Round negotiations in 1994 with the Marrakesh Agreement establishing the WTO in 1995 brought with it, as Hoekman makes clear in Chapter 1, a breakthrough towards the rule of law. Moreover, WTO membership has significantly expanded since that time:

while the Marrakesh Agreement was signed by 123 governments, the WTO membership in late 2016 had reached 164; a further twenty states had the status of observers.[12] The most significant entry was that of China in 2001; another notable addition was Russia, which joined the WTO in 2012.

The partial order to manage *international public health emergencies* also made, as Hunger shows in Chapter 3, important advances during the 1990s. In 1995, the World Health Assembly requested the WHO secretariat to develop new International Health Regulations; the first draft was completed in 1998, but the reforms were adopted only in 2005 and became effective in 2007. The WHO had taken several important initiatives already earlier, however: the Global Outbreak Alert and Response Network (GOARN) was up and working before 2000, and in 2003, the WHO effectively acted in the SARS emergency by applying the as yet unratified norms and rules of the new International Health Regulations.

During the 1990s, significant progress was also made towards deepening the *climate change policy order*: the Kyoto Protocol, which was agreed in 1997 and became effective in 2005, provided for mandatory greenhouse gas emission reduction targets for industrialized countries for the period up to 2012 (see Gupta, Chapter 2). By contrast, the advances made during the 1990s in ordering *cyberspace* were rather limited (see Dunn Cavelty, Chapter 5). This was not very surprising, however, as cyberspace at that time was still only emerging as a new dimension requiring international regulation.

Turning towards the partial orders with uneven performance, the *nuclear order* witnessed significant advances following the end of the Cold War's nuclear confrontation. Several new treaties were negotiated, reducing levels of armament and banning explosive testing among other things; Iraq's nuclear weapons program was uncovered and destroyed by the IAEA on behalf of the UN Security Council; the IAEA's safeguards system was reformed; and agreement was reached on granting the (nuclear) Non-Proliferation Treaty (NPT), initially a twenty-five-year treaty, an indefinite lifetime. Unfortunately, the progress was not sustained. As Walker shows in Chapter 4, those efforts did not prevent India's and Pakistan's and subsequently North Korea's emergence as nuclear powers, arms control suffered from the return of great power rivalry, and international nuclear relations became wracked with dispute over the realization of nuclear disarmament.

The reconfiguration of the *pan-European regional order* proceeded throughout the 1990s into the 2000s, above all through opening the European Communities (which became the European Union in 1993) to thirteen new member states, including a number of Eastern European countries. A second important dimension of "deepening and widening" the pan-European security

[12] With the exception of the Holy See, observers will have to initiate membership accession procedures within five years.

order concerned the introduction of new member states in NATO and the inclusion of all successor states of the former Soviet Union and Yugoslavia in the Conference for Security Cooperation in Europe (renamed *Organization* for Security Cooperation in Europe (OSCE) in 1995). In that context, new institutions, such as the NATO–Russia and the NATO–Ukraine Councils, were added. The adjustment of the pan-European regional order to the new situation was far from peaceful, however, and the wars of disintegration in former Yugoslavia were quelled only in 1994/9 after NATO military interventions. The total number of victims killed in Croatia is presumed to have been around 20,000;[13] in Bosnia, they are estimated, at a minimum, close to 90,000;[14] and in Kosovo, at about 10,000 Kosovar Albanians alone.[15] The war between Armenia and Azerbaijan over Nagorno-Karabakh claimed at least 20,000 lives.[16] Still, as Richter shows (Chapter 6), by 2000 the reconfiguration of the pan-European security order seemed to have been broadly completed.

The *East Asia regional order* continued to experience remarkable stability throughout the 1990s, and there was considerable progress in developing regional institutions for economic as well as political and security interactions (see Morrison and Chun, Chapters 8 and 9, respectively). The *Middle Eastern regional order*, however, failed to make any significant progress: promising initiatives undertaken by the United States with the Soviet Union and Europe after the end of the Gulf War in 1991, and by Israel and the Palestinians with the help of the Norwegian government (Oslo Agreements in 1993 and 1995) ultimately did not result in real progress on the ground (see Perthes and Maull, Chapter 7).

[13] BBC News Europe, Presidents apologize over Croatian war, September 10, 2003, available at http://news.bbc.co.uk/2/hi/europe/3095774.stm [accessed November 16, 2016].

[14] Jan Zwierzchowski and Ewa Tabeau, *The 1992–95 War in Bosnia and Herzegovina: Census-Based Multiple System Estimation of Casualties' Undercount*, Conference Paper for the International Research Workshop on "The Global Costs of Conflict," The Households in Conflict Network (HiCN), and The German Institute for Economic Research (DIW Berlin), February 1–2, 2010, Berlin, available at http://www.icty.org/x/file/About/OTP/War_Demographics/en/bih_casualty_undercount_conf_paper_100201.pdf [accessed November 15, 2016].

[15] Patrick Ball, Wendy Betts, Fritz Scheuren, Jana Dudukovich, and Jana Asher, *Killings and Refugee Flows in Kosovo, March–June 1999*, A Report to the International Criminal Tribunal for the Former Yugoslavia, in Ewa Tabeau (ed.), *Conflict in Numbers: Casualties of the 1990s Wars in the Former Yugoslavia*, Helsinki Committee for Human Rights in Serbia 2009 (= Testimonies no. 33), pp. 877–949, available at http://www.helsinki.org.rs/doc/testimonies33.pdf [accessed November 15, 2016]. See also Patrick Ball, Meghan Lynch, and Amelia Hoover, Revisiting "Killings and Migration in Kosovo," Responses to additional data and analysis, in Tabeau (ed.), *Conflict in Numbers*, pp. 951–75.

[16] Andrew E. Kramer, Fighting Between Armenia and Azerbaijan Flares up in Nagorno-Karabakh, *New York Times*, April 2, 2016, available at http://www.nytimes.com/2016/04/03/world/europe/nagorno-karabakh-fighting-azerbaijan-armenia.html?action=click&contentCollection=Europe&module=RelatedCoverage&region=EndOfArticle&pgtype=article [accessed November 16, 2016].

Since about 2003, the overall picture of international order began to darken, however. This was evident in both the regional and the functional orders surveyed in this volume. In the *pan-European order*, relations between the West and Russia progressively deteriorated over NATO expansion, the EU's neighborhood policy activities in Eastern Europe, and Russia's determination to establish a new sphere of influence in its "near abroad." The war between Russia and Georgia in 2008, and then the events following the popular uprising in Ukraine in the winter of 2013/14, culminated in Russia's military annexation of the Crimea and support for secessionist forces in Eastern Ukraine. Thus, fundamental differences between Russia and the West about how to organize the pan-European order undermined the arrangements of the 1990s, leaving both sides, as well as those countries in-between, to grapple for ways to reconfigure it in line with their own preferences.[17] The *Middle Eastern regional order* was shaken by the US intervention and the following civil war in Iraq, in which first al-Qaida and later the so-called Islamic State emerged as important transnational forces. In *East Asia*, tensions rose on the Korean peninsula around North Korea's nuclear program, missile tests, and military provocations, and China's newly assertive policies in its maritime territorial conflicts with Japan and several ASEAN countries. It also became increasingly obvious in the course of the last ten years that China intended to challenge the dominant position of the United States in this regional order.

A similar tendency towards erosion could be observed in several functional partial orders. In the *world trade order*, the WTO's Doha Development Round failed to reach a conclusion while regional trade arrangements proliferated. The remarkable economic rise of China, together with its gradual shift away from opening and liberalizing its economy towards an industrial strategy that relies heavily on state-owned enterprises and large current account surpluses, created growing tensions with the West. In the *climate change policy order*, the refusal of the United States to join the Kyoto Protocol undermined, as Gupta shows in Chapter 2, the top-down approach based on Western leadership and legally binding commitments. At COP 15 in Copenhagen, this approach collapsed spectacularly, despite (or because of) the presence of 115 world leaders and over 40,000 delegates and observers,[18] giving way to a fundamentally different approach that found its expression in the Paris Agreement. The *nuclear order* was shaken by Russia's return to a Cold War-style use of nuclear weapons in its attempt to recover lost power and influence, the military counter-proliferation intervention of the United States in Iraq 2003, Iran's

[17] See also Samuel Charap and Timothy J. Colton, *Everyone Loses: The Ukraine Crisis and the Ruinous Contest for Post-Soviet Eurasia*, London: Routledge for IISS, 2017.

[18] See UNFCCC, United Nations Framework Convention on Climate Change: Copenhagen Climate Change Conference December 2009, available at https://unfccc.int/meetings/copenhagen_dec_2009/meeting/6295.php [accessed November 15, 2016].

secret nuclear program, and by the DPRK's determined effort to master nuclear weapon and missile technologies. Since 2000, the only major success within that order (apart from the new Strategic Arms Reduction Treaty agreed between Russia and the USA that entered into force in February 2011) has been the Agreement between Tehran and the P5 (the five permanent members of the UN Security Council), the EU, and Germany in 2015.[19] However, the Trump administration has now withdrawn from the JCPOA and thus undermined this achievement. In *cyberspace*, demand for effective and legitimate global governance exploded, far outpacing international efforts to design regulatory measures and defuse conflicts. Only the functional order addressing *international public health emergencies* remained largely unaffected by those symptoms of erosion of order.

Overall, with that one exception and the as yet open question whether the Paris Agreement will be effective in reining in climate change (the election of Donald Trump in November 2016 and his announcement to withdraw the USA from the agreement in June 2017 have lowered the odds considerably), we thus observe a significant deterioration in both the legitimacy and the effectiveness of partial orders since 2000.

2. THE UNITED STATES AND CHINA AS "ORDERING POWERS"

As we have argued in the Introduction to this volume, the United States clearly has been the predominant ordering power over the quarter century of the LIO 2.0, while China recently has assumed an increasingly important role in it. This is borne out by our case studies: other conceivable ordering powers have either failed to realize their potential (as is the case for the European Union, with the partial exceptions of the *climate change* and *international trade* orders), or have too small and lopsided a power base (as with Russia) to sustain an independent role as an ordering power. It therefore seemed justified to confine our analysis to those two powers that will likely be most consequential with their respective policies on international order, and whose relationship—which is based on strong ties of economic and security interdependence, but also on geo-political competition and rivalry—will do much to shape the future of international order.

[19] The full text of the "Joint Comprehensive Plan of Action" is available at http://apps.washingtonpost.com/g/documents/world/full-text-of-the-iran-nuclear-deal/1651/ [accessed November 16, 2016].

2.1. Legitimacy and Effectiveness as Ordering Powers

The United States entered the post-Cold War world with enormous international prestige and remarkable legitimacy as an "ordering power." Its project of a liberal international order (LIO) by 1990 had become universally recognized and broadly accepted. To be sure, non-democratic regimes resisted some of the implications of this new framework, particularly the right to intervene in internal affairs and the de-legitimization of authoritarian political order. There also was resentment of America's "unilateral moment"[20] among its allies and former antagonists—a resentment crystallized in the widely quoted notion of America as a "hyperpuissance" coined by then French foreign minister Hubert Védrine.[21] Yet of the major potential challengers of the LIO, the Soviet Union had disintegrated and its principal successor state, Russia, appeared to be willing to cooperate with the United States (if sometimes grudgingly, as in the Balkan wars of 1990 to 1999) and about to transform itself into a Western capitalist democracy. The People's Republic of China had decided to open up its economy and society already in 1978. In the course of its domestic reforms, Beijing accepted the United States economy in some ways as an important role model and a source of support. In foreign policy terms, the corollary of China's opening policy was to pursue a low profile, "biding its time," as Deng Xiaoping advised. Moreover, the bloody repression of the Chinese democracy movement in June 1989 brought widespread international condemnation and sanctions, underlining the newly acquired strength of the LIO. China's international isolation in the wake of the Tiananmen massacre significantly weakened the country diplomatically and forced it to accommodate the LIO. Thus, resistance to the LIO and US leadership in world politics in the early 1990s was confined to a few maverick non-Western countries such as North Korea, Cuba, and Iran.

This extraordinary level of America's and the LIO 2.0's legitimacy always was unlikely to last, of course, and during the 1990s, it began to erode, at home and abroad. In the USA itself, the erosion began with the "Gingrich revolution" in 1994, carried out by a new Republican majority in the House of Representatives, which undermined the bipartisan consensus on foreign policy. Abroad, it was America's utilitarian attitude towards the multilateral dimensions of the LIO 2.0 and its insistence on imposing its own preferences on others that reduced America's legitimacy.[22] That decline then became precipitous during the first administration of George W. Bush, due to its spurning of

20 Charles Krauthammer, The Unipolar Moment, *Foreign Affairs* 70:1, America and the World 1990/91 (1990–1), pp. 23–33.

21 Hubert Védrine, *L'hyperpuissance américaine*, Paris: Fondation Jean Jaurès, 2000.

22 See, for example, François Heisbourg, American Hegemony? Perceptions of the U.S. Abroad, *Survival* 41:6 (Winter 1999–2000), pp. 5–19.

international institutions and aggressive response ("global war on terror") to the terrorist attacks on New York and Washington on September 11, 2001.[23] As Richter, Perthes and Maull, and Deudney show (in Chapters 6, 7, and 10, respectively), US policies contributed to undermining the foundations of the pan-European and Middle Eastern regional orders; Gupta (Chapter 2) and Walker (Chapter 4) draw similar conclusions about Washington's role in the first climate change order of 1992 and in the nuclear order. Efforts by President G. W. Bush himself in his second term and by his successor Barack Obama to correct the precipitous decline of US legitimacy since 2002 were only partly successful.

Though its standing thus suffered, the USA remained by far the most important ordering power throughout the period under review. Yet America's effectiveness (which, as Deudney (Chapter 10) reminds us, included effective destruction) as an ordering power clearly had declined significantly, though not quite in parallel with its imploding legitimacy, even before the arrival of the Republican presidency of Donald Trump in 2017. The uneven record of US influence in stabilizing partial orders that our case studies reveal (see, in particular, Overhaus in Chapter 11) suggests that the ability of Washington to shape outcomes varied significantly between different partial orders but declined significantly almost across the board. The arrival of the Trump administration and its performance in its first year in office[24] provide little evidence for a revival of American influence and authority as the world's ordering power but much reason for concern about its disruptive potential. For Washington, as well as for the future of international order itself, not only gross mistakes, but also a failure to act can be dangerous: as the most important ordering power, the USA needs to get its policies right.[25]

China, on the other hand, was able to improve its international standing persistently from its low point in 1989, reflecting its dramatic successes in modernizing its economy and society, but also its shrewd international

[23] Thus, those rating the United States favorably or very favorably halved from 60 per cent (2002) to 31 per cent (2008) in Germany; they declined from 60 per cent (2002) to 42 per cent (2008) in France; from 72 per cent to 50 per cent in Japan; and from 30 per cent to 12 per cent in Turkey. One of the few exceptions from this trend was Pakistan, where the favorability rating improved from an abysmal 10 per cent in 2002 to 19 per cent—still far from a supportive attitude towards America. Data taken from Pew Research Center, Global Attitudes and Trends, available at http://www.pewglobal.org/database/ [accessed January 4, 2017].

[24] Richard Haass, *A World in Disarray: American Foreign Policy and the Crisis of the Old Order, With a New Afterword*, New York: Penguin Books, 2018, pp. 309–28.

[25] This was recognized by one of China's most astute foreign policy experts, Jia Qingguo, the Dean of the Department of Diplomacy, at Peking University, in his comments to Evan Osnos. See Evan Osnos, Making China Great Again: How Beijing Learned to Use Trump to its Advantage, *The New Yorker*, January 8, 2018, available at https://www.newyorker.com/magazine/2018/01/08/making-china-great-again [accessed January 8, 2018].

diplomacy within the framework of the LIO 2.0.[26] Nevertheless, as our case studies show, China throughout this period played an important role as "ordering power" only in the *East Asian regional order*, in the *Paris Agreement climate change policy order*, and in *international trade* (WTO order). Of those, the Paris Agreement represents the only example so far where China has actively shaped the global order in line with its own preferences (see Krahl in Chapter 13). Beyond that, China's attitude and policies towards the LIO 2.0—and towards international order in general—have been broadly supportive, though with significant reservations: Beijing wavers between acknowledging the importance of the LIO's continued functioning, on the one hand, and its desire to promote alternative arrangements that would satisfy China's long-term international ambitions, on the other. Thus, China basically recognizes the benefits it receives from the LIO 2.0, not least in its rise to the status of a global power, and is therefore generally willing to go along with efforts to uphold it. The one exception is the *East Asian regional order*, where Beijing has pursued objectives that differ importantly from those of the United States and thus directly challenges the status quo. Even that challenge has been ambivalent, however, as Beijing also sees the advantages of America's implicit containment of Japan as an independent regional great power. Overall, as Pang (Chapter 12) and Krahl (Chapter 13) remind us, China remains profoundly ambivalent about the LIO 2.0: Beijing sees it as an order that greatly has supported its rise but does not carry its own imprint. It therefore wants to revise the international order to reflect its own preferences. In terms of its attitudes towards the international order, this makes China a revisionist, though not a revolutionary power.[27]

2.2. Unilateral Use of Force and Violence

China's ambiguity towards the LIO appears most clearly in its willingness to ignore basic principles of international law if the Chinese Communist Party (CCP) leadership deems this necessary in the pursuit of China's wider ambitions.[28] Although Beijing has not hesitated to use military force

[26] Alastair Iain Johnston, Is China a Status Quo Power? *International Security* 27:4 (Spring 2003), pp. 5–56.

[27] David Shambaugh, China or America: Which is the Revisionist Power? *Survival* 43:3 (2001), pp. 25–30; Jonathan Holslag, The Smart Revisionist, *Survival* 56:5 (October/November 2014), pp. 95–116; Jennifer Lind, The Other Revisionist Power, *Foreign Affairs* 96:2 (March/April 2017), pp. 74–82.

[28] Notably, the United Nations Convention on the Law of the Sea (UNCLOS), as determined by the Permanent Court of Arbitration on June 24, 2016. See the PCA's Press release at https://pca-cpa.org/wp-content/uploads/sites/175/2016/07/PH-CN-20160712-Press-Release-No-11-English.pdf [accessed November 12, 2016].

Table C.4. Military expenditure of the United States and China, 1990 to 2015

	1990	1995	2000	2004	2010	2016
China: Current $US bill	6.1	31.7	42.0	62.5	76.4	145.0
In % of global total	n.a.	3.9	5.2	5.7	5.0	9.6
As % of GDP	1.7	5.7	5.3	3.7	1.30	1.27
United States: current $US bill	289.8	277.8	294.7	455.9	693.6	604.5
In % of global total	n.a.	34.1	36.3	41.6	45.8	40.2
As % of GDP	5.4	3.8	3.0	3.6	4.77	3.26

Source: author calculations, based on data from International Institute for Strategic Studies, *The Military Balance*, various years

unilaterally in the pursuit of its maritime territorial claims in the South China Sea, it has done so cautiously and with circumspection.[29]

Over the last quarter century, China has invested massively in its military power (Table C.4), but it has used force sparingly and primarily to send signals. The United States continues to spend more on its military than the ten next largest military powers (six of which are US allies) combined and, while Washington generally has tried to act with the international legitimacy provided by a mandate of the UN Security Council, it has not been shy in using military force unilaterally to pursue its objectives when an international mandate turned out to be hard to get, as in Iraq in 1997, against Serbia in 1999, and again in Iraq in 2003. Unlike China, the USA in those instances acted with allies (with the UK, in enforcing the no-fly zone in Northern Iraq from 1997 onward, with its NATO allies against Serbia in 1999, and through a "coalition of the willing" with the UK and a few other allies in Iraq in 2003). Also unlike China's use of force, that of the USA resulted in extensive casualties for the fighting forces, and even more deaths and injuries among the civilian populations affected. The justifications for those actions in terms of international law were at best dubious. So was the strategy of targeted killing of al-Qaida and Islamic State terrorist leaders in the context of President Obama's "drone war," pursued in several countries of the Middle East and Africa. The military intervention in Libya in 2011, while originally authorized by UN Security Council Resolution 1973, stretched this mandate considerably—and possibly beyond its limits—by pursuing "regime change."[30]

[29] Robert Ayson and Manjeet S. Pardesi, Asia's Diplomacy of Violence: China–US Coercion and Regional Order, *Survival* 59:2 (April/May 2017), pp. 85–124 (esp. 98–106); Ashley Townshend and Rory Metcalf, Shifting Waters: China's New Passive Assertiveness in Asian Maritime Security, Sydney: The Lowy Institute, April 2016, available at https://www.lowyinstitute.org/publications/shifting-waters-china-s-new-passive-assertiveness-asian-maritime-security [April 25, 2017].

[30] Alan J. Kupelman, A Model Humanitarian Intervention? Reassessing NATO's Libya Campaign, *International Security* 38:1 (Summer 2013), pp. 105–36; Peter Rudolf, Schutzverantwortung und militärische Intervention: Eine ethische Bewertung der 'Responsibility to Protect'

In sum, both the United States and China have demonstrated their willingness to use military force unilaterally if their leaders consider this necessary in the pursuit of important national interests and objectives. The USA has tended to do so massively, together with allies and with a mandate from the UN Security Council wherever possible. China has been much more restrained and cautious, but has tended to act on its own in the use of coercive power.

2.3. Principles, Norms, Rules, and Institutions

As Pang (Chapter 12) and Krahl (Chapter 13) show for China and Deudney (Chapter 10) for the United States, "national security," national prosperity (or "rejuvenation," in the case of China), and international status are key principles underlying the policies and strategies of both the United States and China as "ordering powers." In both countries, "national security" is perceived as being linked to the survival of the respective domestic political orders, albeit in different ways. In the case of the United States, Deudney argues that this link is both tragic and ironic: to sustain the LIO, the government turned America into a national security state that relied on accumulating superior military power, if necessary for total war. As Deudney sees it, this severely damaged America's liberal internationalism and American democracy itself.

In China, national security is perceived as linked to the survival of the Chinese Communist Party's regime at home. The regional and international order that China seeks must at a minimum be compatible with or, better still, promote the CCP's enduring hold on power. Wealth and status are as much means to this as ends in themselves. So is China's version of international order, presently represented by the grand strategy of the "One Belt, One Road" project (more recently known as the Belt and Road Initiative (BRI)) and encapsulated, as Pang argues, in the notion of a "community of human destinies." Yet while the USA was remarkably successful in shaping the LIO, but failed to do so in ways that sustained and supported its own domestic political arrangements, Beijing may risk undermining its own interests in global order by its obsessive search for regime security through coercive power.

Both the United States and China also pursue what Deudney calls "techno-material globalism," the belief in unlimited technological progress and globalization. Yet while this shared principle offers ample opportunities for cooperation between the two powers, it also induces conflict. Each seeks to exploit the forces of globalization for its own purposes in different ways, their societies and economies come from very different starting points and they will often perceive themselves in competition for scarce resources and status.

im Lichte der Libyen-Intervention, Berlin: SWP, 2013, available at https://www.swp-berlin.org/fileadmin/contents/products/studien/2013_S03_rdf.pdf [accessed January 12, 2017].

Moreover, since both America and China so far have not been successful in combining the pursuit of technomaterial globalism with adequate social integration, they provide convenient scapegoats for each other, allowing those in power to channel the fears and frustrations of their own societies' globalization losers against the other country.

2.4. Collective Sanctions and Rules Enforcement

The LIO 2.0 came into its own with the collective reversal of Iraq's occupation and annexation of Kuwait in August 1990. The United Nations Security Council one day after the beginning of the invasion of Kuwait adopted Resolution 660 that—by referring to Articles 39 and 40 of Chapter VII of the Charter of the United Nations—authorized all measures, including the use of force, against this aggression. This legitimized the military operations Desert Shield and Desert Storm that led to the defeat of the Iraqi aggression and the liberation of Kuwait: a textbook example of effective collective security. The United States initiated and led the international coalition, and it contributed most of the military resources. Its diplomacy, including the early exit of its ground forces after the victory, helped to ensure the broad international legitimacy this war enjoyed.[31] Russia and China supported the policy in the UN Security Council.[32]

Russia and China also allowed the UN Security Council to function throughout the 1990s by either supporting or at least abstaining (and thus condoning) economic sanctions or even the use of force to "secure peace and international security" and enforce international law in a number of instances in Europe (e.g., to halt Serbia's policies of dismemberment and ethnic cleansing in Bosnia and Kosovo); in the Middle East (e.g., to stall the proliferation of weapons of mass destruction in Iraq and Iran, and to combat al-Qaida's and IS' terrorism); and in East Asia (e.g., to prevent and, if possible, to roll back North Korea's nuclear weapons program). In all those instances, the Security Council—as the highest authority under the present international order—was able to decide on measures to enforce compliance (output effectiveness); often, the implementation of those Resolutions would significantly affect developments (outcome effectiveness); sometimes, they would contribute to achieving desired results (impact effectiveness, as in the liberation of Kuwait 1991 or in

[31] Lawrence Freedman and Ephraim Karsh, *The Gulf Conflict, 1990–1991: Diplomacy and War in the New World Order*, Princeton, NJ: Princeton University Press, 1993.

[32] China—still weakened by international condemnation of its repression of the Tiananmen Square democracy movement in June 1989—supported the initial UNSC resolution and then abstained in the vote for UNSCR 678 that ordered member states to "use all necessary means... to restore and secure peace and international security in the area" (the key phrase authorizing the military operations to eject Iraqi forces from Kuwait).

the Joint Comprehensive Plan of Action (JCPOA) with Iran 2015). To this positive assessment should be added the WTO order, established in 1995, that has its own, quite effective system of policing and enforcing compliance through its Dispute Settlement Mechanism.

During the 1990s, the international order therefore functioned reasonably well, despite some setbacks and failures (such as the genocide in Rwanda that the UN and the great powers were unwilling and unprepared to prevent). In the UN Security Council, the United States from 1990 to 1999 cast four vetoes (mostly against draft resolutions concerning criticism of Israeli policies in the occupied territories), Russia and China two each (the Chinese vetoes were cast to punish Guatemala and Macedonia for their diplomatic relations with Taiwan).[33]

Since the turn of the century, however, the use of the veto has become more frequent, indicating the gradual weakening of great power cooperation to uphold the international order.[34] In Europe, the West failed to secure Russian and Chinese agreement to authorize NATO intervention in Kosovo in 1999 through a UN Security Council resolution; the accidental bombing of the Chinese Embassy in Belgrade during that conflict[35] contributed to the strengthening of Chinese resistance to such interventions. During the 2000s to 2016, the war between Russia and Georgia in 2008 and the Russian annexation of the Crimea and its intervention in Eastern Ukraine pushed Europe back into a new East–West conflict between Russia and the West.[36]

In the Middle East, the United States insisted on its disastrous military intervention in Iraq without a UN Security Council mandate, as even its close allies France and Germany objected. During the Arab popular uprisings in 2011, the United States persuaded Russia and China to support a UN Security Council resolution (UNSCR 1973) to authorize military intervention in Libya; the West, however, subsequently stretched this mandate to justify their military support for regime change, again with disastrous consequences for the

[33] See Global Policy Forum, Subjects of UN Security Council Vetoes, available at https://www.globalpolicy.org/security-council/40069-subjects-of-un-security-council-vetoes.html [accessed January 3, 2017].

[34] From 2001 to the end of 2016, the United States cast vetoes eleven times (ten times concerning draft resolutions critical of Israeli policies and/or supportive of Palestinian positions). China used its veto seven times, always together with Russia, on issues concerning the Middle East (mostly Syria) and in support of non-intervention against gross human rights violations by the regimes in Zimbabwe and Myanmar. See Dag Hammarskjöld Library: Security Council—Veto List (in reverse chronological order), available at http://research.un.org/en/docs/sc/quick [accessed January 3, 2017].

[35] Yu-ru Lian, Der Kosovokrieg und seine Auswirkungen auf die chinesische Außenpolitik, *Asien* 77 (2000), pp. 48–57; Martin Wagener, Die Bombardierung der chinesischen Botschaft in Belgrad: Ursachen, Reaktionen und Konsequenzen, *Asien* 77 (2000), pp. 23–47; Peter Hays Gries, Chinese Nationalist Reactions to the Belgrade Embassy Bombing, *The China Journal* 46 (July 2001), pp. 25–43.

[36] See Charap and Colton, *Everyone Loses*.

country and its political viability. The most recent failure of regional or international order in the Middle East is marked by the terrible scale of death and destruction in the Syrian civil war, made worse by interventions by various external actors.

The nuclear order was weakened badly by the military counter-proliferation policies of the United States in Iraq and the refusal of the nuclear powers to fulfill their part under the Non-Proliferation Treaty deal; only the nuclear agreement with Iran and the efforts (so far futile) to rein in and, if possible, roll back the North Korean nuclear threat showed some remaining capacity for great power cooperation. The prospects for a functioning partial order for cyberspace were significantly weakened by military competition between the United States and China in this domain, and even the WTO order was affected by growing geopolitical competition between the two great powers. Only the partial order for international public health emergencies and the Paris Agreement on climate change demonstrate some continuing American and Chinese willingness and capacity to work together, though the latter remains untested.

2.5. Dominant Patterns of Interaction with the International Order

The United States leadership in the international order over the last quarter century has been, as our case studies show, important but ambivalent. Its activist approach has often worked through existing international organizations, and at times has made major contributions to strengthening those institutions, as in the cases of the WTO and the NPT. In other instances, however, the United States has caused damage to international order, as in the partial regional orders of the Middle East and Europe, the Kyoto Protocol climate change order, and the non-proliferation regime. To translate its power resources into influence, the United States has relied on diplomacy, on its security alliances, and on multilateral institutions but also, probably too much and too often, on unilateral military power projection.

Overall, America's grand strategy since 1990, such as it was, has been to uphold, preserve, and develop the LIO 2.0 and its own dominant position in it. To this end, it has relied on its alliances, on existing multilateral institutions, and on the strengths and attractions of the US economy. There were some efforts to overhaul and adapt partial orders, but no determined push to strengthen the LIO 2.0 as a whole. Moreover, the USA itself repeatedly destabilized segments of the LIO 2.0, such as the *Middle Eastern regional order* or the *Kyoto Protocol climate change policy order*. All in all, Washington has been unable to compensate for the impact of changes in the international environment and of its own destructive actions that worked to undermine the LIO. In the words of one of America's most experienced former diplomats, R. Stapleton Roy:

> Surveying the international scene in 2017, it is clear that the post-Cold War period has not been good for the United States. This is in large measure because of failures of U.S. leadership and the growing dysfunctionality in the U.S. political system. Such dysfunction poses a major problem in addressing the question of global order. If the leading world power cannot conceptualize its foreign policy goals in terms that reflect global realities rather than an ideological vision, then little can be accomplished.... This is dangerous because Westphalian systems do not function well, or peacefully, without some organizational structure.[37]

Our analyses of China's policies towards the international order show a much less important contribution than that of the United States so far, but also its rising importance for world order. Through its actions, as well as through its refusal to act, China will expand its influence on the future international order. It likely will act in its role as an ordering power with considerable ambivalence, however, for reasons that sometimes are not that different from the ambiguity of the United States towards international order. Thus, both China and the USA see themselves as "exceptional powers," and therefore are reluctant to be constrained by international arrangements. In their respective foreign and security postures, both often appear motivated by an exaggerated sense of threat and a tendency to overinvest in national military (and police) security policies. Moreover, while Beijing usually plays a reasonably constructive role in existing international organizations, it clearly is a "reluctant power" in the context of the LIO 2.0.[38] It therefore has begun to work towards a new international order, and in that context has launched a number of new institutions to complement Western institutions, to hedge against their possible failure and as a means to leverage its influence within those established organizations.[39]

In short, Beijing still seems uncertain whether, how much, and in which ways it would support, or rather modify, the present international order. China's primary foreign policy purpose has been the expansion of its own power and the reclamation of its traditional status as the dominant power, starting with its own region. To this end, it is using economic incentives and political inducements, it relies on existing but increasingly also on its own, newly created multilateral institutions, and it occasionally also uses implicit or explicit coercive threats of its rapidly growing military power. This foreign

[37] J. Stapleton Roy, Sino-Russian Relations in a Global Context: Implications for the United States, in Michael S. Chase et al., *Russia–China Relations: Assessing Common Ground and Strategic Fault Lines*, Seattle, WA: The National Bureau of Asian Research, 2017, pp. 37–49 (47f.) (= NBR Special Report No. 66).

[38] Evan A. Feigenbaum, China and the World: Dealing with a Reluctant Power, *Foreign Affairs* 96:1 (January/February 2017), pp. 33–40.

[39] Moritz Rudolf et al., Chinas Schatten-Außenpolitik: Parallelstrukturen fordern die internationale Ordnung heraus, Berlin: MERICS 2014 (= China Monitor No. 18, available at https://www.merics.org/sites/default/files/2017-09/China_Monitor_18_Schatten-Au%C3%9Fenpolitik_DE.pdf [accessed January 8, 2018].

policy, in turn, ultimately seems designed and implemented to ensure the unchallenged exercise of power by the Chinese Communist Party at home.

2.6. Interference

The major impact the US government seems to have had on the unraveling of international order represents a particularly powerful example of what we call "interference." This concept relates to the (positive or negative) impact that developments in one part of international order have on other parts, between and across the three levels of political order (national, regional/functional, and global). The concept includes the activities that traditionally have been referred to as "interference"—with the Russian efforts to manipulate elections in the United States and Europe in 2016 and 2017 as some recent examples. Yet in this book, we use the concept of interference in a broader sense: it refers, as explained in the Introduction, not only to the direct impact of actions but also to their unintended consequences, as well as to the impact of developments that do not have clearly identifiable actors across the boundaries between different orders across and within the different levels of political order.

Ordering powers by definition interfere in the international order, but as we saw, America and China do so in different ways and to different degrees (Table C.5). In our case studies, we found considerable evidence for America's interference with political order elsewhere, at the national, the regional/functional, and the global level. In the *Arab Middle East*, as Overhaus (Chapter 11) shows, President Clinton was unsuccessful in adapting US policies sufficiently to establish a "winning coalition" and a resilient regional order; his successor President Bush then further undermined the old regional order by "smashing" Iraq (Deudney, Chapter 10). This extreme form of counter-proliferation policy via regime change interfered with the *nuclear order*, as Walker (Chapter 4) points out, in both positive (the Libyan decision to give up its clandestine nuclear program) and negative ways (the loss of legitimacy suffered by Washington). In Europe, Richter (Chapter 6) shows that the Bush administration was at best ambivalent about the post-Cold War *pan-European order* and contributed to its demise. The Bush administration also undermined, as Gupta (Chapter 2) demonstrates, the *climate change policy order I* of the Kyoto Protocol. Even the *international trade order* was weakened by US trade policies that interfered with the WTO. Only in the cases of the—as yet largely inexistent—functional partial orders for *cyberspace* and *international public health emergencies* was US interference of secondary importance.

China, on the other hand, has so far played a major role only in the *East Asian regional* and in the *climate change policy II* orders. The latter case, argues Krahl (Chapter 13), is of particular interest: the Paris Agreement might

Table C.5. The two ordering powers compared

	Legitimacy	Effectiveness	Unilateral use of force	Principles, rules, norms, institutions	Collective sanctions, enforcement of rules	Dominant pattern of behavior in international order	Interference
USA	High during 1990s; contested since 2003	High ambition. Moderate during 1990s, weak since 2003	Large-scale military power; willingness to use force unilaterally without international sanction	National security, national prosperity, status; democracy and HR	Leadership role, broadly successful during 1990s and early 2000s but important failures (Balkan wars to 1994, Rwanda)	Forceful but de facto ambivalent support for LIO; alliances and heavy reliance on military power	Strong, across the board but ambivalent in its impact
China	Growing from low level during the 1990s and early 2000s, declining since 2010 in some countries	Low ambition until 2013. Significant effectiveness in East Asian region.	Rapidly building up military power; willingness to use force unilaterally in border areas and multilaterally in some UN peacekeeping operations	National and regime security, national rejuvenation; status, in East Asia and the world; non-interference	Permissive role to 2000, except where China's interests were directly involved (Taiwan). Willingness to cooperate declines after 2003	Much lower profile; ambivalence; instrumental multilateralism; rejection of alliances; reliance on military	Largely supportive but modest, except in East Asia regional order, where China acts as revisionist power

Source: compiled by the author based on case studies in this volume

still turn out to be a model of how Beijing and Washington may together shape the future international order—despite the serious deterioration of bilateral relations the Trump presidency has brought.

3. HOW IS THE INTERNATIONAL ORDER CHANGING?

Our comparison of the thirteen case studies allows us to draw a picture of how the international order has been changing over the last quarter century. In a nutshell, the LIO 2.0 has become more complex, more driven by power and geo-politics, and more conflictual in several ways.

- First, the playing field of world politics has become *more crowded*. At the most basic level, the number of states has gone up significantly over that period: the United Nations counted 159 member states in 1990; today (in early 2017), there are 193, an increase of about one fifth. The growth in the numbers of other important actors in international affairs, from international and transnational civil society organizations to transnational corporations, has been larger still; most fundamentally, the number of human beings living on the planet increased from 5.3 billion (1990) to 7.6 billion in 2018. This, too, has had important implications for the distribution of power across the globe: the spread of education and knowledge has empowered individuals and civil society actors. As a consequence, more people have been able to take control of their own fate, and some (think of Bill Gates, George Soros, or Osama bin Laden) amassed fortunes that enabled them to become significant actors in world politics. There also have been important additions to what we call partial orders—the regional and functional components of the international order. Thus, new regions, such as Asia-Pacific, Central Asia, or the Caucasus, have (re-)appeared on the geo-political map, and new international regimes, such as those for cyberspace or climate change, have developed in response to new knowledge, challenges, and material realities. The proliferation of significant actors in the international order has been particularly striking in the climate change order: at the COP 21 in Paris 2015, the organizers counted about 10,000 representatives from member or observer state governments, about 14,000 representatives from civil society organizations, and about 3,000 media representatives.[40]
- Second, the actors in the international order have become *more diverse*. In material terms, inequality of wealth and income has been growing

[40] UNFCCC Secretariat, Participation at UN Climate conference in Paris, available at http://newsroom.unfccc.int/paris/participation-at-un-climate-conference-in-paris/ [accessed January 20, 2017].

within and, by some measures, also between nations, despite the remarkable progress made in reducing the share of mankind living in absolute poverty. Domestically, while material inequality did not surface much in the major ideological battles of the last years of the past century despite those socio-economic trends, recently inequality has become politically salient again, fueling the rise of populism in the United States and Europe.[41] International justice, on the other hand, never disappeared from the agenda of world politics. It appears as an important principle in several of our case studies, notably in those on the world trade and the climate change policy orders. Yet the struggle over international justice between the haves and the have-nots has not been the major ideological divide in the LIO 2.0, as the notion of market-based economic development until recently seemed broadly unchallenged in international economic policy-making. Within this consensus, however, there have emerged important differences between variants of a "developmentalist" model practiced in East Asia that is today represented most importantly by China, and the various mixed-economy models practiced in the West. Other dimensions of ideological diversity concern differences between the normative orders of democracy and human rights, on the one hand, and various forms of authoritarian order, on the other; between globalism/cosmopolitanism and nationalism/populism; and between secularism and the varieties of religious fundamentalism, in particularly Islamism.

- Third, while during the Cold War, *the state of world politics* was highly aggregated, it has since become *more disaggregated, diffuse*, and *fluid*. The conflict between the West and the Soviet bloc dominated and structured much of international affairs as the one major conflict formation. There were the opposed nuclear arsenals of the United States and the Soviet Union, which created the precarious stability of Mutually Assured Destruction; there were the two military alliances of NATO and the Warsaw Pact; there were even two international economic orders, the liberal international economic order and that of the (Soviet-led) Council for Mutual Economic Assistance. Exchanges between those two international economies were severely limited by systemic differences and politically imposed constraints. There existed a clear distinction between "high politics" (security) and "low politics" (e.g., economics), and many regional and local conflicts had become frozen by their subordination under the East–West conflict. Last but not least, the Cold War also imposed an element of discipline on many national political orders.

41 One sign of this has been the worldwide success of the study by Thomas Piketty, *Capital in the 21st Century*, Cambridge, MA: Harvard University Press, 2014.

- With the end of the Cold War, that hierarchy and the imposed discipline dissolved. Security issues became regionalized or even localized as some of the frozen conflicts thawed, and the domestic political orders that had been made to support the Cold War were now losing cohesion, sometimes even coming apart. Those fundamental changes shifted the aggregate state of world politics, as it were, from ice to water. This is most apparent in the *pan-European* and the *Middle Eastern regional orders*, but also in the *nuclear order*. The notion of a unipolar world order with an overwhelmingly powerful United States therefore turned out to be something of an optical illusion: governing the world had not become easier, but in fact a lot more complicated after the end of the Cold War.
- The international order since 1990 has also become much *more interconnected*. Interactions of all kinds between governments, business, and societies across borders have grown rapidly and frequently exponentially, driven by the revolution in social communication with the rise of the Internet and mobile telephones.[42] One result of this has been deepened interdependence between and, consequently, more dependence and vulnerability of societies to developments elsewhere.[43] The implications come across particularly strongly in our case study on *cyberspace*, but also in that on the *Middle Eastern regional order*. As Perthes and Maull show in Chapter 7, weaknesses of the state in the Arab world played a critical role in the demise and violent transformation of the Middle Eastern regional order in a double sense: they produced social tensions that exacerbated risks of violence, while they lacked mechanisms to manage those tensions and address shocks from outside constructively. Similarly, weak states in Eastern Europe and in Russia were important preconditions for political instability in the Ukraine and for Russia's intervention in that country (see Richter, Chapter 6). Interferences were

[42] By 2016, almost half of mankind (47 percent) used the Internet, and 95 percent of the world lived within reach of a mobile-cellular network. The Apple iPhone celebrated its tenth anniversary in January 2017; by the end of September 2016, the company had sold more than 1 billion units and 2.6 billion people, i.e., about every third human being living on the planet, owned some form of smartphone. Data are taken from ITU (ed.), ITC Facts and Figures, available at http://www.itu.int/en/ITU-D/Statistics/Pages/default.aspx; see also Don Reisinger, Understanding the iPhone's Impact over the Last Decade, *Fortune Tech*, January 9, 2017, available at http://fortune.com/2017/01/09/apple-iphone-turns-10-stats/ [accessed January 12, 2017].

[43] Thus, in nominal terms world merchandise trade increased from $US3.8 trillion in 1993 to $US16.3 trillion in 2015, a more than fourfold increase; in volume terms, world exports throughout that period grew faster than world Gross Domestic Product (GDP). As a result, world exports of goods and service as a percentage of world GDP grew from just below 20 percent in 1990 to close to 30 percent in 2015: see World Bank, Exports of goods and services (% of GDP), 1960–2015, available at http://data.worldbank.org/indicator/NE.EXP.GNFS.ZS [accessed January 10, 2017]. Interestingly, this trend has been reversed recently: its peak value was reached at 30.8 percent in 2008 and again at 30.6 percent in 2012. Since then, the values have declined. See Bernard Hoekman (ed.), *The Global Trade Slowdown: A New Normal?* London: CEPR Press and European University Institute, 2015.

also evident between partial orders, for example between the regional order in the Arab-Middle East and the nuclear order.

- The international order has also become *more fragmented.* Fragmentation here refers to loss of authority, of the capacity to make binding and broadly respected decisions and to uphold agreed principles, norms, and rules. That capacity seems to have been affected across our three levels of political order as a result of the diffusion of power and the proliferation of normative diversity. This has reduced the effectiveness and the legitimacy of authority, at the national and the global level as well as at the level of partial regional and functional orders. Only in the *international trade order* and the order governing *international public health emergencies* did we find authority holding up reasonably well. The *Paris Agreement climate policy order* effectiveness is still largely untested; in *cyberspace*, prospects of creating a framework of order look dim. The *nuclear order* was seriously damaged and the Kyoto Protocol climate policy order effectively destroyed by United States government activities under President George W. Bush. The *East Asian regional order* still holds but appears to be under growing strain, while the *pan-European* and the *Middle Eastern regional orders* have undergone transformations that have pushed them across the threshold of violence.
- *More power-driven*: Deepening interdependence and political fragmentation have encouraged the return of power politics as an obvious, though not necessarily an effective way to cope with the pressures of change. Power politics, of course, has never been absent since the end of the Cold War, but its characteristics may have changed. The erosion of political order could be seen as a shift away from the politics of checks and balances on power, in which power is embedded in and exercised through rules and institutions, to transactional balance of power politics, in which rules and institutions at best are renegotiated between the most powerful actors or—at worst—simply pushed aside and ignored. The central axis of power politics both unites and opposes the United States and China that frequently aligns with Russia.
- *More conflictual and possibly also again more violent*: Our case studies also reveal the renewed salience of identity in international order. Nationalism has been a potent factor in world politics since the early nineteenth century, of course, and it continues to be one of the major ideological forces of our times. It is the most obvious example of what Michael Gerson calls the "tribalism of ideology,"[44] but not the only one. The fusion of identity with ideology or religion dangerously exacerbates the emotional dimension of social conflict and makes such conflicts particularly difficult to contain and manage. The importance of identity issues also surfaces in our case studies in the salience of status, which

[44] Michael Gerson, The hypocrisy in elevating Assange, *The Washington Post*, January 6, 2017.

seems something of an obsession for both the USA and China. The international order today at all its three levels is therefore riven with criss-crossing lines of conflict that often are difficult to resolve because of their perceived zero-sum characteristics and difficult to manage because they are emotionally highly charged.

- As we have noted already, overall levels of violence in the international order declined significantly since 1990 well into this century, but those favorable trends may recently have been reversed. The progress in pushing back war and violence since 1990 certainly does not suggest, moreover, that the world had become a peaceful place.[45] Even excluding the genocide in Rwanda in 1994 as an isolated event, the toll of violence was generally higher during the 1990s, when it oscillated between 50,000 and 100,000 people killed annually, than during the following decade of the 2000s, when fatalities per year were estimated at between 30,000 and 45,000.[46] Since 2010, however, there seems to have been a significant turn-around for the worse in international violence: according to Peace Research Institute Oslo data, the level of international violence has risen each year, and in 2014 it exceeded, with over 126,000 fatalities, the level of 100,000 for the first time since 1990.[47] While it is too early to interpret this as a secular change, the data on violence certainly appear compatible with a picture that sees the LIO 2.0 as strengthening during the 1990s but eroding since 2002.

4. WHY HAS THE INTERNATIONAL ORDER BEEN CHANGING?

Asking the question why international order has been changing is obviously hazardous: to assume that the path of international politics can be explained

[45] Melander, *Organized Violence in the World 2015.*

[46] Those figures were still lower, however, than the numbers of war-related fatalities during the Cold War, which rarely fell below the threshold of 100,000 battle deaths per year. See Melander, *Organized Violence in the World 2015*, p. 7.

[47] According to the Uppsala Conflict Data Program, between 1989 and 2013, about 1.9 million people died in three types of violent conflicts: state-based conflicts (i.e., conflicts that involved a government and a rebel group within a state, or two or more states); non-state conflicts (conflicts that involved only non-state actors, such as the violence between the so-called Islamic State and Kurdish Peshmerga); and one-sided violence (such as the genocide in Rwanda that accounted for an estimated 500,000 deaths). By comparison, during the Cold War, the estimated total toll of violence was significantly higher still, however: since 1960, the annual number of battle-related deaths collected by the Peace Research Institute Oslo (a much more narrow measure of violence), rarely declined below 100,000 until 1990. See Melander, *Organized Violence in the World 2015*, and SIPRI Yearbook 2016, *Armaments, Disarmament and International Security*, Zusammenfassung auf Deutsch, Hamburg: Berghof Foundation, 2016, p. 5.

through identifying causal links goes against the very nature of history, which always has been turbulent and chaotic. Yet the comparative evaluation of the cases we analyzed does suggest that the pathway of the LIO 2.0 has been shaped by the interaction of two broad dynamics: the advance of scientific knowledge and its transformation into new technologies, which have produced persistent and persistently growing impulses of change, on the one hand, and the dynamics of political responses to those impulses, on the other. More specifically, factors can be discerned that at least may help to explain what has been happening to the LIO 2.0.

Technological innovation: The single most potent force of change in all our case studies has been technological innovation. Even the arguably largest single discontinuity in the international order that we have identified, the change in American foreign policy from 2001 to 2005, had important technological ingredients: the assumption of overwhelming US military power that played a critical role in those policies rested on the belief in a "revolution in military affairs" that seemed to be confirmed by the wars in the Gulf 1991 and in Afghanistan 2001.[48] In world trade, it has been the advances in information, communication, and transportation that have driven the expansion of regional and global production networks; in climate change, itself caused by changes in the energy system resulting from industrialization, technological innovations drive both the supply (e.g., the shale gas revolution) and the demand side of the energy equation and therefore the evolution of the world energy system. With nuclear proliferation and cyberspace, the relevance of technological innovation needs no further elaboration. In the international public health emergencies, the innovations in communication enabled the WHO to establish effective early warning, and those in the pharmaceutical industry have been critical in effectively dealing with new threats.

In more subtle and indirect ways, technological innovation also played a critical role in the evolution of regional order. The very fact that material production processes and markets now tend to be regional or even global reflects technological advances. The concept of "globalization" summarizes processes that affect all dimensions of individual and social life; the dynamics behind those processes are usually technologically induced. Globalization, in turn, has profound implications for socio-economic changes within and between societies that ultimately also affect politics.

An opening gap between the demand for and the supply of governance: Political systems seem to be the social systems most resistant to change, and therefore the least well equipped to adapt to the implications of the technological dynamics of globalization; economies, societies, and even cultures seem to be more malleable. The comparative evaluation of our case studies leaves no

[48] See, e.g., Donald H. Rumsfeld, Transforming the Military, *Foreign Affairs* 81:3 (May/June 2002), pp. 20–32.

doubt that the most important level of political order continues to be the nation-state. State fragility and state failure appear to be closely related to the capacity of governments and polities to adapt to the rapidly changing technological and socio-economic environment engendered by a globalizing world. The barriers to development in the Arab world identified in the Arab Development Report document the failure of the Arab state; this, in turn, helps to understand the failure of the *Middle Eastern order*. Conversely, the strength of the state in *East Asia* reflects its ability to exploit globalization in all its dimensions. The *pan-European order* falls somewhere in-between the two extremes provided by the other two regional orders.

Overall, the range, scope, and speed of change in international relations over the last quarter century induced by technological innovation may well be unprecedented in history outside major wars. The resulting pressure for adjustment has been felt across all three levels of political order and governance, but they may have impacted nation-state political orders most severely. Governments today need to do much more, and are expected to do much more, than in the past. Since they frequently are unable to address the implications of change on their own, however, they will need to cooperate with other states, as well as with non-state actors across boundaries in partial orders beyond the state. Political institutions at all three levels of political order therefore face more variegated, more insistent, and more far-reaching demands in response to globalization's risks and opportunities.

Demand for governance in this sense reflects collective perceptions and expectations. Yet this demand can also be established objectively. Perhaps the most dramatic example for such an "objective" need for more effective global governance is in the area of climate change: if the target of the Paris Agreement to confine global warming to a peak increase of 1.5 to 2°C is to be realized, then national efforts to revise and effectively implement the Intended Nationally Determined Contributions (INDCs) will have to be significantly strengthened.[49]

[49] The most recent IPCC Synthesis Report finds that global anthropogenic GHG (greenhouse gas) emissions would need to be reduced by 40–70 percent by 2050 compared to 2010, and emissions levels would have to be near zero or below in 2100. According to the report, to limit global warming to 2°C would be possible only if CO_2 emissions would be limited to a total of 1,000 gigatonnes of CO_2 equivalent from 2011 to 2050. CO_2 emissions worldwide rose by an average 1.6 percent during the decade from 2005 to 2015, and in the five years from 2012 to 2016 emissions that were related only to the oil, coal, and gas industries—that is, excluding other sources of CO_2 emissions and other GHG emissions—alone added about 166 gigatonnes of CO_2 to the atmosphere. See Intergovernmental Panel on Climate Change (IPCC), *Climate Change 2014: Synthesis Report, Summary for Policy Makers*, p. 20, available at http://ipcc.ch/pdf/assessment-report/ar5/syr/AR5_SYR_FINAL_SPM.pdf [accessed August 28, 2017], and BP Statistical Review of World Energy 2017, available at https://www.bp.com/content/dam/bp/en/corporate/pdf/energy-economics/statistical-review-2017/bp-statistical-review-of-world-energy-2017-full-report.pdf [accessed August 28, 2017].

While demand for governance thus has been growing, its supply through arrangements of political order at all three levels of politics, from national to global, has been adversely affected by some of the same developments that have produced the growing demand in the first place. In particular, as we have seen, political authority has been weakened by the empowerment of citizens and non-state actors through knowledge, and the diminished effectiveness of governance due to increasingly complicated, diverse, and contested policy environments. As demands on political order have expanded, its ability to meet expectations and adapt successfully to changing circumstances has tended to fall behind, despite all efforts to enhance the capacity of political order.

Our metaphor to describe this situation is that of an opening gap between the demand for and the supply of political order. This metaphor may help us in understanding the transformation of the international order over the last quarter century in two ways: one concerns the direct impact on the LIO 2.0 and its arrangements for global governance that were affected pervasively by a growing supply/demand imbalance, the other its indirect impact via growing state weakness and its implications for regional/functional and international order. Our cases suggest that in many instances, weaknesses in partial orders were caused by interferences from domestic political order. The *Middle Eastern* and the *pan-European orders* are the most obvious examples for this.

There are a few examples in our cases, however, that seem to contradict the relevance of our metaphor: the successful adaptation of several of the functional partial orders analyzed, such as the WTO order or the WHO partial order dealing with international public health emergencies, and the forceful (if misguided) policies of the first administration of President George W. Bush, as well as the more recent assertiveness of China in East Asia and world affairs. Yet the successful adaptations of those partial orders were undertaken during the 1990s, that is, at a time when US leadership was significantly more effective than today. The order governing *international public health emergencies* may be the exception that confirms the rule of an eroding international order—an exception rooted above all in the issue and the particular nature of the challenges, but also in the importance of civil society actors and epistemic communities and strong leadership at the helm of the WHO at the time of a window of opportunity.[50]

[50] For indications that even that partial order may not be immune to the problems described by the metaphor of an opening supply/demand gap in global governance, see Donald G. McNeil, How the Response to Zika Failed Millions, *New York Times*, January 16, 2017, available at https://www.nytimes.com/2017/01/16/health/zika-virus-response.html?rref=collection%2Ftimestopic%2FWorld%20Health%20Organization&action=click&contentCollection=timestopics&region=stream&module=stream_unit&version=latest&contentPlacement=24&pgtype=collection [accessed August 28, 2017], and *The Economist*: World Health Organization, Too Big to Ail, December 11, 2014, available at https://www.economist.com/news/international/21636038-ebola-has-laid-bare-failings-worlds-health-authority-too-big-ail [accessed August 28, 2017].

The forceful policies of the first Bush administration that culminated in an ill-conceived counter-proliferation effort through regime change in Iraq were enabled domestically by the shock administered to American society by the terror attacks of September 11, 2011. Those attacks gave the Bush administration an almost completely free hand to mobilize military and financial resources for the "global war on terror." That particular window of opportunity began to close in 2004, despite the re-election of George W. Bush. Moreover, events increasingly demonstrated that the US government had vastly overestimated its power to shape developments in Afghanistan and Iraq in accordance with its own preferences. As a result, US influence in the international order suffered a massive setback from which it has yet to recover. In the context of our metaphor, the first administration of George W. Bush tried to close the opening gap between the demand for and the supply of international order through massive mobilization of military power. For a while, this seemed to work, but over time the logic of the metaphor reasserted itself all the more powerfully.

Finally, the case of China's assertive foreign policy is also more ambivalent than it may seem. Beijing clearly has been very ambiguous in its efforts to challenge and revise the international order in line with its own preferences: it recognized how much China has benefitted from the old LIO 2.0, and it therefore has been reluctant to push too hard for its revision. In fact, in many ways China has chosen to support and uphold, rather than to overturn that old international order. More generally, the Chinese Communist Party under the present leadership of Xi Jinping has been engaged in a massive effort to upgrade its capacity to govern, at home and abroad. Domestically, the regime faces enormous challenges, and while the efforts undertaken are impressive, they also have a price, and it is as yet quite uncertain whether the present leadership will be able to close the supply/demand gap of governance that certainly had been opening in China, too. Abroad, the ambitions of the leadership for regional and even global dominance will require China to massively enhance its global influence and its capacity to underwrite, in cooperation with others, regional and functional partial orders and the emerging future international order, whatever it may be. This will certainly also put huge demands on the abilities, resources, and skills of China's leadership.

5. IMPLICATIONS

All our case studies point to the importance of functioning national political orders as prerequisites for well-governed regional and functional partial orders, as well as for the governance of the international order as a whole. This is hardly surprising: states still are by far the most important actors in international relations. They shape international decisions and policies and ensure their implementation. While international organizations and transnational actors usually have only limited means at their disposal, the resources that functioning, well-governed countries can mobilize in the pursuit of common objectives are potentially enormous. Conversely, decisions and policies in the pursuit of international order will have much less chance to succeed if the contributions of governments are hesitant and half-hearted, if these resources are not available or refused, or if important state resources are mobilized against those decisions and policies.

Functioning, well-governed states, and political orders generally, have the capacity to control their boundaries, withstand external shocks, and adapt to changing external circumstances. For example, the international trade order has so far successfully weathered the geo-political shift and diffusion of power and the trend towards regional trade agreements, at least in part because it resisted attempts to broaden its remit too much. The Kyoto Protocol climate policy order, on the other hand, was unable to defend the boundary between the Annex member countries and the other member states, which confined adjustment efforts to the industrialized countries. The nuclear order also has found it increasingly difficult to defend the privileges of the established nuclear weapon member states vis-à-vis the other member states of the NPT. The old *Middle Eastern order* was unable to prevent external interventions, and it did not survive the implosion of several of its member states; as a result, instability has spilled over into adjacent regions (such as southern Europe and West Africa), which in turn have found it difficult to adapt to those external shocks. The *East Asian regional order*, on the other hand, so far has shown remarkable resilience in the face of change, though the pressure for adjustments is building up. Finally, as far as the two major *ordering powers* are concerned, their ability to draw boundaries between their bilateral conflicts and their cooperation on wider issues of international order will be crucial for the future of international order.

The transformation of LIO 2.0 may well have reached the stage of what Homer-Dixon and his collaborators, in a somewhat related context, call "synchronous failure." Their analysis concerns the socio-ecological system, which they describe as "... the emergence for the first time in human history of a single, tightly coupled socio-ecological system of planetary dimensions." Our analysis dealt with the international order; for very similar reasons, we also see the international order entering what could be called a "synchronous failure" of governance. In this situation, the interferences, that is, the spillover effects of disorder proliferate unpredictably within a system, with crises multiplying in different parts and at different levels (Figure C.2).

This is why the LIO 2.0 by the end of 2016 seemed to have become history. That does not imply, of course, that nothing of it remains. Some of its principles, norms, rules, and institutions may continue to be relevant; others could become

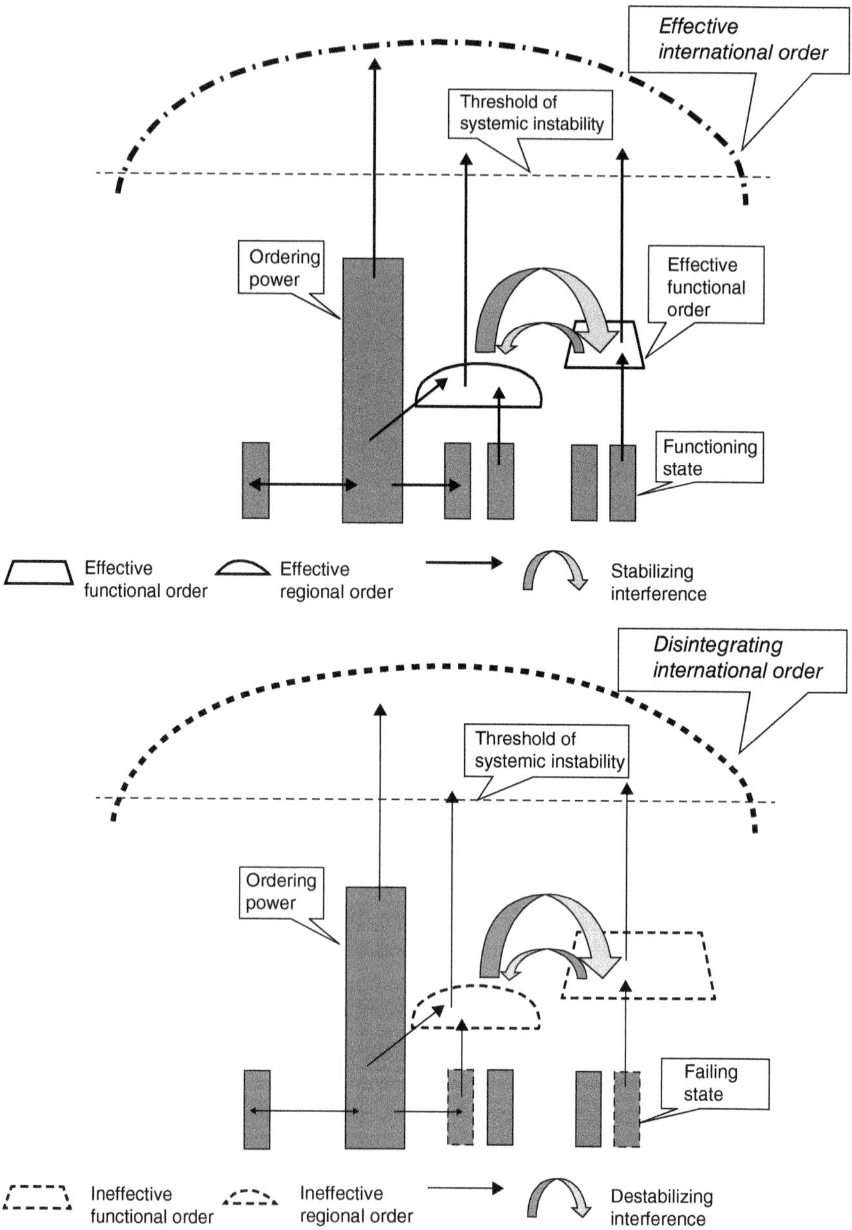

Figure C.2 Effective vs. disintegrating international order
Source: own design

empty facades, resembling Potemkin villages. Yet the underlying power structure that allowed the United States, as the leading power of the Western alliance system, to erect and sustain that LIO no longer exists—not least because its domestic foundations have crumbled. The central axis in the new power structure appears to be the complex and contradictory relationship between the United States and China, which is characterized by both high interdependence and vulnerability and strong competitive impulses. The two countries will need to cooperate if international order is to prevail, but at the same time they will find themselves in bitter rivalry over their respective positions in the East Asian regional order and, in the longer run, in the international order as a whole. How those two ordering powers adapt to each other and the twin exigencies of interdependence and competition will shape the future of international order.

There can be little doubt that the state of international order has deteriorated significantly over the course of this project, which began with a small internal working group at Stiftung Wissenschaft und Politik in Berlin in 2013. Yet it would be wrong to extrapolate from that dire predictions: we cannot *know* the future, we can only try to *shape* it. While political order will always be fragile and incomplete, the search for it appears to be deeply anchored. Together, this produces what might be called a dialectics of politics. The decline of the old liberal international order, the LIO 2.0, may already have begun to kindle impulses and forces that will create a new international order out of its ashes.

Bibliography

Primary Sources

Auswärtiges Amt, Pressemitteilung, February 12, 2015.

BP Statistical Review of World Energy 2017, https://www.bp.com/content/dam/bp/en/corporate/pdf/energy-economics/statistical-review-2017/bp-statistical-review-of-world-energy-2017-full-report.pdf [accessed August 28, 2017].

Centers for Disease Control and Prevention, The 2009 H1N1 Pandemic: Summary Highlights. April 2009–April 2010, updated June 16, 2010, http://www.cdc.gov/h1n1flu/cdcresponse.htm [accessed August 31, 2016].

Centers for Disease Control and Prevention, CDC and the Global Health Security Agenda, Meeting in Seoul, Korea, September 7–9, 2015, http://www.cdc.gov/globalhealth/security/events/default.html [accessed August 31, 2016].

Centers for Disease Control and Prevention, Telebriefing on launch of global health security agenda, Press Briefing Transcript, February 12, 2014, http://www.cdc.gov/media/releases/2014/t0213-global-health-security.html [accessed August 31, 2016].

Council of the European Union, Council Decision 14866/17 establishing Permanent Structured Cooperation (PESCO) and determining the list of Participating Member States. Brussels, December 8, 2017.

Defense Manpower Data Center (DMDC), DoD Personnel, Workforce Reports and Publications, Active Duty Military Strength by Service (Updated Monthly), https://www.dmdc.osd.mil/appj/dwp/dwp_reports.jsp.

Department of Defense, *Sustaining U.S. Global Leadership: Priorities for 21st Century Defense*, Washington, DC: Department of Defense, January 2012.

Department of Defense, *Quadrennial Defense Review 2014*, Washington, DC: Department of Defense, March 2014.

District Court, The Hague, Case number C/09/456689/HA ZA 13–1396, June 24, 2015, http://deeplink.rechtspraak.nl/uitspraak?id=ECLI:NL:RBDHA:2015:7145 [accessed February 15, 2016].

Draft Charter of the Organization for Security and Cooperation in Europe submitted to the OSCE Permanent Council by the Russian Federation, PC.DEL/444/07, May 18, 2007.

Elysée-Vertrag, January 22, 1963, in Auswärtiges Amt (ed.), *Außenpolitik der Bundesrepublik Deutschland.*

European Police Office, Exploring tomorrow's organised crime, 2016, https://www.europol.europa.eu/content/massive-changes-criminal-landscape.

European Security Treaty, Draft of November 29, 2009: President of Russia, Official Web Portal, http://eng.kremlin.ru/text/docs/2009/11/223072.shtml [accessed December 3, 2009].

G20, G20 Leaders' Declaration: Shaping an Interconnected World, Hamburg, July 7–8, 2017, https://www.g20.org/en/g20/timeline [accessed November 28, 2017].

German–French initiative of April 18, 1990, in Auswärtiges Amt (ed.), *Außenpolitik der Bundesrepublik Deutschland.*

Global Health Security Agenda, Action Packages, https://ghsagenda.org/packages.html [accessed September 21, 2016].

Global Health Security Agenda, Events and Updates, https://ghsagenda.org/events.html [accessed September 26, 2016].

Global Health Security Agenda, Membership, https://ghsagenda.org/members.html [accessed September 26, 2016].

Global Health Security Agenda, Seoul Declaration, 2015, http://www.ghsa2015seoul.kr/SeoulDeclaration.pdf [accessed August 31, 2016].

Global Policy Forum, Subjects of UN Security Council Vetoes, https://www.globalpolicy.org/security-council/40069-subjects-of-un-security-council-vetoes.html [accessed January 3, 2017].

Global Polio Eradication Initiative, http://polioeradication.org.

Global Polio Eradication Initiative, Public Health Emergency status, http://polioeradication.org/polio-today/polio-now/public-health-emergency-status/ [accessed November 28, 2017].

Global Trade Alert, http://www.globaltradealert.org/ [accessed December 20, 2017].

Independent International Fact-Finding Mission on the Conflict in Georgia (IIFFMCG/EUSR), Report Volume I, September 30, 2009, http://news.bbc.co.uk/2/shared/bsp/hi/pdfs/30_09_09_iiffmgc_report.pdf [accessed September 8, 2016].

Independent Monitoring Board of the Global Polio Eradication Initiative, Tenth report, October 2014, http://www.polioeradication.org/Portals/0/Document/Aboutus/Governance/IMB/11IMBMeeting/11IMB_Report_EN.pdf [accessed September 28, 2016].

Independent Monitoring Board of the Global Polio Eradication Initiative, Twelfth report, October 2015, http://www.polioeradication.org/Portals/0/Document/Aboutus/Governance/IMB/13IMBMeeting/13IMB_Report_EN.pdf [accessed September 28, 2016].

Intergovernmental Panel on Climate Change (IPCC), *Climate Change 2014: Synthesis Report, Summary for Policy Makers*, p. 20, http://ipcc.ch/pdf/assessment-report/ar5/syr/AR5_SYR_FINAL_SPM.pdf [accessed August 28, 2017].

International Crisis Group, The Politics Behind the Ebola Crisis, Africa Report No. 232 (October 28, 2015), http://www.crisisgroup.org/~/media/Files/africa/west-africa/232-the-politics-behind-the-ebola-crisis.pdf [accessed August 31, 2016].

IPCC-III, *Climate Change 2014: Mitigation of Climate Change*, ed. Ottmar Edenhofer et al., New York: Cambridge University Press, 2014.

ITU (ed.), ITC Facts and Figures, http://www.itu.int/en/ITU-D/Statistics/Pages/default.aspx.

Jackson, Van, Donald Trump's Asia Policy Would Be a Disaster, *The Diplomat*, September 11, 2015, https://thediplomat.com/2015/09/donald-trumps-asia-policy-would-be-a-disaster/.

Joint Comprehensive Plan of Action, http://apps.washingtonpost.com/g/documents/world/full-text-of-the-iran-nuclear-deal/1651/ [accessed November 16, 2016].

Médecins Sans Frontières, Ebola 2014–15 Facts and Figures, http://www.msf.org/sites/msf.org/files/ebola_accountability_report_low_res.pdf [accessed August 31, 2016].

Médecins Sans Frontières, *Pushed to the Limit and Beyond: A Year into the Largest Ever Ebola Outbreak*, March 2015, https://www.doctorswithoutborders.org/sites/usa/files/msf143061.pdf [accessed August 31, 2016].

Ministry of Commerce of the People's Republic of China, Regular News Conference Held by the Ministry of Commerce, January 6, 2016.

Ministry of Foreign Affairs of the People's Republic of China, http://www.fmprc.gov.cn/mfa_eng/wjdt_665385/zyjh_665391/t1148640.shtml [accessed January 13, 2017].

Ministry of Foreign Affairs of the People's Republic of China, http://www.fmprc.gov.cn/mfa_eng/zxxx_662805/t1298420.shtml.

Ministry of Foreign Affairs of the People's Republic of China, Foreign Ministry Spokesperson Lu Kang's Regular Press Conference, February 5, 2016, http://www.fmprc.gov.cn/ce/cech/ger/fyrth/t1338870.htm.

National Security Strategy of the United States of America, December 2017, https://www.whitehouse.gov/wp-content/uploads/2017/12/NSS-Final-12-18-2017-0905.pdf [accessed January 4, 2018].

NATO, *Active Engagement, Modern Defence, Strategic Concept for the Defence and Security of the Members of the North Atlantic Treaty Organization, Adopted by the Heads of State and Government in Lisbon*, November 20, 2010, No. 27, http://www.nato.int/cps/en/natolive/official_texts_68580.htm.

NATO, *Bucharest Summit Declaration*, Issued by the Heads of State and Government participating in the meeting of the North Atlantic Council in Bucharest on April 3, 2008 (= NATO PR(2008)049).

NATO, *Wales Summit Declaration*, Issued by the Heads of State and Government participating in the meeting of the North Atlantic Council in Wales, Press Release (2014) 120, September 5, 2014, in particular Nos. 1, 16–23, http://www.nato.int/cps/en/natohq/official_texts_112964.htm?selectedLocale=en.

NATO, *Warsaw Summit Declaration*, Issued by the Heads of State and Government participating in the Meeting of the North Atlantic Council in Warsaw 8–9 July 2016, Press Release (2016) 100, July 9, 2016, in particular Nos. 37–41, https://www.nato.int/cps/en/natohq/official_texts_133169.htm [accessed November 30, 2017].

NATO–Russia Council, *Rome Declaration*, May 28, 2002, http://www.nato-russia-council.info.

NATO/Russian Federation, *Founding Act on Mutual Relations, Cooperation and Security between NATO and the Russian Federation*, Paris, May 27, 1997, http://www.nato.int/cps/en/natolive/official_texts_25468.htm.

North Atlantic Treaty Organization, *NATO's Enhanced Forward Presence Factsheet*, updated May 2017, https://www.nato.int/nato_static_fl2014/assets/pdf/pdf_2017_05/1705-factsheet-efp.pdf.

Obama, Barack, Statement by President Obama on the Signing of the Trans-Pacific Partnership, February 3, 2016, https://obamawhitehouse.archives.gov/the-press-office/2016/02/03/statement-president-signing-trans-pacific-partnership.

OECD, Aid-for-trade statistical queries, http://www.oecd.org/dac/aft/aid-fortradestatisticalqueries.htm.

Office of the Press Secretary, The White House: President Donald J. Trump's New Strategy on Iran, Washington, DC, October 13, 2017, https://www.whitehouse.gov/briefings-statements/president-donald-j-trumps-new-strategy-iran/ [accessed December 15, 2017].

Office of the Under Secretary of Defense (Comptroller)/CFO, DoD Releases Fiscal Year 2018 Budget Proposal, http://comptroller.defense.gov/Portals/45/Documents/defbudget/fy2018_ERI_J-Book.pdf [accessed November 30, 2017].

OSCE, Agreement on the Adaptation of the Treaty on Conventional Armed Forces in Europe, OSCE (ed.), *OSCE Istanbul Summit 1999*, Istanbul Document 1999, Istanbul 2000, pp. 118–234 (= PCOEW389).

OSCE, CFE Final Act of the Conference of the State Parties to the Treaty on Conventional Armed Forces in Europe, November 19, 1999, in OSCE (ed.), *OSCE Istanbul Summit 1999*, Istanbul Document 1999, Istanbul 2000, pp. 235–51 (= PCOEW389).

OSCE, Charter for European Security, Istanbul, November 1999, in OSCE (ed.), *OSCE Istanbul Summit 1999*, Istanbul Document 1999, Istanbul, 2000, pp. 1–13 (= PCOEW389).

OSCE, Organization for Security and Co-operation in Europe, Ministerial Council Hamburg 2016: *From Lisbon to Hamburg: Declaration on the Twentieth Anniversary of the OSCE Framework for Arms Control*. MC.DOC/4/16 of December 9, 2016.

OSCE, Permanent Council, Decision No. 1162 Extension of the Mandate of the OSCE Special Monitoring Mission to Ukraine, PC.DEC/1162 of March 12, 2015 (= PCOEW5968).

Oxfam, Wealth: Wanting It All and Wanting More, Oxfam Issue Briefing, January 2015, https://www.oxfam.org/sites/www.oxfam.org/files/file_attachments/ib-wealth-having-all-wanting-more-190115-en.pdf [accessed February 15, 2016].

Permanent Court of Arbitration, Press Release on June 24, 2016, https://pca-cpa.org/wp-content/uploads/sites/175/2016/07/PH-CN-20160712-Press-Release-No-11-English.pdf [accessed November 12, 2016].

Pew Research Center, Global Attitudes and Trends, http://www.pewglobal.org/database/ [accessed January 4, 2017].

Plan Bureau Nederland, Are Global Emissions Still Rising? The Hague: Plan Bureau Nederland 2015, http://infographics.pbl.nl/website/globalco2-2015/ [accessed February 15, 2016].

Polio Global Eradication Initiative, List of wild poliovirus by country and year as of November 28, 2017, http://polioeradication.org/wp-content/uploads/2017/11/global-wild-poliovirus-2012-2017-29112017.pdf [accessed November 28, 2017].

President of the United States, *National Security Strategy of the United States of America*, Washington, DC, December 2017.

Presse und Informationsamt der Bundesregierung, *Weißbuch 1973/1974, Zur Sicherheit der Bundesrepublik Deutschland und zur Entwicklung der Bundeswehr*, Bonn: BMVg, 1974.

Putin, Wladimir, *Rede auf der 43. Münchener Sicherheitskonferenz*, AG Friedensforschung (online), February 14, 2007, http://www.ag-friedensforschung.de/themen/Sicherheitskonferenz/2007-putin-dt.html [accessed November 10, 2017].

Rio Declaration and Agenda 21, Report on the UN Conference on Environment and Development, Rio de Janeiro, June 3–14, 1992, New York: United Nations, 1992 (= A/CONF.151/26/Rev.1 (Vols.1–III).

Robert Koch Institut, Nationaler Pandemieplan II, RKI: 2016, p. 15, http://www.rki.de/DE/Content/InfAZ/I/Influenza/Pandemieplanung/Downloads/Pandemieplan_Teil_II_gesamt.pdf?__blob=publicationFile [accessed August 31, 2016].

Save the Children, *A Wake-up Call: Lessons from Ebola for the World's Health System*, London: Save the Children, 2015, http://www.savethechildren.org.uk/resources/online-library/wake-call-0 [accessed August 31, 2016].

Schlussakte von Helsinki 1.8.1975, in Auswärtiges Amt (ed.), *20 Jahre KSZE, 1973–1993*, Second Edition, Bonn: Ausw. Amt, 1993, pp. 18–81.

Statements of the G7 summits in Elmau, Germany, 2015, https://sustainabledevelopment.un.org/content/documents/7320LEADERS%20STATEMENT_FINAL_CLEAN.pdf [accessed September 26, 2016].

Statements of the G7 summits in Iseshima, Japan, 2016, http://www.mofa.go.jp/files/000160266.pdf [accessed September 26, 2016].

Stavridis, James, *Testimony of Admiral James Stavridis, United States Navy Commander, United States European Command, Before the 113th Congress*, Stuttgart: European Forces Command (EUCOM), 2013.

Steinmeier, Frank-Walter, Deutscher OSZE-Vorsitz 2016, in *Ständige Vertretung der Bundesrepublik Deutschland bei der OSZE*, Vienna, Deutscher OSZE Vorsitz, 2016, http://www.wien-osze.diplo.de/Vertretung/wienosce/de/011Vorsitz/Vorsitz_202016.html [accessed November 20, 2017].

The Atlantic Charter, *Declarations of Principles issued by the President of the United States and the Prime Minister of the United Kingdom*, August 14, 1941, http://www.nato.int/cps/en/natohq/official_texts_16912.htm [accessed January 12, 2017].

The Austrian or Humanitarian Pledge, http://www.bmeia.gv.at/fileadmin/user_upload/Zentrale/Aussenpolitik/Abruestung/HINW14/HINW14vienna_Pledge_Document.pdf.

The Embassy of the Russian Federation to the United Kingdom of Great Britain and Northern Ireland, Russian views of the OSCE activities, http://www.rusemb.org.uk/osce/ [accessed September 8, 2016].

Trail Smelter Arbitration (United States vs. Canada), April 16, 1938, March 11, 1941, *Reports of International Arbitration Awards, Volume III* (2006), pp. 1905–82, http://legal.un.org/riaa/cases/vol_III/1905–1982.pdf.

Treaty between the United States of America and the Union of Soviet Socialist Republics on the Elimination of their Intermediate-Range and Shorter-Range Missiles, December 1987, Selected Documents No. 25, Department of State Publications 9555, Washington, DC: Dept of State, December 1987 (reprint July 1990).

US Army Europe Public Affairs Office, *Atlantic Resolve Fact Sheet*, updated April 1, 2017, http://www.eur.army.mil/AtlanticResolve/.

US–China Economic and Security Review Commission, China Seeks a “New Type of Major-Country Relationship” with the United States, June 25, 2013, https://www.uscc.gov/sites/default/files/Research/China%20Seeks%20New%20Type%20of%20Major-Country%20Relationship%20with%20United%20States_Staff%20Research%20Backgrounder.pdf.

US Congress, Countering America’s Adversaries Through Sanctions Act, https://www.congress.gov/bill/115th-congress/house-bill/3364 [accessed December 15, 2017].

US Department of Defense, *Freedom of Navigation Report for Fiscal Year 2014*, http://policy.defense.gov/Portals/11/Documents/gsa/cwmd/20150323%202015%20DoD%20Annual%20FON%20Report.pdf.

UNFCCC, http://unfccc.int/kyoto_protocol/doha_amendment/items/7362.php.

UNFCCC, COP 21 Decision, FCCC/CP/2015/L.9/Rev.1/III (22), https://unfccc.int/resource/docs/2015/cop21/eng/l09r01.pdf.

UNFCCC, *Kyoto Protocol to the United Nations Framework Convention on Climate Change*, New York: UNFCCC, 1997.

UNFCCC, Newsroom: China submits its climate action plan ahead of 2015 Paris summit, June 30, 2015, http://newsroom.unfccc.int/unfccc-newsroom/china-submits-its-climate-action-plan-ahead-of-2015-paris-agreement/ [accessed October 17, 2016].

UNFCCC, Paris Agreement, December 12, 2015, http://unfccc.int/files/home/application/pdf/paris_agreement.pdf [accessed February 15, 2016].

UNFCCC, Synthesis Report on the Aggregate Effect of Intended Nationally Determined Contributions, UNFCCC 2015, http://unfccc.int/files/focus/indc_portal/application/pdf/synthesis_report_-_overview.pdf.

UNFCCC, *United Nations Framework Convention on Climate Change*, New York: UNFCCC, 1992.

UNFCCC Secretariat, Participation at UN Climate conference in Paris, http://newsroom.unfccc.int/paris/participation-at-un-climate-conference-in-paris/ [accessed January 20, 2017].

UN General Assembly, *Transforming our World: The 2030 Agenda for Sustainable Development*, New York: United Nations General Assembly Resolution A/Res/70/01 of September 25, 2015.

United Nations, High-Level Panel on the Global Response to Health Crises: Protecting Humanity from Future Health Crises (advance unedited copy), January 25, 2016, http://www.un.org/News/dh/infocus/HLP/2016-02-05_Final_Report_Global_Response_to_Health_Crises.pdf.

United Nations, *Transforming Our World: The 2030 Agenda for Sustainable Development*, New York: United Nations, 2015.

United Nations, *United Nations Framework Convention for Climate Change*, 1992, https://unfccc.int/resource/docs/convkp/conveng.pdf [accessed October 17, 2016].

United Nations Development Programme, Arab Fund for Economic and Social Development, *Arab Human Development Report 2002*, http://hdr.undp.org/sites/default/files/rbas_ahdr2002_en.pdf.

United Nations Framework Convention on Climate Change, Copenhagen Climate Change Conference December 2009, https://unfccc.int/meetings/copenhagen_dec_2009/meeting/6295.php [accessed November 15, 2016].

United States Objectives and Programs for National Security, *National Security Council Report 68*, April 1950, https://www.trumanlibrary.org/whistlestop/study_collections/coldwar/documents/pdf/10-1.pdf.

United States Trade Representative, *2015 Report to Congress on China's WTO Compliance*, https://ustr.gov/about-us/policy-offices/press-office/reports-and-publications/2015/2015-report-congress-chinas-wto [accessed August 9, 2016].

US Senate Resolution 98 on Global Warming, Congressional Record, Senate, pp. S10308–S10311, October 3, 1997 ("Byrd/Hagel Resolution").

Vertrag über die abschließende Regelung in Bezug auf Deutschland (September 12, 1990), Art. 3, in Bundesgesetzblatt 1990 II.

World Bank, Exports of goods and services (% of GDP), 1960–2015, http://data.worldbank.org/indicator/NE.EXP.GNFS.ZS [accessed January 10, 2017].

World Bank, Gross National Income per capita, http://data.worldbank.org/indicator/NY.GNP.PCAP.CD/countries?display=default.

World Bank, NDB chief KV Kamath, July 9, 2015, http://economictimes.indiatimes.com/news/economy/finance/not-here-to-compete-with-imf-world-bank-ndb-chief-kv-kamath/articleshow/48002259.cms?utm_source=contentofinterest&utm_medium=text&utm_campaign=cppst [accessed August 29, 2016].

World Bank, Pandemic Emergency Facility: Frequently Asked Questions, http://www.worldbank.org/en/topic/pandemics/brief/pandemic-emergency-facility-frequently-asked-questions [accessed August 31, 2016].

World Bank, Topics, pandemic: Overview, 2015, http://www.worldbank.org/en/topic/pandemics/overview [accessed August 31, 2016].

World Bank, Trade (% of GDP), http://data.worldbank.org/indicator/NE.TRD.GNFS.ZS?end=2015&start=2013.

World Health Assembly, Global Health Security: Epidemic Alert and Response (2001), A54/9.

World Health Assembly, Revision and Updating of the International Health Regulations, WHA 48.7 (1995), http://apps.who.int/iris/bitstream/10665/178403/1/WHA48_R7_eng.pdf [accessed September 21, 2016].

World Health Organization, A research and development Blueprint for action to prevent epidemics, http://www.who.int/csr/research-and-development/en/ [accessed September 29, 2016].

World Health Organization, Closing Remarks at the Sixty-Ninth World Health Assembly, Dr Margaret Chan, Director-General of the World Health Organization, Geneva, Switzerland, May 28, 2016, http://www.who.int/dg/speeches/2016/wha69-closing-remarks/en/ [accessed September 29, 2016].

World Health Organization, Constitution, http://www.who.int/governance/eb/who_constitution_en.pdf [accessed August 31, 2016].

World Health Organization, Disease outbreak news, http://www.who.int/csr/don/en/ [accessed September 25, 2016].

World Health Organization, Emergencies preparedness, response: Director-General statement following the ninth meeting of the emergency committee (2010), http://www.who.int/csr/disease/swineflu/9th_meeting_ihr/en/ [accessed August 31, 2016].

World Health Organization, Emergencies preparedness, response: Influenza A(H1N1)—update 47 (2009), http://www.who.int/csr/don/2009_06_11/en/ [accessed August 31, 2016].

World Health Organization, Emergencies preparedness, response: Pandemic (H1N1)—update 112 (2010), http://www.who.int/csr/don/2010_08_06/en/.

World Health Organization, Emergencies preparedness, response: Partners: Global Outbreak Alert and Response Network (GOARN) (2016), http://www.who.int/csr/disease/ebola/partners/en/ [accessed August 31, 2016].

World Health Organization, Emergency Preparedness: Response, http://www.who.int/csr/alertresponse/epidemicintelligence/en/ [accessed August 31, 2016].

World Health Organization, Final report of the Ebola Interim Assessment panel, July 2015, http://www.who.int/csr/resources/publications/ebola/report-by-panel.pdf?ua=1 [accessed August 31, 2016].

World Health Organization, Global Advisory Committee on Vaccine Safety, June 16–17, 2010, http://www.who.int/vaccine_safety/committee/reports/Jun_2010/en/ [accessed September 28, 2016].

World Health Organization, Global Outbreak Alert and Response, Report of a WHO meeting (2000), WHO/CDS/CSR/2000.3, http://www.who.int/csr/resources/publications/surveillance/whocdscsr2003.pdf.

World Health Organization, International Health Regulations (1969), http://apps.who.int/iris/bitstream/10665/96616/1/9241580070.pdf [accessed August 31, 2016].

World Health Organization, International Health Regulations (2005), http://www.who.int/ihr/9789241596664/en/ [accessed August 31, 2016].

World Health Organization, International Health Regulations: Global Outbreak Alert and Response Network, http://www.who.int/ihr/about/IHR_Global_Outbreak_Alert_and_Response_Network_respond.pdf?ua=1 [accessed August 31, 2016].

World Health Organization, Joint External Evaluation Tool: International Health Regulations (2005), 2016, http://apps.who.int/iris/bitstream/10665/204368/1/9789241510172_eng.pdf [accessed September 29, 2016].

World Health Organization, Reform of WHO's work in health emergency management, document A69/30, May 5, 2016, http://apps.who.int/gb/ebwha/pdf_files/WHA69/A69_30-en.pdf [accessed September 29, 2016].

World Health Organization, *Severe Acute Respiratory Syndrome (SARS): Status of the Outbreak and Lessons for the Immediate Future*, Geneva: WHO, 2003, http://www.who.int/csr/media/sars_wha.pdf [accessed August 31, 2016].

World Health Organization, Situation Report, Zika-Virus, Microcephaly, Guillain–Barré Syndrome, December 1, 2016, http://apps.who.int/iris/bitstream/10665/251811/1/zikasitrep1Dec2016-eng.pdf?ua=1 [accessed November 28, 2017].

World Health Organization, Strengthening health security by implementing the International Health Regulations (2005), http://www.who.int/ihr/procedures/ihr_committees/en/ [accessed August 31, 2016].

World Health Organization, The history of Zika virus, http://www.who.int/emergencies/zika-virus/history/en/ [accessed September 24, 2016].

World Health Organization, World Health Organization issues emergency travel advisory, March 15, 2003, http://www.who.int/csr/sars/archive/2003_03_15/en/ [accessed August 31, 2016].

World Health Organization, Zika strategic response plan, June 2016, http://apps.who.int/iris/bitstream/10665/246091/1/WHO-ZIKV-SRF-16.3-eng.pdf?ua=1&ua=1&ua=1 [accessed September 24, 2016].

Xi Jinping, Forging a Strong Partnership to Enhance Prosperity of Asia, Institute for Southeast Asian Studies (ISEAS), Singapore, November 7, 2015, http://www.fmprc.gov.cn/mfa_eng/wjdt_665385/zyjh_665391/t1313923.shtml [accessed January 13, 2017].

Xi Jinping, *Secure a Decisive Victory in Building a Moderately Prosperous Society in All Respects and Strive for the Great Success of Socialism with Chinese Characteristics for a New Era*, Report of October 18, 2017 to the 19th Congress of the Chinese Community Party. English text available at http://news.xinhuanet.com/english/special/2017-11/03/c_136725942.htm.

Xi Jinping, speech in Seattle, September 22, 2015, https://www.ncuscr.org/content/full-text-president-xi-jinpings-speech [accessed September 24, 2016].

Secondary Sources

AccessNow, A Human Rights Response to Government Hacking, 2016, https://www.accessnow.org/governmenthackingdoc/.

Acharya, Amitav, *The End of American World Order*, Cambridge: Polity Press, 2014.

Acharya, Amitav (ed.), *Why Govern? Rethinking Demand and Progress in Global Governance*, Cambridge: Cambridge University Press, 2016.

Acton, James M., *Silver Bullet: Asking the Right Questions about Conventional Prompt Global Strike*, New York: Carnegie Endowment for International Peace, 2013.

Alagappa, Muthiah (ed.), *Asian Security Order: Instrumental and Normative Features*, Stanford, CA: Stanford University Press, 2002.

Allison, Graham, The Thucydides Trap: Are the U.S. and China Headed for War? *The Atlantic*, September 24, 2015, https://www.theatlantic.com/international/archive/2015/09/united-states-china-war-thucydides-trap/406756/.

Andrews, David (ed.), *The Atlantic Alliance Under Stress: US–European Relations after Iraq*, Cambridge: Cambridge University Press, 2005.

Applebaum, Anne, Obama and Europe: Missed Signals, Renewed Commitments, *Foreign Affairs* 94:5 (September/October 2015), pp. 37–44.

Armitage, David, *The Declaration of Independence: A Global History*, Cambridge, MA: Harvard University Press, 2007.

Arquilla, J. and D. F. Ronfeldt (eds.), *In Athena's Camp: Preparing for Conflict in the Information Age*, Santa Monica, CA: RAND Corporation, 1997.

Ayson, Robert and Manjeet S. Pardesi, Asia's Diplomacy of Violence: China–US Coercion and Regional Order, *Survival* 59:2 (April/May 2017), pp. 85–124.

Bacevich, Andrew, *America's War for the Greater Middle East: A Military History*, New York: Random House, 2016.

Ball, Patrick, Wendy Betts, Fritz Scheuren, Jana Dudukovich, and Jana Asher, *Killings and Refugee Flows in Kosovo, March–June 1999*, A Report to the International Criminal Tribunal for the Former Yugoslavia, in Ewa Tabeau (ed.), *Conflict in Numbers: Casualties of the 1990s Wars in the Former Yugoslavia*, Helsinki Committee for Human Rights in Serbia 2009 (= Testimonies no. 33), pp. 877–949, http://www.helsinki.org.rs/doc/testimonies33.pdf [accessed November 15, 2016].

Ball, Patrick, Meghan Lynch, and Amelia Hoover, Revisiting "Killings and Migration in Kosovo," Responses to additional data and analysis, in Ball et al., *Killings and Migration in Kosovo*, Washington, DC: AAAS and ABA/CEELI, 2002, pp. 951–75.

Balzacq, T. and M. Dunn Cavelty, A Theory of Actor-Network for Cyber-Security, *European Journal of International Security* 1:2 (2016), pp. 176–98.

Baracat, E., J. M. Finger, R. L. Thorne, and J. Nogués, *Sustaining Trade Reform: Institutional Lessons from Peru and Argentina*, Washington, DC: World Bank, 2013.

Barlow, J. P., A Declaration of the Independence of Cyberspace, 1996, http://homes.eff.org/~barlow/Declaration-Final.html [accessed December 7, 2017].

Barmé, Geremie R. and Jeremy Goldkorn (eds.), *Civilising China*, Canberra: Australia National University, 2013.

BBC News Europe, Presidents apologize over Croatian war, September 10, 2003, http://news.bbc.co.uk/2/hi/europe/3095774.stm [accessed November 16, 2016].

Beckett, Margaret, A World Free of Nuclear Weapons, Keynote Address to the Carnegie Endowment's Non-Proliferation Conference, Washington, DC, June 25,

2007, https://carnegieendowment.org/2007/06/25/keynote-address-world-free-of-nuclear-weapons-event-1004.

Beeson, Mark, Hegemonic Transition in East Asia? The Dynamics of Chinese and American Power, *Review of International Studies* 35:1 (2009), pp. 95–112.

Berkowitz, B. D., *The New Face of War: How War will be Fought in the 21st Century*, New York: Free Press, 2003.

Betz, D. and T. Stevens, *Cyberspace and the State: Toward a Strategy for Cyber-Power*, London: IISS, 2011.

Bhagwati, J. and H. Patrick (eds.), *Aggressive Unilateralism: America's Trade Policy and the World Trading System*, New York: Harvester-Wheatsheaf, 1990.

Bisley, Nick, *Building Asia's Security*, London: Routledge for IISS, 2009.

Bisley, Nick, Neither Empire nor Republic: American Power and the Regional Order in the Asia-Pacific, *International Politics* 43 (2006), pp. 197–218.

Bodansky, D., Legitimacy in International Law and International Relations, APSA 2011 Annual meeting Paper, http://papers.ssrn.com/sol3/papers.cfm?abstract_id=1900289 [accessed August 31, 2016].

Bodansky, D., The United Nations Framework Convention on Climate Change: A Commentary, *Yale Journal of International Law* 18 (2003), pp. 451–558.

Bodansky, Daniel, *The Copenhagen Climate Change Conference: A Post-Mortem*, 2010, http://www.fao.org/fileadmin/user_upload/rome2007/docs/Copenhagen_Climate_Change.pdf [accessed November 26, 2016].

Bodansky, Daniel, The Paris Climate Change Agreement: A New Hope? *American Journal of International Law* 110 (May 2016), https://papers.ssrn.com/sol3/papers.cfm?abstract_id=2773895 [accessed November 26, 2016].

Borghard, E. D. and S. W. Lonergan, The Logic of Coercion in Cyberspace, *Security Studies* 26:3 (2017), pp. 452–81.

Bozeman, Adda B., *Politics and Culture in International History*, Second Edition, Piscataway, NJ: Transaction Publishers, 2002.

Brady, Anne-Marie, *Making the Foreign Serve China: Managing Foreigners in the People's Republic*, Lanham, MD: Rowman & Littlefield, 2003.

Breedlove, Philip, *Statement of General Philip Breedlove, Commander U.S. Forces Europe, Congressional Posture Statement*, Stuttgart: European Forces Command (EUCOM), April 1, 2014.

Brodie, Bernard (ed.), *The Absolute Weapon: Atomic Power and World Order*, New York: Harcourt, Brace, and Company, 1946.

Brookes, T., *Behind the Mask: How the World Survived SARS*, Washington, DC: American Public Health Association, 2005.

Brunnee, J., M. Doelle, and L. Rajamani, *Promoting Compliance in an Evolving Climate Regime*, Cambridge: Cambridge University Press, 2012.

Bukovansky, Mlada, Ian Clark, Robyn Eckersley, Richard Price, Christian Reus-Smit, and Nicholas J. Wheeler, *Special Responsibilities: Global Problems and American Power*, Cambridge: Cambridge University Press, 2012.

Bull, Hedley, *The Anarchical Society: A Study of Order in World Politics*, London: Macmillan, 1977.

Butler, D., Web Data Predict Flu, *Nature* 456 (November 2008), pp. 287–8.

Buzan, Barry, China in International Society: Is "Peaceful Rise" Possible? *The Chinese Journal of International Politics* 3:1 (2010), pp. 5–36.

Buzan, Barry, *People, States and Fear: The National Security Problem in International Relations*, Brighton: Wheatsheaf Books, 1983.

Buzan, Barry and Ole Wæver, *Regions and Powers: The Structure of International Security*, Cambridge: Cambridge University Press, 2003.

Buzan, B., O. Wæver, and J. de Wilde, *Security: A New Framework for Analysis*, Boulder, CO: Lynne Rienner, 1998.

Cai, Fang and Yang Lu, Take-Off, Persistence, and Sustainability: The Demographic Factor in Chinese Growth, East Asia Bureau of Economic Research, Working Paper 96, 2015, http://papers.ssrn.com/sol3/papers.cfm?abstract_id=2808296.

Calder, Kent and Min Ye, *The Making of Northeast Asia*, Stanford, CA: Stanford University Press, 2010.

Callahan, David, Chinese Visions of World Order: Post-Hegemonic or a New Hegemony? *International Studies Review* 10:4 (2008), pp. 749–61.

Callahan, William, *China: Pessoptimist Nation*, Oxford: Oxford University Press, 2010.

Cardin, Ben, The South China Sea is the Reason the United States Must Ratify UNCLOS, *Foreign Policy*, July 13, 2016, http://foreignpolicy.com/2016/07/13/the-south-china-sea-is-the-reason-the-united-states-must-ratify-unclos/ [accessed December 15, 2016].

Carter, Ashton B. and William James Perry, *Preventive Defense: A New Security Strategy for America*, Washington, DC: Brookings Institution Press, 1999.

Center for Strategic and International Studies (CSIS), *Global HIV/AIDS: A Strategy for U.S. Leadership*, Washington, DC: CSIS, 1994.

Chan, Steve, *China, the U.S., and the Power-Transition Theory: A Critique*, New York: Routledge, 2008.

Charap, Samuel and Timothy J. Colton, *Everyone Loses: The Ukraine Crisis and the Ruinous Contest for Post-Soviet Eurasia*, London: Routledge for IISS, 2017.

Chi Zhang, *The Domestic Dynamic of China's Energy Diplomacy*, Singapore: World Scientific Press, 2015.

Chin, Gregory and Hugo Dobson, China as G20 Host in 2016: Dawn of Asian Global Leadership? *Global Policy Journal*, March 3, 2015, http://www.globalpolicyjournal.com/blog/03/03/2015/china-g20-host-2016-dawn-asian-global-leadership [accessed August 20, 2016].

Christensen, Thomas J., Obama and Asia: Confronting the China Challenge, *Foreign Affairs* 94:5 (September/October 2015), pp. 28–36.

Christou, G., *Cybersecurity in the European Union: Resilience and Adaptability in Governance Policy*, London: Palgrave Macmillan, 2016.

Clark, Ian, *Hegemony in International Relations*, Oxford: Oxford University Press, 2011.

Climate Action Tracker, http://climateactiontracker.org/ [accessed February 15, 2016].

Cohen, Raphael S. and Gabriel M. Scheinmann, Can Europe Fill the Void in U.S. Military Leadership? *Orbis* 58:1 (Winter 2014), pp. 39–54.

Coker, Christopher, *The Improbable War: China, the United States and the Continuing Logic of Great Power Conflict*, Oxford: Oxford University Press, 2015.

Corasaniti, Nick, Alexander Burns, and Binyamin Appelbaum, Trump Takes Aim at Trade Deals and "Globalism," *New York Times*, June 28, 2016, p. A1.

Cornish, P., R. Hughes, and D. Livingstone, *Cyberspace and the National Security of the United Kingdom: Threats and Responses*, a Chatham House Report, 2009, https://www.chathamhouse.org/sites/files/chathamhouse/public/Research/International%20Security/r0309cyberspace.pdf.

Costanza, Robert, Ralph d'Arge, Rudolf de Groot, Stephen Farber, Monica Grasso, Bruce Hannon, and Karin Limburg, The Value of the World's Ecosystem Services and Natural Capital, *Ecological Economics* 25:1 (April 1998), pp. 3–15.

Crocker, Chester A., The Strategic Dilemma of a World Adrift, *Survival* 57:1 (February/March 2015), pp. 7–30.

Cullen, Patrick, The Rebalance to Asia under Trump: What Comes Next? *The RUSI Journal* 162:2 (April/May 2017), pp. 8–15.

Dag Hammarskjöld Library, Security Council—Veto List (in reverse chronological order), http://research.un.org/en/docs/sc/quick [accessed January 3, 2017].

Deibert, R. J., *Black Code: Inside the Battle for Cyberspace*, Toronto: McClelland & Stewart, 2013.

Deibert, Ronald J., Cyberspace Under Siege, *Journal of Democracy* 26:3 (July 2015), pp. 64–78.

Demchak, C. and P. Dombrowski, Rise of a Cybered Westphalian Age, *Strategic Studies Quarterly* 5:1 (Spring 2011), pp. 32–61.

Deudney, Daniel H., *Bounding Power: Republican Security Theory from the Polis to the Global Village*, Princeton, NJ: Princeton University Press, 2007.

Deudney, Daniel and G. John Ikenberry, Unraveling America the Great, *The American Interest* 11:5 (May/June 2016), pp. 7–17.

Deudney, Daniel and G. John Ikenberry, The Unraveling of the Cold War Settlement, *Survival* 51:6 (December/January 2009/10), pp. 39–62.

Dittmer, Lowell, China and the Developing World, in Lowell Dittmer and George T. Yu (eds.), *China, the Developing World, and the New Global Dynamic*, Boulder, CO: Lynne Rienner, 2010, pp. 1–12.

Dollar, David, China's Rise as a Regional and Global Power: The AIIB and the "One Belt, One Road," *Horizons* 4 (Summer 2015), pp. 162–72.

Dollar, David, *Is China's Development Finance a Challenge to the International Order?* Brookings Institution Report, November 2017.

Dosch, Jörn, Relations between China and Southeast Asia: A New Regional Order in the Making?, in Lowell Dittmer and George T. Yu (eds.), *China, the Developing World, and the New Global Dynamic*, Boulder, CO: Lynne Rienner, 2010, pp. 61–82.

Dunn Cavelty, M., *Cyber-Security and Threat Politics: US Efforts to Secure the Information Age*, London: Routledge, 2008.

Dunn Cavelty, M., Militarizing Cyberspace: Why Less may be Better, in C. Czosseck, R. Ottis, and K. Ziolkowski (eds.), *Proceedings of the 4th International Conference on Cyber Conflict*, Talinn: NATO, 2012, pp. 141–53.

Dunn Cavelty, M., The Normalization of Cyber-International Relations, in O. Thränert and M. Zapfe (eds.), *Strategic Trends 2015: Key Developments in Global Affairs*, Zurich: Center for Security Studies, 2015, pp. 81–98.

Dunn Cavelty, M., M. Kaufmann, and K. S. Kristensen, Resilience and (In)security: Practices, Subjects, Temporalities, *Security Dialogue* 46:1 (2015), pp. 3–14.

Dunn Cavelty, M. and K. S. Kristensen, Introduction: Securing the Homeland: Critical Infrastructure, Risk, and (In)Security?, in M. Dunn Cavelty and K. S. Kristensen (eds.), *The Politics of Securing the Homeland: Critical Infrastructure, Risk and Securitization*, New York: Routledge, 2008, pp. 1–14.

Dunn Cavelty, M. and M. Suter, The Art of CIIP Strategy: Taking Stock of Content and Processes, in J. Lopez, R. Setola, and S. D. Wolthusen (eds.), *Critical Infrastructure Protection: Information Infrastructure Models, Analysis, and Defense*, Berlin: Springer, 2012, pp. 15–38.

Dunn Cavelty, M. and M. Suter, Public–Private Partnerships are no Silver Bullet: An Expanded Governance Model for Critical Infrastructure Protection, *International Journal of Critical Infrastructure Protection* 2:4 (2009), pp. 179–87.

Dunn Cavelty, M. and R. Van der Vlugt, A Tale of Two Cities: Or How the Wrong Metaphors Mess With Our Security, *Georgetown Journal for International Affairs, International Engagements on Cyber V*, October 2015, pp. 21–9.

Elbe, S., *Virus Alert: Security, Governmentality, and the AIDS Pandemic*, New York: Columbia University Press, 2009.

Elias, Norbert, *Über den Prozess der Zivilisation*, 2 vols. Frankfurt am Main: Suhrkamp, 1976.

Elsig, M., B. Hoekman, and J. Pauwelyn, Thinking about the Performance of the World Trade Organization: A Multi-Disciplinary Perspective, in M. Elsig, B. Hoekman, and J. Pauwelyn (eds.), *Assessing the World Trade Organization: Fit for Purpose?* Cambridge: Cambridge University Press, 2017, pp. 12–42.

Engel, Jeffrey A. (ed.), *Four Freedoms: FDR and the Evolution of an American Idea*, Oxford: Oxford University Press, 2016.

Farwell, J. and R. Rohozinski, Stuxnet and the Future of Cyber-War, *Survival, Global Politics and Strategy* 53:1 (2011), pp. 23–40.

Feigenbaum, Evan A., China and the World: Dealing with a Reluctant Power, *Foreign Affairs* 96:1 (January/February 2017), pp. 33–40.

Fidler, D. P., Epic Failure of Ebola and Global Health Security, *The Brown Journal of World Affairs* 21:2 (2015), https://www.brown.edu/initiatives/journal-world-affairs/sites/brown.edu.initiatives.journal-world-affairs/files/private/articles/Fidler.pdf [accessed September 24, 2016].

Fidler, D. P., From International Sanitary Convention to Global Health Security: The New International Health Regulations, *Chinese Journal of International Law* 4:2 (2005), pp. 325–92.

Fineberg, H. V. et al., Strengthening response to pandemics and other public health emergencies, Report of the Review Committee on the Functioning of the International Health Regulations (2005) and on Pandemic Influenza (H1N1) 2009 (2010), http://apps.who.int/iris/bitstream/10665/75235/1/9789241564335_eng.pdf?ua=1 [accessed August 31, 2016].

Finnamore, Barbara, Sam Geall, Angel Hsu, Johanna Lewis, and Li Shuo, Beijing Is Finally Getting Serious About Climate Change, *Foreign Policy*, July 11, 2015, http://foreignpolicy.com/2015/07/11/china-climate-change-greenhouse-united-states-policy/ [accessed October 17, 2016].

Fiorini, M. and B. Hoekman, Services Trade Policy and Sustainable Development, EUI RSCAS Working Paper 2017/41, Florence: European University Institute, 2017, http://cadmus.eui.eu/handle/1814/47684 [accessed December 10, 2017].

Fitzgerald, Frances, *Way Out There in the Blue: Reagan, Star Wars and the End of the Cold War*, New York: Simon & Schuster, 2008.

Fontaine, Richard, Salvaging Global Order, *The National Interest*, March 10, 2015, http://nationalinterest.org/feature/salvaging-the-global-order-12390 [accessed July 22, 2016].

Fontaine, Richard and Mira Rapp-Hooper, The China Syndrome, *The National Interest* 143 (May/June 2016), pp. 10–18.

Fonte, John, Sovereignty or Submission: Will Americans Rule Themselves or be Ruled by Others? New York and London: Encounter Books, 2011.

Frear, Thomas, Russia–West Dangerous Brinkmanship Continues, European Leadership Network, March 2015, https://www.europeanleadershipnetwork.org/commentary/russia-west-dangerous-brinkmanship-continues/.

Freedman, Lawrence and Ephraim Karsh, *The Gulf Conflict, 1990–1991: Diplomacy and War in the New World Order*, Princeton, NJ: Princeton University Press, 1993.

Friedberg, Aaron L., Ripe for Rivalry: Prospects for Peace in a Multipolar Asia, *International Security* 18:3 (Winter 1993–4), pp. 5–33.

Fu Ying, China and the Future of International Order, Lecture at Chatham House, London, July 6, 2016, https://www.chathamhouse.org/sites/files/chathamhouse/events/special/2016-07-08-China-International-Order_0.pdf.

Fu Ying, Speech at the MSC 2016, https://www.securityconference.de/en/activities/munich-security-conference/msc-2016/speeches/speech-by-fu-ying/.

Fu Ying, Under the same roof: China's view of world order, *The Huffington Post*, November 11, 2016, http://www.huffingtonpost.com/fu-ying/china-global-order_b_8537918.html [accessed January 14, 2017].

Futter, Andrew, *Cyber Threats and Nuclear Weapons: New Questions for Command and Control, Security and Strategy*, London: RUSI Occasional Papers, 2016.

Gawande, K., B. Hoekman, and Y. Cui, Determinants of Trade Policy Responses to the 2008 Financial Crisis, *World Bank Economic Review* 29:1 (2015), pp. 102–28.

Gill, Bates, *Rising Star: China's New Security Diplomacy*, Washington, DC: Brookings Institution Press, 2007.

Gillingham, John R., *The EU: An Obituary*, London and New York: Verso, 2016.

Giorgetti, C., *A Principled Approach to State Failure: International Community Actions in Emergency Situations*, Leiden: Koninklijke Brill NV, 2010.

Glosny, Michael A., China and the BRICS: A Real (but Limited) Partnership in a Unipolar World, *Polity* 42:1 (2010), pp. 100–29.

Godehardt, Nadine and Daniel Krahl, "Friedensmission 2010": China als zentralasiatischer Akteur? *GIGA focus*, October 2010, https://www.giga-hamburg.de/de/system/files/publications/gf_global_1010.pdf [accessed October 16, 2016].

Godlee, F., Conflicts of interest and pandemic flu, *British Medical Journal* 340 (June 2010), p. c2947.

Goldberg, Jeffrey, The Obama Doctrine: The U.S. President talks through his hardest decisions about America's role in the world, *The Atlantic*, April 2016, https://www.theatlantic.com/magazine/archive/2016/04/the-obama-doctrine/471525/ [accessed January 4, 2018].

Goldstein, Avery and Edward D. Mansfield, *The Nexus of Economics, Security, and International Relations in East Asia*, Stanford, CA: Stanford University Press, 2012.

Gompert, D. C. and M. Libicki, Cyber Warfare and Sino-American Crisis Instability, *Survival* 56 (2014), pp. 7–22.

Gore, A., An Inconvenient Truth, documentary directed by Davis Guggenheim, produced by Lawrence Bender Productions and Participant Productions, 2006.

Gotev, Georgi, EU loses Armenia to Russia's Customs Union, September 4, 2013, http://www.euractiv.com/europes-east/eu-loses-armenia-russia-customs-news-530224.

Gottwald, Jörn-Carsten and Niall Duggan, Hesitant Adaptation—China's New Role in Global Policies, in Sebastian Harnisch, Cornelia Frank, and Hanns W. Maull (eds.), *Role Theory in International Relations: Approaches and Analysis*, London: Routledge, 2011, pp. 234–51.

Gray, Alexander and Peter Navarro, Donald Trump's Peace Through Strength Vision for the Asia-Pacific, *Foreign Policy*, November 7, 2016, http://foreignpolicy.com/2016/11/07/donald-trumps-peace-through-strength-vision-for-the-asia-pacific/ [accessed December 15, 2017].

Gries, Peter Hays, Chinese nationalist reactions to the Belgrade embassy bombing, *The China Journal* 46 (July 2001), pp. 25–43.

Grissom, Adam, The United States, in Clara Marina O'Donnell (ed.), *The Implications of Military Spending Cuts for NATO's Largest Members*, Washington, DC: Brookings Institution, July 2012 (= Analysis Paper).

Gupta, J., Climate Change: Governance History, Future, and Triple Loop Learning? WIRES Climate Change, *Wiley Interdisciplinary Reviews*, 2016, doi: 10.1002/wcc.388.

Gupta, J., *The History of Global Climate Governance*, Cambridge: Cambridge University Press, 2014.

Gupta, J., A History of International Climate Change Policy, WIRES Climate Change, *Wiley Interdisciplinary Reviews* 1:5 (2010), pp. 636–53, doi: 10.1002/wcc.67.

Gupta J., Leadership in the Climate Regime: Inspiring the Commitment of Developing Countries in the Post-Kyoto Phase, *Review of European Community and International Environmental Law* 7:2 (1998), pp. 178–88.

Gupta, J. and K. Arts, Achieving the 1.5°C Objective: Just Implementation through a Right to (Sustainable) Development, INEA, 2018, https://doi.org/10.1007/s10784-017-9376-7.

Gupta, J., E. Chu, K. Bos, and T. Kuijten, The Geo-Ecological Risks of Oil Investments by China and the Global South: The Right to Development Revisited, in M. P. Amineh and L. Guang (eds.), *Geopolitical Economy of Energy and Environment: China and the European Union*, Leiden: Brill, 2017.

Gupta J. and C. Vegelin, Sustainable Development Goals and Inclusive Development, *International Environmental Agreements: Politics, Law and Economics* 16:3 (2016), pp. 433–48.

Gurtov, Mel, Changing Perspectives and Policies, in Lowell Dittmer and George T. Yu (eds.), *China, the Developing World, and the New Global Dynamic*, Boulder, CO: Lynne Rienner, 2010, pp. 13–36.

Haass, Richard, *A World in Disarray: American Foreign Policy and the Crisis of the Old Order, With a New Afterword*, New York: Penguin Books, 2018.

Hanauer, Larry and Morris Lyle, *Chinese Engagement in Africa: Drivers, Reactions and Implications for U.S. Policy*, Santa Monica, CA: RAND Corporation, 2014.

Hanrieder, Wolfram, *Germany, America, Europe: Forty Years of German Foreign Policy*, New Haven, CT and London: Yale University Press, 1989.

Hansen, L. and H. Nissenbaum, Digital Disaster, Cyber Security, and the Copenhagen School, *International Studies Quarterly* 53 (2009), pp. 1155–75.

Hardus, S., Chinese National Oil Companies in Ghana: The Cases of CNOOC and Sinopec, *Perspectives on Global Development and Technology* 13 (2014), pp. 588–612.

Hawken, Paul, Amory B. Lovins, and L. Hunter Lovins, *Natural Capitalism*, Boston, MA: Little, Brown, 1999.

He Kai, Institutional Balancing and International Relations Theory: Economic Interdependence and Balance of Power Strategies in Southeast Asia, *European Journal of International Relations* 14:3 (2008), pp. 489–518.

He Lichao, China's Climate-Change Policy from Kyoto to Copenhagen: Domestic Needs and International Aspiration, *Asian Perspective* 34:3 (2010), pp. 5–33.

Heilmann, Sebastian, Moritz Rudolf, Mikko Huotari, and Johannes Buckow, China's Shadow Foreign Policy: Parallel Structures Challenge the Established International Order, *China Monitor* No. 18 (2014), http://merics.org/fileadmin/templates/download/china-monitor/China_Monitor_No_18.pdf [accessed September 28, 2016].

Heisbourg, François, American Hegemony? Perceptions of the U.S. Abroad, *Survival* 41:6 (Winter 1999–2000), pp. 5–19.

Held, David, Anthony McGrew, David Goldblatt, and Jonathan Perraton, *Global Transformations: Politics, Economics and Culture*, Stanford, CA: Stanford University Press, 1999.

Held, David and Charles Roger (eds.), *Global Governance at Risk*, Cambridge: Polity Press, 2013.

Herbst, Jeffrey, Terence McNamee, and Greg Mills, *On the Fault Line: Managing Tensions and Divisions within Societies*, London: Profile Books, 2012.

Hey, E., The Climate Change Regime: An Enviro-Economic Problem and International Administrative Law in the Making, *International Environmental Agreements: Politics, Law and Economics* 75 (2001), pp. 75–100.

Heymann, D. L. et al., Zika Virus and Microcephaly: Why is this Situation a PHEIC? *The Lancet*, February 10, 2016, http://www.thelancet.com/pb/assets/raw/Lancet/pdfs/S0140673616003202.pdf [accessed August 31, 2016].

Hoekman, B., Fostering Transatlantic Regulatory Cooperation and Gradual Multilateralization, *Journal of International Economic Law* 18:3 (2015), pp. 609–24.

Hoekman, B. and P. C. Mavroidis, Embracing Diversity: Plurilateral Agreements and the Trading System, *World Trade Review* 14:1 (2015), pp. 101–16.

Hoekman, Bernard (ed.), *The Global Trade Slowdown: A New Normal?* London: CEPR Press and EUI, 2015.

Hoffmann, Stanley (ed.), *Conditions of World Order*, Boston, MA: Houghton Mifflin, 1968.

Hogan, Michael J., *A Cross of Iron: Harry S. Truman and the Origins of the National Security State, 1945–1954*, Cambridge: Cambridge University Press, 1998.

Hokayem, Emile and Becca Wasser, *The Gulf States in an Era of American Retrenchment*, London: Routledge for IISS, 2014 (= Adelphi Series No. 447–8).

Holslag, J., China's New Mercantilism in Central Africa, *African and Asian Studies* 5:2 (2006), pp. 133–69.

Holslag, Jonathan, The Smart Revisionist, *Survival* 56:5 (October/November 2014), pp. 95–116.

Homer-Dixon, Thomas et al., Synchronous Failure: The Emerging Causal Architecture of Global Crisis, *Ecology and Society* 20:3 (2015), http://dx.doi.org/10.5751/ES-07681-200306.

Hoogenboom, B., Latin America and China's Transnationalizing Oil Industry: A Political Economy Assessment of New Relations, *Perspectives on Global Development and Technology* 13 (2014), pp. 626–47.

Horesh, Niv, Hyun Jin Kim, and Peter Mauch, *Superpower China: Historicizing Beijing's New Narratives of Leadership and East Asia's Response Thereto*, Singapore: World Scientific, 2015.

Horsburgh, Nicola, *China & Global Nuclear Order: From Estrangement to Active Engagement*, Oxford: Oxford University Press, 2015.

Howe, Neil and Richard Jackson, Global Aging and the Crisis of the 2020s, *Current History* 110:732 (January 2011), pp. 20–5, https://csis-prod.s3.amazonaws.com/s3fs-public/legacy_files/files/publication/110104_gai_jackson.pdf.

Hurrell, Andrew, *On Global Order: Power, Values and the Constitution of International Society*, Oxford: Oxford University Press, 2007.

Hurst, Steven, Parties, Polarization, and U.S. Foreign Policy, in Inderjeet Parmar, Linda B. Miller, and Mark Ledwidge (eds.), *Obama and the World: New Directions in U.S. Foreign Policy*, London and New York: Routledge, 2014 (Second Edition), pp. 95–106.

Huxley, Tim and Benjamin Schreer, Trump's Missing Asia Strategy, *Survival* 59:3 (June/July 2017), pp. 81–9.

Ikenberry, G. John, The Liberal International Order and its Discontents, *Millennium* 38:3 (2010), pp. 509–21.

Ikenberry, G. John, *Liberal Leviathan: The Origins, Crisis, and Transformation of the American World Order*, Princeton, NJ: Princeton University Press, 2011.

Inglesby, T. and J. E. Fischer, Moving Ahead on the Global Health Security Agenda, *Biosecurity and Bioterrorism* 12:2 (2014), pp. 63–5.

Inkster, N., Information Warfare and the US Presidential Election, *Survival* 58 (2016), pp. 23–32.

International Institute for Strategic Studies (ed.), *The Military Balance*, London: IISS, 2016.

Ioffe, Julia, Russia's Game Plan in Syria Is Simple, *Foreign Policy*, September 25, 2015, http://foreignpolicy.com/2015/09/25/russias-game-plan-in-syria-is-simple putin-assad/.

Jervis, Robert, *American Foreign Policy in a New Era*, New York: Routledge, 2005.

Ji, Z. and F. Sha, The Challenges of the Post-COP21 Regime: Interpreting CBDR in the INDC Context, *International Environmental Agreements: Politics, Law and Economics* 15:4 (2015), pp. 421–30.

Jia Qingguo, The Shanghai Cooperation Organization: China's Experiment in Multilateral Leadership, Japan Slavic Research Center (SRC), 2007, http://src-h.slav.hokudai.ac.jp/coe21/publish/no16_2_ses/05_jia.pdf [accessed September 9, 2016].

Jin Kai, Can China Build a Community of Common Destiny?, http://thediplomat.com/2013/11/can-china-build-a-community-of-common-destiny/.

Jin Liqun, *Building Asia's New Bank*, Washington, DC: Brookings Institution, October 21, 2015, http://www.brookings.edu/~/media/events/2015/10/21-aiib-jin-liqun/20151021_asia_infrastructure_bank_transcript.pdf [accessed August 29, 2016].

Johnston, Alastair Iain, How New and Assertive Is China's New Assertiveness? *International Security* 37:4 (Spring 2013), pp. 7–48.

Johnston, Alastair Iain, Is China a Status Quo Power? *International Security* 27:4 (Spring 2003), pp. 5–56.

Jones, Bruce and Thomas Wright, *The State of the International Order*, Washington, DC: Brookings Institution, 2014 (Policy Paper 33).

Kagan, Robert, *The Twilight of the Liberal World Order*, Brookings Institution, January 24, 2017, https://www.brookings.edu/research/the-twilight-of-the-liberal-world-order/?utm_campaign=Brookings+Brief&utm_source=hs_email&utm_medium=email&utm_content=41517002 [accessed January 30, 2017].

Kang, David, *China Rising: Peace, Power, and Order in East Asia*, New York: Columbia University Press, 2007.

Kavanagh, C., *The United Nations, Cyberspace and International Peace and Security: Responding to Complexity in the 21st Century*. UNIDIR Resources, 2017, http://www.unidir.org/publications/report-of-the-international-security-cyber-issues-workshop-series.

Keohane, R. and D. Victor, The Regime Complex for Climate Change, Kennedy School Discussion Paper, Harvard University, 2010, pp. 10–33.

Kerr, Malcolm H., *The Arab Cold War, 1958–1964: A Study of Ideology in Politics*, Chatham House Essays, London: Oxford University Press, 1965.

Kilbourne, E. D., Influenza Pandemics of the 20th Century, *Emerging Infectious Diseases* 12:1 (2006), pp. 9–14, http://wwwnc.cdc.gov/eid/article/12/1/pdfs/05-1254.pdf [accessed August 31, 2016].

Kinkel, Klaus, Rede des Bundesministers des Auswärtigen, Dr. Kinkel, vor dem Deutschen Bundestag am 2.12.1992 anlässlich der Verabschiedung des Ratifikationsgesetzes zum Vertrag von Maastricht, in Auswärtiges Amt (ed.), *Deutsche Außenpolitik nach der Einheit 1990–1993*, Bonn: Eine Dokumentation, 1994, pp. 204–6.

Kirby, William C. and F. Warren McFarlan, China still isn't ready to be a true global leader, *Harvard Business Review*, January 5, 2015, https://hbr.org/2015/01/china-still-isnt-ready-to-be-a-true-global-leader [accessed September 9, 2016].

Kissinger, Henry, *World Order: Reflections on the Character of Nations and the Course of History*, New York: Penguin, 2014.

Kitchen, Nick, Hegemonic Transition and U.S. Foreign Policy, in Inderjeet Parmar, Linda B. Miller, and Mark Ledwidge (eds.), *Obama and the World: New Directions in U.S. Foreign Policy*, London and New York: Routledge, 2014 (Second Edition), pp. 80–92.

Kohl, Helmut, Ansprache des Bundeskanzlers, Dr. Kohl, aus Anlass des dreißigjährigen Bestehens des Elysée-Vertrags, in Auswärtiges Amt (ed.), *Deutsche Außenpolitik nach der Einheit 1990–1993*, Bonn: Eine Dokumentation, 1994, pp. 235–8.

Kohl, Helmut, *Vom Mauerfall zur Wiedervereinigung, Meine Erinnerungen*, Munich: Knaur Verlag, 2014.

Korb, Lawrence J. and Daniel de Wit, Beyond Iraq: Lasting Issues for the U.S. in the Middle East, in Robert E. Looney (ed.), *Handbook of U.S.–Middle East Relations: Formative Factors and Regional Perspectives*, London and New York: Routledge, 2009, pp. 25–37.

Krahl, Daniel, China: Aus den BRICS herausgewachsen? *Aus Politik und Zeitgeschichte (APuZ)* 63:50–1 (2013), pp. 36–41, http://www.bpb.de/apuz/173803/china-aus-den-brics-herausgewachsen?p=all [accessed October 16, 2016].

Krasner, Stephen D., *Defending the National Interest: Raw Materials Investments and U.S. Foreign Policy*, Princeton, NJ: Princeton University Press, 1978.

Krauthammer, Charles, The Unipolar Moment, *Foreign Affairs* 70:1 (Winter 1990/1), pp. 23–33.

Kshetri, N., *The Quest to Cyber Superiority: Cybersecurity Regulations, Frameworks, and Strategies of Major Economies*, Cham, Switzerland: Springer International, 2016.

Kupchan, Charles A. and Peter L. Trubowitz, Dead Center: The Demise of Liberal Internationalism, *International Security* 32:2 (Fall 2007), pp. 7–44.

Kupelman, Alan J., A Model Humanitarian Intervention? Reassessing NATO's Libya Campaign, *International Security* 38:1 (Summer 2013), pp. 105–36.

Kurlantzick, Joshua, *Charm Offensive*, New Haven, CT: Yale University Press, 2007.

Kydd, Andrew, In America We (Used to) Trust: U.S. Hegemony and Global Cooperation, *Political Science Quarterly* 120:4 (2005–6), pp. 619–36.

Lake, David A., *Hierarchy in International Relations*, Ithaca, NY: Cornell University Press, 2011.

Layne, Christopher, The Unipolar Illusion Revisited: The Coming End of the United States' Unipolar Moment, *International Security* 31:2 (Fall 2006), pp. 7–41.

Layne, Christopher and Bradley Thayer, *American Empire: A Debate*, New York: Routledge, 2006.

Ledbetter, James, *Unwarranted Influence: Dwight D. Eisenhower and the Military–Industrial Complex*, New Haven, CT: Yale University Press, 2011.

Lee, Sheryn, *Crowded Waters: Naval Competition in the Asia-Pacific*, Australian Strategic Policy Institute: ASPI Special Report, July 2015, https://www.files.ethz.ch/isn/192241/Crowded%20waters_%20naval%20competition%20in%20the%20Asia-Pacifi.pdf.

Leung, G. M. and A. Nicoll, Reflections on Pandemic (H1N1) 2009 and the International Response, *Public Library of Science Medicine* 7:10 (2010), e1000346.

Li, (David) Daokui, The AIIB as China's Pilot Attempt to Reform the Global Economic Governance, *Foreign Affairs Journal* (Beijing) (Summer 2015), pp. 27–36.

Li, L. and M. Yu, Impact of the WTO on China's Rule of Law in Trade: Twentieth Anniversary of the WTO, *Journal of World Trade* 49:5 (2015), pp. 837–72.

Li, Mingjiang and Kalyan Kemburi (eds.), *China's Power and Asian Security*, Abingdon: Routledge, 2015.

Lian, Yu-ru, Der Kosovokrieg und seine Auswirkungen auf die chinesische Außenpolitik, *Asien* 77 (2000), pp. 48–57.

Lieber, Keir and Daryl G. Press, The New Era of Counterforce: Technological Change and the Future of Nuclear Deterrence, *International Security* 41:4 (Spring 2017), pp. 9–49.

Lind, Jennifer, The Other Revisionist Power, *Foreign Affairs* 96:2 (March/April 2017), pp. 74–82.

Lipset, Seymour Martin, *The First New Nation: The United States in Historical and Comparative Perspective*, New York: Basic Books, 1963.

Louis, William Roger, *Imperialism at Bay: The United States and the Decolonization of the British Empire, 1941–1945*, Oxford: Oxford University Press, 1978.

Low, D. E. and A. McGeer, Pandemic (H1N1) 2009: Assessing the Response, *Canadian Medical Association Journal* 182:17 (2010), pp. 1874–8.

Lustick, Ian S., The Absence of Middle Eastern Great Powers: Political "Backwardness" in Historical Perspective, *International Organization* 51:4 (Autumn 1997), pp. 653–83.

MacDonald, Paul K. and Joseph M. Parent, Graceful Decline? The Surprising Success of Great Power Retrenchment, *International Security* 35:4 (Spring 2011), pp. 7–44.

Madoff, L. C. and J. P. Woodall, The Internet and the Global Monitoring of Emerging Diseases: Lessons from the First 10 Years of ProMED-mail, *ARCMED* 36.6 (2005), pp. 724–30, doi: http://dx.doi.org/10.1016/j.arcmed.2005.06.005.

Mancinelli, Paul, Conceptualizing "New Type Great Power Relations": The Sino-Russian Model, *Jamestown Foundation China Brief* 14:9 (May 7, 2014), pp. 12–16.

Manyin, Mark E., Stephen Daggett, Ben Dolven, Susan V. Lawrence, Michael F. Martin, Ronald O'Rourke, and Bruce Vaughn, *Pivot to the Pacific? The Obama Administration's "Rebalancing" Toward Asia*, Congressional Research Service, March 28, 2012, https://china.usc.edu/sites/default/files/legacy/AppImages/crs-2012-pivot-pacific.pdf.

Mastanduno, Michael, System Maker and Privilege Taker: U.S. Power and the International Political Economy, *World Politics* 61:1 (2009), pp. 121–54.

Maull, Hanns W., European Policies Towards China and the United States: Can They Support a Strategic Triad? *European Foreign Affairs Review*, 21, Special Issue (2016), pp. 29–46.

Maull, Hanns W., *Oil and Influence: The Oil Weapon Examined*, Adelphi Paper No. 117, London: IISS, 1975.

Maull, Hanns W., The Politics of the EU: China's Relationship with Europe, *Asian Journal of Comparative Politics* 2:1 (2016), pp. 55–69, http://journals.sagepub.com/doi/pdf/10.1177/2057891116662343 [accessed January 16, 2017].

Maull, Hanns W., The Rise of New Powers: Implications for the Transatlantic World, in Daniel Hamilton and Kurt Volcker (eds.), *Transatlantic 2020: A Tale of Four Futures*, Washington, DC: Center for Transatlantic Relations, 2011, pp. 71–92.

May, J. R. and E. Daly, *Global Environmental Constitutionalism*, Cambridge: Cambridge University Press, 2014.

Mazarr, Michael, George W. Bush, Idealist, *International Affairs* 79:3 (2003), pp. 503–22.

Mead, Walter Russell, *Special Providence: American Foreign Policy and How It Changed the World*, New York: Routledge, 2002.

Mearsheimer, John J., *The Tragedy of Great Power Politics*, New York: W. W. Norton, updated edition, 2014.

Mearsheimer, John J. and Stephen M. Walt, The Case for Offshore Balancing: A Superior U.S. Grand Strategy, *Foreign Affairs* 95:4 (July/August 2016), pp. 70–83.

Medeiros, Evan, *China's International Behavior*, Santa Monica, CA: RAND Corporation, 2009.

Mehta, Aaron, Revealed: Trump's $110 Billion Weapons List for the Saudis, *Defense News*, June 8, 2017, https://www.defensenews.com/breaking-news/2017/06/08/revealed-trump-s-110-billion-weapons-list-for-the-saudis/ [accessed December 15, 2017].

Meister, Stefan and Marie-Lena May, *Die Östliche Partnerschaft der EU—ein Kooperationsangebot mit Missverständnissen*, Berlin, September 2009 (DGAP-Standpunkt 7).

Melander, Erik, *Organized Violence in the World 2015: An Assesment [sic] by the Uppsala Conflict Data Program*, http://www.pcr.uu.se/digitalAssets/61/c_61335-l_1-k_brochure2.pdf [accessed January 10, 2017].

Menzel, Ulrich, *Die Ordnung der Welt: Imperium oder Hegemonie in der Hierarchie der Staatenwelt*, Berlin: Suhrkamp, 2015.

Merritt, Giles, *Slippery Slope: Europe's Troubled Future*, Oxford: Oxford University Press, 2016.

Mian, Zia, After the Nuclear Weapons Ban Treaty: A New Disarmament Politics, *Bulletin of the Atomic Scientists*, July 7, 2017, https://thebulletin.org/after-nuclear-weapons-ban-treaty-new-disarmament-politics10932.

Mierzejewski, Dominik, From Morality to Morality: The Rhetoric of Chinese Foreign Policy over Four Decades, in Bin Wu, Yao Shujie, and Chen Jian (eds.), *China's Development and Harmonization*, Abingdon: Routledge, 2013, pp. 41–59.

Migdal, Joel S., *Shifting Sands: The United States in the Middle East*, New York: Columbia University Press, 2014.

Monteiro, Nuno P., Unrest Assured: Why Unipolarity is Not Peaceful, *International Security* 36:3 (Winter 2011/12), pp. 9–40.

Moon, S. et al., Will Ebola change the game? Ten essential reforms before the next pandemic, The report of the Harvard–LSHTM Independent Panel on the Global Response to Ebola, *The Lancet* 386 (2015), pp. 2204–21, http://www.thelancet.com/pdfs/journals/lancet/PIIS0140-6736%2815%2900946-0.pdf [accessed August 31, 2016].

Morris, Ian, *Why the West Rules—for Now: The Patterns of History, and What They Reveal About the Future*, New York: Farrar, Straus & Giroux, 2010.

Morse, C. and R. O. Keohane, Contested Multilateralism, *Review of International Organizations* 9 (2014), pp. 385–412.

Morse, Edward L. and Amy Myers Jaffe, OPEC—Can the Cartel Survive another Fifty Years?, in Jan H. Kalicki and David L. Goldwyn (eds.), *Energy and Security: Foreign Policy Strategies for a World in Transition*, Second Edition, Washington, DC and Baltimore, MD: Wilson Center Press/Johns Hopkins University Press, 2013, pp. 121–39.

Mueller, M., A. Schmidt, and B. Kuerbis, Internet Security and Networked Governance in International Relations, *International Studies Review* 15:19 (2013), pp. 86–104.

Muller, Wim, China: An Illiberal, Non Western State in a Western-Centric, Liberal Order? *Baltic Yearbook of International Law* 15:1 (2015), pp. 216–37, http://papers.ssrn.com/sol3/papers.cfm?abstract_id=2575643 [accessed September 6, 2016].

Mungo, P. and B. Clough, *Approaching Zero: The Extraordinary Underworld of Hackers, Phreakers, Virus Writers, and Keyboard Criminals*, New York: Random House, 1993.

Murdock, Clark, Samuel J. Brannen, Thomas Karako, and Angela Weaver, *Project Atom: A Competitive Strategies Approach to Defining U.S. Nuclear Strategy and Posture for 2025–2050*, Washington, DC: Center for Strategic & International Studies, 2015.

National Intelligence Council, *Global Trends 2030: Alternative Worlds*, Washington, DC: NIC, December 2012.

Nye, J., The regime complex for managing global cyber activities, Global Commission on Internet Governance Paper Series No. 1, 2014, https://www.cigionline.org/sites/default/files/gcig_paper_no1.pdf.

Nye Jr., Joseph S., *Bound to Lead: The Changing Nature of American Power*, New York: Basic Books, 1990.

Nye Jr., Joseph S., East Asia: The Case for Deep Engagement, *Foreign Affairs* 74:4 (July/August 1995), pp. 90–102.

Obani, P. and J. Gupta, The Impact of Economic Recession on Climate Change: Eight Trends, *Climate and Development* 8:33 (2015), pp. 211–23.

O'Dowd, A., Council of Europe Condemns "Unjustified Scare" Over Swine Flu, *British Medical Journal* 340 (June 2010), p. c3033.

Olson, Mancur, *The Rise and Decline of Nations: Economic Growth, Stagflation, and Social Rigidities*, New Haven, CT: Yale University Press, 1984.

Olson, Stephen and Clyde Prestowitz, *The Evolving Role of China in International Institutions*, Prepared for the US–China Economic and Security Review Commission, January 2011, http://origin.www.uscc.gov/sites/default/files/Research/TheEvolvingRoleofChinainInternationalInstitutions.pdf [accessed November 26, 2016].

Osgood, Robert E., *Ideals and Self-Interest in America's Foreign Affairs: Great Transformation of the Twentieth Century*, Chicago, IL: University of Chicago Press, 1953.

Osterhammel, Jürgen, *China und die Weltgesellschaft*, Munich: Beck, 1989.

Osterhammel, Jürgen, *Die Verwandlung der Welt, Eine Geschichte des 19. Jahrhunderts*, Munich: Beck, 2009.

Pang, Zhongying and Hongying Wang, Debating International Institutions and Global Governance: The Missing Chinese IPE Contribution, *Review of International Political Economy* 20 (2013), pp. 1189–214.

Park, Joon-Woo, Gi-Wok Shin, and Donald Keyser (eds.), *Asia's Middle Powers? The Identity and Regional Policy of South Korea and Vietnam*, Asia-Pacific Research Center Books, Stanford, CA: Walter H. Shorenstein, 2013.

Patrick, Stewart, World Order: What, Exactly, are the Rules? *The Washington Quarterly* 39:1 (2016), pp. 7–27.

Pattberg, P., F. Biermann, S. Chan, and A. Mert, *Public–Private Partnerships for Sustainable Development: Emergence, Influence and Legitimacy*, Cheltenham, UK and Northampton, MA: Edward Elgar, 2012.

Pelling, M., D. Manuel-Navarrete, and M. Redclift, *Climate Change and the Crisis of Capitalism*, London: Routledge, 2012.

Perelman, L. J., Shifting Security Paradigms: Toward Resilience, in J. A. McCarthy (ed.), *Critical Thinking: Moving from Infrastructure Protection to Infrastructure Resilience*, CIP Program Discussion Paper Series, Arlington, VA: George Mason University, 2007, pp. 23–48.

Perkovich, George, The Nuclear Weapon Ban Treaty: What would follow?, Carnegie Endowment for International Peace, Washington, DC, June 8, 2017, https://carnegieendowment.org/2017/05/31/nuclear-ban-treaty-what-would-follow-pub-70136.

Perkovich, George and James Acton, *Abolishing Nuclear Weapons*, London: IISS, 2008 (= Adelphi Paper 396).

Perthes, Volker, *Das Ende des Nahen Ostens, wie wir ihn kennen—Ein Essay*, Berlin: Suhrkamp Verlag, 2015.

Piketty, Thomas, *Capital in the 21st Century*, Cambridge, MA: Harvard University Press, 2014.

Posen, Barry, *Restraint: A New Foundation for U.S. Grand Strategy*, Ithaca, NY and London: Cornell University Press, 2014.

Preble, Christopher, *The Power Problem: How American Military Dominance Makes Us Less Safe, Less Prosperous, and Less Free*, Ithaca, NY: Cornell University Press, 2009.

Press-Barnathan, Galia, The Impact of Regional Dynamics on U.S. Policy toward Regional Security Arrangements in East Asia, *International Relations of the Asia-Pacific* 14:3 (2014), pp. 357–91.

Radio Free Europe/Radio Liberty, EU Officials Warn Yerevan Over "U-Turn," September 4, 2013, http://www.rferl.org/content/armenia-eu-customs-union/25095145.html.

Rattray, G., *Strategic Warfare in Cyberspace*, Cambridge, MA: MIT Press, 2001.

Record, Jeffrey, *Wanting Iraq: Why the Bush Administration Invaded Iraq*, Washington, DC: Potomac Books, 2010.

Reisinger, Don, Understanding the iPhone's Impact over the Last Decade, *Fortune Tech*, January 9, 2017, http://fortune.com/2017/01/09/apple-iphone-turns-10-stats/ [accessed January 12, 2017].

Rengger, Nicholas J., *International Relations, Political Theory and the Problem of Order*, London: Routledge, 2000.

Ross, Lester, Changing Climate: What the Paris Accord means for China, *Law360*, New York, March 18, 2016, http://www.law360.com/articles/767558/changing-climate-what-the-paris-accord-means-for-china [accessed October 17, 2016].

Roy, J. Stapleton, Sino-Russian Relations in a Global Context: Implications for the United States, in Michael S. Chase et al., *Russia–China Relations: Assessing Common Ground and Strategic Fault Lines*, Seattle, WA: The National Bureau of Asian Research, 2017, pp. 37–49 (= NBR Special Report No. 66).

Rudolf, Moritz, et al., *Chinas Schatten-Außenpolitik: Parallelstrukturen fordern die internationale Ordnung heraus*, Berlin: MERICS, 2014 (= China Monitor No. 18, https://www.merics.org/sites/default/files/2017-09/China_Monitor_18_Schatten-Au%C3%9Fenpolitik_DE.pdf [accessed January 8, 2018]).

Rudolf, Peter, Schutzverantwortung und militärische Intervention, Eine ethische Bewertung der 'Responsibility to Protect' im Lichte der Libyen-Intervention, Berlin: SWP, 2013, https://www.swp-berlin.org/fileadmin/contents/products/studien/2013_S03_rdf.pdf [accessed January 12, 2017].

Rumsfeld, Donald H., Transforming the Military, *Foreign Affairs* 81:3 (May/June 2002), https://www.foreignaffairs.com/articles/2002-05-01/transforming-military.

Russet, Bruce, *Grasping the Democratic Peace: Principles for a Post-Cold War World*, Princeton, NJ: Princeton University Press 1993.

Sacerdoti, G., The Future of the WTO Dispute Settlement System: Confronting Challenges to Consolidate a Success Story, in C. Braga and B. Hoekman (eds.), *Future of the Global Trade Order*, Second Edition, Florence: EUI, 2017, http://cadmus.eui.eu/handle/1814/49384 [accessed December 20, 2017].

Sally, Razeen, *Regional Economic Integration in Asia: The Track Record and Prospects*, ECIPE Occasional Paper, 2 (2010), http://ecipe.org/app/uploads/2014/12/regional-economic-integration-in-asia-the-track-record-and-prospects.pdf.

Samuel, Charap and Timothy J. Colton, *Everyone Loses: The Ukraine Crisis and the Ruinous Contest for Post-Soviet Eurasia*, London: IISS/Routledge, 2017.

Scherlis, W. L., S. L. Squires, and R. D. Pethia, Computer Emergency Response, in P. Denning (ed.), *Computers Under Attack: Intruders, Worms, and Viruses*, Reading: Addison-Wesley, 1990, pp. 495–504.

Schlein, L., New Africa Regional Chief Aims to Shake Up Maligned WHO Office, *Voice of America*, January 31, 2015, http://www.voanews.com/a/ebola-who-africa-director/2622985.html [accessed September 28, 2016].

Schmitt, M. N. (ed.), *Tallinn Manual on the International Law Applicable to Cyber Warfare*, Cambridge: Cambridge University Press, 2013.

Schmitt, Michael N., Below the Threshold Cyber Operations: The Countermeasures Response Option and International Law, *Virginia Journal of International Law* 3 (2014), pp. 697–732.

Schneier, B., The Battle for Power on the Internet. *The Atlantic*, 2013, http://www.theatlantic.com/technology/archive/2013/10/the-battle-for-power-on-the-internet/280824.

Schneier, B., When It Comes to Security, We're Back to Feudalism. *Wired*, 2012, http://www.wired.com/opinion/2012/11/feudal-security/.

Schüler-Zhou, Yun and Margot Schüller, *Trump's Shadow over U.S.–China Economic Relations*, Hamburg: German Institute for Global and Area Studies, July 2017, https://www.giga-hamburg.de/en/system/files/publications/gf_asien_1704_en.pdf [accessed December 15, 2017].

Sen, Amartya, Democracy as a Universal Value, *Journal of Democracy* 10:3 (1999), pp. 3–17.

Senghaas, Dieter, *Zum irdischen Frieden*, Frankfurt am Main: Suhrkamp, 2004.

Shambaugh, David, *China goes Global: The Partial Power*, Oxford and New York: Oxford University Press, 2013.

Shambaugh, David, China or America: Which is the Revisionist Power? *Survival* 43:3 (2001), pp. 25–30.

Sheldon, J. B., Deciphering Cyberpower: Strategic Purpose in Peace and War, *Strategic Studies Quarterly* 5:2 (Summer 2011), pp. 95–112.

Shih Chiyu, Assigning Role Characteristics to China: The Role versus the Ego State, *Foreign Policy Analysis* 8:1 (2012), pp. 71–91.

Shih Chiyu and Yin Jinwu, Between Core National Interest and a Harmonious World: Reconciling Self-Role Conceptions in Chinese Foreign Policy, *The Chinese Journal of International Politics* 6:1 (2013), pp. 59–84.

Shimkin, Michael B., The World Health Organization, *Science* 104:2700 (1946), pp. 281–3, doi: 10.1126/science.104.2700.281.

Shirk, Susan, *China: Fragile Superpower*, Oxford: Oxford University Press, 2007.

Simurina, Jurica, *China's Approach to the CEE-16*, ECRAN Short-Term Policy Brief 85, January 2014, http://eeas.europa.eu/archives/docs/china/docs/division_ecran/ecran_is107_paper_85_chinas_approach_to_the_cee-16_jurica_simurina_en.pdf.

SIPRI Yearbook 2016, *Armaments, Disarmament and International Security*, Zusammenfassung auf Deutsch, Hamburg: Berghof Foundation, 2016.

Spafford, E. H., The Internet Worm: Crisis and Aftermath, *Communications of the ACM* 32:6 (1989), pp. 678–87.

Sparrow, Bartholomew, From the Outside, in B. Sparrow, *World War II and the American State*, Princeton, NJ: Princeton University Press, 1996.
Steinberg, James B. and Michael O'Hanlon, Keep Hope Alive: How to Prevent U.S.-Chinese Relations from Blowing Up, *Foreign Affairs*, June 16, 2014, https://www.foreignaffairs.com/articles/asia/2014-06-16/keep-hope-alive [accessed April 21, 2017].
Steinberg, James B. and Michael O'Hanlon, *Strategic Reassurance and Resolve: U.S.-China Relations in the Twenty-First Century*, Princeton, NJ: Princeton University Press, 2014.
Stephens, Brat, What Obama Gets Wrong: No Retreat, No Surrender, *Foreign Affairs* 94:5 (September/October 2015), pp. 13–16.
Stevens, T., A Cyberwar of Ideas? Deterrence and Norms in Cyberspace, *Contemporary Security Policy* 33:1 (2012), pp. 148–70.
Stevens T. and D. J. Betz, Analogical Reasoning and Cyber Security, *Security Dialogue* 44:2 (2013), pp. 147–64.
Sutter, Robert, East Asian Security, Policy Debates, and American Leadership, in Elena Atanassova-Cornelis and Frans-Paul van der Putten (eds.), *Changing Security Dynamics in East Asia*, Basingstoke and New York: Palgrave Macmillan, 2014, pp. 27–46.
Sutter, Robert, *Foreign Relations of the PRC: The Legacies and Constraints of China's International Politics since 1949*, Lanham, MD: Rowman & Littlefield, 2013.
Swaine, Michael D., Perceptions of an Assertive China, *China Leadership Monitor* No. 32 (May 2010), http://carnegieendowment.org/2010/05/03/perceptions-of-assertive-china-pub-40724.
Swaine, Michael D. with Wenyang Deng and Aube Rey Lescure, *Creating a Stable Asia: An Agenda for a U.S.-China Balance of Power*, Washington, DC: Carnegie Endowment for International Peace, 2017.
Tang, M. and S. J. Wei, The Value of Making Commitments Externally: Evidence from WTO Accessions, *Journal of International Economics* 78:2 (2016), pp. 216–29.
Tannenwald, Nina, *The Nuclear Taboo: The United States and the Non-Use of Nuclear Weapons since 1945*, Cambridge: Cambridge University Press, 2007.
Task Force on Cooperation in Greater Europe, Position Paper III: Avoiding War in Europe: how to reduce the risk of a military encounter between Russia and NATO, August 2015, https://www.europeanleadershipnetwork.org/wp content/uploads/2017/10/Task-Force-Position-Paper-III-July-2015-English.pdf.
Taubenberger, Jeffery and David M. Morens, 1918 Influenza: The Mother of all Diseases, *Emerging Infectious Diseases* 12:1 (January 2006), pp. 15–22, http://wwwnc.cdc.gov/eid/article/12/1/05-0979_article [accessed August 31, 2016].
Terada Takashi, Japan and Geo-Economic Regionalism in Asia: The Rise of TPP and AIIB, East Asia Institute Issue Briefing, February 3, 2016, http://www.eai.or.kr/data/bbs/eng_report/20160203166284.pdf.
Terhalle, Maximilian, *The Transition of Global Order, Legitimacy and Contestation*, Basingstoke: Palgrave Macmillan, 2015.
The Lancet, Another Kind of Zika Public Health Emergency (editorial), *The Lancet* 389:10069, p. 573, February 11, 2017, http://www.thelancet.com/pdfs/journals/lancet/PIIS0140-6736(17)30325-2.pdf [accessed November 28, 2017].

Townshend, Ashley and Rory Metcalf, *Shifting Waters: China's New Passive Assertiveness in Asian Maritime Security*, Sydney: The Lowy Institute April 2016, https://www.lowyinstitute.org/publications/shifting-waters-china-s-new-passive-assertiveness-asian-maritime-security [accessed April 25, 2017].

Turner, Oliver, The U.S. "Pivot" to Asia Pacific, in Inderjeet Parmar, Linda B. Miller, and Mark Ledwidge (eds.), *Obama and the World: New Directions in U.S. Foreign Policy*, London and New York: Routledge, 2014, Second Edition, pp. 219–30.

Tyrrell, Ian and Jay Sexton (eds.), *Empire's Twin: U.S. Anti-Imperialism from the Founding Era to the Age of Terrorism*, Ithaca, NY: Cornell University Press, 2015.

United States of America. Department of Defense, Office of the Secretary of Defense: Nuclear Posture Review 2018, issued February 2018, https://media.defense.gov/2018/Feb/02/2001872886-1/-1/1/2018-NUCLEAR-POSTURE-REVIEW-FINAL-REPORT.PDF [accessed June 15, 2018].

Valeriano, B. and R. C. Maness, The Dynamics of Cyber Conflict between Rival Antagonists, 2001–11, *Journal of Peace Research* 51:3 (2014), pp. 347–60.

Van Asselt, H., *The Fragmentation of Global Climate Governance: Consequences and Management of Regime Interactions*, Cheltenham, UK and Northampton, MA: Edward Elgar, 2013.

van Schaik, L. and R. van de Pas, *Transnational Governance and Democratic Legitimacy: The Case of Global Health*, Clingendael: Netherlands Institute of International Relations, July 2014, https://www.clingendael.nl/sites/default/files/Transnational%20Governance%20and%20Democratic%20Legitimacy%20-%20Global%20Health.pdf [accessed September 28, 2016].

Védrine, Hubert, *L'hyperpuissance américaine*, Paris: Fondation Jean Jaurès, 2000.

Wacker, Gudrun, *Security Cooperation in East Asia: Structures, Trends, and Limitations*, Berlin: SWP (German Institute for International and Security Affairs), 2015 (= SWP RP 4, May 2015).

Wagener, Martin, Die Bombardierung der chinesischen Botschaft in Belgrad: Ursachen, Reaktionen und Konsequenzen, *Asien* 77 (2000), pp. 23–47.

Walker, William, *A Perpetual Menace: Nuclear Weapons and International Order*, London: Routledge, 2012.

Walpuski, Günter, *Verteidigung + Entspannung = Sicherheit, Texte und Materialien zur Außen- und Sicherheits-politik*, Second Edition, Bonn: Verlag Neue Gesellschaft, 1975.

Waltz, Kenneth, The Stability of a Bipolar World, *Daedalus* 93:3 (Summer 1964), pp. 881–909.

Wang, Jianwei, China's Multilateral Diplomacy in the New Millennium, in Yong Deng and Fei-Ling Wang (eds.), *China Rising: Power and Motivation in Chinese Foreign Policy*, Lanham, MD: Rowman & Littlefield, 2004, pp. 159–200.

Wang, Jisi, China's Search for a Grand Strategy: A Rising Great Power Finds Its Way, *Foreign Affairs* 90:2 (March/April 2011), pp. 68–79.

Wang, Yizhou, Rethinking State Interests, in Cai Tuo (ed.), *Chinese Perspectives on Globalization and Autonomy*, Leiden: Brill, 2012, pp. 157–80.

Wang, Zheng, *Never Forget National Humiliation*, New York: Columbia University Press, 2012.

Wark, McKenzie, *Molecular Red: Theory for the Anthropocene*, London: Verso, 2015.

Westphal, Kirsten, Marco Overhaus, and Guido Steinberg, *The U.S. Shale Revolution and the Arab Gulf States: The Economic and Political Impact of Changing Energy Markets*, Berlin: SWP (German Institute for International and Security Affairs), November 2014 (= Research Paper RP 11).

White, Hugh, *The China Choice: Why We Should Share Power*, Oxford: Oxford University Press, 2012.

White, John Kenneth, Terrorism and the Remaking of American Politics, in William Crotty (ed.), *The Politics of Terror: The U.S. Response to 9/11*, Boston, MA: Northeastern University Press, 2004, pp. 37–63.

White, Matthew, Necrometrics: Part of the Historical Atlas of the Twentieth Century, http://necrometrics.com/20c5m.htm#Second [accessed January 15, 2017].

Winters, L. A., China and the World Trading System: Will "In and Up" be replaced by "Down and Out"? RSCAS Working Paper 2015/82, Florence: European University Institute, 2015, http://cadmus.eui.eu/handle/1814/37823 [accessed December 10, 2017].

Wohlforth, William, The Stability of a Unipolar World, *International Security* 24:1 (Summer 1999), pp. 5–41.

Wolfe, R., First diagnose, then treat: what ails the Doha Round? *World Trade Review* 14:1 (2015), pp. 7–28.

Wolfers, A., National Security as an Ambiguous Symbol, *Political Science Quarterly* 67:4 (1952), pp. 481–502.

Wright, Lawrence, *The Looming Tower: Al-Qaeda and the Road to 9/11*, New York: Knopf, 2006.

Wuthenow, Joel, *Chinese Diplomacy and the UN Security Council: Beyond the Veto*, New York: Routledge, 2012.

Xinhua, China Focus: China's Xi proposes security concept for Asia, May 21, 2014, http://news.xinhuanet.com/english/china/2014-05/21/c_133351210.htm [accessed August 20, 2016].

Yang Jiemian, The Self-Consciousness of Chinese-Characteristic Diplomatic Practice and Theory, in Jinjun Zhao and Zhirui Chen (eds.), *China and the International Society: Adaptation and Self-Consciousness*, Hackensack, NJ: World Century Publishing Cooperation, 2014.

Yong Chool Ha and Chaesung Chun, North Korea's Brinkmanship and the Task to Solve the "Nuclear Dilemma," *Asian Perspective* 34:1 (2010), pp. 87–109.

Yong Deng, Better than Power: "International Status" in Chinese Foreign Policy, in Yong Deng and Fei-Ling Wang (eds.), *Power and Motivation in Chinese Foreign Policy*, Lanham, MD: Rowman & Littlefield, 2005, pp. 51–72.

Yu Hongjun, The OBOR is for the community of human destiny, interview with the author January 11, 2016, in Zhuhai, China.

Yun Sun, *Xi and the 6th Forum on China–Africa Cooperation, Major Commitments, but with Questions*, Washington, DC: Brookings Institution, 2015, https://www.brookings.edu/blog/africa-in-focus/2015/12/07/xi-and-the-6th-forum-on-china-africa-cooperation-major-commitments-but-with-questions/ [accessed September 12, 2016].

Zhang Jun, China's Pursuit of a New World Order, http://www.project-syndicate.org/commentary/china-new-world-order-by-jun-zhang-2015-06?barrier=true [accessed January 11, 2017].

Zhao Kejin, Guiding Principles of China's New Foreign Policy, Carnegie-Tsinghua Center for Global Policy, September 9, 2013, http://carnegietsinghua.org/2013/09/09/guiding-principles-of-china-s-new-foreign-policy-pub-52902 [accessed November 26, 2016].

Zheng Bijian, China's "Peaceful Rise" to Great Power Status, *Foreign Affairs* 84:5 (September/October 2005), https://www.foreignaffairs.com/articles/asia/2005-09-01/chinas-peaceful-rise-great-power-status [accessed September 9, 2016].

Zheng Yongnian, What the reform of "supply-side" answers [in Chinese], http://www.zaobao.com/forum/expert/zheng-yong-nian/story20160216-582045/page/0/1 [accessed September 9, 2016].

Zhou Xiaochuan, Statement on Reforming the International Monetary System, http://www.cfr.org/china/zhou-xiaochuans-statement-reforming-international-monetary-system/p18916.

Zwierzchowski, Jan and Ewa Tabeau, *The 1992–95 War in Bosnia and Herzegovina: Census-Based Multiple System Estimation of Casualties' Undercount*, Conference Paper for the International Research Workshop on "The Global Costs of Conflict," The Households in Conflict Network (HiCN), and The German Institute for Economic Research (DIW Berlin), February 1–2, 2010, Berlin, http://www.icty.org/x/file/About/OTP/War_Demographics/en/bih_casualty_undercount_conf_paper_100201.pdf [accessed November 15, 2016].

Newspapers and Magazines

Ananthakrishnan, G., China, Russia, Venezuela and Arab states support Paris Agreement, *The Hindu* online, December 13, 2015, http://www.thehindu.com/sci-tech/energy-and-environment/cop21-climate-change-summit-at-paris-china-russia-venezuela-and-arab-states-support-paris-agreement/article7983278.ece [accessed February 15, 2016].

Asahi Shimbun, http://www.asahi.com/ajw/articles/AJ201711160052.html.

Broad, William J. et al., This Missile Could Reach California. But Can North Korea Use It With a Nuclear Weapon? *New York Times*, September 3, 2017, https://www.nytimes.com/interactive/2017/08/22/world/asia/north-korea-nuclear-weapons.html [accessed December 15, 2017].

Caixin Online, October 12, 2014, http://english.caixin.com/2014-12-10/100761304.html [accessed October 16, 2016].

China Daily, Inclusive AIIB to boost sustainable growth, January 15, 2016, http://www.chinadaily.com.cn/opinion/2016-01/15/content_23096770.htm.

Cohen, Roger, China's Monroe Doctrine, *New York Times*, May 8, 2014, http://www.nytimes.com/2014/05/09/opinion/cohen-chinas-monroe-doctrine.html [accessed August 20, 2016].

Deibert, R. and R. Rohozinski, The new cyber military-industrial complex, *The Globe and Mail*, March 28, 2011, http://www.theglobeandmail.com/news/opinions/opinion/the-new-cyber-military-industrial-complex/article1957159/.

Den Boer, Andrea and Valerie Hudson, The Security Risks of China's Abnormal Demographics, *Washington Post*, April 30, 2014.

Financial Times, New BRICS bank in Shanghai to challenge major institutions, July 21, 2015, http://www.ft.com/cms/s/0/d8e26216-2f8d-11e5-8873-775ba7c2ea3d.html#axzz4JGzZw7Bk [accessed August 29, 2016].

Gall, Carlota, How Kosovo was turned into fertile ground for ISIS, *New York Times*, May 22, 2016, p. A1.

Gerson, Michael, The hypocrisy in elevating Assange, *Washington Post*, January 6, 2017.

Greenwald, G. and E. MacAskill, Obama orders US to draw up overseas target list for cyber-attacks, *The Guardian*, June 7, 2013, http://www.theguardian.com/world/2013/jun/07/obama-china-targets-cyber-overseas.

Kramer, Andrew E., Fighting Between Armenia and Azerbaijan Flares up in Nagorno-Karabakh, *New York Times*, April 2, 2016, http://www.nytimes.com/2016/04/03/world/europe/nagorno-karabakh-fighting-azerbaijan-armenia.html?action=click&contentCollection=Europe&module=RelatedCoverage&region=EndOfArticle&pgtype=article [accessed November 16, 2016].

Liptak, A. and C. Davenport, Supreme Court Deals Blow to Obama's Efforts to Regulate Coal Emissions, *New York Times* online, February 2016, http://www.nytimes.com/2016/02/10/us/politics/supreme-court-blocks-obama-epa-coal-emissions-regulations.html?_r=0 [accessed February 15, 2016].

Loh, Christine, As the U.S. dithers, China cements its climate leadership role, *South China Morning Post*, November 22, 2017, http://www.scmp.com/comment/insight-opinion/article/2120923/us-ditherschina-cements-its's-climate-leadership-role-opening [accessed December 22, 2017].

Ludwig, Michael, Ein hoher Preis, Weshalb Armenien Russland der EU vorzieht, *Frankfurter Allgemeine Zeitung*, October 8, 2014.

Lynas, Mark, How do I know China wrecked the Copenhagen deal? I was in the room, *The Guardian* online, December 22, 2009, http://www.guardian.co.uk/environment/2009/dec/22/copenhagen-climate-change-mark [accessed September 13, 2016].

McNeil, Donald G., How the Response to Zika Failed Millions, *New York Times*, January 16, 2017, https://www.nytimes.com/2017/01/16/health/zika-virus-response.html?rref=collection%2Ftimestopic%2FWorld%20Health%20Organization&action=click&contentCollection=timestopics&region=stream&module=stream_unit&version=latest&contentPlacement=24&pgtype=collection [accessed August 28, 2017].

Osnos, Evan, Making China Great Again: How Beijing Learned to Use Trump to its Advantage, *The New Yorker*, January 8, 2018, https://www.newyorker.com/magazine/2018/01/08/making-china-great-again [accessed January 8, 2018].

Pastreich, Emanuel, Interview: Joseph Nye, *The Diplomat*, October 30, 2015, http://thediplomat.com/2015/10/interview-joseph-nye-2/ [accessed September 24, 2016].

Perlez, Jane, China Creates a World Bank of Its Own, and the U.S. Balks, *New York Times*, December 4, 2015, http://www.nytimes.com/2015/12/05/business/international/china-creates-an-asian-bank-as-the-us-stands-aloof.html?_r=0 [accessed October 16, 2016].

Prasad, R., I Think WHO Should Declare an Emergency, *The Hindu*, January 31, 2016, http://www.thehindu.com/sci-tech/health/zika-i-think-who-should-declare-an-emergency/article8172249.ece [accessed August 31, 2016].

Quinn, B. and J. Ball, UK's top companies condemned for prolific use of tax havens, *The Guardian* online, May 12, 2013, http://www.theguardian.com/uk/2013/may/12/uk-companies-condemned-tax-havens [accessed November 19, 2015].

Rogin, Jeff, Bannon Is Right About North Korea, *Washington Post*, August 17, 2017.

Sanger, David E. and Maggie Haberman, Transcript: Donald Trump on NATO, Turkey's Coup Attempt and the World, *New York Times*, July 21, 2016, https://www.nytimes.com/2016/07/22/us/politics/donald-trump-foreign-policy-interview.html [accessed December 15, 2017].

Shambaugh, David, The Coming Chinese Crackup: The Endgame of Communist Rule in China Has Begun, *Wall Street Journal*, March 6, 2015.

Shultz, George P., William J. Perry, Henry A. Kissinger, and Sam Nunn, A World Free of Nuclear Weapons, *Wall Street Journal*, January 4, 2007.

South China Morning Post, China, EU step up ties to fight climate change, September 18, 2017, http://www.scmp.com/news/china/policies-politics/article/2111657/china-eustep-ties-fight-climate-change [accessed December 22, 2017].

South China Morning Post, Japan ready to cooperate with China on global trade plan, Shinzo Abe says, December 4, 2017, http://www.scmp.com/news/china/diplomacy-defence/article/2122846/japan-ready-cooperate-china-global-trade-plan-shinzo [accessed December 22, 2017].

Taylor, Adam, Despite Campaigns' Rhetoric, Majority of Americans Polled Favor Globalization, *Washington Post*, September 7, 2016, p. A7.

The Economist, World Health Organization, Too Big to Ail, December 11, 2014, https://www.economist.com/news/international/21636038-ebola-has-laid-bare-failings-worlds-health-authority-too-big-ail [accessed August 28, 2017].

Tilghman, Andrew, EUCOM Base Closure Will Not Affect Force Levels, *The Military Times* (online), January 9, 2015, http://www.militarytimes.com/story/military/pentagon/2015/01/08/eucom-base-closures-will-not-affect-force-levels/21453321/ [accessed April 17, 2107].

Vandiver, John and Michael Darnell, Army Looking to Store Tanks, Equipment in Eastern Europe, *Stars and Stripes* (online), January 25, 2015, https://www.stripes.com/army-looking-to-store-tanks-equipment-in-eastern-europe-1.325693 [accessed April 17, 2017].

Vidal, John and David Adam, China overtakes U.S. as world's biggest CO2 emitter, *The Guardian* online, June 19, 2007, https://www.theguardian.com/environment/2007/jun/19/china.usnews [accessed September 13, 2016].

Yushchenko, Victor, Interview, *Die Welt*, September 11, 2008, http://www.welt.de/politik/article2429300/Ukraine-will-Russland-in-die-Grenzen-weisen.html.

Index